SANDRA GUSTAFSON'S

CHEAP

SLEEPS IN

ITALY

Florence • Rome • Venice

THIRD EDITION

**A Traveler's Guide to the
Best-Kept Secrets**

CHRONICLE BOOKS

SAN FRANCISCO

Printed in the United States of America.

THIRD EDITION
ISBN 0-8118-1839-X
ISSN 1074-5076

Cover design: Yeong Sun Park
Cover photograph: Allan Friedlander/SuperStock
Book design: Words & Deeds
Original maps: Françoise Humbert

Distributed in Canada by
Raincoast Books
8680 Cambie Street
Vancouver, B.C. V6P 6M9

10 9 8 7 6 5 4 3 2 1

Chronicle Books
85 Second Street
San Francisco, CA 94105

www.chroniclebooks.com

For Samantha Durell, whose love of Venice and boundless enthusiasm for it has enriched the lives of all of us fortunate enough to know her

Contents

To the Reader

Italy is my magnet.

—Lord Byron

I realize that every day my heart is Italian.

—Stendhal

Italy has played host to visitors for more than two thousand years. Despite tangled red tape, long lines, and the Italian fascination with complicating simple issues, if you develop a sense of *pazienza* (patience), you will survive. And with a healthy dose of *pazienza* and your copy of *Cheap Sleeps in Italy* in hand, your trip should be nothing short of marvelous.

It is important that you know *Cheap Sleeps in Italy* is not for those travelers who are looking for a list of the cheapest beds in Florence, Rome, and Venice. It is for those who are concerned with having a better trip by saving money and not sacrificing comfort, convenience, and well-being in the bargain. Life is too short not to treat it as a grand adventure. Have fun, and the rest will fall into place, especially when you accept that value is not always measured by how much you spend. There are times when spending the least amount possible is necessary and smart. Then there are those times when spending a little more can yield a great deal of extra comfort and enjoyment. To achieve this balance and get the most out of your trip, it is important that you know what you want, which things you can and cannot do without, and the trade-offs you will accept to hold down your costs. Travel with an open mind and a light suitcase. When you leave home, do not expect to encounter your familiar way of life. Enjoy all the new sights, people, and sounds around you. Sample different foods, make an attempt at a few words of the language, and remember that a smile is understood worldwide. If you can do these things, you will come home a more knowledgeable person, with a lifetime of happy memories.

Not long ago the hotel situation in Italy was easy. If you wanted luxury, you got it without breaking the bank. If you wanted a simple, clean pensione with charm, character, and a low rate, you would find it. Things have changed, not for the better from a Cheap Sleeper's point of view. Remodeling and redecorating worn-out hotels have become almost growth industries in Italy. What used to be cheap and charming is now more expensive and modern, with extras such as minibars, hair dryers, and color televisions, many of which beam CNN around the clock. These features add nothing to your trip, but they are the justification for doubling or triple the rates. The result is that what was once an affordable family hotel is now inching perilously close to $200 per night . . . without breakfast.

There are some significant extra costs the savvy Cheap Sleeper must watch out for. First is breakfast. What a rip-off! This is a real moneymaker for the hotel and an absolute budget-killer for you. If the strong coffee does not wake you, the high cost of the hotel breakfast will. Convenience is the reason why so many eat at the hotel, but the cost is usually exorbitant, if not downright extortion, when you pay between L8,000 to 25,000 per person for food that may cost the hotel less than L2,000. Hotel laundries often charge more than a garment is worth, and the minibar bottles are real budget-blowers. Finally, the telephone surcharges in some hotels can be as much as 250 percent of the cost of the call. Despite all of these gloomy realities, it is still possible to find suitable accommodations that are reasonably priced, and, of course, *Cheap Sleeps in Italy* will show you how.

Some of the hotels in *Cheap Sleeps in Italy* are cozy, quaint, and rustic, full of charm and personality and boasting views you will never forget. Others are just right for romantic stays, while a few will be a bit faded around the edges but have enough redeeming virtues. Still others may have been renovated and have the latest word in bathroom plumbing. Some are cheap, others not very, and yet others fall into the Big Splurge category.

The way smaller hotels hold down prices is by keeping the decor simple, limiting services, and, in general, running a no-frills operation. This may translate to Formica furniture, linoleum floors, fewer pictures on the walls, skimpy curtains, and limited room and closet space. It may also mean you will carry your own luggage up several flights of stairs, look for the shower and toilet down the hall, and do without air-conditioning—or pay a supplement and even then find that it is available only during a few short hours in the morning and again late in the afternoon and not at all at night. Almost invariably it will mean the absence of a shower curtain, though you'll find this even in some three-star hotels. The concept of the shower curtain has not yet been embraced by hoteliers in Italy. "The water eventually evaporates" is what they say when asked why this civilized invention is so often missing.

One of the benefits and joys of my job is discovering hidden treasures and passing them along to you. In the name of that research, on my last trip to Italy I walked hundreds of miles in every type of weather, wearing out several pairs of shoes in my daily search. For me, it is the perfect job and I love every minute of it. For you, it is this edition of *Cheap Sleeps in Italy,* full of wonderful hotels in all price ranges, which I hope will make your stay truly special and set the stage for many return trips.

It is important for readers to know that I do not include any hotel or shop, no matter how highly recommended it may be, or how many letters I've received praising it, that I have not personally visited. Where other guidebooks often send a questionnaire to be filled out by someone at the hotel, or have a few on-site stringers employed to stop by a random selection of the entries, I have been to every address in this book—plus hundreds of others I tossed into the rejection heap. On all of my unannounced visits, in addition to making sure the hotel is a Cheap Sleep monetary value, I assess the facilities, the attitude of the management, and the overall cleanliness and ambience of the hotel. I am on the lookout for dust, mold, mildew, bugs, thin towels, scratchy or waxed toilet tissue, creaking floors, peeling paint, no-watt bulbs, and cigarette burns on the bedspreads. I look for somewhere to store the luggage, a place in the bathroom to put a toothbrush and cosmetics, and enough closet space to hold the contents of more than a carry-on flight bag. The goal is to find the best values for the best prices in all Cheap Sleeping categories, from shoestring budget to Big Splurge.

In addition to offering budget-minded travelers the best advice about hotel values in Florence, Rome, and Venice, *Cheap Sleeps in Italy* provides Cheap Chic shopping tips for the smart consumer who feels that no trip is complete without at least a few hours spent browsing and buying.

Cheap Sleeps in Italy is not an ordinary guide. I wrote it just for you . . . it was great fun, and hard work, and I can't wait to go back to Italy and do it all over again. I want to thank all of the faithful Cheap Sleepers who have used my guides in the past, and extend a warm welcome to those of you who are first-time Cheap Sleepers in Italy. I ask you all to please write to me and tell me about your experiences, whether to disagree with something I have said, or to pat me on the back, or to point me toward some new or special place you want me to check out on my next trip. At the back of the book is an address where you can write to me. Your comments and suggestions are very important; I read every letter and answer all of my mail personally. In the meantime, I wish you *buona fortuna* and *buon viaggio*.

Tips for Cheap Sleeps in Italy

All saints can do miracles, but few of them can keep a hotel.
—*Mark Twain (sign in a hotel in Florence)*

1. For a successful trip kept within a reasonable budget, plan ahead. Research where you want to go, how to get there, and the things you want to do along the way. Make hotel reservations in advance to ensure that you get the hotel of your choice in the location you want—and at the price you can afford.

2. Try to go in an off-season, when rates are lower and tourists are fewer.

3. Whatever time of year you are reserving, ask if there are any special lower rates for businesspeople, teachers, extended stays, cash versus a credit card . . . anything you can think of that might apply. If a hotel has an 800 number, the operator may not be authorized to grant discounts. When you call or fax the hotel yourself, do it during Italian working hours; at night, the person receiving the request will have no authority to make discount decisions. Be sure the quoted rate includes taxes and service charges, and get the rate you have agreed to pay in writing, and take it with you for the check-in.

4. Ask to have the cost of the hotel breakfast deducted from your total bill, even if the hotel policy states that breakfast is included. In some cases, hotels charge up to L20,000 per person for a daily breakfast consisting of a roll, coffee, jam, and butter—and, if you are lucky, a glass of processed juice and prepackaged cheese. Multiply this by two or three people over several days, and it becomes a ridiculous amount of money poorly spent. It is so much better, and more interesting, to have a cappuccino and *cornetto* (roll) at the corner *caffè* with the locals.

5. If you do eat the hotel breakfast, remember that is just what you are having . . . breakfast ONLY. Please do not take advantage of the buffet and consider it a place to load your pockets and bags with enough extra food to sustain you and your family for lunch and/or dinner. Hoteliers take a very dim view of this cheap trick.

6. A room with a double bed (*matrimoniale*) and shower on the back of the hotel will be cheaper than a twin-bedded room (*due letto*) with a bathtub and a balcony or a view. Also, if you are in a bathless room and the hotel has a shower or towel surcharge, consider whether this is most economical. If there are two of you, a room with a private shower might cost about the same as one without

once you add in the surcharges, to say nothing of the inconvenience of waiting your turn to bathe and, when it comes, of finding there is no hot water.

7. Major Italian cities are not known for their peaceful tranquillity. In fact, Rome has the dubious distinction of being the noisiest city in Europe. If you are a light sleeper, bring earplugs and ask for a quiet room—but be prepared to stay in a dark room with no view and limited ventilation on the back of the hotel.

8. Find out what the hotel refund policy is should you have to cancel a reservation or cut short your stay. Some have only one policy: You do not get your money back, period. This is a critical point if you are renting an apartment, and you should seriously consider trip cancellation insurance. (For more on this, plus apartment renting tips, see page 13.)

9. Insist on checking out the room before checking in: make sure everything works, it is clean, there are towels, and it is what you reserved. This is the time to reconfirm the room price and discuss extra charges such as telephone calls. Pleading ignorance to extra charges at checkout time is no excuse not to pay them.

10. Italian law states that hotel guests are not allowed to have any unregistered guests or visitors in their rooms, no matter how short a time they may be staying. In small hotels, this is strongly enforced.

11. Hotels detest any kind of eating in the room, so if you do have room snacks, please dispose of your papers, crumbs, and cores discreetly.

12. It is not the washing of clothes that hotels object to, it is the dripping. Wet clothes have ruined many carpets and stained walls. If you must rinse out a few things in the room, please let them drip-dry over the tub, sink, or bidet. If you have jeans or other heavy articles to wash, inquire about the nearest coin-operated laundromat. Hotel laundry services are sky-high, and so are finish laundries. Your best bet is to go to a laundromat and mix with the locals while washing and drying your clothes. Who knows, it could turn out to be one of your more interesting encounters with the Italians.

13. Many hotels in all categories turn on the heat and air-conditioning only between 7 and 9 A.M. and again from 4:30 or 5 P.M. until 11 P.M., turning it off completely after midnight and during the middle of the day no matter how high or low the thermometer may dip. If this poses a problem for you, ask if your hotel room has individually controlled heat and/or air-conditioning that you may regulate at your discretion.

14. If you are staying in Florence or Venice from spring through fall, bring mosquito spray. The mosquitoes during this time of year are lethal, and *very* few hotels have window screens. Hotels do provide a *machina por zanzare* (machine for mosquitoes), but often this is not enough.

15. BYO (Bring Your Own) lightbulbs if you are staying in a two-star-or-lower hotel and want to do any work or read after dark in your room. Italians must have developed the power to read by the light of the moon! I have never seen such low-watt bulbs masquerading as light. I travel with my own folding halogen light, but you can pump up the watts by using stronger bulbs that you can buy in an Italian corner convenience store.

16. *Never* change money in a hotel, restaurant, or shop. Go to a bank, the American Express office (if you have their traveler's checks, there is no commission), or use an ATM.

17. Take a Xeroxed copy of your passport, credit cards, airline tickets, hotel confirmation letters, and any other important documents without which you would be either in trouble or very inconvenienced. Leave a second copy with someone at home. This one precautionary step could save you hours of time should something happen to these vital papers.

18. Stay alert. Be aware of your immediate surroundings, and do not take any chances you would not take back home. Pickpockets are everywhere and often strike when you least expect them. Carry your valuables in a money belt or keep them locked up in the hotel safe. Women should carry purses crosswise in front of their body and hold the purse away from the traffic side of the sidewalk.

19. If you are planning to be in Rome anytime during the year 2000, when Catholics around the world celebrate the Jubilee Year and plan pilgrimages to Rome to reaffirm and celebrate their faith, make your reservations *today.* Some hotels were fully booked in 1998! The small, independent hotels will probably be the least affected, but if you plan to stay in student, hostel, or Holy Hotel accommodations, start working on your reservations now!

20. Last but not least . . . three special people: Frank Peters, Tom Rankin, and Samantha Durell. These three personal tour guides will enhance your trip to Florence, Rome, and Venice in ways you never thought possible. In addition to being bilingual and extremely well qualified to guide you, they are all passionate about what they do. Each one possesses an intimate, detailed knowledge of the city they cover, one they have come to love and call their own through many years of living and working there. Whether it is your first visit, or you consider yourself a seasoned veteran, time

spent with them will allow you to see their cities with new eyes and a deeper understanding. As you bid them farewell, you will feel you have made a wonderful friend you will want to tell others about, and certainly be eager to see again. For details, please refer to the following pages: Frank Peters (Florence), page 76; Tom Rankin (Rome), Scala Reale, page 134; and Samantha Durell (Venice), Venice Advisory Service, page 219.

Tips on Renting an Italian Apartment

1. MOST IMPORTANT: *Know the cancellation policy and buy cancellation insurance.* It is beyond the scope of this book to detail the various apartment rental policies you will encounter, but I can assure you they are not favorable to you and always hit the hardest when the chips are down and you must change your plans as far as forty-five days ahead or, worse, in the middle of your stay. To protect yourself, purchase trip insurance. The Automobile Club of American has a list of carriers, some of which are Access America, Inc., (800) 284-8300; Carefree Travel Insurance, (800) 323-3149; and Travel Guard International, (800) 782-5151.

2. When renting, state your needs clearly: the size of apartment you want, the number of people in your group, the types of beds needed (i.e., orthopedic mattresses essential or will a sofa bed do?), stall shower versus handheld shower nozzle in a tub with no curtain, and so on. Do you want CNN, or will you be happy watching Italian TV?

3. Is there a telephone specifically for your unit and how much are you charged per call? Is there an answering machine available, a fax, sufficient wiring to support your computer?

4. In an individual rental, it is almost certain that you will pay for all utilities. How much will this be? Chances are that heating and/or air-conditioning will be needed and will either be deducted from a hefty deposit that will be collected upon reserving, and the remainder of which will be refunded as long as three months *after* you have gone home, or charged at a fixed rate you will be required to pay up front or upon arrival.

5. How far is the flat from what *you* want to see in Rome, Florence, or Venice? Ask for photos of the apartment inside and out, and a city map with the flat location marked on it.

6. How far is the nearest market, laundry and dry cleaner, public transportation, pharmacy, restaurant, and so on?

7. Is maid service included, and if not, is it available and for how much extra? How much is the final cleaning fee. (Even if you leave the flat surgically clean, you will pay a final cleaning fee.)

8. Who is responsible for laundering sheets and towels? If you are, you will probably want a washing machine in the flat, or at least in the building.

9. Is the apartment childproofed? Suitable for someone with special needs? Is there a park or playground nearby?

10. Is there a lift to your flat? While that fifth-floor penthouse has a million-dollar view, do you really want to lug suitcases up and down, as well as daily bags of groceries and shopping finds? Think about this one carefully—stairs get old in a hurry.

11. Upon arrival, will someone meet you at the apartment to show you the ropes, or do you have to go to an office somewhere to get the keys.

12. What back-up services are provided? Is there a twenty-four-hour hot line to call if the heater blows up (don't laugh, it happened to me), the plumbing quits (that, too), or you face some other household crisis.

General Information

Discounts

Hotels

Every *Cheap Sleeps in Italy* hotel listing states if seasonal discounts are offered. The amounts of the discount are not given because they vary with the time of the year, room availability, and often the whim of the owner. In most cases, you can count on a 10 to 15 percent discount in the off-season. In some cases, discounts are granted year-round to readers of this book who mention the book when reserving and show a copy upon arrival. These hotels are indicated. Finally, just because a hotel did not offer any sort of discount at press time doesn't mean they won't if you ask. Don't be timid about this . . . always ask.

Senior Citizens

It is great to be young, but it pays to be older. Today, more and more people over fifty find themselves with time and extra money on their hands. Statistics show that the bulk of travelers are between forty-five and seventy years of age. Italy is not the best place to find senior citizens discounts, but there are a few savings out there.

Travelers over sixty can buy the Senior Citizen's Silver Card (*Carta d'Argento*), a rail pass good for a 20 percent reduction on Italian train tickets. This pass can *only* be bought in Italy, costs around L50,000, and is valid for one year. The blackout periods are Friday, Saturday, Sunday, June 26 to August 14, and December 18 to 28.

Any person sixty or older is given free or reduced admission to state and some private museums, national monuments, cultural events, and cinemas. The key is to ask at the ticket booth, and be prepared to show a passport.

These three U.S.-based organizations aimed at seniors are worth checking into if you are planning any trip, not just one to Italy.

American Association of Retired Persons (AARP)
601 E. Street NW, Washington, D.C. 20049
Tel: (202) 434-2277, (800) 424-3410, Mon–Fri 8 A.M.–8 P.M.

Elderhostel
75 Federal Street, third floor, Boston, MA 02110
Tel: (617) 426-7788, Mon–Fri 8 A.M.–5 P.M.

Hostelling International (HI/AYH)
P.O. Box 37613, Washington, D.C. 20013-7613
Tel: (202) 783-6161, Mon–Fri 8 A.M.–5 P.M.

Students

If you have youth and energy on your side and are twenty-six years old or younger, bargains abound.

Accommodations: Youth hostels are the cheapest beds, provided you can get one. You will need an International Youth Hostel Association card. Contact American Youth Hostels, 733 15th Street NW, Suite 840, Washington, D.C. 20005, or call (202) 783-6161. They can also provide books listing all the European hostels.

Discount Cards: The Italian railroads offer a Carta Verde for any person under twenty-six. This is valid for three years, costs around L50,000, and entitles cardholders to a 20 percent reduction off any Italian state rail fare year-round. It is available only in Italy and can be bought at railroad stations.

For discounts on transportation, museums, and other attractions, it is smart to buy the International Student Identity Card (ISIC) if you are a student, or the International Youth Card (IYC) if you are not but are under twenty-six. They also have deals for teachers. In the United States both cards cost $20 and are available through Council Travel (see below). In addition to discounts for museums and ground and air travel, holders receive hotel, restaurant, and cultural discounts at participating establishments as well as accident and medical emergency benefits. It is a card no person under twenty-six or teacher traveling to Italy should leave home without! For more information, brochures, and their *Student Travel* magazine, contact the Council Travel Office at CIEE headquarters, 205 East 42nd Street, 16th floor, New York, NY 10017, or call (212) 661-1450 or (800) 2-COUNCIL. For information about their educational programs, call (888) COUNCIL. There are also branches in most major U.S. cities. Check your telephone directory or call the New York office for the location nearest you.

One of the best student discount cards is the Rolling Venice Card, but it is available for purchase and use only in Venice. You save on food, hotels, admissions, and in many stores. See Venice, page 218, for more details.

Travel Agencies: The Centro Turistico Studentesco (CTS) is a student travel agency in Italy, and the only representative in Italy of the ISIC Association, dedicated to furthering travel opportunities for students (see above for more on ISIC). This organization has offices in major Italian cities and helps students find accommodations and low airfares, and it's a good place to get plugged into the travel-on-a-shoestring crowd. The main Rome office is at Via Genova, 16, tel: 06-462-0431; fax: 06-462-04326; e-mail: ctsinfo@cts.it; Internet: www.cts.it. The branch offices are at Corso Vittorio Emanuele II, 297, tel: 06-687-2672-3-4; and Air Terminal Ostiense, tel: 06-574-7950, 06-575-8514.

Getting There

Getting there can cost you a fortune . . . or be half the fun if you get a discounted ticket. Options for finding these cheap tickets include student ticket agencies (see "Discounts," above), courier flights, bucket shops, the Internet, and frequent-flyer miles. When dealing directly with the airlines, the point to remember is that *you* must ask them what discounts they have, since they would rather you pay the full fare. If at first you don't succeed, hang up and call again. The next operator may be able to get you a deal. If you are going through a travel agent, do a little advance homework on airfares yourself so you will know whether or not the "discounted" fare your agent offers really is a good deal. The following airlines have daily nonstop flights from various U.S. cities to Italy.

Alitalia, (800) 223-5730
Direct flights daily to Rome and Milan from Boston, Chicago, New York, Miami, and Los Angeles.

American Airlines, (800) 433-7300
Direct flights from Chicago and Miami to Milan with other airline connections to Rome.

Delta, (800) 221-1212
Some of the best fares from New York to Rome.

TWA, (800) 892-4141
One of the best for variety in the discount-fare circus. For young people, two of the best are the Youth Fare (for ages twelve to twenty-four), with discounts varying according to time of year and days of travel, and the Youth Travel Pack, a four-coupon book for four U.S. flights that must be purchased in the United States—a fifth coupon allows 20 percent off on any international flight. Seniors (sixty-two or older) can buy an eight-coupon Travel Pack and apply the ninth coupon for a 20 percent discount on any international flight. They also have companion-fare discounts ranging from 10 to 15 percent, plus senior promotional fares during the year.

High and Low Seasons

Wouldn't it be wonderful to drop everything and fly to Italy whenever the spirit moved us? Unfortunately, most of us do not lead such charmed lives; we are bound by schedules, budgets, family considerations, and deadlines on all sides. To get the most out of your hotel dollar, the high and low seasons must be given careful attention.

Throughout Italy, the high season is generally from the first of April through October and again the two weeks around Christmas and New Year's. Venice has an additional high season during the two weeks before Lent, when Carnivale is celebrated and the city is filled with unbelievable numbers of partying tourists. As one wag put it, you could drop dead and still be standing upright in the crowds that pack St. Mark's Square during the last few days of Lent. I have been there and I know; you literally cannot move one inch in any direction, and it is scary. It is beyond the beyonds for most people, let alone a claustrophobic. Prices on everything during this time in Venice are out of this world. August is the traditional vacation month for most in Rome, while Venetians vacation in the damp months of January and February. In Florence, vacations seem to be in July and August, when the heat, humidity, and mosquitoes are at their peak.

Holidays

The following is a list of legal holidays in Italy, when banks and most stores are closed. Restaurants tend to go with the moment: if business is slow, they will close; otherwise they may be open. It is impossible to nail down exact policies. Hotels are always open, but the third-string staff may be on duty. On the eve of important holidays such as Christmas, New Year's, and the Feast of the Assumption, some stores close for the day at 1 P.M. and the banks close at 11:30 A.M. If the holiday falls on a Thursday or a Tuesday, the Friday and Monday may also be taken to create long weekends. This is called "building a bridge" (*ponte*) from one holiday to another. For example, if May Day falls on a Thursday, many shops will close from Wednesday afternoon until Monday afternoon or Tuesday morning.

January 1	Capi d'Anno	New Year's Day
Dates vary	La Befana	Epiphany
Dates vary	Pasqua	Easter Sunday
Dates vary	Lunedi Pasqua	Easter Monday
April 25	Venticinque Aprile	Liberation Day
May 1	Primo Maggio	Labor Day
June 2		National Day
August 15	Ferragósto	Assumption of the Virgin
November 1	Tutti Santi	All Saints' Day
December 8	Festa dell'Immacolata	Feast of the Immaculate Conception
December 25	Natale	Christmas
December 26	Santo Stefano	Boxing Day
Patron Saints' Days		
Florence:	June 24	St. John the Baptist's Day
Rome:	June 29	St. Peter's Day
Venice:	April 25	St. Mark's Day

Reservations

People always ask me, "Do I need reservations? I am only going to be in Rome (or Florence or Venice) for a few days." The answer is *absolutely yes,* no matter how long or short your stay will be or the time of year. It is not unusual for hotels in the central parts of these cities to be fully booked, even in the off-season. Unless you do not mind spending major portions of time securing hotel accommodations, taking chances on a cancellation, paying more than your budget allows, or staying on the fringes and commuting into tourist central, reservations are essential.

Today the best way to reserve is by fax or telephone. When you consider the cost of this convenience against the entire cost of the trip, it is nothing. When you make your reservations, the following points should be covered.

1. The dates of the stay, time of arrival, and number of people in the party.

2. The size and type of rooms (double or twin beds, extra beds needed, adjoining rooms, suite, etc.).

3. The facilities needed: private toilet and shower or bathtub, or hall facilities if these are acceptable to you.

4. The location of the room: view, on the street, on the courtyard, or a quiet room on the back of the hotel (which will have no view at all).

5. The rates. Determine ahead what the nightly rates will be and state whether or not you will be eating breakfast at the hotel (you will save considerable money if you do not). If you do not eat breakfast at the hotel, *be sure* it is deducted from the quoted rate. Most hotel rates include taxes and services: be sure your hotel rates do. Some apartment rentals do not, and it can run close to 10 percent.

6. Determine the deposit required and the form of payment. Also inquire about the cancellation policy.

7. Request a confirmation in writing from the hotel for both your reservation and deposit, and carry this confirmation with you to the registration desk when you check in. You may have to prove that there is a record of your reservation, or that you are *not* booked into the presidential suite (or maybe you are).

E-mail/Internet

More and more Italian hotels are plugging into cyberspace, but it is hardly comparable to the frenzied addiction we see in the States. Whenever applicable, the hotel's e-mail and Internet website has been given. In some cases the hotels subscribe to a general service rather than have their own website. Because technology is in the early stages in Italy, please be understanding, expect some changes along with occasional snafus.

Fax

If you and the hotel both have a fax number, this is the best way to make and confirm a reservation. To fax a message to Italy, use 011-39, then the city code (Florence: 055, Rome: 06, Venice: 041), and then the fax number of the hotel. All fax and telephone numbers now include the zero in the city code. Rome, for example, would have 06-444-4444 (see "Telephone," below).

Telephone

It has been said that even the Pope is at the mercy of the Italian telephone system. In June 1998, area codes became an integral part of all Italian telephone and fax numbers. For calls to Italy from the United States, this means you must dial the area code with the 0 before it before dialing the number. For example, when dialing Rome, it is 011-39-06 plus the number. If you are already in Rome, and want to dial a number within the 06 area code, you will dial the 06 and the number. Dialing directions from city to city within Italy and from Italy to another country are unchanged.

If you are telephoning for reservations, time the call during the hotel's weekday business hours to avoid talking to a night clerk who has no authority to make any sort of discount arrangements, and who perhaps cannot even accept a telephone reservation from abroad. Before calling, write down all your requests and questions. Ask the hotel to send you a written confirmation and, in turn, send them a confirmation of the conversation. If you send the confirmation by mail (see below for reasons not to), send it certified, so you will know the hotel has actually received it, and keep a copy. In your confirmation, cite the details of the conversation, the name of the person with whom you spoke, and the date and time of the call. To dial direct to Italy, dial 011-39, then the city code (Florence: 055, Rome: 06, Venice: 041) and the number of the hotel. Don't forget—telephone numbers now include the zero in the city code.

Letter

In this day of the fax, e-mail, and every other electronic convenience, why anyone would want to write for reservations is a complete mystery to me, and to most hoteliers as well. Many have laughingly pointed out to me a stack of *months*-old letters from prospective guests requesting reservations and/or price information. Managers have told me they do not have time to answer their letters. In addition, everyone who has had any experience with the Italian mail service will tell you the same thing: it is, without question, terrible—worse even than the telephone system. Delays of up to two to three months are commonplace, and often mail simply does not reach its destination . . . and that is when there are no strikes to make matters even more frustrating. If you still insist on this out-of-date method of reserving, allow plenty of time and expect long delays. Also, be prepared to leave on your trip without ever having heard from the three hotels you wrote to, or to have corresponded with the hotel, sent a deposit, but never to have heard back. Believe me, this is *not* the way to plan a trip today.

Making Reservations in Italian

If the hotel in question has no English-speaking staff, or you just want to try your luck with Italian, here are a few simple phrases (also see the "Glossary," page 328).

When you are telephoning, after hearing the hotel greeting, you may want to start with *Parla inglese?* If they don't, move on to *Potrei prenotare una camera singola (doppia) con/senza bagno per il tre Aprile?* Can I reserve a single (double) room with/without bath for the third of April? *È compresa la prima colazione?* Is breakfast included? *Quanto costa?* How much is it? *Ha niente che costa di meno?* Do you have anything cheaper? *Va bene, la prendo.* Okay, I will take it. *Mi chiamo ____.* My name is ____. *Arriverò alle sedici.* I will arrive at 1600. (Note: Italians use a twenty-four-hour clock, or military time as we know it. *Sedici* is 1600, or 4 P.M.) *Mille grazie.* Many thanks.

Deposits

After making your reservations, most hotels will require at least a one-night deposit, even if you have been a guest there before. This is good insurance for both sides. It should mean you are guaranteed the room you want for the number of nights you requested. The easiest way to handle a deposit is with a credit card. If the hotel does not take credit cards, there are other options. The next best thing is to send the hotel an international money order in U.S. dollars. This can be converted into Italian lire by the hotel and saves you having to get the money order in Italian lire on this side of the Atlantic. While this option is more convenient for you, it is added work, time, and expense for the hotel, and those in the lower-priced Cheap Sleep categories will not do it. They will insist on a deposit made out to them in Italian lire. Check with your local bank to find out where you can obtain a foreign-currency money order.

If your local bank cannot provide you with a foreign-currency draft (highly probable), then contact Ruesch International at 825 14th Street NW, Washington, D.C. 20005, or call (800) 696-7990. This currency specialist can perform a variety of transactions for individual travelers. The service fee is nominal, and their services run from issuing and converting foreign bank drafts to wiring any amount of money. In addition to the D.C. office, they have branches in New York, Atlanta, Boston, Chicago, and Los Angeles. Abroad, they are in London and Zurich. No orders are processed after 4 P.M.

Arrivals and Departures

Early Arrival

If you have an early morning arrival flight, chances are good your hotel room will not be ready. Checkout time is noon, and rooms may not be made up until midafternoon. If you must have a room *before* noon, and the hotel cannot guarantee it, perhaps you should consider booking the room for the day before. That way you can have a hot shower and regroup after a long flight rather than hanging out in the lobby or wandering around the neighborhood in a jet-lagged daze waiting for your room to be ready.

Late Arrival

Hotel guests are expected to arrive by 6 P.M. If you have a reservation, even with deposit and confirmation, the hotel does not have to hold the room for you beyond this time unless they have been forewarned that you will be late arriving. To allow for travel delays, always ask your hotel to hold your room for you, then call the minute you know you will be late, if that is possible. If you are arriving by plane or train, give the hotel the name of the airline and the flight number, or the train arrival time. Asking for the room to be held will probably oblige you to pay for it, even if you arrive one day late.

Departures

Checkout time in most Italian hotels is noon. If you have a later plane or train to catch, most hotels will be glad to hold your luggage for you at no additional cost. In fact, if you are making some side trips, and don't want to take all the luggage you brought with you, arrangements can be made to store your luggage at the hotel. A few hotels may give a day rate, or offer an extended checkout time, if you need the use of your room until your plane or train leaves. Make these arrangements as soon as possible.

Money Matters

If you will be a traveller, have always two bags very full . . . one of patience and another of money.

—John Florio

No part of your trip will cause you more grief than money, even if you have enough of it. If you are on a limited budget, try to have a little cushion that will enable you to enjoy a cappuccino at St. Mark's Square in Venice, to stay in a romantic pensione in Florence with a view to the Tuscan hills, or to splurge on a great meal in Rome. Life is too short *not* to have the happy memories that come from just enjoying where you are in the moment, without trying to squeeze every penny.

Carrying large amounts of cash, even in a money belt, is risky business. If you remember to have traveler's checks, charge big items on your credit card, convert lire as you go, and use ATMs, you will do well. Also, remember to carry some of your own personal checks. If you suddenly run out of money, you can use them to get cash advances or buy traveler's checks, provided the credit cards you have allow you to do this. Try to have a few lire on hand when you arrive. True, you may pay more for this convenience, but if you change $100 or so before you leave home, you will never miss the few extra dollars it may cost against the peace of mind of knowing you have some money to tide you over until you can get to a bank or ATM. Airport and train station change booths have long lines and poor rates. They should be used in emergencies only. If you cannot get lire locally, you can order them by telephone and they will be Federal Expressed to you within two days. Please contact Thomas Cook Currency

Service, 630 Fifth Avenue, New York, NY 10101; tel: (800) 287-7362; fax: (202) 237-0026. Hours are Monday through Friday, 8:30 A.M. to 9 P.M., Eastern Standard Time.

Banks offer the best exchange rate, much better than hotels or exchange windows, which are identified by signs reading "Cambio," "Wechsel," or "Change." Estimate your needs carefully. If you overbuy lire, you will lose twice, both in buying and in selling. Every time you change money, someone is making a profit, and I can guarantee that it is not you.

NOTE: Italian banking hours are Monday through Friday from 8:30 A.M. to 1:30 P.M., and 3 or 3:30 P.M. to 4 or 4:30 P.M. All are closed on holidays, and sometimes the afternoon before a major holiday.

ATM Cards

If your ATM card is part of a network that works abroad, you are in business. You use the machines in Italy the same way you do here, by punching in your personal identification number (PIN) and the amount of cash you want. It is essential that you check in advance on the limits of withdrawals and cash advances within specific time periods. Also ask whether your bank card or credit card PIN number will need to be reissued for use in Italy, since Italian ATM machines only accept four-digit PIN numbers. Your U.S. bank or credit card will also charge you for using a foreign ATM, but you will be getting a wholesale conversion rate that is better than you would get at a bank or currency exchange office. Finally, plan ahead. Find out the ATM locations and the names of corresponding affiliated cash machine networks before you leave home. For Cirrus locations, call (800) 4-CIRRUS. For Plus locations, call (800) THE-PLUS. To enroll in the American Express foreign ATM program, call (800) CASH-NOW.

Credit Cards

Despite the fact that Italy is the world's fifth-largest industrial nation, some smaller hotels, especially in the student, hostel, and Holy Hotel categories, and *madre e padre* shops have not kept pace with the rest of the world in accepting plastic instead of cash. Quite often a place will accept a particular credit card, and then stop for no apparent reason, only to start again. All the *Cheap Sleeps in Italy* listings indicate which credit cards, if any, are accepted.

Despite this, I recommend using a credit card whenever possible. A credit card can be a lifesaver in emergencies when you need quick cash, as most cards have instant cash advance benefits. Also, carrying plastic eliminates the need for carrying large sums of cash, which must be purchased by standing in line at a bank or other money-changing facility. Credit card receipts also provide you with a record of your purchases. Best of all, you often get delayed billing of up to four to six weeks after purchase. It is also important to remember that the currency conversion rate is made at the time of processing, not at the time of purchase. In Italy, and all of Europe, MasterCard is Eurocard, and Visa is Carte Bleu. Here are a few other credit card tips:

1. If the dollar is falling, use cash. If the dollar is going up, charge like crazy.

2. Before using your credit card, ask the store or hotel if there is any discount or incentive to pay in cash.

3. Keep a copy of all your credit card numbers with you and leave another copy at home.

4. Save your receipts to check against the statement when it arrives. Errors are all too frequent.

5. Report the loss of your card immediately. Contact both the local police and the U.S. consular office, then report the loss to the credit card company. When you get home, contact your insurance agent to see if the loss is covered.

American Express	(800) 528-0480, (212) 477-5700 (collect), 1678-64046 (card emergencies), 1678-72000 (traveler's check emergencies)
Diner's Club	(800) 234-6377, or (214) 680-6480 (collect), 1678-64064
MasterCard	(800) 307-7309, 1678-74299
Visa	1678-19014, or 1678-77232 (toll-free from Italy to the United States)

6. Finally, emergency check cashing is a benefit for many cardholders, as is free car-rental insurance. Check with your issuing bank to determine the list of benefits you have; you may be pleasantly surprised.

Personal Checks

Yes, you should definitely take some with you. Personal checks are not widely accepted, but some stores and a very few hotels will accept them. The main reason to take personal checks is that you can use them to get cash advances with your credit cards at participating Italian banks and at all American Express offices.

Tipping

Tipping is definitely part of the Italian way of life and is expected on almost all levels of service. However, you are not required to tip if the service is poor or rude.

Beauty parlors and barber shops	10 to 15 percent for each person who serves you

Caffès and bars	L100–200 for whatever you drink standing at a coffee bar; L1,000 for table service in a sidewalk *caffè*
Hotels:	
Maids	L1,000 per day
Doorman for calling a taxi	L2,000
Bellboys and porters	L1,500 per bag; L5,000–10,000 for extra services
Concierge	L3,500 for each service given
Room service	L1,000
Guides	L2,000 per person
Museum and church offerings	L2,000 per person
Restaurants	15 percent service is often included in or added to the bill—this *is* the tip. If service has been exceptional, leave 10 percent more.
Service stations	Nothing expected
Taxis	10 to 15 percent of metered fare
Theater usher	L1,000 per person
Train station and airport porters	They charge a fixed rate per bag. Tip an extra L500 per bag, more if they have been very helpful.
Washroom attendants	L100–300

The Tipping Scam

There is a practice in some restaurants in the Italian/tourist industry of writing the amount of the bill, to which a 12 to 15 percent service charge has *already* been added, or included in the basic cost, in the top box of the charge slip, leaving the boxes marked "gratuity" or "tip" and "total" empty. Do not fall for this. If the service has already been added or included, draw a line from the top figure to the total at the bottom of the sheet, then write in the total figure yourself. If you are leaving a tip on top of this total, leave it in cash. Often tips left on credit cards are not properly distributed. It is better to leave any tip in cash.

Traveler's Checks

You will always get a better exchange rate for traveler's checks than for cash, but the real cost lies in what you spent to get the traveler's checks in the first place and what commission you pay to cash them. American Express cardholders can order traveler's checks by phone, at banks, or at credit unions free of charge with a gold card, or for a 1 percent commission with a green card. Nonmembers also pay the 1 percent commission. American Automobile Association (AAA) members can purchase American Express traveler's checks commission free from their local AAA office, but there is usually a limit. You can exchange American Express traveler's checks to lire without paying a commission at any American Express office, and they are located in Rome, Florence, Venice, and twelve other Italian cities. American Express cardholders can also write a personal check for traveler's checks at any of these offices. For a directory of American Express services and offices, ask for the American Express Traveler's Companion. Call (800) 673-3782 to order checks or get further information.

American Express is the best when it comes to traveler's checks in Italy, but there are others that for various reasons may work for you. Remember that you may have to pay a commission to cash traveler's checks, even if you did not pay one to buy them.

Citicorp banks sell traveler's checks that give the holder access to a twenty-four-hour SOS line that provides travel-related services. For information, call (800) 645-6556.

MasterCard International issues traveler's checks that are widely accepted. Call (800) 223-7373 for general information, or (800) 423-3630 to buy them over the phone using your MasterCard.

Visa sells traveler's checks through Bank of America, many travel agencies, and at any bank with a VISA logo displayed. They do not sell them by telephone. For further information, call (800) 227-6811.

A final note: *Always* Xerox your passport and keep a separate record of your traveler's check numbers. Keep one copy in your money belt and another with a trusted person at home. This precaution will save the day if your checks are lost or stolen.

Wiring Money from Home

Sometimes we need a little help from home, especially if our money becomes history on our trip before we do. You can have someone send you an American Express MoneyGram. You do not have to be an American Express cardholder to send or receive a MoneyGram. You can send up to $10,000 using a credit card or, if you only have cash, you can send up to $1,000. A MoneyGram can be sent and ready for you to pick up in less than an hour! Fees vary according to the amount of money sent, but they average from 3 to 10 percent. When you pick up your money, you will have to know the transaction number from the sender at home and show ID. For American Express MoneyGram locations, call (800) 926-9400.

If you don't use an American Express MoneyGram, your next choices are either wiring the money (from one cent to $20,000) through a company called MoneyGram, tel: (800) 696-7990, or through Western Union, tel: (800) 325-6000.

Packing: Do You Really Need All That?
On a long journey, even a straw weighs heavy.
—Spanish proverb

Lay out all the clothes you think you will need, then put half of them back into the closet. Trust me on this; you will be glad you did when you are lugging your suitcases up the stairway in that charming little pensione in Rome on the fifth floor of a building with no elevator. Coordinate around one color, and use every nook and cranny of your suitcase to its fullest: stuff your shoes, roll your sweaters and underwear, lay plastic garment bags between layers to prevent wrinkling, and pack the suitcase full so things will not slide to a pile at one end. Take clothes you would wear in any major metropolitan city. Short shorts, baseball caps, jogging outfits (when not jogging), and bare midriffs, no matter what the temperature, will label you as a gauche tourist. Sleeveless, backless, or otherwise abbreviated dresses and bare chests are always unwelcome in restaurants and in many museums and churches. There are dress codes for St. Peter's in Rome and St. Mark's in Venice. Women must not have bare shoulders, but heads may be uncovered. Short shorts are out for both sexes.

If you are in Italy in summer, bring comfortable, light cottons. Synthetics do not breathe and add to the heat discomfort. Even though the days can be very hot, nights are often cool, so include a sweater or lightweight jacket. For winter visits, you will want a warm coat or lined raincoat, a hat (70 percent of body heat goes out through your head), extra sweaters for layering, and perhaps a set of silk underwear and warm night wear. Many hotels turn off the heat or air-conditioning around midnight, and central heating in many buildings and restaurants is antique at best. No matter what time of year, include an extra pair of walking shoes, an umbrella, a plastic bag for damp or dirty laundry, blow-up hangers for drip-dry laundries, rubber flip-flops if you are staying in bathless rooms, a money belt, and an extra pair of eyeglasses.

Pack your toiletries and cosmetics in a waterproof bag. You only need one experience with the mess caused by airline pressure blowing off the top of your shampoo to know what I am talking about. If you are coming in summer, don't forget the bug repellent.

The bottom line in packing is this: you are not going to a desert island but to Italy, where hundreds of shops sell everything you forgot to bring or may suddenly find you need. It is always fun to have to go shopping and then to bring back something new and different that all of your friends can admire.

Telephone

Any country whose telephone numbers range from four to eight digits has got to be exciting and full of surprises.

—*Michael Jackson*

The wide range of digits in telephone numbers is just the start of the fun, fascination, and challenge of the Italian telephone system. As mentioned in the section on telephoning and faxing for hotel reservations, all telephone and fax numbers in Italy now include the 0 in dialing any number in the country. For instance, if you are calling from the United States to Italy, or from one address in Florence to another, you must dial 055 plus the number.

Outside your hotel or apartment, there are three types of telephones in Italy: token phones (*gettoni*), coin telephones, and card phones. The *gettoni* are holdovers from the days of Caesar and are slowly being phased out. If you get a handful of L200 *gettoni* coins as change in a bar, insist on real coins. *Gettoni* are heavy, and chances are you will use a card phone. If you do use a *gettone* phone, one *gettone* buys five minutes.

The easiest way to make a call from a public telephone is to use a phone card (*carte telefoniche*). You can buy these phone cards from *tabacci* or news agents, and they come in denominations of L5,000 and L10,000. When you insert the card, a meter subtracts lire from it as you speak and displays the remaining value. Don't leave your card behind; chances are you still have time left on it. Please remember that unless they are toll-free, *all* calls made from any phone in Italy, even if it is just next door, cost the caller. Toll-free numbers begin with 1678.

Long-Distance Calling

The cheapest and easiest way to make an international call is to use AT&T Direct Service, MCI, or one of the other international calling services that are so prevalent today. These are competitive, money-saving programs, so shop around and find the one that suits you best. Italian telephone charges are lowest from 10 P.M. to 8 A.M. Monday through Saturday and all day Sunday.

Hotels are well known for sticking guests with as much as a 200 percent surcharge for long-distance and international calls. Check with the desk, and if they do add a surcharge, go to a Phone Center, where operators will assign you a booth, help you place your call, and collect payment after you are through at no additional charge.

Calls Made from Italy

If you want to make a collect call, or bill a call to your calling card (which will be cheaper than billing it to a credit card), dial 172-1011. An English-speaking operator will come on the line to assist you. To call the United States and Canada and have it billed to your Italian telephone, which is the more expensive way to do it, dial 00 plus the country code

(1 for the United States and Canada), then the area code and the number you are calling.

Calls Made to Italy

To call Italy direct, dial 011, the country code, the city code (including the 0 preceding it), and then the number you are calling. For example, the prefix for a call to Florence would be 011-39-055.

Country code for Italy 39
City code for Florence 055
City code for Rome 06
City code for Venice 041

Safety and Security

Caution and common sense should be exercised on a trip to Italy, just as they should be when traveling anywhere. It is best to leave all jewelry, expensive watches, and high-visibility wardrobes at home. Try to blend in. It is also smart to carry all valuables in a money belt or a necklace purse worn *inside* your clothing. Even if it feels bulky and uncomfortable, it beats having essential documents and money stolen. Money belts and necklace purses will also protect you against skilled thieves who use razors to slash open backpacks and fanny packs. If you do carry a purse, buy a sturdy one with a secure clasp and zipper, and carry it crosswise with the clasp against you and on the side of your body away from the street. Thieves on darting Vespas ride through the streets searching for likely victims. If you use a fanny pack, wear it in front, not in back. For backpacks, buy a small combination padlock, and slip it through the zippers. If you don't have a lock, use a safety pin and thread it through the zippers. Keep a hand on your bags at all times. When standing still, clutch them close to you, or hold them between your legs with one foot through the straps. When leaving a bank, ATM, or other change facility, or anytime for that matter, *never* count money in public. In cars, do not leave luggage locked inside, and open the door of the glove compartment to show potential thieves that nothing is there. Remove the radio when you leave your car. Never travel with your car unlocked. The U.S. State Department warns that every car, whether parked, stopped at a traffic light, or even moving, can be a potential target for armed robbery.

If you are staying in a student accommodation, or in any place where you cannot lock up your valuables, always carry them on your person, even if it means taking your camera and wallet with you to the showers. It goes without saying that you should leave nothing of value in your hotel room, and nothing is gained by locking valuables in your suitcase. What is to prevent someone from just taking the entire suitcase? It has happened often.

Every society has its criminals, and you must be alert at all times. The biggest threat, particularly in Rome, is the menace of pickpockets and bands of gypsies, especially children. Thieving groups can be thick around the Colosseum and the Forum, the Vatican, Piazza di Spagna, and Via del Corso, where they operate in a swarming mass with fluttering newspapers to divert your attention so they can get in and out of your pockets before you know what hit you. Extreme caution should be exercised on crowded buses, certainly on the tourist-infested 64, 85, and 492 in Rome. If you are on a bus and know you have been robbed, immediately alert the driver, who will lock the doors and drive to the nearest police station. It is also wise to avoid the Via Veneto in the evening, when hookers, who may or may not be female, and wallet-snatching gypsy children make it an unsafe free-for-all.

At night, women should stay on brightly lit streets and walk with purpose. It is also smart to walk in groups at night and to avoid the underground metro.

If you are robbed, file a report (*denunctare*) with the police. You will need it for your own insurance, and it is helpful in case anything is eventually found.

Anywhere you are in Italy, if you find yourself in a dangerous situation, call 113, the Public Emergency Assistance number for the State Police and First Aid. The military police, at 112, might be of help, and so could the Italian automobile club (ACI), at 116, if you need immediate assistance due to a crisis on the road.

There is a zero-tolerance law in Italy regarding drugs, and possession of even the smallest amount of *any* narcotic, including marijuana, is now illegal. All foreigners are subject to Italian law. If you are caught with drugs, the U.S. government can do little to help you: they send consular officers to visit you in jail, provide a list of attorneys, and inform your family of your stupidity. They cannot repatriate you to a prison on U.S. soil, and they have nothing to do with your sentencing, let alone your trial. For further information, read *Travel Warning on Drugs Abroad,* a free pamphlet put out by the Bureau of Consular Affairs, Department of State, Washington, D.C. 20520, tel: (202) 647-1488.

Some Last-Minute Hints

1. Italian Tourist Offices in the United States:
   630 5th Avenue, Suite 1565, New York, NY 10011
   (212) 245-5618, or (212) 245-5027

   500 N. Michigan Avenue, Chicago, IL 60611
   (312) 644-0990, or (312) 644-0996

   12400 Wilshire Boulevard, Suite 550, Los Angeles, CA 90025
   (310) 820-0098, or (310) 820-1898

2. American Express Global Assist can be reached at (800) 554-2639. This is a service for any American Express cardholder who needs emergency medical, legal, or financial assistance while traveling. All cases are verified. Operators at this number will accept collect calls and give information on currency rates, weather, visa/

passport requirements, customs, and embassy and consular telephone numbers and addresses.

3. Use *only* legitimate taxis, not the maverick independents, no matter how cheap they quote a fare. If you are coming from the airport, worries about flight safety pale compared with the horrors of riding in a taxi driven by the "Cabbie from Hell," who listens to a blaring tape recorder or radio, keeps the beat with the gas pedal, and turns his head in every direction but that of the road. Before you get in the taxi, determine the rate, and make sure the starting rate is showing on the meter when you get in, or you may find yourself paying for someone else's ride.

   If possible, keep your bags, or at least your most important pieces of luggage, with you in the cab. In case of fare confrontation, you won't be at the further mercy of a dishonest cabdriver.

4. In Italy, a *piano* is not always a musical instrument; it is also a floor in a building. *Piano terra,* or T, as you will see it on elevator indicators, means ground floor. *Primo piano,* or 1, means the first floor above the ground level (or what we would consider the second floor).

5. For a last-minute check on the weather in Italy before you leave the States, call (900) WEATHER. It costs under a dollar a minute and gives hourly updated weather information and three-day accurate weather forecasts for six hundred cities in the United States and the rest of the world.

How to Use Cheap Sleeps in Italy

Abbreviations
The following abbreviations are used to denote which credit cards a hotel or shop will accept:

American Express	AE
Diners Club	DC
MasterCard	MC
Visa	V

Big Splurges
Some hotels covered in *Cheap Sleeps in Italy* fall into the Big Splurge category because of their higher prices. These hotels are included for readers with more flexible budgets, exacting tastes, or greater needs. Even though the prices are higher, the hotels all offer good value for money. It is important to point out that while the prices are considered to be Big Splurges during the high season, which is generally from late March until November 1, many of these hotels offer significantly lower rates during the low season, making them affordable to a wider group of travelers. In some cases, weekend rates are offered year-round. To indicate that a hotel is a Big Splurge, a dollar sign ($) will appear in parentheses after the star(s) in the hotel's write-up and in all listings.

Stars
Hotels in Italy are controlled by a government rating system that ranks them from no stars to five-star deluxe. The star rating depends on things like number of lights in a room, whether or not the hotel has an elevator, number of private showers and toilets, and the size of the rooms. It has nothing to do with service, attitude of management, cleanliness, or cross-ventilation.

A no-star hotel is basic; some might say primitive. A one-star hotel has minimum facilities and seldom an elevator. Two stars means a comfortable room with a telephone, but not necessarily an elevator or private bathroom. Three stars usually guarantees a private bathroom, a color television, possibly air-conditioning, maybe a room safe, and perhaps an elevator. A four-star hotel has most luxuries you need, including a lift and usually a uniformed staff and a restaurant. A five-star deluxe hotel in Italy is a slice of heaven on earth as viewed from fabulous surroundings. Please note that many Italian hotels *do not* have elevators.

This does not mean that the hotel is not a good one. It usually means that the hotel is in a historically designated building that does not allow the renovations necessary to install an elevator.

Accommodations: Checking In

When you arrive at the hotel, always ask to see the room assigned to you before accepting it. If you are dissatisfied, ask to see another. After accepting the room, reconfirm the rate and whether or not you will be eating breakfast at the hotel. If not, be sure the breakfast price is deducted per day, per person, from the quoted price. If it is summertime, be sure you know the cost of air-conditioning. In some hotels it can be as much as L15,000–20,000 *extra* a day. This advance work prevents any unpleasant surprises when you check out.

The Italian hotel day begins and ends at noon. If you overstay without notifying the desk, you could be charged the price of an extra day.

In most hotels, you pay for the room, not for the number of people in it. Thus, if you are alone and occupy a triple, you could end up paying the triple price. Most hotels have two kinds of single and double rooms. First there is the usual single, which can too often be nothing more than a cell on the back of the hotel with no view, little ventilation, and very little living space. If you are a solo Cheap Sleeper and are willing to pay extra for a better room, ask for a double that is sold as a single. Double rooms are those with one double bed (*matrimoniale*) and usually smaller than those with twin beds (*due letto*). If you ask for a room with a bath, specify if you want a bathtub or will settle for a shower, but please remember . . . even in some three-star Italian hotels, there is no shower curtain or door. Prudent Cheap Sleepers also know that a room with a double bed and a shower will cost less than a room with twins and a bathtub. When reserving, be specific about the type of arrangements you want, get them confirmed in writing, take that confirmation with you to the hotel check-in, and then insist on them when you arrive.

Rates: Paying the Bill

Hotel rates and the number of stars must be posted, and the rates *should* include all services and taxes. In some residence hotels, services and taxes are extra (sometimes up to 10 percent).

Italian hotel rates are no longer tightly controlled by the government. As a result, hotels now offer different rates at different times of the year, getting the most they can, even in the off-seasons. It always makes good Cheap Sleeping sense to ask for the lowest rate possible, and to go in the off-season if your schedule permits.

All of the rates listed in *Cheap Sleeps in Italy* are for full price and do not reflect any discounts or deals. The listings also state if lower off-season rates apply, or if special rates are granted to readers of *Cheap Sleeps in Italy*. These special rates can vary widely depending on the time of year, if the hotel is fully booked, length of stay, and, in some smaller hotels, if you pay in cash or by credit card. *No matter when you go, ask for a discounted rate.* You never know, you may get lucky.

The hotel listings state which credit cards are accepted. In most *Cheap Sleeps* listings, payment is required one night in advance to hold your room. Some low-priced hotels, and almost all youth hostels and Holy Hotels, do not take credit cards. It is cash up front, in advance, in Italian lire only, and these hotels do not bend.

Hotel money exchange rates are terrible and never in your best interest. If you must pay your bill in lire, convert your money at a bank.

Before leaving the hotel, go over your bill carefully, question anything you do not understand, and get a receipt marked *paid* before leaving.

Breakfast

Most hotels listed in *Cheap Sleeps in Italy* serve at least a Continental breakfast consisting of a roll, butter, jam, and coffee, tea, or chocolate. Hotels stand to make an enormous profit on this meal, and in some instances, the cost per person, per day, can be as much as L20,000! If you want anything extra, it costs dearly and is usually not worth the additional outlay. Many three-star hotels now offer a buffet breakfast with cereals, yogurt, meat, cheese, and fruit added to the basic Continental offering. Sometimes the buffet may be worth the price if you plan to skip lunch. However, it is *never* anything but a show of very poor manners and a world-class cheap trick to load your purse or sack with enough food from the breakfast buffet to sustain you through lunch and/or dinner. Please refrain from taking advantage of your hotel in this way. Some hotels charge extra for breakfast, some include it in the room rate no matter what, and some include it in the room rate but allow you to deduct it if you don't want breakfast. If you are trying to save money, however, omit every hotel breakfast you can, insist that the cost be deducted from your bill, and join the locals standing at the corner *caffè*. You will have more fun and save a bundle.

English Spoken

All the listings tell you whether English is spoken. If you can dust off a few Italian phrases, smile, and display goodwill, you will find that the hotel staff will probably be warm and friendly and go out of their way to serve you. If you do not speak any Italian at all, it is important to know whether or not someone at the hotel can speak English. While it is fun to practice your broken Italian, it is definitely not fun to be unable to communicate when facing a crisis.

Facilities and Services

A brief summary at the end of each hotel listing tells what facilities and services the hotel offers. Generally, the more facilities, the more money you will spend.

Nearest Tourist Attractions

The hotels are listed in each city alphabetically by geographic location, with tourist attractions that are within a reasonable walking distance noted.

Maps

Each hotel listing in *Cheap Sleeps in Italy* is given a number that appears in parentheses beside its name and corresponds to a number on the appropriate map. Letters in parentheses have been used instead of numbers for shops listed in Cheap Chics. Establishments located outside the boundaries of these maps have been given no number or letter.

FLORENCE

Of all the places I have seen in Italy, it is the one by far I should most covet to live in. It is the ideal of an Italian city, once great, now a shadow of itself.
>   —*William Hazlitt,*
>   Notes of a Journey through
>   France and Italy, *1826*

Florence, the world's greatest celebration of the triumph of the human spirit, has long been regarded as the birthplace of the Renaissance and the Athens of modern civilization. Under the ruling of the powerful Medici family, Florence was decorated with churches and palaces, making it one of the most incredible living museums in the world.

If you like to walk, Florence is your city. Almost everything a visitor wants to see and do is easy to manage on foot. Explore her beautiful history by wandering down medieval streets and narrow lanes that have not changed in centuries. Wherever you turn, elegant Florence is a feast for the eyes and the soul, whether you are looking at the River Arno where the Ponte Vecchio stretches over it, strolling through the Boboli Gardens with the hazy Tuscan hills in the distance, or losing yourself for hours in one of her many churches and museums.

Many of the grand old villas of Florence have been converted into hotels. These now range from simple pensiones on the fourth floor (no elevator, of course) to grand luxury palaces. If possible, take advantage of lower rates between November and February, with the exception of Christmas and New Year's, and again during July and August. If you come in July or August, be prepared to share your stay with swarms of very aggressive mosquitoes. To ward off the onslaught, arm yourself with bug repellent, citronella candles, and apply Skin-So-Soft by Avon. Only a handful of hotels have window screens.

Street addresses in Florence are difficult to understand without a little advance knowledge. To the unknowing visitor, they can lead to hair pulling, serious arguments, and every other form of sheer frustration you can imagine. However, once you get the system, they are easy to decipher. Here is how: the addresses are numbered in red and black sequences. The red numbers are for commercial establishments (restaurants and shops) and the black are for residences and hotels. Black addresses will usually appear as a number only, while red addresses will appear as a number followed by the letter *r*. The numbers follow their own sequences. You will see 21r, 23r, 45, 47, and 49 all on the same side of the street, next to one another on the same block. You just have to remember whether you are looking for a red or a black number.

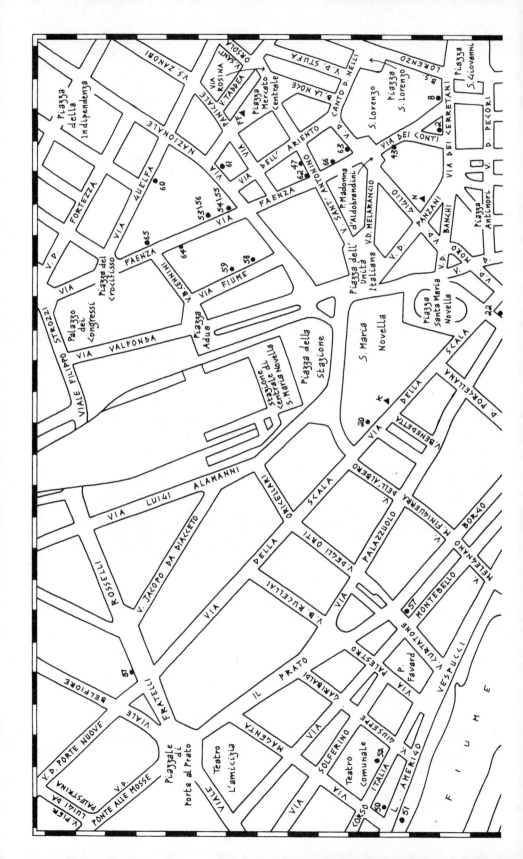

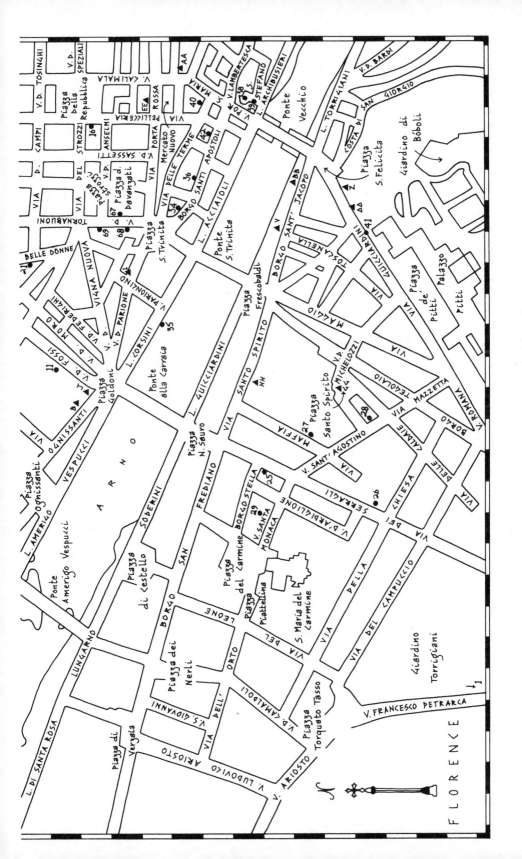

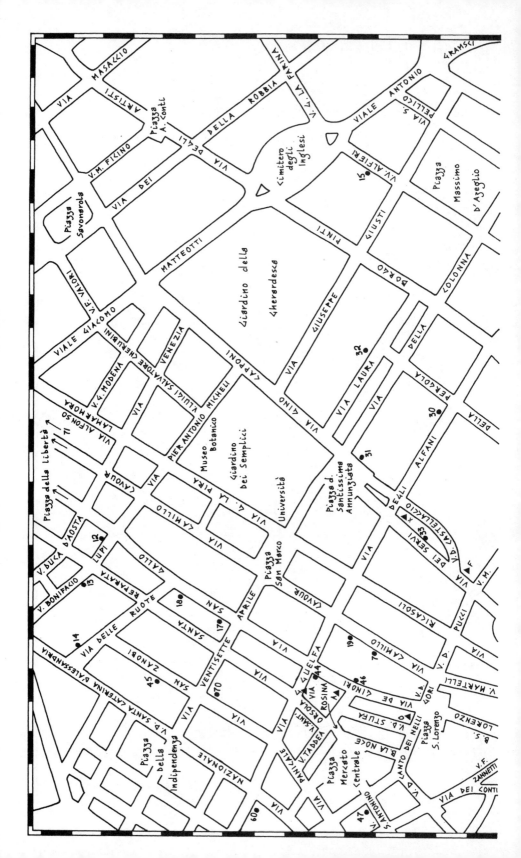

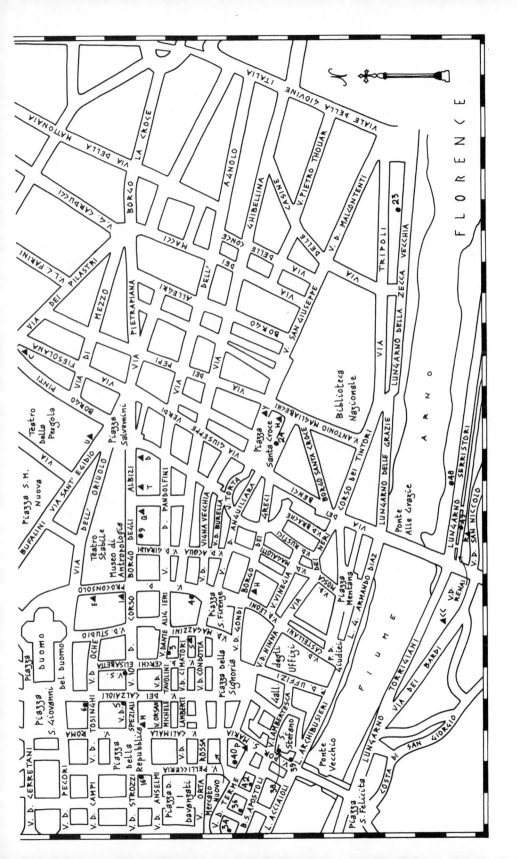

Useful Information

Emergencies

Police, Fire, Ambulance   113

Doctor, Dentist, or Pharmacy

Tourist Medical Service   Viale Lorenzo Il Magnifico, 055-475-411

Cardiology Emergency Service   055-283-394, 055-244-4444

Night Doctor   055-477-891

AVO (Association Volontari
Ospedalieri)   Volunteer interpreters who help with medical problems; Mon, Wed, Fri 4–6 P.M., Tues, Thurs 10 A.M.–noon, 055-425-0126, 055-234-4556

Homeopathic Pharmacy   Mon–Sat, 9 A.M.–1 P.M., 4–8 P.M. (they speak English), 055-211-159

Twenty-Four-Hour Pharmacies

Communale (Train Station)   055-289-435

Molteni, Via Calzaioli   7r, 055-215-472 (they speak English)

All'Insegna del Moro   Piazza San Giovanni, 20r, 055-211-343 (some English spoken)

Consulates

Great Britain   Lungarno Corsini, 2r, 055-212-594, Mon–Fri 9:30 A.M.–12:30 P.M., 2:30–4:30 P.M.;

United States   Lungarno Amerigo Vespucci, 28r, 055-239-8276, Mon–Fri 9 A.M.–2 P.M.

Getting Around

Airports   Galileo Galilei Airport, Pisa, 58 miles from Florence, 050-500-707; Amerigo Vespucci, 3½ miles from Florence, 055-373-498 (airport information), 055-306-1700 (flight information)

Taxi   4242, 4390, 4798, 4386

Train   055-565-0222 (general information), 055-212-319 (luggage service)

Currency Exchange

Cassa di Risparmio di Firenze
(bank with a 24-hour ATM)   Via dei Servi, 38r, Via degli
Speziali, 16r, Via Tornabuoni, 23r

Deutsch Bank   Via Strozzi, 16r, tel: 055-50-981,
Mon–Fri 8:30 A.M.–1:20 P.M.,
2:40–4 P.M.

Main Post Office   Via Pellicceria, 3, first floor, tel:
055-211-127, Mon–Sat 8:15 A.M.–
6 P.M.

Post Office

Main Post Office   Via Pellicceria, 3, first floor, 055-
211-127, Mon–Sat 8:15 A.M.–6 P.M.

Telephones

All numbers have six or seven digits plus the 055 at the beginning.
Toll-free numbers begin with 167 or 1678.

Code for Florence   055

Code for United States   001

Operator Assistance and Local
Directory Assistance   12

American Express

American Express   Via Dante Alighieri, 22r, Mon–
Fri 9 A.M.–5:30 P.M., Sat 9 A.M.–
12:30 P.M., tel: 055-50-981. Call
1678-72000 toll-free in Italy to
report lost or stolen credit cards; to
get balance of account, call 1678-
74333.

Consumer Complaints

To report unfair treatment at a hotel, restaurant, shop, or any other
location in Florence.

SOS Turistica   Via Cavour, 1r, 055-276-0382,
winter Mon–Sat 10 A.M.–1 P.M.;
summer Mon–Sat 10 A.M.–1 P.M.,
3–6 P.M.

Tourist Office

Tourist Office   Via Cavour, 1r, 055-290-832,
Winter (Nov–Feb): Mon–Fri
8:15 A.M.–1:45 P.M.; summer (Mar–
Oct): Mon–Sat 8:30 A.M.–7 P.M.,
Sat–Sun 8:30 A.M.–1:45 P.M.

Two Important Tips for Florence

1. How to Avoid Spending Your Vacation Time Standing in the LONG Line to Get into the Uffizi Gallery

The line starts forming at daybreak and by 9 A.M. is snaked to the street and at least a block or two along the river. Who needs this? No one, especially during rainy weather or on hot summer days. Now you can avoid this and buy your tickets ahead of time over the Internet. Isn't cyberspace wonderful?

By clicking onto Weekend in Florence at the website listed below, you can buy tickets for concerts, the theater, and, most important, the Uffizi Gallery for a certain day and time. You pay for the tickets from the comfort of your home, and save yourself lots of grief and wasted time standing in line. Weekend in Florence also specializes in high-quality handcrafted Italian goods. The choices are updated regularly, delivery is by air, and you can pay by credit card. If you wish you had bought that beautiful leather purse or silk scarf when you were in Florence, this could be your chance to find it again:

E-mail   waf@waf.it
Internet   www.waf.it/mall

2. Parking Your Car in Florence

If you drive *to* Florence, fine, but do yourself a favor and do not try to drive *in* Florence. The narrow one-way streets, lack of parking spaces, and general mental attitude of crazy Italian drivers is not conducive to a stress-free vacation. Instead, park your car and forget it until you are ready to leave town. Now that you have decided to park the car, the next questions are, "Where do I park it?" and "How much will it cost?" It could be far away, and cost you a pretty lira if you are not a smart Cheap Sleeper (and car parker).

The Parterre Parcheggio parking company has special rates for motorists who spend at least one night in a Florentine hotel. Leaving your car in their lot costs only L12,000 per day. The lot is in Piazza della Libertà, about a ten-minute walk from the Santa Maria del Fiore Cathedral. They will loan you a free bike to get back to your hotel. They also issue a taxi voucher for L5,000 to be used if bicycling doesn't appeal. Look for or ask for the taxi voucher at the cash counter of the garage. For more information, ask about the Parterre Parcheggio company at your hotel reception desk. Many hotels have parking arrangements with nearby garages, but the daily rate can run much higher, sometimes up to four times. It is up to you, your budget, and your desire for convenience.

Hotels in Florence by Area

The number in parentheses before each hotel corresponds to a number that marks the hotel's location on the Florence map (an entry with no number before it is located outside the parameters of the map); a dollar sign ($) indicates hotels in the Big Splurge category.

HOTELS

Boboli Gardens
 (1) Classic Hotel ★★★   48

Il Duomo
 (2) Albergo San Giovanni ★   49
 (3) Dei Mori ★★   50
 (4) Grand Hotel Cavour ★★★ ($) 51
 (5) Hotel Aldini ★★   52
 (6) Hotel Calzaioli ★★★ ($)   53
 (7) Hotel Casci ★★   54
 (8) Hotel Il Perseo ★   54
 (9) Hotel Orchidea ★   55
 (10) Pensione Maria Luisa de' Medici ★ 56

Piazza Goldoni
 (11) Hotel Unicorno ★★★ ($)   57

Piazza della Indipendenza
 (12) Residenza Johanna (NO STARS) 58

Piazza della Libertà
 (13) Hotel Cimabue ★★   59
 (14) Hotel Royal ★★★ ($)   60

Piazza Massimo d'Azeglio
 (15) Pensione Losanna ★   61

Piazza della Repubblica
 (16) Hotel Pensione Pendini ★★★ ($) 62

Piazza San Marco
 (17) Hotel Splendor ★★★   63
 (18) Hotel Tina ★   65
 (19) Il Guelfo Bianco ★★★ ($)   66

Piazza Santa Maria Novella
 (20) Hotel Aprile ★★★   67
 (21) Hotel Pensione Ferretti ★   68
 (22) Pensione Ottaviani ★   69

Piazza Santa Croce
 (23) Hotel Privilege ★★★ ($)   70
 (24) Palazzo Antellesi (see "Apartment Rentals," page 111)

OTHER OPTIONS

Boboli Gardens

Designed by Tribolo and extended over 45,000 square meters on the hill behind the Pitti Palace, the Boboli Gardens are one of the greatest examples of Italian-style gardens. The beautiful site affords wonderful views of the city and is a good place to bring children to feed the ducks and fish, and to run, play, and have fun.

The Pitti Palace was built in 1457 for Luci Pitti, a rival of the Medicis, but less than a century later, the impoverished Pitti family was forced to sell the palace to the Medici family. The sprawling building now consists of six museums showcasing a vast collection of Medici paintings, silver, and art.

(1) CLASSIC HOTEL ★★★
Viale Machiavelli, 25
20 rooms, all with shower or bath and toilet

TELEPHONE
055-229-351

FAX
055-299-353

CREDIT CARDS
AE, MC, V

CLOSED
2 weeks in Aug

RATES
Single L140,000, double L200,000, suite/apt L310,000; lower off-season rates; Continental breakfast (L12,000 extra)

Set in a residential area next to the Boboli Gardens, the Classic Hotel was a beautiful old villa until Connie Bernabei invested her heart, soul, and plenty of lire in turning it into an alluring garden hotel. For some, the out-of-the-mainstream location might be a deterrent, but not for those who know and love Florence. Here you have the best of everything: peace and quiet in elegant parklike surroundings, with everything on a tourist's Florence itinerary an easy twenty- to thirty-minute bus ride away. Motorists will also appreciate the free parking the hotel provides.

On my first visit to the Classic Hotel, I thought it offered the quintessential Florentine experience, with high molded ceilings, crystal chandeliers, inlaid hardwood floors, fireplaces, marble bathrooms, and well-appointed bedrooms perfectly in keeping with the hotel's history as a private home. On subsequent visits I have not changed my mind . . . much. The rooms, with their polished hardwood floors, are still lovely and so are the bathrooms. Favorites include No. 105, a two-level garden suite with an upstairs sitting room and a double bed downstairs. Frescoed ceilings and antiques add to the charm. The bath is excellent, but it has a shower only, no tub. There are three suites similar to this. Number 5 is a double on the garden with closets lining the entry. Standouts include the high ceiling, pink settee, and an old fireplace. I also like No. 102 because of its private balcony and No. 106 with its quiet garden view.

A Continental breakfast is served in a glassed-in area of the garden, in the breakfast room surrounded by a wallpaper of trellised pink petunias, or in your room. Questionable taste seems to have invaded and remained in place in the public sitting areas near the entrance. Why Sra. Bernabei has invested so much effort and money in the other parts of the hotel and kept the ugly slipcovered couch, the worn-out brown chair in the entry, and several other badly mismatched pieces of furniture remains a mystery to me. Hopefully they will have been redone or removed by the time of your visit. Because the bedrooms themselves are so nice, try not to judge the hotel from these decorating blips.

NOTE: To get to Boboli Gardens and the Classic Hotel from central Florence, take bus number 11, 36, or 37 from Piazza Santa Maria Novella or the railway station to Porta Roma.

ENGLISH SPOKEN Yes

FACILITIES AND SERVICES Bar, direct-dial phones, elevator, hair dryer available, free parking, TVs, office and in-room safes, room service

NEAREST TOURIST ATTRACTIONS Boboli Gardens; twenty-minute bus ride into Florence for tourist sites

Il Duomo

The Duomo, or the House of God, was begun in 1296 by Arnolfo di Cambio. His goal was to create a cathedral of "the greatest lavishness and magnificence possible." Today it reigns supreme as the heart, soul, and symbol of Florence. Every visitor to Florence usually begins their tour of the city standing on the Piazza del Duomo, looking at the octagonal Baptistry and the splendid bronze doors Michelangelo called the "gates of paradise." The massive dome, designed by Brunelleschi, dominates the city landscape for miles around and is the model for the larger but not more beautiful dome of St. Peter's in Rome.

(2) ALBERGO SAN GIOVANNI ★
Via dei Cerretani, 2
9 rooms, 2 with shower or bath and toilet

Cheap Sleepers who want to be in the thick of things and at the doorstep of Il Duomo check into this basic but clean one-star hotel—and yes, there will be some noise. The building, which now houses the Haitian Consulate

TELEPHONE
055-213-580, 288-385

FAX
055-213-580

CREDIT CARDS
AE, DC, MC, V

CLOSED
Never

RATES
Single L60,000, double
L80,000–90,000, triple
L110,000; lower off-season
rates; Continental breakfast
(L7,000 extra, served in
your room)

in addition to this nine-room pensione, was the home of the first bishop of Florence. From some rooms guests can look onto the present bishop's house and Il Duomo. Actually, there is just one room with no view at all (No. 9). Keep in mind that this is a one-star, so furnishings will not be in the spirit of the architectural details, which include inlaid floors and hand-painted seventeenth-century ceilings, some of which have been chopped in half by room partitions. However, the rooms have homey little touches, such as ruffles around the sinks, the hall facilities are acceptable, off-season rates apply, there is a lift from the street level to the hotel, and the simpatico owner, Sr. Zanobetti, loves children. In fact, some of his grandchildren's framed artwork hangs in the reception area and one grandchild designed the room-number plaques.

ENGLISH SPOKEN Yes

FACILITIES AND SERVICES Lift to hotel, office safe

NEAREST TOURIST ATTRACTIONS As central as it gets

(3) DEI MORI ★★
Via Dante Alighieri, 12
6 rooms, 3 with shower and toilet

TELEPHONE AND FAX
055-211-438

E-MAIL
deimori@bnb.it

CREDIT CARDS
MC, V

CLOSED
Never

RATES
Single L90,000–110,000,
double L120,000–140,000;
lower rates for longer stays
year-round; Continental
breakfast included

Hats off to owners Daniele and Franco for completing the renovation of the year in two-star hotels in Florence! Eek! *Sporka! Vecchio!* Ugh! are only a few of the negative words used to describe the absolute wreck of a hotel that was here before these two foresighted and hardworking friends transformed it into one of the snazziest little two-stars going. It took five people, working all day, seven days a week, for six months to totally gut and redo the hotel. If you don't believe me, just ask them to show you the photo album they have showing the "before" pictures. I am sure you will agree that the difference is nothing short of amazing.

Now you will find six rooms, either with or without private baths, all nicely furnished with individual touches. Wherever possible, original ceilings and floors were restored. Four rooms have air-conditioning, and all come equipped with duvets on orthopedic mattresses, robes, and a large marble workspace that doubles as a dining table if you decide to take advantage of the kitchen privileges extended to guests. Decorative pieces, pictures collected from their various travels, and oil paintings by Daniele add just the right notes of artistic interest. Bathrooms are fully stocked with towels and toiletries. In fact, both of the beautiful green-tiled communal bathrooms have a huge supply of toiletries you are welcome to use in case you forgot to bring your own. Should you come down with a cold or other ailment, not to worry . . . they provide a fully stocked medicine cabinet. Dirty clothes can be washed in their washer and can hang to dry on their drying lines. Breakfast is served in their kitchen, which is stocked with pots, pans, dishes, a coffeemaker, and staples such as tea, coffee, sugar, and milk for the guests' use. Quiet classical music is played in the sitting room, where you are welcome to look through their library of books on Florence or watch TV. On a warm afternoon, you can sit on the side balcony and read or relax with a drink. Smokers take note: this balcony area and the kitchen are the only two places you are allowed to light up. The rest of the hotel, including all of the bedrooms, are smoke-free. As you can imagine, this is a very popular Florence address . . . so get your reservation request in as soon as possible.

ENGLISH SPOKEN Yes

FACILITIES AND SERVICES Air-conditioning in four rooms, bar, direct-dial phones, kitchen privileges, bathrobes, TV in the sitting room, washing machine, no smoking in any part of the hotel except the kitchen and on the outside balcony

NEAREST TOURIST ATTRACTIONS Heart of Florence, great shopping, can walk to everything

(4) GRAND HOTEL CAVOUR ★★★ ($)
Via del Proconsolo, 3
92 rooms, all with shower or bath and toilet

If you like elegant surroundings with all the services and extras, you will love the Grand Hotel Cavour, directly opposite the Bargello Museum in the heart of Florence. It is also close to Il Duomo and the Palazzo della Signoria and within walking distance of the Uffizi Gallery and the Ponte Vecchio.

The hotel is a former thirteenth-century palace built by the Cerchi family. Despite renovations and changes over the years, the hotel has respected its architectural heritage and is magnificent throughout. The old chapel of the palace is now an independent restaurant that offers half-board for dinner to hotel guests. An air of luxury in the dining room is enhanced by the beautiful hand-painted ceilings, stained-glass windows, and the original altar and confessional. The main lounge of the hotel

TELEPHONE
055-282-461

FAX
055-218-955

CREDIT CARDS
AE, DC, MC, V

CLOSED
Never

RATES
Single L150,000, double L250,000, triple L325,000; half-board available with restaurant; some lower off-season rates; buffet or Continental breakfast included

has a polished marble floor, a fountain, massive gold mirrors, and sectional sofas designed especially for the room. In the center pillar of the lobby you can see the high-water mark from the disastrous 1966 Florence flood.

The comfortable bedrooms keep pace with the rest of the hotel. They are uniformly done with carpets, walnut furniture, and coordinated bedspreads and curtains. They have large closets, good drawer and luggage space, and fully stocked baths outfitted with fluffy towels. On every floor there is a room with a bathroom specially equipped for the disabled. Views from most of the rooms are not spectacular. However, single guests will like No. 409, which has a view of the Bargello, and couples will enjoy No. 411, a double with a large bathroom that has the same view. If you want quiet, those rooms on the interior courtyard will be the ones to book, but these have no views at all.

However, the Michelangelo breakfast room and adjoining terrace on the sixth floor have a panoramic view of the city. A large buffet breakfast is served here, either inside or out, depending on the weather. A Continental breakfast can be brought to your room, and half-pension for dinner (except Monday) can be arranged.

ENGLISH SPOKEN Yes

FACILITIES AND SERVICES Air-conditioning, direct-dial phones, hair dryers, elevator, minibars, parking (L40,000 per day), TVs, in-room and office safes, laundry service, porters, half-pension (dinner, L50,000 per person; beverages extra)

NEAREST TOURIST ATTRACTIONS Within walking distance of everything Florence has to offer

(5) HOTEL ALDINI ★★
Via dei Calzaioli, 13
15 rooms, all with shower and toilet

TELEPHONE
055-214-752, 212-448

FAX
055-291-621

CREDIT CARDS
MC, V

CLOSED
Never

RATES
Single L130,000, double L210,000, triple L270,000, quad L320,000; some off-season rates; Continental breakfast included

The Aldini receives Cheap Sleeps honors for its comfortable accommodations and desirable location, which is about as central as you will find in Florence. Plus, the front-desk staff is knowledgeable and attentive without being overly familiar. The clean white rooms are freshly painted and have dark Italian Country reproduction furniture sitting on terra-cotta floors. Bright floral spreads add a needed splash of color, and matching fabric-covered headboards tie everything together. There is enough wardrobe and drawer space for longer stays. To buffer noise, the windows are double-glazed, and to keep you cool in the sizzling summer months, the rooms are fully air-conditioned . . . a real luxury in most two-star hotels in Florence.

Room No. 101, a huge triple with a fabulous view of Il Duomo, has a large bathroom suitable for handicapped guests. Number 109 has a peek at Il Duomo, but the shower leaves something to be desired. Perennial favorites are No. 102, the Tower Room, a triple with a long-necked view of Il Duomo and a better shower, and No. 105, which has two streetside windows with a view of the patchwork of Florentine rooftops and a sweet old fireplace painted pink and gilded in gold. All rooms display a selection of the owner's impressive print collection, which he has also hung throughout the rest of the hotel.

ENGLISH SPOKEN Yes

FACILITIES AND SERVICES Air-conditioning, direct-dial phones, elevator to hotel (it is all on one floor), hair dryers, TVs, office safe

NEAREST TOURIST ATTRACTIONS Central Florence, convenient to everything on foot

(6) HOTEL CALZAIOLI ★★★ ($)
Via dei Calzaioli, 6
45 rooms, all with shower or bath and toilet

If you pinpointed the best central location in Florence, anything on the pedestrian-only Via dei Calzaioli would come up a winner. At this restored forty-five-room hotel, you'll begin in the boring commercial lobby and lounge and continue up the original stone staircase through handsome halls lined in muted wallpaper. In addition to space, a rarity in most hotels in this old section of Florence, the streamlined rooms have coordinated colors and tiled bathrooms—some with spout showers and all with curtains. Room 405, a nicely done twin in rose with a ceiling border added for interest, has good luggage space and light. If you are a single traveler and space is a priority, one of the best choices is No. 215, but you will sacrifice a view to get it. I would avoid No. 105 on the back—although the high-ceilinged room is large, the dated bathroom is too small for comfort. Many of the rooms have good views directly onto the street below. Unless you count horse-drawn carriages, this is a traffic-free zone where you can people-watch from your open window instead of sealing it shut and still being

TELEPHONE
055-212-456/7/8

FAX
055-268-310

CREDIT CARDS
AE, DC, MC, V

CLOSED
Never

RATES
Single L195,000, double L285,000; extra person L95,000; Continental breakfast included

able to count horn honks from passing cars and backfires from racing mopeds.

ENGLISH SPOKEN Yes

FACILITIES AND SERVICES Air-conditioning, direct-dial phones, elevator, minibars, parking (L45,000 per day), satellite TVs, in-room safes, laundry service

NEAREST TOURIST ATTRACTIONS Center of Florence

(7) HOTEL CASCI ★★
Via Camillo Cavour, 13
25 rooms, all with shower or bath and toilet

TELEPHONE
055-211-686

FAX
055-239-6461

E-MAIL
CASCI@pn.itnet.it

CREDIT CARDS
AE, DC, MC, V

RATES
Single L120,000, double L170,000, triple L225,000, quad L280,000; buffet breakfast included

The Casci is owned and managed by the Lombardi family: Armando, Carla, Paolo, and their dog, Spunky. All are fluent in several languages (even Spunky understands more than one language) and do a fine job of taking personal care of their guests. The hotel is centrally located in a fifteenth-century palace that was once home to the famous nineteenth-century musician Gioacchino Rossini. From the doorstep, guests are close to Il Duomo, many museums, the core of Florence shopping, and many restaurants listed in *Cheap Eats in Italy*. The comfortable rooms are upgraded and maintained on a regular schedule. All have private bathrooms, luggage and closet space, and pleasing colors. Number 6 is called the "Honeymoon Room" because it overlooks a garden with a lovely magnolia tree in it. Breakfast is served in a large dining room with its original frescoed ceiling. While I was at the hotel, Carla's comment to me proved true: "We say kindness and cleanliness go a long way."

ENGLISH SPOKEN Yes

FACILITIES AND SERVICES Air-conditioning in ten rooms (others have fans), bar, direct-dial phones, hair dryers, elevator, laundry service, satellite TVs, individual safe-deposit boxes in the office for each guest, effort made to keep a few rooms for nonsmokers

NEAREST TOURIST ATTRACTIONS Il Duomo and all of central Florence

(8) HOTEL IL PERSEO ★
Via dei Cerretani, 1
19 rooms, 7 with shower and toilet

TELEPHONE
055-212-504

FAX
055-288-377

E-MAIL
hotelperseo@dada.it

It is what it is . . . a nice one-star near Il Duomo, cheerfully run by Susan and Giacinto, a friendly Australian/Italian couple. Susan, the Australian, is a designer who, with the help of her mother, has pulled the hotel together. Her husband, Giacinto, is an artist whose modern paintings hang in the dining room. The others scattered throughout the hotel were left by cash-strapped guests.

The bright rooms have plain white walls and curtains, wood or tile floors, and light modern furnishings. Only five rooms are viewless, and the views from the others are of Forte Belvedere, Santa Maria Maggiore, and Il Duomo. The hall facilities are cleaned several times a day.

ENGLISH SPOKEN Yes

FACILITIES AND SERVICES Bar, direct-dial phones, fans available, elevator, office safe

NEAREST TOURIST ATTRACTIONS Everything

CREDIT CARDS
AE, MC, V

RATES
Single L75,000, double L115,000–140,000; extra bed 35 percent of room rate; lower off-season rates; Continental breakfast included

(9) HOTEL ORCHIDEA ★
Borgo degli Albizi, 11; first floor
7 rooms, 1 with shower only

For twenty-plus years, Maria Rosa Cook, a former English teacher, and her daughter, Miranda, have been welcoming guests at their cozy Hotel Orchidea. The twelfth-century building overlooks Gemma's Tower, named after Gemma Donati, the wife of Dante, Italy's greatest poet. This tower can be seen from the nearby S. Pier Maggiore square, which is one of the most characteristic in this part of Florence.

The seven-room, first-floor lodging offers exceptionally clean large rooms painted in soft pink. Several, including No. 5, a great single, and No. 4, with a balcony, have quiet views of the garden below, which is especially wonderful when the wisteria vines are in bloom. Some disagree, but the only room I would avoid is No. 6, because of its opaque window. The hall facilities are just fine. The area around the hotel is interesting because in addition to being close to all the tourist musts, there is good shopping, ranging from the Standa department store (the K-Mart of Italy) to artists' boutiques, newsstands, and fruit stalls. Reservations during high season are difficult to nail down, so if this is your spot, plan far in advance. Early morning risers take note, they do not serve breakfast.

ENGLISH SPOKEN Yes

FACILITIES AND SERVICES Elevator to hotel, office safe

NEAREST TOURIST ATTRACTIONS Il Duomo, Santa Croce, good shopping

TELEPHONE AND FAX
055-248-0346

CREDIT CARDS
None

CLOSED
Jan 15–31, Aug 12–19 (dates can vary)

RATES
Single L60,000, double L89,000 (with shower L130,000)

(10) PENSIONE MARIA LUISA DE' MEDICI ★
Via del Corso, 1
9 rooms, 2 with shower or bath and toilet

TELEPHONE AND FAX
055-280-048

CREDIT CARDS
None

CLOSED
Never

RATES
One or two persons
L110,000–137,000,
triple L150,000–190,000,
quad L185,000–245,000;
large Continental breakfast
included and served in the
room (the breakfast cannot be
deducted)

Welsh-born Evelyn Morris and her partner, Angido Sordi, bought this property with the intention of developing it into a rehabilitation facility for the elderly. These plans never materialized, and the rooms stood empty for twelve years until they decided to open it as a pensione in 1986. For those not well versed in sixteenth-century Baroque art or early twentieth century furniture designers, the second-floor pensione may appear to be a dusty mishmash of odds and ends with the kind of faded elegance that appeals to artistic types who love retro clothing discovered in cluttered thrift stores. How wrong that impression turns out to be.

Angido Sordi is a lifelong collector of Baroque paintings and statuary as well as early to mid-twentieth-century furniture. Every item you see standing, hanging, or squeezed into a corner is original, authentic, and has artistic merit. I will admit I thought the plastic and metal chairs were patio quality, and dismissed the metal lights altogether. Wrong again. The aluminum chairs date from the 1920s and are museum quality. The plastic chairs were designed by Gae Aulenti, the most famous Italian *female* architect, who was commissioned to redo one of the train stations in Paris. The red and blue chair you see at the entrance cost L2,000,000 thirty years ago! Designed by Gerrit Rietveld, and represented in the permanent collection of the New York Modern Art Museum, it is considered to be one of the finest chair designs of the twentieth century. In addition to the works of art, Sr. Sordi has a wonderful collection of art books that he will show to interested guests.

Each eccentric room in the pensione is named after one of the last dukes of the Medici, is adorned with one of their portraits, and displays an eclectic mixture of almost-antiques and many of the modern pieces that have been collected over the years by Sr. Sordi. The overall atmosphere of the hotel is chummy, especially for the residents of the seven bedrooms sharing the three hall bathrooms. In order to keep in close contact with her guests, Ms. Morris serves a large breakfast to them in their rooms. The meal includes juice, cereal, yogurt, eggs, a choice of breads, and a piece of cheese. For a one-star hotel, this is a good value.

Usually hotel rooms along this traffic-free patch of real estate cost a pretty lire, but for three or four friends, or a family willing to share either of the enormous family rooms with its own bathroom and Ping-Pong table (in No. 5), the price is very attractive when you consider that the cost of the big breakfast is included.

ENGLISH SPOKEN Yes

FACILITIES AND SERVICES Elevator to pensione (which is on one floor), office safe

NEAREST TOURIST ATTRACTIONS Piazza della Repubblica, Il Duomo, Central Market, Uffizi Gallery, Ponte Vecchio

Piazza Goldoni

Named after the playwright Carlo Goldoni, this piazza is a crossroads leading over the Ponte alle Carraia along the river on Via dei Fossi to the center of Florence.

(11) HOTEL UNICORNO ★★★ ($)
Via dei Fossi, 27
28 rooms, all with shower or bath and toilet

Contemporary simplicity prevails at the Unicorno, a smart, stylish hotel done in wicker, red-and-white slipcovered sofas and chairs, and effective lighting. To keep pace with the times, a computer with Internet capabilities is available for guests in the mezzanine sitting room. The breakfast room is a cheerful place to begin your day. You are bound to be uplifted by the orange-and-white tablecloths, cream-colored wallpaper with its tiny floral accents, and the large buffet, which includes eggs, salami, cheese, and fruit, along with the usual breads, jams, and beverages. The twenty-eight rooms are reached through green enameled doors opening onto understated accommodations with hardwood floors, gray built-ins, cotton bedspreads, and soft yellow textured walls. Bathrooms are equally nice, with sink space, good light, and curtains for the showers. The rooms are air-conditioned and have a private safe. The only one I would avoid is No. 202, which is sold as a double but is too small to accommodate a chair or proper shower. The location is close to Piazza Goldoni, good shopping, and the Arno.

ENGLISH SPOKEN Yes, and Japanese

FACILITIES AND SERVICES Air-conditioning, bar, direct-dial phones, hair dryers, elevator, minibars, parking can be arranged, satellite TVs, in-room safes

TELEPHONE
055-287-313

FAX
055-268-332

E-MAIL
unicorno@usa.net

CREDIT CARDS
AE, DC, MC, V

CLOSED
Never

RATES
Single L160,000, double L250,000, triple 310,000; lower off-season rates; breakfast with bacon and eggs included

NEAREST TOURIST ATTRACTIONS Arno, shopping, most of Florence

Piazza della Indipendenza

This wide green space is populated by retirees, who gather on their benches to gossip and while away the day.

(12) RESIDENZA JOHANNA (NO STARS)
Via Bonifacio Lupi, 14
12 rooms, 2 with shower or bath and toilet

TELEPHONE
055-481-896
FAX
055-482-721
CREDIT CARDS
MC, V
CLOSED
Never
RATES
Single L75,000, double L120,000; some lower off-season rates; Continental breakfast included

Savvy Cheap Sleepers in Florence who already know about the Residenza Johanna have been keeping it a closely guarded secret. They do not want their favorite place spoiled by eager tourists who cannot appreciate it or, worse yet, to find it full when they want to return. I do not blame them—this is a find. But it is not for corporate climbers who travel with portable faxes, laptop computers, and have cellular telephones glued to their ears wherever they go, or for those who want to kick up their heels and paint the town red. This is a true get-away—no telephones, no radios or televisions, and no noise—about a half-hour walk from the heart of Florence in a neighborhood where children play after school, matrons shop for dinner, and retirees sit in the small parks to gossip and feed the pigeons. It is great for motorists. You will be minutes away from the arteries leading in and out of Florence. Is it cheap? Well, that depends on your budget and how you look at it. Is it a good deal with value? I think so. Is it attractive? Positively.

The twelve rooms are in a nineteenth-century villa that has been restored by Evelyn Arrighi and her partner, Lea Gulmanelli, both transplants from France. They brought their native French chic and élan with them, and the result is the Residenza Johanna, which has the warmth and charm of a private home. The rooms are coordinated in pastels and small print fabrics, and feature antiqued furnishings, comfortable seating, good beds, and a sink and a bidet hidden behind a screen in those without private bathrooms. The shared hall facilities are first-class. Numbers 3, 6, and 10 have a balcony, but every room has an electric kettle with complimentary coffee and tea packets. There is also a small library for guests to use. Breakfast is prepared on a tray and set out in the rooms.

NOTE: There is a second Residenza Johanna at Via delle Cinque Giornate, 12. The six-room pensione is every bit as nice as the first Residenza Johanna, with a television in each room, cellular telephones guests can rent, a garden, and free parking. Quite frankly, however, the location is beyond Mars for most visitors in Florence and the neighborhood holds absolutely nothing of interest . . . and that includes restaurants and *caffès*. Unless you do not mind this distant location, be sure to specify which Residenza Johanna you want when you reserve. The telephone and fax number at the second Residenza Johanna is 055-473-377. Rates are: single or double L130,000, triple L155,000.

ENGLISH SPOKEN Yes

FACILITIES AND SERVICES Elevator to hotel

NEAREST TOURIST ATTRACTIONS Must use bus, car, or walk about thirty minutes to nearest attractions

Piazza della Libertà

On the northeastern edge of Florence, this piazza serves as a good exit point if driving away from the city.

(13) HOTEL CIMABUE ★★
Via Bonifacio Lupi, 7
15 rooms, all with shower or bath and toilet

The Cimabue is a two-star Cheap Sleeps winner. It is owned by Igino Rossi, a former director of Trusthouse Forte Hotels, and his pretty Belgian wife, Danièle Dinau, who is responsible for the painting you see at the entrance of the hotel and all the sponge painting and hand-painting on the bedroom doors. Sr. Rossi has been in the hotel business for years and carefully follows the guidelines that separate a two-star Italian hotel from a three-star. For instance, in a two-star, a single is normally eight square meters, but a large single can be sold as a double if the room measures eleven square meters; a regulation double measures fourteen square meters. Two-star hotels are required to change the towels every two days and the sheets twice a week in rooms occupied that long by the same people. I am telling you this because I have had several inquiries from readers about room size and laundry issues, not only in this hotel, but in others in all three cities covered in this book. Naturally, many

TELEPHONE
055-471-989

FAX
055-475-601

CREDIT CARDS
AE, DC, MC, V

CLOSED
2 weeks at Christmas

RATES
Single L135,000, double L185,000; extra bed L50,000; discount for *Cheap Sleeps* readers; buffet breakfast included (deduct L5,000 if not taken, in low season only)

two-star hotels change the towels daily and the sheets more than twice a week, but it is important for future guests to know that they are not required to do so.

A few well-placed pieces of vintage furniture and interesting photos of old Florence decorate the hallways. Wood-framed doors painted by Danièle lead to the well-proportioned bedrooms, which have cool terra-cotta floors, frescoed ceilings, and balconies. All have an interesting assortment of marble-topped dressers, carved wooden headboards, and mirrored armoires, as well as tiled baths with showers. A buffet breakfast is served in a pink-and-green room with banquette seating just off the reception and bar areas. The hotel is located at the corner of Via Zara, about twenty or thirty minutes by foot from most touristy things to do, but this neighborhood is quiet, appealing, and also safe . . . the Central Police Station is right here. And I have saved the best for last: you will receive a discount if you mention *Cheap Sleeps in Italy* when reserving.

ENGLISH SPOKEN Yes

FACILITIES AND SERVICES Bar, direct-dial phones, parking nearby by arrangement (L12,000 per day with in-and-out privileges), TVs, office safe

NEAREST TOURIST ATTRACTIONS Nice neighborhood; near exits from the city, so good for motorists; about a twenty-five-minute walk or a ten-minute bus ride to center of Florence

(14) HOTEL ROYAL ★★★ ($)
Via delle Ruote, 50–54
41 rooms, all with shower or bath and toilet

TELEPHONE
055-483-287, 490-648, 495-274

FAX
055-490-976

CREDIT CARDS
AE, MC, V

CLOSED
Never

RATES
Single L180,000, double L300,000; extra person 35 percent of room rate; lower off-season rates; buffet breakfast included

The Hotel Royal was built in the 1800s as the private villa for a noble Florentine family. After World War II, it became a hotel, and since then it has aged beautifully. Set off the street in a large garden not far from the train station and exhibition halls, it is considered one of the better three-star hotels in Florence.

Light gray and soft blue walls accented with white moldings, massive crystal chandeliers, highly polished hardwood floors with Oriental rugs, and a circular bar and sitting area strategically arranged for intimate conversations make up the downstairs portion of the hotel. In spring and summer, breakfast is served in the garden, which is filled with roses and other blooming plants. At other times, guests are served in a glass-enclosed dining room overlooking the garden.

The bedrooms display well-planned decor and comfort. All are large and invite long, lingering stays. Most have large shuttered windows with floor-to-ceiling white linen curtains gently pulled back to let in just enough sunshine. The rooms are all quiet and most have views of the gardens. Framed botanical prints, excellent lighting, and roomy bathrooms add the touches that make the difference between just a place to sleep and a memorable hotel stay.

NOTE: After the compliments, a warning is in order. While not a routine practice, the hotel does overbook, especially when there are large shows at the nearby exhibition center. Because of this it is extremely important that you or your travel agent guarantee your room with a credit card as far in advance as possible and get a written confirmation stating exact accommodations and dates of your stay. Also determine the price you will be expected to pay, especially if you have been quoted a special off-season rate. While this advice is good in any hotel you book, it is especially prudent here because there have been a few problems. If you follow these guidelines, you should not experience any unpleasant surprises.

ENGLISH SPOKEN Yes

FACILITIES AND SERVICES Air-conditioning, bar, direct-dial phones, hair dryers, elevator, minibars, free parking, satellite TVs, in-room safes (L3000), office safe (free)

NEAREST TOURIST ATTRACTIONS None; most sites a fifteen-minute walk or a bus ride away

Piazza Massimo d'Azeglio

This pretty green square anchors a residential neighborhood a few blocks north of the Sant' Ambrogio market.

(15) PENSIONE LOSANNA ★
Via Vittorio Alfieri, 9
8 rooms, 5 with shower and toilet

There are several other pensiones in the same building, all with too many problems of one sort or another to make them serious contenders. The Pensione Losanna, run by Sra. Vittoriana Martini, is a decent, clean Cheap Sleep if you don't mind living on the edge of action central. The good news is that the area is quiet and tourist-free, and if you are driving, you are positioned for

TELEPHONE AND FAX
055-245-840

CREDIT CARDS
MC, V

CLOSED
Never

RATES
Single L65,000–75,000, double L95,000–120,000, triple L130,000–165,000, quad L165,000–205,000; Continental breakfast included

quick exits that do not involve crossing the one-way nightmare of streets in the center of Florence. Close to the *albergo* (hotel) is a pretty green park where I like to go and while away an hour or so watching Florentines playing with their children, gossiping, or just doing what I am doing . . . people-watching. The rooms pass the white-glove test with honors. For a single Cheap Sleeper, No. 1 is a feminine choice, with a brass bed topped with a pink chenille spread. The overhead light is bright and the view of neighboring laundry lines tells you that this is a real neighborhood.

ENGLISH SPOKEN Limited

FACILITIES AND SERVICES Direct-dial phones, office safe

NEAREST TOURIST ATTRACTIONS Nothing, must use public transportation

Piazza della Repubblica

This large piazza was once the Roman Forum and, until 1888, when the surrounding medieval buildings were torn down, the Mercato Vecchio. The huge square is now ringed by outdoor *caffès* and expensive shopping opportunities.

(16) HOTEL PENSIONE PENDINI ★★★ ($)
Via dei Strozzi, 2
42 rooms, all with shower or bath and toilet

TELEPHONE
055-211-170

FAX
055-281-807

E-MAIL
pendini@dada.it

INTERNET
www.tiac.net/users/pendini/
hotel.html

CREDIT CARDS
AE, DC, MC, V

CLOSED
Never

RATES
Single L180,000, double L260,000; lower off-season rates; Continental breakfast included

The Pendini passed its century mark as a Piazza della Repubblica landmark hotel, offering guests continuous gracious service in a comfortable air of cosmopolitan dignity. The Abolaffio family, consisting of the parents and their two sons, always strives to offer guests all the services of a large hotel in the intimate and pleasant surroundings of a private residence. The public areas reflect the hotel's old-fashioned charm, with oversize sofas and chairs positioned either for quiet talks or just being alone with your newspaper. There is a sunny bar open twenty-four hours a day and a more formal dining room inside one of the building's archways with a view of the Strozzi Palace. The collection of black-and-white photos and posters near the reception desk showing the piazza over the years is wonderful. It is interesting to note the different spellings of the Pensione Pendini . . . until Mussolini's time, the elegant French version of pensione (*pension*) was used, but when Mussolini and the

Fascists came to power, the *e* was added, and it has stayed.

It is hard to select a favorite bedroom because no two are the same. If it's elbow room you need, No. 27 is a spacious choice. Here you will sleep on twin beds flanked by marble-topped side tables. For relaxing during the day there is a blue sofa, and from the windows, you will have a picture-perfect view of the Piazza della Repubblica, plus the tip of Il Duomo. Number 210 is a lovely quiet, inside-court room with brass twin beds and a floral theme carried out on the quilt spreads. The inlaid desk is an antique. Rooms 221, a narrow twin, and 222, a larger double-bedded room, can be joined to make a family suite. Number 221, reached by a winding wooden staircase, has a small high-walled terrace with a sighting of Il Duomo's dome. The wicker furnishings give it a casual feel. The great inner-city location is in shopping heaven *and* within walking distance to museums, galleries, and churches. For trips further afield, it has all the bus stops.

ENGLISH SPOKEN Yes

FACILITIES AND SERVICES Air-conditioning, twenty-four-hour bar, direct-dial phones, hair dryer available, elevator, satellite TVs, office safe, computer modems (on request when reserving), every effort taken to provide nonsmoking rooms

NEAREST TOURIST ATTRACTIONS Central to everything a visitor wants to see in Florence

Piazza San Marco

Cosimo il Vecchio (a Medici) built the Dominican monastery of San Marco and funded a public library full of Greek and Latin classical works. It is now the Museo di San Marco, which occupies the convent beside the church and is dedicated to the works of Fra Angelico of Fiesole, a fifteenth-century spiritual artist.

(17) HOTEL SPLENDOR ★★★
Via San Gallo, 30
31 rooms, 23 with shower or bath and toilet

I love this hotel . . . and every time I am here I find more to compliment and praise. No, it is not new and flashy, but therein lies its charm. This family owned hotel, occupying the top three floors of an apartment

TELEPHONE
055-483-427

FAX
055-461-276

CREDIT CARDS
AE, MC, V

CLOSED
Never

RATES
Single L155,000, double
L180,000–230,000, triple 35
percent of room rate, suite
L200,000 per room; buffet
breakfast included

building in a residential neighborhood, is splendid in every respect. As you approach the building, look for the flowering window boxes on the nine windows that face the street, then walk through the large doors and up a flight of carpeted graystone steps (or take the lift) to the reception desk, where you will be greeted by Marieangela Masoero or a member of her family.

The sitting room, with its big television set, armchairs covered in rich fabrics, and lovely chandelier hanging from a magnificent 155-year-old hand-painted ceiling, is an inviting place to while away an hour or so. Breakfast can be served on the sunny roof terrace, where you hear the chimes from the San Marco Church, or in the flower- and plant-filled dining room, which has original murals on the walls.

The large, spotless bedrooms are quiet, well maintained, and suitable for relaxing, comfortable stays. I have always liked No. 24, a double with an inlaid floor, three-door armoire, comfortable chair, nice bath, high ceilings, and bright exposure. Other delightful choices are Nos. 14 or 15, both with hand-painted furniture and good space. Bathrooms in these have half-tubs with handheld shower nozzles and floral tiles. Number 26 can serve as a double, triple, or quad with its massive armoire, four-drawer dresser, crystal chandelier, and large tiled bathroom with a tub. A wall of windows lets in light all day long in No. 30, a top-floor twin with turn-of-the-century clawfoot beds plus matching dresser and wardrobe. This room can combine with No. 31 to make a mini-suite for a family. I can also happily recommend No. 20, which is done in pink . . . from the velvet headboard, three matching chairs, and delicately hand-colored armoire, desk, and dressing table to the completely pink-tiled bathroom. I could go on forever, but I suggest you stay and see for yourself.

ENGLISH SPOKEN Yes

FACILITIES AND SERVICES Most rooms have air-conditioning, direct-dial phones, elevator, hair dryers, satellite TVs, in-room safes, 1 A.M. lockout

NEAREST TOURIST ATTRACTIONS Accademia Gallery, twenty-minute walk to Central Market and Il Duomo

(18) HOTEL TINA ★
Via San Gallo, 31
16 rooms, 10 with shower or bath and toilet

TELEPHONE
055-483-519, 483-593

FAX
055-483-593

CREDIT CARDS
MC, V

CLOSED
Never

RATES
Single L65,000, double L80,000–100,000, triple L120,000; Continental breakfast (L10,000 extra, served in your room)

Several years ago a reader wrote to me about the Hotel Tina, and in the last edition of *Cheap Sleeps in Italy* her praise-filled letter was printed in full. In the letter, she told of staying at the hotel with her elderly parents for an extended period of time, and said, "They were pleased beyond measure with the service provided."

The reader went on to say, "Lorenzo Aiello, the owner, who is the grandson of Tina, the original owner, speaks English. He is assisted by Pietro, who speaks less but understands enough. Between them they know where every wonderful out-of-the-way art treasure is to be found. The decor of the hotel is not worth mentioning, but the place is clean. The hall bathroom I shared was spotless, and there was a shower curtain and mop to sop up the water after. The beds were comfortable and our rooms quiet. During the last week of our stay, my father had his eighty-fourth birthday. Lorenzo, Pietro, and Eleanora, the cleaning lady, came to my parents' door with a bottle of champagne and a fruit tart with two big candles stuck in it and stayed to celebrate the birthday. It was a memorable party."

Finally, the reader says, "Had I spent only one night at the Hotel Tina, I would still consider it worth mentioning as a place with good beds, quietness, cleanliness, and nice management. Since we were there long enough to become 'regulars' we experienced more of the homey, caregiving qualities of the hotel management. And Florence was more welcoming because of them."

As long as it's been since that letter was written, little has changed at the Hotel Tina, including the Siberian husky, Niki, who doubles as a greeter. Lorenzo and Pietro are still delightful and do their best to accommodate their guests. To this I will add that I like No. 28, the only room with a small balcony. The bathroom has red accents and a tassel-printed shower curtain. I would avoid rooms facing the inside courtyard and those with a shower "booth" in one corner, specifically No. 24. Otherwise, this continues to be a happy Cheap Sleep.

ENGLISH SPOKEN Yes

FACILITIES AND SERVICES Direct-dial phones, double-glazed windows on the street, office safe

NEAREST TOURIST ATTRACTIONS Piazza San Marco, Central Market, Il Duomo

(19) IL GUELFO BIANCO ★★★ ($)
Via Camillo Cavour, 29
29 rooms, all with shower or bath and toilet

TELEPHONE
055-288-330/1

FAX
055-295-203

CREDIT CARDS
AE, MC, V

CLOSED
Never

RATES
Single L200,000, double
L290,000–330,000; lower off-
season rates; Continental
breakfast included (deduct
L15,000 if not taken)

Il Guelfo Bianco is an ideal upmarket midtown choice for those wanting to be a heartbeat away from the artistic and architectural treasures of Florence. For business-people, it is a short taxi ride to the convention center. For the shopper, call it mecca.

The hotel, skillfully owned and run by Lusia Ginti, whose good taste and decorating talents are evident throughout, is divided into two parts: the main portion and the annex, called the Cristallo. In the main part of the hotel, the bedrooms, several of which have balconies, are small but furnished with imagination and style. All are soundproofed and air-conditioned, a true blessing in summer, when temperatures rise and the mosquitoes arrive in great hordes. The rooms are uniformly done with coordinated colors. The beautiful bathrooms have nice fixtures and good lighting and are large enough to turn around in and lay out things.

In the Cristallo, however, the rooms are wonderful, impeccably done in soft colors that allow the original parts of the building to show off. Each room is different and may include original doors or beam-and-brick ceilings, hand-painted bathroom tiles, large windows, or a fireplace. Number 101 is a perfect example. The huge room has two armchairs, the original marble fireplace, old doors, and a cherub-motif ceiling. The pink-and-white-tiled bathroom is a dream with its long tub, good shelf space, and light. Room 42 has the best view of Il Duomo. Number 46, a nice single, overlooks the court-yard and is quiet. Reaching No. 55 requires climbing a few steps, but you will be rewarded with views of the San Lorenzo Chapel and the rooftops of Florence. Scattered in the rest of the hotel and annex are warm touches of welcome . . . a hall table with current magazines, a bouquet of fresh flowers, a lovely painting, or a comfortable chair.

Breakfast for all hotel guests is served in an Art Deco–style room highlighted by modern artwork. In summer, umbrella-shaded tables are placed in the court-yard for your morning meal. Athletically inclined guests can rent the hotel bikes for full- or half-day trips. Since the traffic here does not approach the insanity found in Rome, this is a unique and fun way to see the splendors of this wonderful Renaissance city.

ENGLISH SPOKEN Yes

FACILITIES AND SERVICES Air-conditioning, bar, direct-dial phones, hair dryers, elevator, minibars, parking (L35,000–55,000 per day), TVs, in-room safes

NEAREST TOURIST ATTRACTIONS Piazza San Marco, Piazza SS. Annunziata, Central Market, Il Duomo

Piazza Santa Maria Novella

The Santa Maria Novella Church was the headquarters of the Dominicans, a fanatical order that urged followers to strip and whip themselves before the altar. The oldest part of the convent in the cloisters dates from 1270, and the square in front is one of the largest in the city.

(20) HOTEL APRILE ★★★
Palazzo dal Borgo, Via della Scala, 6
29 rooms, 26 with shower or bath and toilet

The Aprile has been preserved by the Commission of Fine Arts as a historic monument. Converted from a fifteenth-century Medici palace, it retains its original frescoes and hand-decorated vaulted ceilings. Because of its busy location, there is noise, but if you are on the back side, uninterrupted sleep will be possible. It is not a spacious hotel, but that does not take away from its overall appeal. Downstairs is a modest reception area presided over for almost thirty years by Antonio. Next to it is a lounge and bar, both filled with healthy green plants. The bar has an arched ceiling and comfortable chairs scattered among leather couches. Breakfast is served in a room with a ceiling dating from the 1700s. On warm mornings, you can enjoy your cappuccino and rolls in the adjacent garden.

Wide halls with sitting areas and more plants lead to the rooms, which are big enough and scrupulously clean. Many have tiled baths, walnut or wrought-iron furnishings, frescoed ceilings, and a view of the Piazza Santa Maria Novella. Number 3, a huge ground-floor choice with a palatial ceiling, can house four and still feel roomy. Number 9 can be either a double or triple. It has green metal twin beds, a built-in armoire, a garden view, a pull-down desk, two armchairs, and a sofa that makes into a bed for the third person. The ceiling is painted a beautiful blue with a soft floral trim. Blue cotton bedspreads and good reading lights round out the package.

TELEPHONE
055-216-327, 289-147

FAX
055-280-947

CREDIT CARDS
AE, MC, V

CLOSED
Never

RATES
Single L120,000–180,000, double L190,000–260,000, suite/apt for four L390,000; lower off-season rates; breakfast (L15,000 extra)

Room 16 is a back double with a frescoed ceiling. To make up for the lack of a view is a bathroom that has space, a window, and a half-tub with a handheld shower nozzle and a curtain. Three rooms have mixed facilities: one has its own shower and the other two have a basin only. Toilets for all three are "hall variety." If you want to save money, sleep in one of these rooms. If you select No. 11, you will have a shower, but it will consist of a "cabin" in the corner of your room. Also be wary of No. 16, a small double with a pretty ceiling but with a window you can't see out of and a bathroom with a half-tub you can't stretch out in. For those desiring more space, reserve No. 24, a two-room suite with a tiny balcony overlooking the garden. Number 29, a small double but a better single, has its original beamed ceiling and a sunny exposure to the church.

ENGLISH SPOKEN Yes

FACILITIES AND SERVICES Most rooms with air-conditioning, bar, direct-dial phones, elevator, some hair dryers, some minibars, TVs, office safe, small library of English paperbacks

NEAREST TOURIST ATTRACTIONS Arno and Il Duomo; almost everything on this side of the river is within walking distance

(21) HOTEL PENSIONE FERRETTI ★
Via delle Belle Donne, 17
16 rooms, 8 with shower and toilet

TELEPHONE
055-238-1328

FAX
055-219-288

INTERNET
www.emmeti.it/Hferretti

CREDIT CARDS
AE, DC, MC, V

CLOSED
Never

RATES
Single L70,000–90,000, double L110,250–131,250, triple L141,000–161,000; sometimes lower rates; Continental breakfast included

Luciano Michel spent twenty years working in a four-star hotel in Florence. Finally, he realized his dream of being his own boss, and the one-star Hotel Pensione Ferretti is the result. It is a quantum leap away from a four-star, but for a fixer-upper work-in-progress one-star, it is indeed a good choice for a Cheap Sleep in Florence. I think the best thing about staying here, aside from the price, is Luciano . . . a friendly, outgoing man with a desire to please his guests. He bought the hotel in 1996, and started bringing it up to speed by installing new mattresses, brightening up the paint, and installing some bathrooms. He plans to have five rooms for non-smoking guests, so be sure to inquire about them when reserving. Best roosts are Nos. 3 or 5, with new bathrooms and street views; No. 10, a simple inside twin with a pink-tiled bathroom; or No. 8, a single with sun and a bathroom hidden behind folding doors. Unless the hall facilities have been revamped, you probably don't want a bathless room, or one with a phone-booth-style shower in the corner.

ENGLISH SPOKEN Yes

FACILITIES AND SERVICES Fans for the inside courtyard rooms, direct-dial phones, office safe, Internet terminal and free e-mail

NEAREST TOURIST ATTRACTIONS All of central Florence within a five- to thirty-minute walk; good *Cheap Eats in Italy* restaurants in the neighborhood

(22) PENSIONE OTTAVIANI ★
Piazza Ottaviani, 1; second floor
19 rooms, 4 with shower or bath and shower

A lift from the ground floor takes you to the second floor, where this nineteen-room pensione is located. A 12:30 A.M. curfew and lockout is emphatically enforced. If you stay out past that time, you will not be sleeping here. The best part about this one is that the prices are kind to those on a budget, especially during the low season. If you stay in Sara Rino Tarchi's Cheap Sleep at the corner of Piazza Santa Maria Novella, you can count on clean rooms, with no musty odors, that are uniform in their total simplicity. Sra. Tarchi and her husband labor long and hard to maintain high standards. When I visited one time, a section of the hotel had been torn apart to be cleaned, and she was doing it on her hands and knees. Her husband was on his way out the door to jump onto his bicycle to get something for their lunch. The amazing part of this is their ages: he is a decorated World War II hero and she is into her seventh decade.

The rooms are kept painted, the colors match well enough, the linoleum floors are washed daily, and the communal baths are cleaned several times a day. If you value sleep, reserve a back room on the top floor. If you are along the front, please bring industrial-strength earplugs: the traffic roars like a racetrack day and night. If you stay in a bathless room, you will shower down the hall in a room with a wall spout and a floor drain. Remember, this is Italy and shower curtains are not standard issue. Breakfast is served in a cheery room facing the street. For small groups, provided they request it when reserving, Sra. Tarchi will cook lunch and/or dinner.

ENGLISH SPOKEN Yes

FACILITIES AND SERVICES Elevator to hotel, TVs on request for small fee, office safe

TELEPHONE
055-239-62-23

FAX
055-293-355

CREDIT CARDS
None

CLOSED
2 to 3 weeks at Christmas

RATES
Single L70,000–85,000, double L80,000–100,000, triple L108,000–135,000; lower off-season rates; Continental breakfast included; lunch or dinner served to small groups by arrangement, prices on request

Piazza Santa Croce

The piazza was once the site of tournaments, games, and spectacles, including Florentine football in the sixteenth century. Today it is a meeting place for the neighborhood dog walkers, and a common gossip ground for the people who live in the old *palazzos* ringing the square. Shops selling leather goods line the streets leading to the piazza, and in back of the church is the well-known Leather School, which was founded by the priests but is now a privately run commercial business. The Santa Croce Church began as a Franciscan order in 1228. By the thirteenth century, the church was considered inadequate and was replaced by a building that was supposed to be the largest in Christendom. It is not, but it is the richest medieval church in Florence, with a chapel by Brunelleschi, frescoes by Giotto, and tombs of Michelangelo, Galileo, and other famous Florentines, including a memorial tomb to Dante (who is actually buried in Ravenna).

(23) HOTEL PRIVILEGE ★★★ ($)
Lungarno della Zecca Vecchia, 26; first floor
18 rooms, all with shower or bath and toilet

TELEPHONE
055-247-8220, 234-1221

FAX
055-243-287

E-MAIL
privilege@travelita.com

INTERNET
www.travelita.com/privilege

CREDIT CARDS
AE, DC, MC, V

CLOSED
Never

RATES
Single L200,000–220,000, double L260,000, triple L290,000, quad L310,000; lower off-season rates; buffet breakfast included

What is a good three-star city hotel supposed to be all about? Check into the all-purpose Privilege and see for yourself. This is the type of hotel that appeals to small groups, particular maiden aunts, sprightly senior citizens, or anyone who does not want to take a chance on their accommodations. The rooms along the front with views of the Arno have some noise and cost just the same as the quiet rooms on the back with no view. Take your pick. All the rooms are similar: coordinated wall coverings, bland fabrics, amenity rich, good space, and mostly marble bathrooms. If you are alone, ask for either No. 114, facing the river, or No. 108, a quieter nest on the back that looks over the hotel's small terrace and a corner of the carpark. Number 115 is still one of my choices. It is a view double with a sofa, two chairs, an entry with closets, and a desk for all my paperwork. I also like No. 110, a back double with a quiet interior atrium view and a bath with good shelf space and a big shower with a curtain. The double-glazed windows keep out most of the noise in No. 112, a double facing the Arno. I like the breakfast room, too, with its stained-glass skylight and tables covered in red linen with a vase of flowers to welcome me each morning. From the hotel doorstep you are five minutes from Santa Croce Church and good shopping. In another ten you will be in Il Duomo. In the other direction, it is a beautiful ten-minute walk to the Ponte Vecchio, where you can eye the magnificent jewelry shops that line this historic bridge.

ENGLISH SPOKEN Yes

FACILITIES AND SERVICES Air-conditioning, bar, direct-dial phones, hair dryers, minibars, radios, satellite TVs, parking (L20,000 per day, reserve when booking), office safe; no lift (hotel on first level above the street)

NEAREST TOURIST ATTRACTIONS Santa Croce, Ponte Vecchio

Piazza Santo Spirito

The Augustinian monks of Santo Spirito gave up one meal a day for fifty years to help pay for the construction of this church. The walls inside are separated into a series of thirty-eight chapels. The piazza in front is alive every day but Sunday with a morning market, then, on the second Sunday of the month with a flea market, and on the third Sunday, a biological market. Good trattorias and bars dot the piazza and the streets surrounding it.

(26) ISTITUTO GOULD (NO STARS)
Via dei Serragli, 49
33 rooms, 27 with shower or bath and toilet

The Istituto Gould was founded by American Emily Gould in 1871 when she opened her Florence home to young victims of a flood disaster. Today it is part of the Protestant Church of Italy and is a home for approximately twenty-five boys and girls from eight to eighteen who because of severe family problems (not drugs) cannot live with their own families. There is also an afterschool program in which other children come and stay until they are picked up either before or after dinner. On the second floor of the main house, the institute operates a type of hostel, open year-round to guests of all ages. For more than fourteen years, the institute has been run by a kind, gentle man named Paolo.

TELEPHONE
055-212-576

FAX
055-280-274

CREDIT CARDS
None, cash only

CLOSED
Never

RATES
Single L48,000–55,000, double L70,000–78,000, triple L84,000–102,000, quad L135,000, five L140,000; breakfast is included only for groups, otherwise not served; group rates for lunch or dinner on request

In doing my research for the *Cheap Sleeps* series, I have seen my share of hostels, but let me assure you, this is the Ritz of all hostels, and that is why it is listed here rather than in "Student Accommodations." This is a place in which a Cheap Sleeper of any age can stay comfortably. One side is newer than the other, but all of the rooms are exceptionally nice. Although not lavish, they are crisp and functional and kept clean and neat. You will not have to live with hideous color mismatches, unsightly tears, or tacky, beat-up furniture. Four of the rooms open onto a lovely shared terrace; others overlook the mimosa trees in the institute's gardens and Fort Belvedere in the distance. Still others have mezzanine sleeping areas with nice living spaces below. Meal service is available for groups of twenty or more. But I think the wonderful part about staying here is that the money goes directly to the institute to help children. What better way to spend your hotel lire?

NOTE: Office hours are Monday to Friday 9 A.M. to 1 P.M. and 3 to 7 P.M., and Saturdays 9 A.M. to 1 P.M. They are closed Sunday.

ENGLISH SPOKEN Yes

FACILITIES AND SERVICES None

NEAREST TOURIST ATTRACTIONS Piazza Santo Spirito; brisk walk to Pitti Palace

(28) PENSIONE SORELLE BANDINI ★
Piazza Santo Spirito, 9
10 rooms, 5 with shower or bath and toilet

TELEPHONE
055-215-308

FAX
055-282-761

CREDIT CARDS
None, cash only

CLOSED
Never

RATES
Single L99,000–130,000 (no singles in April), double L135,000–160,000; extra bed 35 percent of room rate; lower off-season rates; Continental breakfast included; other meals for groups only by arrangement

Warning: This hotel is not for everyone. The magnificent (in its day) *palazzo* was owned and occupied by the Bandini sisters until 1978. During their lifetimes, and certainly since, not much was or has been done to the building other than an occasional paint job. Guests who stay here either fiercely defend it or would not stay again for free. If you like shiny chrome and glass, slick bathrooms, and heel-clicking room service on a twenty-four-hour basis, better skip this one. On the other hand, if you like laid-back management, appreciate faded and wrinkled charm, love huge, sunny view rooms filled with oversize antiques in need of varying doses of elbow grease, and enjoy reading or napping with the house feline population on verandas with sweeping views of the Piazza Santo Spirito, then you will be a dedicated fan of the Pensione Sorelle Bandini.

From April to October, meals are served to groups in a baronial banquet dining room with a wrought-iron chandelier and oils hung on the walls. On the second Sunday of every month a flea market is held on the square, and the neighborhood has some interesting arty-type boutiques (See "Shopping in Florence," page 295).

ENGLISH SPOKEN Yes

FACILITIES AND SERVICES Lift to pensione office, office safe

NEAREST TOURIST ATTRACTIONS Piazza Santo Spirito; good walk to Pitti Palace

Piazza SS. Annunziata

The square is surrounded on three sides by lovely arcades and distinguished in the center by an equestrian statue of the Grand Duke Ferdinando I. The Ospedale degli Innocenti, designed by Brunelleschi in 1419, was built as a hospital for foundlings, who were the abandoned babies of domestic slaves. The blue-and-white medallions of babies are by Andrea della Robbia. The church was founded by the Seravite Order in 1250, and rebuilt by Michelozzo between 1444 and 1480.

(30) ALBERGO MIRELLA ★
Via degli Alfani, 36
10 rooms, 4 with shower, none with shower or bath and toilet

Frill-free and functional, not to mention cheap and *hygenico* (hygienic), describes the Albergo Mirella, owned for ten years by the energetic Lilia, who not only runs her ten-room *albergo*, but cleans it to make sure everything meets her rigorous standards. Your stay in her sweet hotel will not incite scary nightmares from fighting color schemes or worrying about budget burnout. Her spiffy, bright white rooms are quiet and have flowers at the windows in spring and summer. The furniture is decent, the mattresses are good, and there are bedside reading lights. The hall facilities meet Lilia's stringent cleanliness requirements. Room laundries are prohibited and so is smoking in the breakfast room.

ENGLISH SPOKEN Limited

FACILITIES AND SERVICES Office safe

NEAREST TOURIST ATTRACTIONS Easy walk to Il Duomo and central Florence

TELEPHONE AND FAX
055-247-8170

CREDIT CARDS
None, cash only

CLOSED
Never

RATES
Single L70,000, double L105,000, triple L150,000; Continental breakfast included

(31) HOTEL LOGGIATO DEI SERVITI ★★★ ($)
Piazza SS. Annunziata, 3
29 rooms, all with shower or bath and toilet

TELEPHONE
055-289-592/3
FAX
055-289-595
E-MAIL
Loggiato.dei.Serviti@
italyhotel.com
CREDIT CARDS
AE, DC, MC, V
CLOSED
Never
RATES
Single L220,000, double
L325,000, suite L440,000–
555,000; lower off-season rates;
buffet breakfast included

The Loggiato dei Serviti occupies one of Florence's most beautiful Renaissance buildings on the Piazza SS. Annunziata. The hotel was not always the wonderful site it is today . . . believe me. Years ago I stayed here when it was a dilapidated no-star pensione. I have vivid memories to this day of several sleepless summer nights I spent here swatting kamikaze mosquitoes and lying under damp towels in an effort to keep cool. Things have changed . . . dramatically.

I am happy to say that now, thanks to meticulous restoration work by the Budini-Gatti family, the Loggiato is an elegant and tranquil place to stay with every modern convenience and comfort. The sixteenth-century architecture has been left unchanged, and everything about the hotel is in keeping with the spirit of its heritage as a former monastery. The breakfast room, with its arched ceiling and yellow-and-white linen-dressed tables, is a charming place to start your day. Polished terra-cotta floors, hand-colored prints on the walls, magnificent dried and fresh floral arrangements, and enviable Italian antiques throughout will carry you back to an era when graciousness and etiquette mattered.

Each of the bedrooms has individual character. Some, particularly the singles, are definitely small, with bathrooms squeezed into corners and closet space cut to the minimum. Many other rooms, however, are large, with views of Il Duomo or the Accademia where Michelangelo's *David* is on display. Number 31, a two-room suite, has a formal sitting room papered in green-and-white stripes. A large drop-leaf table serves as a writing desk. There are two separate bathrooms in addition to ample closet and drawer space. The view of Il Duomo is perfect. Number 14 is a large single with a beamed ceiling, antique bed, and marble-topped desk. The view over the square in front of the hotel is a cheerful one.

Because the Loggiato is so well done and nicely run, I recommend it as a Big Splurge for those looking for a special hotel with the true feel of Florence.

ENGLISH SPOKEN Yes

FACILITIES AND SERVICES Air-conditioning, bar, direct-dial phones, hair dryers, elevator, minibars, satellite TVs, in-room safes, parking (L32,000–45,000 per day)

NEAREST TOURIST ATTRACTIONS Church of SS. Annunziata, Foundling's Hospital, Il Duomo, Central Market, San Marco Square and Church, Accademia Gallery

(32) HOTEL MORANDI ALLA CROCETTA ★★★
Via Laura, 50
10 rooms, all with shower or bath and toilet

TELEPHONE
055-234-4747
FAX
055-248-0954
E-MAIL
Hotel.Morandi@dada.it
INTERNET
www.dada.it/Hotel.Morandi
CREDIT CARDS
AE, DC, MC, V
CLOSED
Never
RATES
Single L130,000, double L230,000, triple L330,000, quad L450,000; lower off-season rates; Continental breakfast (L18,000 extra)

The Morandi alla Crocetta is an absolute jewel that combines the best of modern comfort with the warmth of antique furnishings in an exquisitely restored convent dating from 1511. At this quiet and distinguished hotel, staff members pride themselves on giving four-star service and personal attention to all of their guests. English owner Katherine Doyle and her son, Paul, who is the architect responsible for this stunningly restored hotel, have worked diligently to keep the spirit of the original building alive. By ingeniously blending exposed parts of the original structure with pieces from other old buildings and authentic antiques, they have created a charming hotel with a definite sense of its past.

From the street, you pass by two large red clay pots and walk up a red-carpeted stairway to the front door. You will be ushered into a comfortable sitting room, where easy chairs are well placed for conversation or for sitting and reading the morning papers. The rooms vary in size and magnitude and are all unique. One of the best is No. 29, the chapel, with original frescoes that show the artist's brush strokes. Number 1 is a double, with four pieces of Mass vestments framed and hung as a backdrop for the bed. Two rooms have terraces, Nos. 23 and 26, as does the suite, No. 30. In No. 23 the bedroom is hung with Victorian prints and has a desk along one wall. Room 26 can serve as a double or triple, thanks to a sofa bed. Two doors from the 1700s have been placed together and add interest to the room, as does the framed Greek icon over the bed. Room 25 has an 1800s theme, with a wrought-iron bed and side tables accented in mother-of-pearl. The sitting area has a mirrored armoire and a mahogany desk with beveled-glass doors. The beautiful marble bath features a corner sink with double mirrors and a great tub. Number 30 is a spacious new suite, with a dressing area and tiled bath (complete with a full-length mirror and heated towel rack) off the entry. The large bedroom, which opens onto a terrace with an antique fountain, has a brick fireplace with a painting of the owner, Mrs. Doyle, showcased above it.

A comfortable sofa, a glass writing table, and a series of antique Florentine prints add to the enjoyment of staying in this special suite.

Once people discover the Morandi, they never consider staying elsewhere. With only ten rooms, reservations fill up months in advance, so you must plan far ahead to get a spot.

NOTE: If you want to appreciate and understand Florence beyond what the usual tourist sees, please consider a private tour with one of the Morandi's own staff, Frank Peters, an extremely knowledgeable and personable American-born guide who conducts wonderful private tours. He has lived in and loved Florence for many years and is full of fascinating facts, figures, tidbits of historical lore, art history, and much, much more, which will make Florence come alive in ways you never imagined. These tours last at least four hours, or longer if guests wish, and can be tailored to suit your particular area of interest. However, his expertise is not solely limited to Florence. If your travels are taking you to cities in Italy beyond Florence, Frank's vast wealth of information will greatly enhance these portions of your trip as well. I highly recommend one of his fascinating tours, which will be one of the best travel investments you ever make. Reservations are mandatory and can be made through the hotel. Rates upon request. You do not need to be a guest of the hotel to take advantage of one of Frank's guided tours.

ENGLISH SPOKEN Yes

FACILITIES AND SERVICES Air-conditioning, bar, direct-dial phones in rooms and bathrooms, hair dryers, magnifying mirrors in bathrooms, minibars, radios, satellite TVs, in-room safes, private tours of Florence and other parts of Italy available by advance reservation

NEAREST TOURIST ATTRACTIONS Accademia Gallery, Piazza SS. Annunziata, Archeological Museum

(33) SOGGIORNO PANERAI (NO STARS)
Via dei Servi, 36
5 rooms, none with shower or bath and toilet

TELEPHONE
055-264-103
(guests are asked to reserve by phone and call back to confirm, telling the time of arrival)

CREDIT CARDS
None, cash only

CLOSED
Never

The residentially challenged who seek a Cheap Sleep in Florence should check into the Soggiorno Panerai, where the occupants of the five rooms share two hall bathrooms. The building dates from 1510, and there are original exposed beams in three rooms. Room 5, a multipurpose affair that can be divided by screens into a single or expanded into a triple, is better than No. 3 because you can at least open the window to see out and check the weather. Number 2 provides direct access to the communal bathroom, and No. 4 enjoys a view over the parking spaces on Piazza Brunelleschi. Newly white-washed walls, a sitting area with a refrigerator and coffee machine, and one of the sweetest women in Florence will welcome you after a long journey or day hoofing it through the city. A bonus for many is that the rooms are quiet, there are lockers for stashing valuables, and there is no curfew, but you must pay for your room in advance . . . in cash only.

ENGLISH SPOKEN Yes

FACILITIES AND SERVICES None

NEAREST TOURIST ATTRACTIONS Reasonably central, not far from Il Duomo, Accademia Gallery, good shopping

RATES
One or two persons L65,000, triple L85,000

Piazza S. Trinita

The column in the center of the piazza was taken from the Baths of Caracalla in Rome and given to Cosimo I by Pope Pius I in 1560. The statues at either end of the Ponte Santa Trinita are of the four seasons.

(34) HOTEL CESTELLI ★
Borgo SS. Apostili, 23; first floor
7 rooms, 1 with shower and toilet

In the first edition of *Cheap Sleeps in Italy,* I wrote about this gem, which was then called Soggiorno Cestelli. In 1934, Ada Cestelli's mother opened the door of their seven-bedroom home to paying guests. When her mother could no longer run it, Ada took over and, through the years, developed a loyal following that appreciated her gracious hospitality . . . and very low prices. Although it was hidden from the narrow street, it was well located for all the main sights in Florence. The approach, up two flights of stairs, was never inspiring, but once you reached the small entrance hall and saw the family antiques, you knew you had arrived in a special place. You saw wonderful touches everywhere: decorative tassels holding back heavy curtains, tables displaying small collectibles, a pretty chair here, a nice painting or print there. Number 2 was a huge room with a massive armoire, bed, and matching bureau. A three-panel screen shielded the sink and bidet from the rest of

TELEPHONE AND FAX
055-214-213

CREDIT CARDS
V

CLOSED
Never

RATES
Single L65,000, double L110,000–130,000; Continental breakfast (L10,000 extra, served in the room)

the room, an ornate coatrack sat in one corner, and a gold standing mirror occupied another.

When I returned to review the hotel for the following edition of this book, it was closed. No one in the neighborhood was able to tell me anything about what had happened, only that it was closed. I subsequently learned that Ada had died, but did not know what had happened to her little hotel. On my last trip to do the research for this edition, I had the address on my list, just on the off-chance that someone had bought and reopened it. While I was rechecking the Florence and Abroad rental agency (see page 114), Karen Brennan Piemonte told me about a good friend who had recently purchased a small hotel in the center of Florence. I put two and two together and realized that her friend, Ivana Camillo, had bought Ada's hotel. I am pleased to report that the Cestelli is up and running once again.

Ivana modernized the name of the hotel and made some needed improvements. In No. 2, she added a private bathroom, but left everything else beautifully in place. The six other rooms are still bathless, but she hopes to add one or two very soon. A paint job, fresh curtains, and a new mattress picked up No. 1, but the view (of a wall) will never improve. From the pebbled-glass window in No. 4 you have a corner sighting of the river. The pretty window made of colored glass at the end of the entry, flanked by two armchairs, is still here, but most of the other valuable antiques were removed by the family. Nevertheless, the hotel still retains its air of dignity and charm, thanks in no small measure to the engaging Ivana, who I hope will have as many years of success and pleasure in running the hotel as her predecessors did.

NOTE: During the winter months, the heat is turned on from 7 to 9 A.M and again from 4:30 or 5 P.M. to 11 P.M. This is not unusual. Please see "Tips for Cheap Sleeps in Italy," page 11.

ENGLISH SPOKEN Yes

FACILITIES AND SERVICES Office safe

NEAREST TOURIST ATTRACTIONS Il Duomo, museums and galleries, shopping

(35) HOTEL PENSIONE BRETAGNA ★★
Lungarno Corsini, 6
18 rooms, 10 with shower or bath and toilet

If you have some discretionary money to invest in a Florentine hotel, this is it. All this one needs to lift it into the sensational category is that too often missing ingredient . . . money. In its day, the villa, so beautifully positioned along the Arno River and near everything wonderful in Florence, must have been something indeed. Now it is a two-star pensione with faded-rose qualities owned by Antonio Castaldini. Sr. Castaldini appreciates the building's past (starting in 1820, Louis Napoleon lived here for ten years) but is running it on a shoestring by slowly doing most of the renovation and repair work himself. To his great credit, I must say he has worked hard to improve things by cleaning it up considerably, removing the majority of mismatched colors, and adding some showers and toilets.

For those who require modern comforts in a coordinated atmosphere, go on to the next hotel write-up—this is *not* your Florence address. But for those who appreciate history, river views, original architectural touches—such as inlaid-wood floors, marble fireplaces, a collection of Japanese and Chinese ceramic plates from the 1700s mysteriously embedded into a cement wall by the family of the saint who owned them (you can see her picture by the reception desk), and graceful old ceilings—this *could* be your address. The location is great and the view from the enormous salon across the river is a genuine photo op. Lower winter prices also help. Unfortunately, there is only one bedroom with a river view, No. 34, which also has its own shower and sink and the toilet off the entryway. The best rooms are Nos. 22 and 30, both overlooking the courtyard of the neighboring British Consulate. These rooms can be either a double or a triple—if you unfold the sofa in 30, or sleep in the twin bed in an alcove in 22. Number 22 has the best bathroom (includes a shower curtain), while No. 20 offers a small balcony and a desk, but its bathroom has one of those sawed-in-half tubs with a shower over it (no curtain). But in No. 21 you will have a big bathroom, white walls, a blue ceiling, and a little stairway to climb if you want to see out the window. If you are traveling with a small child, they do have cribs.

ENGLISH SPOKEN Yes

TELEPHONE
055-289-618

FAX
055-289-619

INTERNET
www.dbweb.agora.stm.it/market/bretagna

CREDIT CARDS
AE, MC, V

CLOSED
Never

RATES
Single L70,000–85,000, double L110,000–130,000, triple L160,000–175,000; lower off-season rates; Continental breakfast included

FACILITIES AND SERVICES Air-conditioning in four rooms, direct-dial phones, hair dryer available, TVs, lift to hotel, office safe

NEAREST TOURIST ATTRACTIONS Walking distance to almost everything

(36) PENSIONE ALESSANDRA ★★
Borgo SS. Apostoli, 17
25 rooms, 16 with shower or bath and toilet

TELEPHONE
055-283-438, 217-830

FAX
055-210-619

E-MAIL
htlalessandra@mcilnk.it

CREDIT CARDS
AE, MC, V

CLOSED
Dec 10 or 15–Dec 27

RATES
Single L100,000–135,000, double L155,000–195,000, triple L205,000–255,000, quad L270,000–300,000; Continental breakfast included

The Gennarini family–run hotel is an excellent midpriced value that provides old-fashioned charm in a friendly setting. It was clear to me that the family cares about the hotel and all of their guests. The rooms are not plush, but they are larger-than-average, spotlessly clean retreats.

Three rooms have views of the Arno: Nos. 11, 21, and 22. Number 22 is a huge bathless double, with a minimum of creature comforts, that could accommodate four with no problem. The best of the river-view rooms is No. 21, a double with a tango-size bathroom and coordinating fabrics on the little round table and chairs, bedspread, and window detailing. Number 6 is a big single with a glass-topped desk, spacious armoire, and pink-tiled shower. The row of makeup lights over the bathroom shelf is another pleasing factor. For a quiet choice, No. 9 on the back overlooks a church. If you book room 10, you will be in a double with air-conditioning and a rooftop view, but no private facilities. Don't worry about booking a bathless room: the hall facilities are excellent.

To reach the hotel, you must walk up one flight of stairs and then take an elevator. The hotel is spread out over three floors. The public rooms are all gracious. Soft sofas and chairs in the sitting rooms are comfortable places to watch television or read the newspaper. Breakfast is served in a room with matching yellow-linen-covered tables and window curtains.

ENGLISH SPOKEN Yes

FACILITIES AND SERVICES Air-conditioning in sixteen rooms, direct-dial phones, elevator to hotel (which is on three levels), hair dryer available, parking (L30,000 per day), TVs in sixteen rooms, office safe

NEAREST TOURIST ATTRACTIONS Within ten to twenty minutes walking distance of almost everything

Piazzale di Porta al Prato

This is one of the old gates of Florence.

(37) HOTEL VILLA AZALEE ★★★ ($)
Viale Fratelli Rosselli, 44
24 rooms, all with shower or bath and toilet

It is always hard to be objective when you are in love, and I fell head over heels in love with the Villa Azalee the minute I arrived. After every meeting, I will admit I am more in love than ever. This romantic hotel is simply without peer in Florence.

The entire hotel is done with great taste and style, and no effort has been spared to create a haven of beauty and charm. The garden surrounding it is a beautiful oasis, filled with seasonal blooming plants and flowers, including azaleas and camellias in late winter. It has that small-hotel look and feel, which is achieved through an imaginative personal touch and a dedicated staff that is willing to go the extra mile to provide service and attention to each valued guest.

The floral bedrooms are all different, and it is absolutely impossible to select a favorite—I adore them all. Number 28, on the first level, streetside, is marvelous, with a net canopy over a pink quilted headboard and an eyelet-ruffled duvet cover. Two chairs plus a long sofa provide the seating. The bath has a stretch tub and plenty of sink and shelf space. Number 21 has a violet theme carried out on the quilt spread, rug, settee, and two wing chairs. Over the bed is a lacy white canopy appliquéd with pink flowers. The bathroom is divine, with the convenience of a four-line drying rack hung over a walk-in shower. Number 24 is also fabulous. Here you will have a floral frescoed ceiling and a crown-held drape over the twin or king-size beds. There's a large double dresser to hold all of your clothes, a comfortable armchair, a terrace on the back, and an excellent marble-tiled bathroom with a stall shower. If noise is a problem, and there will be some, consider reserving a room in the back section. The eight rooms here are somewhat smaller but offer no shortage of appeal. In No. 29 you will be sleeping in an iron canopy bed from the 1800s and showering in a pink and green floral tiled bathroom. Some rooms here (33 and 34) have open closets, but trust me, it all works together in perfect harmony.

On the entry level is a glass sunroom and another, more formal, sitting room around the corner. The

TELEPHONE
055-214-242, 284-331

FAX
055-268-264

E-MAIL
villaazalee@Fl.Flashnet.it

CREDIT CARDS
AE, DC, MC, V

CLOSED
Never

RATES
Single L185,000, double L275,000, triple L370,000; buffet breakfast included

sunroom is filled with light and attractive furnishings, and is accented with multitudes of green plants and flowers. The sitting room has a fireplace and is lined with old paintings and arranged with comfortable seating on overstuffed chairs and sofas. Be sure to notice the antique Chinese glass screen on display here. Your breakfast will be served on Richard Ginori china in an adorable pink-and-white room with a sideboard along one wall. If you do not want to come down for breakfast, call for room service.

Despite its distant location (for some) from the heart of Florence, there is excellent bus service just around the corner. If you take the number 1 or 17, you will go directly to Il Duomo. Or, for L5,000 per day, you can rent one of the hotel bicycles and pedal your way through Florence.

ENGLISH SPOKEN Yes

FACILITIES AND SERVICES Air-conditioning, bar, direct-dial phones, hair dryers, clothes-drying racks in bathrooms, minibars, room service, TVs, parking (L40,000 per day), office safe, window screens in some rooms, bicycles for rent (L5,000 per day)

NEAREST TOURIST ATTRACTIONS None, must take a bus or walk about fifteen minutes

Ponte Vecchio

Crossing the narrowest point of the Arno, this stone bridge was built in 1345 to replace a twelfth-century structure swept away by flood in 1333. Its shops were originally for tanners, but in the sixteenth century, butchers occupied them. The butchers were thrown out in 1593 by Grand Duke Ferdinandi I, who objected to their foul smells, and replaced with goldsmiths and jewelers, whose picturesque and very expensive shops still line the bridge.

The Uffizi Gallery is the most glorious Renaissance art museum in Europe, with masterpieces of Italian painting from every age, including works by Giotto, Fra Angelico, Botticelli, Leonardo, Raphael, Michelangelo, Titian, and Tintoretto, to name only a few. Two of the most famous paintings in the Uffizi Gallery are in Room 10, Botticelli's *Birth of Venus* and *Primavera*. Please note: The lines to enter the Uffizi are as legendary as the art inside. To get around this, see page 44.

(38) AILY HOME ★
Piazza San Stefano, 1
4 rooms, none with shower or bath and toilet

A stay at the Aily Home may not make you feel pampered, but you will walk away happy to have saved so much money. This is the sort of Cheap Sleep that will go the way of the wrecking ball, or be renovated into something far more expensive, once the present elderly owner leaves. As of now, this four-room, third-floor walk-up is convenient to the Uffizi Gallery and the Ponte Vecchio, good shopping, and fine restaurants (see *Cheap Eats in Italy*). The rooms are dark but clean, and the furniture relatively modern. If you plan to read at night, BYO reading lamp. All four rooms in the pensione must share one hall toilet and shower. Heat is kept to an absolute minimum. On the winter day I was there, the owner wore three sweaters. She has been here twenty-five years and does not believe in serving breakfast. As you can see, this is definitely nothing special, but it is too cheap to ignore.

ENGLISH SPOKEN No

FACILITIES AND SERVICES None

NEAREST TOURIST ATTRACTIONS Ponte Vecchio, Uffizi Gallery, Arno, all of central Florence

TELEPHONE
055-239-6505

FAX
None

CREDIT CARDS
None, cash only

CLOSED
Aug

RATES
Single L30,000, double L60,000; showers L3,000 per person

(39) HOTEL HERMITAGE ★★★ ($)
Vicolo Marzio, 1
29 rooms, all doubles with shower or bath and toilet

One of my favorite hotels in Florence has always been the Hermitage, located in a building on the Piazza del Pesce, overlooking the Ponte Vecchio and the Arno River. Everything about this charming hotel is appealing, from the plant-filled terrace with its spectacular top-floor views to the well-thought-out bedrooms and sitting areas. Recent improvements include twenty Jacuzzis and several extra rooms the hotel added when it was able to absorb a small hotel in the same building. The cozy living room has a bar along one side and a fireplace for cool winter evenings. Oriental rugs are tossed on the tile floors, and yellow slipcovers add a touch of brightness to comfortable chairs and sofas that are perfect for sinking into with a good book.

No two of the bedrooms are alike, but all are done with good taste and flair. They have muted wallpaper, a mixture of antique and reproduction furniture, and

TELEPHONE
055-287-216

FAX
055-212-208

E-MAIL
hermitage@italyhotel.com

INTERNET
www.italyhotel.com/firenze/hermitage

CREDIT CARDS
MC, V

CLOSED
Never

RATES
No single rooms, but a double for single use L210,000, double L330,000; suite for four L470,000; lower off-season rates; buffet breakfast included

double-glazed windows to buffer the noise along the river. Of the eight rooms with river views, one is No. 409, a twin with a corner Jacuzzi in the marble bathroom. My absolute favorite rooms are Nos. 601 and 602, located on the top floor and reached by a small stairway. Aside from the comfortable, beautifully appointed rooms, the real payoff is the terrace, with a spectacular wraparound view of Florence. To alleviate the impossible parking situation, they have a garage where you can leave your car while staying here. However, the hotel is so central to everything in Florence that a car would only be a nuisance.

ENGLISH SPOKEN Yes

FACILITIES AND SERVICES Air-conditioning, bar, direct-dial phones, hair dryers, satellite TVs, elevator, parking (L30,000–40,000 per day), office and in-room safes, laundry service, some Jacuzzis

NEAREST TOURIST ATTRACTIONS Ponte Vecchio, River Arno, Uffizi Gallery, all of central Florence

(40) HOTEL DELLA SIGNORIA ★★★ ($)
Via delle Terme, 1
27 rooms, all with shower or bath and toilet

Judging from the wide audience of devoted regulars, owner Rita Lippolis's actions have met her words for more than twenty years: "The best thing we have is our service. We try to satisfy all our clients because this is our best publicity." Situated between Piazza Signoria and the Ponte Vecchio, her attractive hotel is perfectly located at Via delle Terme and Via Por S. Maria, ground zero for visitors hoping to explore all the beauty of Florence. The mirrored dining room with white iron chairs and tables covered in pink linens trimmed in white has a view of the Ponte Vecchio. During the day, drinks are served here or at the mezzanine bar that faces the street. In summer, breakfast is moved to a canopied, plant-lined terrace. The halls leading to the twenty-seven bedrooms showcase paintings by local artists. The guest rooms are all decorated individually with an eye for refinement. For instance, No. 523, a large sunny single or cozy double, has a pink hand-appliquéd bedspread. In No. 433, the furnishings are similar to those you would find in a rustic Tuscan farmhouse and the view is of the Ponte Vecchio and Palazzo Vecchio. The exceptional bathroom has its own window, two corner glass shelves, and a bathtub with a handheld shower

TELEPHONE
055-214-530, 239-6598, 268-402

FAX
055-216-101

E-MAIL
dellasignoria@italyhotel.com

INTERNET
www.italy.com/firenze/dellasignoria/
dellasignoria@italyhotel.com

CREDIT CARDS
AE, DC, MC, V

CLOSED
Never

RATES
Single L190,000–230,000, double L285,000; extra bed L55,000; lower off-season rates; Continental breakfast included

nozzle above it. The rooms on the first floor have balconies, and I think No. 114 is the best twin-bedded choice, thanks to its brass beds, two wing chairs, and larger bathroom.

ENGLISH SPOKEN Yes

FACILITIES AND SERVICES Air-conditioning, bar, direct-dial phones, hair dryers, elevator, minibar, parking (L40,000 per day), satellite TVs, office safe, laundry service

NEAREST TOURIST ATTRACTIONS Perfectly located to walk in every direction and see all of Florence

(41) HOTEL LA SCALETTA ★★★
Via Guicciardini, 13; second floor
11 rooms, 10 with shower or bath and toilet

Hotel guests here are a convivial mixture of international travelers, who know that obtaining a room here is no mean feat, but that their efforts will be rewarded by its pivotal location and near-perfect setting just over the Ponte Vecchio on Via Guicciardini, the street that leads to the Pitti Palace and Piazza Santo Spirito. There is a lift from the ground floor to the hotel, which is on the second floor of an old *palazzo* near the American Express office. Once inside, the halls seem to go on forever, and numerous steps lead from one end of the rambling hotel to the other, which prompted the owner's son to jokingly say to me, "We give our guests a city map and a hotel map." The 360-degree view from the roof garden is nothing short of sensational. On a clear day, you can see all the way to Fiesole. Closer in, your view is of the Pitti Palace and the Boboli Gardens.

The hotel is frankly old-fashioned, without any sort of upgrades or apologies. For its devoted fans, that is the appeal. And so is the cat, Micia, who moves from one warm spot to another throughout the day. Rooms facing the garden require reservations one month in advance. Some of the rooms are huge, with marble fireplaces and high ceilings; others are smaller but still roomy. All are furnished in assorted styles, colors, and fabrics. Only a few have full tubs; otherwise you get a shower or a half-size tub that you cannot sit in without having your knees under your chin. For longer stays, towels are changed every other day and sheets twice a week. A three-course dinner is available upon request. Just let them know in the morning if you will be staying for dinner.

ENGLISH SPOKEN Yes

TELEPHONE
055-283-028, 214-255

FAX
055-289-562

E-MAIL
lascaletta.htl@dada.it

CREDIT CARDS
MC, V

CLOSED
Never

RATES
Single L75,000–110,000, double L125,000–180,000; lower off-season rates; discounts given to readers of *Cheap Sleeps in Italy* if you mention the book when making reservations . . . not when you are leaving and paying your final bill; buffet breakfast included; dinner by request (L20,000 per person)

FACILITIES AND SERVICES Bar, direct-dial phones, TVs on request (L10,000 per day), office safe, elevator to reception, dinner by request (L20,000 per person)

NEAREST TOURIST ATTRACTIONS Ponte Vecchio, Arno, Pitti Palace, Piazza Santo Spirito, central Florence

(42) HOTEL TORRE GUELFA ★★
Borgo S.S. Apostoli, 8
15 rooms, all with shower or bath and toilet

TELEPHONE
055-239-6338
FAX
055-239-8577
E-MAIL
zucconi@Fol.it
CREDIT CARDS
DC, MC, V
CLOSED
Never
RATES
Single L175,000, double L255,000; Continental breakfast included

If you are looking for one of the best two-star hotels in Florence, you have found it. The words on the brochure capture the great spirit of this exceptional hotel: "What could be better than looking toward the twenty-first century from a thirteenth century Florentine tower? Located fifty meters from the Ponte Vecchio in the tallest private building in Florence, the *Torre Guelfa* (Guelfa Tower) offers an incredible view, a beautiful atmosphere, and fifteen select rooms for a few, select clients."

Everything about the hotel is smart and sophisticated. To describe it to you, I will start with the top floor, work my way down to the baronial stone living room, then take you back up to two spectacular roof terraces. Yes, No. 15 is a twenty-two-step climb, but once there, *wow!* is the only word to describe the massive terrace with table and chairs positioned for taking in the beautiful view. The double room comes with a pleasing marble bathroom. No stair-climbing is required to reach No. 3, done in shades of green, with a marble bathroom and a detailed ceiling. One wall is faced with lovely seventeenth-century mirrors, the floor is parquet, and the double bed is outlined by a swagged curtain. Singles in No. 4 will sleep in a four-poster metal bed and shower in a small marble bathroom. Twin-bedded No. 13 has a view of the street and a small garden. For breakfast, guests gather in a glass-enclosed winter garden with glass-topped tables surrounded by black wrought-iron chairs.

Two large rooms make up the impressive hotel living room, where stone columns frame a second room with a wall of wood-carved bookshelves along one side. Glass doors open onto a long wooden seventy-two-step stairway that leads to the Guelfa Tower and its two view terraces. Once you reach the first landing, I urge you to go the additional sixteen steps to the top perch, where you will have a spectacular 360-degree view of all of Florence and the surrounding hillsides. Don't forget your camera!

ENGLISH SPOKEN Yes

FACILITIES AND SERVICES Air-conditioning, direct-dial phones, hair dryer available, elevator, minibars, TVs, office safe

NEAREST TOURIST ATTRACTIONS Walking distance to almost everything

San Lorenzo Central Market

Inside the nineteenth-century market hall you find the beautiful bounty of Tuscany: fruit, vegetables, meat, fish, and dairy products displayed in stalls covering two floors. Surrounding it are stalls selling the good, the bad, the indifferent, and the ugly in clothes, gloves, bags, paper and leather goods, and, of course, T-shirts.

The San Lorenzo Church, built between 1419 and 1469, was the parish church of the Medici family, and its massive dome is almost as big as that of Il Duomo. The inside of the basilica is a pure example of Renaissance art due to the genius of Brunelleschi and Michelangelo, who designed the interior facade. Also of great interest are the Old Sacristy and the Medici Chapels, designed by Michelangelo as a Medici mausoleum.

(43) HOTEL BELLETTINI ★★
Via dei Conti, 7
28 rooms, all with shower and toilet

Without inside information, chances are slim that you would find this one on your own. While central to the action in Florence, it is tucked away through a courtyard entrance near the Medici Chapel by the San Lorenzo Central Market. Originally it served as a lodging for workers at the Medici Palaces. For decades it was a *very* basic one-star operated by two aged sisters. A few years ago, a new page was turned: two stars now shine and have been polished to a bright luster by the present owners, the Cini and Delli families.

Form the moment you walk in there is a sense of comfort, from the attractive reception area to the halls scattered with antiques. An old mantel has an original papal insignia hanging over it, which serves as the hotel's logo. Before you leave, be sure to take a peek at the

TELEPHONE
055-213-561, 282-980

FAX
055-283-551

CREDIT CARDS
AE, DC, MC, V

E-MAIL
hotel.bellettini@dada.it

INTERNET
www.firenze.net/hotelbellettini

CLOSED
Never

RATES
Single L130,000, double L180,000, triple L240,000, quad L310,000; lower off-season rates; buffet breakfast included

kitchen to admire the lovely ceiling. In the rest of the hotel, you can admire the Florentine oil paintings, stained-glass windows, and more painted ceilings.

The bedrooms are very nice. One of their best features, from an American standpoint, is that most of the bathrooms have stall showers *with* doors (there are no tubs). Number 20, a twin with hand-painted furnishings, has red-tiled floors and a huge bathroom with a separate enclosed toilet. In one of the singles, No. 25, you feel as though you can almost touch the dome of the Medici Chapel, but the shower here has no base, only a drain in the floor. It does, however, come with a curtain. Numbers 28 and 45 have views of Il Duomo, the Medici Chapel, and the Library of Lorenzo the Magnifico. In No. 45, you can lie in bed and watch the sun rise every morning over Il Duomo. Room 44, the only one with a balcony, has nice reproduction furniture and watercolors of Florence decorating the walls.

ENGLISH SPOKEN Yes

FACILITIES AND SERVICES Air-conditioning, bar, direct-dial phones, hair dryer available, some TVs (L32,000 per day), elevator to reception, in-room and office safes

NEAREST TOURIST ATTRACTIONS Central Florence, easy access to all important tourist destinations

(44) HOTEL CENTRO ★★
Via de' Ginori, 17
16 rooms, 14 with shower and toilet

TELEPHONE
055-230-2901

FAX
055-230-2902

CREDIT CARDS
AE, MC, V

CLOSED
Never

RATES
Single L100,000–125,000, double L125,000–175,000, triple L230,000; Continental breakfast included

The Hotel Centro is in a former palace that was Raphael's favorite residence during his time in Florence. In 1996 the hotel was redone, and it now offers moderately priced Cheap Sleeping options between the Central Market and Il Duomo. The hotel is attractively dressed with bright green trim, which highlights the collection of live plants and modern paintings in the public areas. In the rooms, good mattresses, modern furniture, individual safes, air-conditioning, and CNN should help to make your stay more comfortable. In No. 211, you will have your own balcony; if there are three of you, ask for No. 104, a triple with a shower.

ENGLISH SPOKEN Yes

FACILITIES AND SERVICES Air-conditioning, direct-dial phones, hair dryers, elevator from first level of hotel, satellite TVs, in-room safes

NEAREST TOURIST ATTRACTIONS Central Market, Medici Chapel, Il Duomo

(45) HOTEL ENZA ★
Via San Zanobi, 45
16 rooms, 8 with shower or bath and toilet

During one of my stays in Florence to research this book and *Cheap Eats in Italy,* I walked by this hotel coming and going to my apartment nearby. I could not tell much because it is up a flight of stairs from the street entrance. Finally I went in and met the English-speaking owner, Eugenia Del Mazza, who greets guests carrying her little dog, a Hungarian Chihuahua named Trycchy. She and her husband live in the hotel, but he is not involved in the day-to-day operations. As she put it, "He is busy with his own business. The hotel is mine."

Eugenia aims to provide budget-priced rooms to shoestring travelers and students looking for low-cost places to stay. Remember, it is a one-star, so *Architectural Digest* has not been by to do a spread, and there are a few instances of wild wallpaper and mismatched fabrics. The best rooms are on the second floor because they all have private facilities and the least amount of clashing colors. Number 22 has white walls, a single bed, and an enclosed stall shower, sink, and toilet. Number 24 has white walls and a view of the red rooftops. Number 25 is also a good bet, with decent furniture, three pictures on the walls, and a blue-tiled bathroom with a shower but no curtain. Number 26, for three or four, has a mezzanine area designed to increase the living space of the room.

The location is good. From here you can walk to the Central Market, the Piazza SS. Annunziata, and the train station. Lots of good Cheap Eats are near, and a bakery across the street sells delicious sandwiches, salads, and cool drinks. Breakfast is not included or served, but there are dozens of local spots for your morning cappuccino and *cornetto.* When reserving, please be sure to say you are a *Cheap Sleeps in Italy* reader.

ENGLISH SPOKEN Yes

FACILITIES AND SERVICES Office safe, no towels in rooms without facilities

NEAREST TOURIST ATTRACTIONS Central Market, Piazza SS. Annunziata, Il Duomo, Arno River

TELEPHONE
055-473-672, 490-990

FAX
055-292-192

CREDIT CARDS
None; cash only, in advance

CLOSED
Never

RATES
Single L80,000, double L90,000, triple L120,000, quad L140,000; special group rates; no breakfast served

(46) HOTEL GINORI ★
Via de' Ginori, 24
7 rooms, all with shower or bath and toilet

TELEPHONE
055-218-615, 210-454, 211-392

FAX
055-211-392

CREDIT CARDS
MC, V

CLOSED
Never

RATES
Single L120,000, double L150,000 (must mention *Cheap Sleeps in Italy* to get these rates); Continental breakfast included

For a super one-star in Florence, check into Daniela Nerozzi's Hotel Ginori, a small, well-located Cheap Sleepers' dreamland near the Piazza San Marco, the Medici Chapel, and Central Market. The seven-room abode is immaculate, comfortable, and safe, and it displays no garage-sale furnishings. The rooms are either doubles or triples and are very popular with *Cheap Sleeps* readers who want to stay several steps above bare-bones basic, yet still keep within a budget. The walls are white and so is the modern furniture. Most rooms have a writing desk, more than enough closet space, and a framed watercolor print or open fan. All have private bathrooms and five have air-conditioning, an almost unheard-of feature in one-star hotels in Florence. Breakfast is served at two communal tables in an air-conditioned room with a television.

ENGLISH SPOKEN Yes

FACILITIES AND SERVICES Air-conditioning in five rooms, direct-dial phones, TVs, office safe

NEAREST TOURIST ATTRACTIONS Between the Central Market and Piazza San Marco; can walk to almost everything

(47) HOTEL GLOBUS ★
Via Sant' Antonino, 24; third floor
23 rooms, 6 with shower or bath and toilet

TELEPHONE
055-211-062

FAX
055-239-6225

E-MAIL
hotel.globus@firenzealbergo.it

INTERNET
www.traveleurope.it/h17.htm

CREDIT CARDS
AE, MC, V

CLOSED
Never

RATES
Single L80,000–100,000, double L115,000–140,000, triple L150,000–190,000; lower off-season rates; large Continental breakfast included (deduct L5,000 in low season only if not taken)

I always admire hard work and am happy to see it pay off. The friendly owners, Michele and his wife, Serena, have worked diligently to improve their twenty-three-room hotel and are proud of the results . . . as they should be. At the one-star Globus you will be staying *centralissimo* in a third-floor walk-up hotel that was redone in 1992. The simply coordinated bedrooms are done in the Cost Plus school of rattan decorating. The cream-colored rooms have carpeted floors, a picture or two, and are generally spacious. All rooms on the first floor and No. 209 on the second have window screens. After one summer night spent swatting the beetle-size mosquitoes that invade Florence every summer, you will know how important window screens can be, but only a handful of hotels provide them. Some rooms have views of the Medici Chapel. Number 304 is a grand-slam winner with not only a view but a balcony and a bathroom.

Numbers 102 and 208 and 209 offer views and baths; 203 and 309 have only views, no private baths. Others (Nos. 104 and 303) have little to write home about. Breakfast, which is served by Serena's mother, includes juice, cereal, cheese, and a brioche. It can be deducted (L5,000) in the low season only. It is served in a pleasant room with square marble-topped tables and black-cane-seated bistro chairs. A series of fruit prints hangs on the walls.

NOTE: If you are a winter guest, the heat will only be on from 6:30 to 9 A.M., 3 to 5 P.M., and 8 P.M. to midnight.

ENGLISH SPOKEN Yes

FACILITIES AND SERVICES Fans in all rooms, bar, direct-dial phones, hair dryer available, office safe, e-mail and Internet services for guests (for a fee)

NEAREST TOURIST ATTRACTIONS Central Market, Medici Chapel; can walk to almost everything else

San Niccolò

Legend has it that Michelangelo hid in the bell tower of this church to avoid being rounded up with the other political activists during the fall of the Republic in 1529. Inside the church today are lovely frescoes, and in the Sacristy, *Madonna della Cintola* from the fifteenth century. The streets in the area are dotted with the ateliers of working artists and craftsmen.

(48) HOTEL SAN REMO ★★★
Lungarno Serristori, 13
20 rooms, all with shower or bath and toilet

The San Remo is a three-star riverside site owned for more than forty years by the Montagnaini family. Within a leisurely walk along the Arno, you can be standing on the beautiful piazza in front of Santa Croce Church, crossing the Ponte Vecchio, or lining up to get into the Uffizi Gallery.

For me, the bottom line for a hotel, besides the price, is always: How clean is it? I can assure you the San Remo scores well, with no cracks, peeling paint, telltale odors, or creeping mildew. When the hotel is closed in January or February, the family rolls up its collective sleeves and turns the place inside out—cleaning, painting, and re-doing anything that may show signs of wear and tear.

TELEPHONE
055-234-28-23/4

FAX
055-234-22-69

CREDIT CARDS
AE, DC, MC, V

CLOSED
Jan or Feb

RATES
Single L160,000, double L220,000, triple L300,000; lower off-season rates; buffet breakfast included

Each room is individually decorated and has little touches that make it homey: a vase of dried flowers, a pretty picture, a comfortable chair, beautiful handmade wrought-iron wall lamps or chandeliers. Five rooms have private terraces. The two top-floor rooms, reached by a set of stairs, are ideal for a family or two couples traveling together. Of course, the rooms have separate facilities, but they share a lovely terrace that has a panoramic view of Florence. I have always liked No. 30, which is rather small, but its terrace view of the tower on Porta San Niccolò and nice bathroom, with space for makeup and other toiletries, make it special. Number 27, with a view of the Arno River, has a new bathroom with a separate tub and stall shower with a massage water nozzle. Number 22, a two-room family suite on the street, has a wooden ceiling and a bathroom with a tub and a window. Number 35 has interesting metalwork in the bathroom, on the bedside lights, and on the mirror. This metalwork, which appears throughout the hotel, is the artistry of Walter Certini, a friend of the owner who has his workshop and studio around the corner from the hotel (see "Shopping in Florence," page 295, for details about this unique work that can be successfully shipped back to your home).

In the basement dining room, guests admire the original curved brick ceiling and a memorabilia collection that includes an old record player, a radio, an original Monarch typewriter, and a salt grinder. Beyond this is a sitting room with a fireplace, low leather armchairs, and a long trestle table. Upstairs is another, smaller sitting room where most of the guests seem to gather to watch whatever sporting event is on. Hanging throughout the hotel is an impressive display of paintings.

NOTE: Many hotel rooms in Italy do not have individually controlled heating and air-conditioning systems. Instead they have a master switch in the front office. This means that the owners decide when to heat or cool the rooms, and the majority of them turn off the air-conditioning during the night. This is the policy followed by the Hotel San Remo.

ENGLISH SPOKEN Yes

FACILITIES AND SERVICES Air-conditioning (please see note, above), bar, direct-dial phones, hair dryers, satellite TVs, elevator, in-room and office safes

NEAREST TOURIST ATTRACTIONS Piazzale Michelangelo, interesting shopping along Via Guicciardini, thirty-minute walk to Pitti Palace, fifteen-minute walk to Ponte Vecchio, Uffizi Gallery, and Santa Croce

(49) HOTEL SILLA ★★★ ($)
Via dei Renai, 5
36 rooms, all with shower or bath and toilet

TELEPHONE
055-234-2888, 234-2889

FAX
055-234-1437

CREDIT CARDS
AE, DC, MC, V

CLOSED
Dec

RATES
Single L190,000, double L250,000, triple L300,000, quad L340,000; lower off-season rates; buffet breakfast included

The stately Hotel Silla earns its laurels as one of the most comfortable hotels on the left bank of the Arno River. The hotel skillfully evokes the spirit of Florence by blending the charm and grace of its past as a fifteenth-century palace with the modern comforts that today's travelers appreciate. The street entrance is through a pretty courtyard and up a wide stone stairway padded with an Oriental runner. This gentle walk up will be the extent of your stair-climbing requirements, as there is an elevator once you reach the hotel itself. Twelve rooms face the river, but when the foliage is in full form on the lime-scented trees banking the front of the hotel, your outlook will be filtered. Backside rooms look onto the medieval quarter of San Niccolò.

Every room on the second and third floor has been rejuvenated, with the first-floor bedchambers to follow suit shortly. The Florentine tiled rooms are open and spacious, with walnut furniture composed of a mirrored bureau, desk, comfortable chairs, and bedside lights. The baths are also roomy, with adequate light, heated towel racks, and many housing a tub and separate enclosed stall shower.

Breakfast is served in a formal room with round tables draped in salmon-colored cloths. Along the back wall, a china cabinet beautifully displays the owner's collection of hand-painted ceramic Tuscan plates. On warm days, the riverside terrace is a delightful place to have your breakfast or sip a cool early evening drink. Doing the honors at the reception desk is the delightful Laura, who speaks beautiful English and takes a genuine interest in all the guests.

ENGLISH SPOKEN Yes

FACILITIES AND SERVICES Air-conditioning, bar, direct-dial phones, hair dryers, elevator, minibars, private parking (L25,000 per day), satellite TVs, in-room safe

NEAREST TOURIST ATTRACTIONS Piazzale Michelangelo, San Niccolò quarter, ten- to fifteen-minute walk to Santa Croce, Ponte Vecchio, and Uffizi Gallery, thirty to Pitti Palace

Teatro Comunale and Piazza Vittorio Veneto

The Teatro Comunale is the home of the city's opera, symphony orchestra hall, ballet company, and theater productions. In May, the Maggio Musicale Firoentino Festival, which is the oldest festival in Italy and one of the oldest in Europe, is held here. The Piazza Vittorio Veneto is on the edge of the city, leading to the Casine, a park with a swimming pool and tennis courts.

(50) CASA DEL LAGO ★★
Lungarno Amerigo Vespucci, 58; fourth floor
17 rooms, 13 with shower or bath and toilet

TELEPHONE
055-216-141
FAX
055-214-149
CREDIT CARDS
AE, DC, MC, V
CLOSED
Never
RATES
Single L85,000–115,000,
double L140,000–170,000;
lower off-season rates;
Continental breakfast included
(deduct L10,000 if not taken)

Good views of the Arno can be savored from ten rooms at the Ricciarini family's riverside Casa del Lago. To make this sleep even cheaper, book one without a bath, and don't worry . . . the communal baths are excellent. If you want to spend a little more, I recommend a renovated view room with a bath, perhaps Nos. 12 or 15, which have white walls, sunshine, space, and a nicely tiled bathroom with a shower stall. From these rooms you feel you can almost dive into the river. Views along the back in Nos. 16, 18, and 19, all with private bathrooms, are toward Fiesole and Monte Morello. The breakfast room also has a tranquil view of the Florentine hills. The hotel is close to the Teatro Comunale, so performers often stay here. In the off-season, rates drop and it becomes an even better Cheap Sleep.

ENGLISH SPOKEN Yes

FACILITIES AND SERVICES Room fans, direct-dial phones, elevator, hair dryer available, office safe

NEAREST TOURIST ATTRACTIONS None, must use bus or walk thirty minutes to Ponte Vecchio

(51) HOTEL CONSIGLI ★★★ ($)
Lungarno Amerigo Vespucci, 50
16 rooms, all with shower or bath and toilet

TELEPHONE
055-214-172
FAX
055-219-367
CREDIT CARDS
AE, MC, V
CLOSED
Never

What a view! Positioned on the Arno, the Consigli commands a sweeping river vista from its second-floor terrace, where umbrella-shaded tables and chairs offer perfect vantage points. It is about a twenty-minute stroll along the river to most of the places you came to see in Florence. The Renaissance Palace was once the residence of Princess Demidoff. Beautifully restored, it has been transformed into a hotel warmed by period furnishings, glossy wooden floors, and quality artwork, some of which is by the artist owner of the hotel. The only flaw I can see are those snap-on stretch pink slipcovers used on furniture in the lobby sitting room.

The rooms are ideal roosts for romantics who do not like the feeling of a big hotel but want the comforts of one. Of the sixteen rooms, Nos. 21 and 22 open onto the terrace and four face the river. Room 21 has a small, white-tiled bathroom, cream-colored armchair, reproduction furniture, and a pull-down desk. Room 22 is a large twin with a crystal chandelier and matching set of vintage furniture, including an armoire, a black marble-topped dresser, and side tables. There are two overstuffed chairs and a tub in the bathroom. Best room in the house? No. 11, a two-room suite set off by a high frescoed ceiling (discovered when the old wallpaper was ripped off during renovation) and marble fireplace. It has a 1920s style and a bathroom with a stall shower.

ENGLISH SPOKEN Yes

FACILITIES AND SERVICES Bar, direct-dial phones, elevator, hair dryers, minibars, parking (L10,000 per day), satellite TVs, office safe

NEAREST TOURIST ATTRACTIONS Not much, need to walk or ride the bus

(52) HOTEL CROCINI ★★
Corso Italia, 28
20 rooms, 17 with shower and toilet

In the later part of the nineteenth century, when Florence was the capital of Italy, this neighborhood around the opera house was home to many embassies. On a short walk through the area, looking at the stately town houses, you can imagine what they must have been like in their regal glory.

The Hotel Crocini is one of these old mansions, complete with an interior garden that is pretty in an overgrown way, but one look tells you some TLC wouldn't hurt, and neither would some fertilizer. Never mind . . . you aren't going to sleep in the garden, it is the rooms you need to know about. It is a good thing owner Lorenzo Peroni has youth and enthusiasm on his side, because his twenty bedchambers are similar to his garden . . . fundamentally appealing, but in need of upgrades and refitting. This sounds rather discouraging, but it is not meant to be, because despite its wrinkles here and there, the hotel is sound and I like it. The

RATES
Single L180,000, double L230,000, suite for two to four L250,000–300,000; lower off-season rates; Continental breakfast included

TELEPHONE
055-212-905

FAX
055-210-171

E-MAIL
hotel.crocini@firenze.net

INTERNET
www.firenze.net/hotel.crocini

CREDIT CARDS
AE, DC, MC, V

CLOSED
Never

RATES
Single L135,000, double L170,000; Continental breakfast included

rooms are generally large and especially suited to family living. Your children will love sitting on the velvet seat in the 1930s-style elevator, with its frosted windows, or looking at the fish tank by the wood-burning fireplace downstairs. Antique buffs will appreciate the pieces that are sprinkled about, especially the chest in the second building worth 300 million lire. The light in the rooms is good, and with only a few exceptions (No. 3), the colors go together. Rooms 21 and 23 have private terraces, and there are two small but pleasant ground-level singles.

ENGLISH Yes

FACILITIES AND SERVICES Bar, direct-dial phones, elevator in one part of the hotel, fans, parking (L20,000 per day), TVs, office safe

NEAREST TOURIST ATTRACTIONS Other than the opera, not much; will need to use public transportation or walk

Train Station

Located on the western side of Florence, the train station provides easy access to city bus routes, almost all of which flow through the Piazza della Stazione in front.

(53) ALBERGO MARCELLA ★
Via Faenza, 58; third floor
7 rooms, 1 with shower and toilet

TELEPHONE
055-213-232

CREDIT CARDS
None, cash only

CLOSED
Never

RATES
Single L60,000, double L80,000–90,000; extra person 35 percent of room rate

The Albergo Marcella is another bargain for Cheap Sleepers who want to be near the train station. Actually, the area is far superior to most "train station neighborhoods," despite the fact that it is overrun with hotels, pensiones, and rooms geared to every type of pocketbook. Maria Noto and her husband have been running their seven-room place since 1973, and have never tried to make it more than it is: a plain, no-frills Cheap Sleep. The rooms are freshly painted, the curtains clean, and the hall facilities perfectly acceptable. The top-floor rooms are sunny, with no gloomy interior views. If you land in No. 3, you will be in an enormous double with a nice balcony, but you will have to shower down the hall. That is not the case in No. 4, the only room with its own shower and toilet. The view from No. 1, a big room for three with marginally better furnishings, has a view over the Florentine rooftops. Breakfast is not served, and there is a 1 A.M. lockout, but for most this will not be a problem because Florence has few hot spots to tempt all-night revelry.

ENGLISH SPOKEN Yes

FACILITIES AND SERVICES None, 1 A.M. lockout

NEAREST TOURIST ATTRACTIONS Can walk to many attractions on this side of the Arno, and most on the other side if you are hearty

(54) ALBERGO MARINI ★
Via Faenza, 56; second floor
12 rooms, 6 with shower or bath and toilet

Neat, clean, and uniform in its plainness, the Albergo Marini is short on innate charm but very serviceable. The antiseptically clean rooms and hall facilities, with separate toilets for men and women, are swabbed daily by Lucia, the owner's wife, and Angela, their daughter. The rooms have blond, college dormitory–style furnishings, some with good views and others looking onto a courtyard. Viewless No. 3 has twin beds and facilities outside, but is fresh and appealing. Number 7 is a double with a balcony and an armchair, while No. 8, a triple or quad, has lace curtains at the windows that overlook a tall tree. The ceiling is knotty pine, and the posters are prints by Czech artist Muncha. In No. 13, you will have metal-frame twin beds, two chairs, and your own bathroom. Breakfast is extra, so you will probably do better by going to one of the neighborhood *caffès* for an authentic Italian morning experience.

NOTE: If you mention *Cheap Sleeps in Italy* when reserving and show the book upon arrival, there will be a 10 percent discount.

ENGLISH SPOKEN Very limited

FACILITIES AND SERVICES Office safe

NEAREST TOURIST ATTRACTIONS Can walk to Central Market, Il Duomo, and Ponte Vecchio in under forty minutes, lots to see along the way

TELEPHONE
055-284-824

CREDIT CARDS
None, cash only

CLOSED
Never

RATES
Single L65,000–75,000, double L85,000–125,000, triple L125,000–140,000; lower off-season rates; 10 percent discount for *Cheap Sleeps* readers; Continental breakfast

(55) ALBERGO MERLINI ★
Via Faenza, 56; third floor
12 rooms, 3 with shower or bath and toilet

The building houses several Cheap Sleep possibilities, but for my sleeping lire, the family owned Merlini is the best of the bunch. The twelve-room, third-floor walk-up (no elevator) has a homey atmosphere presided over by a typical Italian family that is happy to share its TV viewing with guests.

Pretty antique pieces and above-average paintings and prints fill the wide hallways, and a sunny glassed-in

TELEPHONE
055-212-848

FAX
055-283-939

CREDIT CARDS
MC, V (must tell them which one you are using one day before departure)

CLOSED
Never

RATES
Single L60,000, double
L80,000–100,000, triple
L105,000; sometimes special
rates; Continental breakfast
(L10,000 extra)

terrace doubles as a breakfast area during the summer season. In winter, guests eat at a big table in a salon crowded with a computer setup, a large breakfront, and two armoires. The rooms are definitely a notch above the usual one-star standard, and the hall facilities are clean— even if the shower consists of a spout in the wall and no curtain. Just remember, you don't have to mop. Most of the rooms have at least one or two nice pieces of furniture and nonthreatening fabric mixes. Naturally there are some lapses, but if you end up in a bright room with your own little balcony, or in any of the seven that have a view of Il Duomo, you won't mind, will you?

ENGLISH SPOKEN Yes

FACILITIES AND SERVICES Office safe

NEAREST TOURIST ATTRACTIONS Can walk to Central Market and Il Duomo

(56) ALBERGO MIA CARA ★
Via Faenza, 58; second floor
24 rooms, 9 with shower or bath and toilet

TELEPHONE
055-216-053
FAX
055-230-2601
CREDIT CARDS
None, cash only
CLOSED
Never
RATES
No single rooms, double
L70,000–90,000; extra person
35 percent of room rate;
Continental breakfast (L7,000 extra)

The hotel has been owned and operated since the early seventies by the Noto family. Their approach is friendly, but guests must toe the line when it comes to drip-dry laundry and room feasts, and they enforce the 2 A.M. lockout without exception. The large, bare rooms are clean, light, and airy, with baths that do not have shower curtains or soap. Some of the rooms are better than others in this one-star, second-floor site, but they are *never* empty. Number 26 is a double with its own bathroom, decent furniture, and no color mixes that will blind you. Number 8 is the smallest double, also with a bath, but the view is over a weed-infested garden that can only improve or be torn out by the time you arrive. The rooms to avoid are the quads with beds that are no more than cots. From March through June the hotel is host to many small student groups. The rest of the year it is home to backpackers and other thrift-minded travelers seeking a midtown budget place to have a Cheap Sleep and not much more.

ENGLISH SPOKEN Yes

FACILITIES AND SERVICES None, lockout at 2 A.M.

NEAREST TOURIST ATTRACTIONS Train station; can walk to everything on this side of the Arno

(57) HOTEL ARGENTINA ★★★ ($)
Via Curtatone, 12
30 rooms, all with shower or bath and toilet

In addition to warm hospitality, the Scatizzi family delivers good value, comfortable accommodations, and a desirable location in one of the nicest three-star hotels in Florence. The senior Scatizzi first opened the hotel in the late thirties. It is now run by his charming daughter, Maria Angela, and her nephew Lorenzo. When you register, notice the framed picture of the Ponte Vecchio hanging nearby. It was done by her other nephew, Alberto, who is now a lawyer, when he was in the first grade. The large lobby has Oriental rugs laid over tiled floors, leather-upholstered barrel chairs, and all the necessary plants, paintings, and attitude to remind you this *is* Florence. A filling breakfast buffet is presented in a formally clad dining room, or you can order a Continental one brought to your room.

Upstairs, the bedrooms are conservatively decorated in soft greens, grays, and corals, with classic furnishings, inlaid flooring, plenty of space for luggage and impulse purchases, and more than adequate baths. Lorenzo has compiled a packet of valuable information about Florence and placed it in each guest room. The quality and depth of the material goes far beyond the usual tourist brochures found in other hotels.

ENGLISH SPOKEN Yes

FACILITIES AND SERVICES Air-conditioning, bar, direct-dial phones, minibars, TVs, some hair dryers, elevator, office safe, Internet and e-mail terminal for guests (small charge)

NEAREST TOURIST ATTRACTIONS Train station; close to the Arno, and about a thirty-minute walk to Il Duomo

TELEPHONE
055-239-8203, 215-408, 239-8616

FAX
055-216-731

E-MAIL
info@hotelargentina.it

INTERNET
www.hotelargentina.it

CREDIT CARDS
AE, DC, MC, V

CLOSED
Never

RATES
Single L190,000, double L250,000; lower off-season rates; buffet breakfast included

(58) HOTEL BEATRICE ★★
Via Fiume, 11
20 rooms, 16 with shower or bath and toilet

Via Fiume is a pensione-packed street close to the train station. Four decades ago it was strictly residential. When Adriano Chinaglia opened his flat as a pensione with full- or half-board, it was a scandal—neighbors were up in arms. Since then, they have joined the lucrative bandwagon, and you will be hard-pressed to find many single-family dwellings on Via Fiume today.

Since those early days, the pensione has expanded to twenty rooms, but it is still run by Adriano and his

TELEPHONE
055-216-790, 239-6137

FAX
055-280-711

CREDIT CARDS
AE, MC, V

CLOSED
Never

RATES
Single L100,000–120,000,
double L150,000–180,000,
triple L210,000; 20 percent
discount for stays longer than
three days; Continental
breakfast included (deduct
L10,000 if not taken)

family: granny, babies, and in-laws all get into the act. Breakfast, if you decide to spring L10,000 for juice, rolls, and coffee, is served in the family dining room. You will also be welcome to share their sitting room, which doubles as a TV room, living area, and place for children to leave their toys. It is a popular rendezvous in summer months because it is the only room with air-conditioning.

The guest rooms are big, and there are no garish color schemes. Two of them have balconies. All is clean and in good order, especially the 1920s-style furniture. Many of the baths have either tubs (some half-size) or showers with a curtain. But watch out for those cotton dish towels masquerading as bath towels.

ENGLISH SPOKEN Yes

FACILITIES AND SERVICES Elevator to reception, direct-dial phones, TVs in some rooms, office safe

NEAREST TOURIST ATTRACTIONS Train station, Central Market; thirty-minute walk to most everything else

(59) HOTEL DESIRÉE ★★
Via Fiume, 20; second floor
25 rooms, all with shower or bath and toilet

TELEPHONE
055-268-236
FAX
055-291-439
CREDIT CARDS
AE, MC, V
CLOSED
Sometimes 15 days in Aug
(dates can vary)
RATES
Single L140,000, double
L180,000; extra bed 35 percent
of room rate; buffet breakfast
included

The beauty of this hotel lies in the original stained-glass windows and doors that grace the entrance and the breakfast room, which also has a corner fireplace and green bower of plants thriving happily on an adjoining balcony. The rooms have been rejuvenated and all have private facilities, but not all of them are equal in my estimation. The best choices are the seven in the Cellini section of the hotel, which was added when the family merged two hotels in the building under the Desirée banner. In the Cellini part, No. 202 provides you with two balconies, large Oriental rugs tossed on parquet floors, and white furniture detailed in gold. Number 203 (also in the Cellini section) is a spacious room with a balcony view of Fiesole and Il Duomo. In No. 204, still Cellini, you will live in a smaller double with a floral tiled floor and have a stall shower. The view will be the same as from No. 203, but you won't have a balcony.

It must be the decorating that turns me off in some of the rooms in the Desirée portion of the hotel. I like Nos. 125 and 127, a double and triple with wooden doors, antiqued furnishings, and eighty-year-old stained-glass windows, but No. 138 comes off as a depressing single with questionable artwork consisting of a painting of the backsides of three horses feeding in their stalls, and for No. 121, done in shocking hot pink, you will have to get out the blinders.

ENGLISH SPOKEN Yes

FACILITIES AND SERVICES Air-conditioning (Cellini only), direct-dial phones, elevators, some hair dryers, TVs, in-room safes

NEAREST TOURIST ATTRACTIONS Fifty meters from the railway station; ten-minute walk to Central Market, Medici Chapel; fifteen-minute walk to Il Duomo

(60) HOTEL IL BARGELLINO ★
Via Guelfa, 87
10 rooms, 5 with shower or bath and toilet

Looking for a friendly Cheap Sleep in Florence? Like to enjoy the fruits of hard work, dedication, and pounds of elbow grease that results in a well-deserved success story? If the answer is yes, please read on about this super one-star hotel.

Carmel Coppola is an expatriate American from Boston who came to Florence to study. She met Pino, now her husband, and the rest is history . . . and the Hotel Il Bargellino. They bought the hotel in 1992 and have slowly but surely brought it into the twentieth century. Pino is a one-man decorating team and construction crew, doing most of the renovations himself. He also haunts country auctions and picks up some amazing antiques and artwork, which he uses in all of the rooms. This is not to suggest that Carmel is idle. One of my favorite things about this hotel is the wraparound roof terrace that is filled in spring and summer with tables, chairs, lemon trees, and roses . . . all lovingly tended by Carmel. In summer, breakfast is served here, and guests are encouraged to enjoy it all day long.

Rooms 8, 9, and 10 open onto the terrace. Number 8 has a ship-style bathroom, but at least you won't have to share; No. 9 showcases one of Pino's antique finds: a pine armoire; and No. 10, a great double with a shower and sink but no toilet, is just next door. Pino installed a new bathroom in No. 1 and painted the picture hanging over the bed. The best point about Room 6 is its spacious bathroom, and No. 7, which looks onto the terrace, is very quiet but bathless. (Note that there is only one public bathroom.) All the beds have new mattresses and down comforters.

TELEPHONE
055-238-2658

FAX
055-238-2698

CREDIT CARDS
V

CLOSED
Sometimes for a few days at Christmas

RATES
Single L65,000, double L110,000–120,000; extra person 35 percent of room rate; Continental breakfast (L10,000 extra)

To top it all off, the neighborhood is full of favorite *Cheap Eats in Italy* spots and Carmel is friendly, energetic, and full of great information on how to make your stay in Florence even better than you imagined.

ENGLISH SPOKEN Yes

FACILITIES AND SERVICES Office safe, parking (L15,000 per day)

NEAREST TOURIST ATTRACTIONS Train station, Central Market

(61) HOTEL NAZIONALE ★
Via Nazionale, 22; second floor
9 rooms, 5 with shower or bath and toilet

TELEPHONE
055-238-2203

FAX
055-238-1735

CREDIT CARDS
MC, V

CLOSED
Never

RATES
Single L65,000–85,000, double L95,000–115,500, triple L122,000–147,000; lower off-season rates; Continental breakfast included (deduct L5,000 in low season only if not taken)

French-born and delightful—that is Marie-Claude Hanotel, the owner of this clean, one-star accommodation close to the railroad station. Her policy is simple: "We are always trying to do something better." She succeeds in keeping up with ongoing maintenance and daily cleaning duties. Although not luxurious by any stretch of the imagination, the rooms are pleasing to the eye, with freshly whitewashed walls, plain but scratch-free furniture, and good wardrobe space. The rooms along the frantically busy Via Nazionale are noisy, but the windows are double-glazed to help quell the roar. Of course, if you open them, you will not have the sound-proofing. For better sleeping prospects, request a quiet room on the back with a sunny exposure. Breakfast is served in your room.

ENGLISH SPOKEN Yes, and French

FACILITIES AND SERVICES None

NEAREST TOURIST ATTRACTIONS Can walk or get a bus to everything

(62) HOTEL NUOVA ITALIA ★★
Via Faenza, 26
21 rooms, all with shower or bath and toilet

TELEPHONE
055-287-508, 268-430

FAX
055-210-941

CREDIT CARDS
AE, MC, V

CLOSED
Never

RATES
Single L95,000, double L145,000, triple L200,000, quad L250,000; lower off-season rates; Continental breakfast included

During all of my trips to Italy, I have seen literally hundreds of hotels. I will tell you that I have seen *fewer than five* hotels in all of the star categories combined that provide something as simple as screens on their windows. It may not seem like much, but Italy, especially Florence and Venice, is invaded in the warm months by relentless, carnivorous mosquitoes. Many hotels provide mosquito coils and bug-burning lights, but I have not found them to be 100 percent effective, so I always warn readers to pack plenty of extra-strength mosquito repellent. After you have spent a night chasing that last elusive mosquito around the room, or wakened to one buzzing in your ear, you will appreciate the Hotel Nuova Italia: In addition to air-conditioning in every room, *they provide screens on the windows!* I cannot emphasize this enough in terms of comfort during your stay.

Okay, so they provide screens, but what about the rooms and the rest of the hotel? At the Nuova Italia, owned by Luciano Viti, his Canadian wife, and their family, care and personal attention are extended to all their guests. Pride of ownership is evident from the reception desk onward. A lovely stone stairway with an iron rail leads guests to the rooms, which, in addition to being air-conditioned, are repainted annually, uniformly carpeted, and done in easy-care laminated wood furniture. All the rooms have private bathrooms, and the showers have curtains. Some of the rooms along the front can be noisy, especially in the early morning when market vendors pull their carts along the cobblestones. There are triple-glazed windows—called Airport Windows—but for ensured quiet, reserve an inside room, perhaps No. 18, which is Luciano's favorite. A downstairs sitting room showcases the family collection of Italian watercolors. This is where Marina will serve your Continental breakfast in the morning. The hotel is close to many good restaurants (see *Cheap Eats in Italy*), interesting shopping (see "Cheap Chic," page 291), and most of the places visitors have on their Florence list.

ENGLISH SPOKEN Yes

FACILITIES AND SERVICES Air-conditioning, direct-dial phones, hair dryer available, no lift (two floors), some TVs, office safe, and . . . *screens on the windows*

NEAREST TOURIST ATTRACTIONS Central Market, Il Duomo, and most other tourist sites

(63) HOTEL PALAZZO BENCI ★★★ ($)
Via Faenza, 6-R
35 rooms, all with shower or bath and toilet

The Hotel Palazzo Benci (on Via Faenza at Piazza Madonna degli Aldobrandini, 3) is the renovated sixteenth-century mansion of the Benci family of Florence. It is now an attractive uptown hotel owned and personally run by the Braccia family. The service they provide is quietly cordial and always discreet, appealing to many government officials and top businesspeople when they are in Florence. The compact, well-decorated bedrooms

TELEPHONE
055-217-049, 238-2821, 213-818

FAX
055-288-308

CREDIT CARDS
AE, DC, MC, V

CLOSED
Never

RATES
Single L190,000, double
L280,000, triple L240,000;
lower off-season rates;
Continental breakfast included

provide guests with all the creature comforts and are quiet, soothing retreats after a long day of sightseeing and shopping in Florence. The rooms along the back overlook the Medici Chapel. All the rooms have double-glazed windows and air-conditioning. They also have another invaluable feature, especially in summer, when Florence is overrun by big mosquitoes. At the Benci, you will have screens on the windows . . . a convenience that I have found in only two other hotel in Florence (see the Hotel Nuova Italia, above, and the Globus on page 90).

The hotel's enclosed, flower-filled garden has tables with umbrellas for summer alfresco breakfasts or afternoon drinks. A new lounge area has tufted red leather sofas and chairs and a marble floor. Also on view is a glass-covered eleventh-century well, which is older by far than the building. To get to the breakfast room, guests cross the ornate upstairs sitting room, with a handsome, heavily scrolled ceiling, which served as a guest room in the mansion in the 1700s. In the breakfast room guests can admire the wooden ceiling, which once graced a room on the third floor of the palace, and can look out the windows for a direct view of the Medici Chapel.

ENGLISH SPOKEN Yes

FACILITIES AND SERVICES Air-conditioning, bar, direct-dial phones, hair dryers, minibars, satellite TVs, elevator, office safe, window screens

NEAREST TOURIST ATTRACTIONS Central Market, Il Duomo, and most other destinations

(64) MARIO'S ★★★ ($)
Via Faenza, 89
16 rooms, 15 with shower or bath and toilet

TELEPHONE
055-216-801
FAX
055-212-039
CREDIT CARDS
AE, DC, MC, V
CLOSED
Never
RATES
Single L200,000, double
L240,000, triple L300,000;
lower off-season rates; large
Continental breakfast included

While you may find rooms in Florence for less, you will not be able to top Mario Noce's fine establishment for general ambience and friendly staff. The many Cheap Sleepers who have stayed here have become devoted regulars because the hotel reflects the best in quality, value, and comfort. Everything is well executed, whether in the form of decor (Oriental runners cushion the picture-gallery hallways) or amenities (the attractive bedrooms might have a corner writing desk, a small balcony, or a stained-glass window). Mario's warmth and hospitality are evident at every turn, from the welcome in four languages to the bowls of fresh fruit and greenery that warm each guest room. On request, for one to four people, Mario will give personal day tours of Tuscany in his own car. Guests are encouraged to mingle and get to know one another at the bar in the early evening, or while seated at the communal breakfast tables under the watchful eyes of the stuffed boar's head.

ENGLISH SPOKEN Yes

FACILITIES AND SERVICES Air-conditioning, bar, direct-dial phones, hair dryers, satellite TVs, in-room safes (L2,000 per day), Mario's day tours of Tuscany for up to four people (rates on request)

NEAREST TOURIST ATTRACTIONS Central Market; twenty-minute walk to train station, Il Duomo

(66) PENSIONE ACCADEMIA ★★
Via Faenza, 7
16 rooms, 13 with shower or bath and toilet

The Accademia has sixteen rooms on three floors in a distinguished building on the hotel-studded Via Faenza, at Piazza Madonna, in an area known as hotel heaven because no matter what your price range or needs you will have many choices. This hotel was formerly a clean, safe, family run spot with prices that would not leave you breathless. It is still family run and just as clean and safe, but the prices are another matter. After a massive renovation project, another star was added and the prices rank right at the top of the second-star tier. I am including it because the renovation was a great success and the hotel still offers good value in what is now one of the prettiest two-stars in the neighborhood.

Many of the best features of the old hotel were kept and improved upon. The original eighteenth-century stained-glass windows and a painted ceiling create a dramatic entry area. The hotel is reached by going through this entry and up red-carpeted stone stairs. Once inside, you will be impressed by the breakfast room, which also has a frescoed ceiling, corner fireplace, huge gilt mirror, stained-glass doors attributed to the Bernardo Cennini school of design (Cennini designed the magnificent door of the baptistery on Il Duomo), and a collection of framed photos of Florence mixed in with watercolors of Tuscany. The colors in the coral marble floor are carried out in the table linens, and accented by black chairs.

Room No. 6, for two or three, has hardwood floors, matching colors, and a tiled bathroom with a shower and curtain. Number 5 looks great, all in yellow, and so does

TELEPHONE
055-293-451

FAX
055-291-771

E-MAIL
hotaccad@tin.it

CREDIT CARDS
AE, MC, V

CLOSED
Never

RATES
Single L110,000–140,000, double L170,000, triple L220,000; lower off-season rates; buffet breakfast included

No. 4, a large twin with plenty of moving-around space. If you are handicapped, No. 2 has a special bathroom. If you don't mind being near the reception area, No. 3, which is on a little garden, might appeal to you. Solo Cheap Sleepers willing to pad down the hall for a shower can book one of the three singles that are bathless.

ENGLISH SPOKEN Yes

FACILITIES AND SERVICES Air-conditioning, bar, direct-dial phones, TVs, office safe

NEAREST TOURIST ATTRACTIONS Il Duomo, most of Florence within a ten- to thirty-minute walk

Via Tornabuoni

This elegant shopping street is lined with houses of the Florentine nobility, the most famous of which is Palazzo Strozzi, whose golden stone facade dominates the street.

(67) HOTEL LA RESIDENZA ★★★ ($)
Via dei Tornabuoni, 8
24 rooms, all with shower or bath and toilet

TELEPHONE
055-218-684

FAX
055-284-197

E-MAIL
la.residenza@italyhotel.com

CREDIT CARDS
AE, DC, MC, V

CLOSED
Never

RATES
Single L160,000, double L270,000, triple L360,000; Continental breakfast included; half-board (dinner only, L45,000 per person, beverages extra)

La Residenza is a throwback to the days when people came to Florence for "the season." Back then, people checked into a favorite pensione, where they slept *and* ate all of their meals. While it is almost impossible to find such a rare accommodation in Florence today, all hope is not lost. There is still Gianna Vasile's La Residenza, which offers a prix fixe dinner to guests in addition to breakfast.

La Residenza, next to the Palazzo Strozzi, occupies the top three floors of a fifteenth-century Renaissance palace built by descendants of the Medici family. To get to the reception desk, you will ride up from the ground floor in one of the first elevators in Florence. Greeting you will be Lara, or one of the other staff members who have worked here all of their lives. The sitting area on the main level of the hotel is filled with Sra. Vasile's collection of furniture, antiques, and a mirrored bar, and on the top floor, a sunny lounge room has an interesting group of old photos of Florence. The welcoming dining room, with it original ceiling, is set with linens, nice china, and silverware. Fresh flowers add a lovely touch, as do the paintings that various guests have left behind.

No two bedrooms are alike, and there is no denying their "old slipper" appeal. Best bets are the havens on the top floors with their own plant-filled terraces or balconies. Otherwise, No. 8, one of the better doubles, has a comfortable chair, matching fabrics, an above-average bathroom, and a feeling of space created by an entryway. Room No. 3 is a miniature double on the street with limited drawer space and an orange sorbet–colored bathroom. A quieter choice in terms of noise is No. 16, which faces the inner courtyard. The bed is covered in chenille and there is a pretty Venetian-style painted armoire and table. The strawberry-colored bathroom is prefab but serviceable.

ENGLISH SPOKEN Yes, and French and German

FACILITIES AND SERVICES Air-conditioned, bar, direct-dial phones, hair dryers, elevator to all but fourth floor, minibars, parking (can be arranged for L30,000 per day), satellite TVs, office safe, half-board, full-board for groups with advance notice given at time of reservation

NEAREST TOURIST ATTRACTIONS Shopping, heart of Florence

(68) HOTEL SCOTI ★
Via dei Tornabuoni, 7
7 rooms, none with shower or toilet

For Cheap Sleeping on one of the toniest stretches of upscale-shopping real estate in Florence, Doreen and Carmelo's Hotel Scoti is a good pick. What you save sleeping cheap you can apply to your purchases at Hermès, Gucci, and Ferragamo, to name only a few of the famous fashion boutiques with addresses on Via dei Tornabuoni. The hotel exudes a friendly family atmosphere, with seven quiet bedchambers sweetly furnished with a collection of this-and-that furniture. Three people living in No. 2 will look out on the bell tower of Santa Trinita. The single Cheap Sleeper in No. 6 will have an antique brass bed, marble dresser, table, chair, washbasin, and a cheerful sighting of tiled Florentine rooftops. Breakfast is served family style at a large table in the main room, which also has an upright piano should you feel musically inclined.

ENGLISH SPOKEN Yes (Doreen is Australian)

FACILITIES AND SERVICES Hair dryer available, elevator, office safe

NEAREST TOURIST ATTRACTIONS Shopping, shopping, shopping, and then Il Duomo, and the core of Florence

TELEPHONE AND FAX
055-292-128

E-MAIL
hotelscoti@iol.it

CREDIT CARDS
None, cash only

CLOSED
Never

RATES
Single L60,000, double L90,000; extra bed L39,000; Continental breakfast (L5,000 extra)

(69) HOTEL TORNABUONI BEACCI ★★★ ($)
Palazzo Minerbetti-Strozzi, Via Tornabuoni, 3; third floor
30 rooms, all with shower or bath and toilet

TELEPHONE
055-212-645, 268-377, 294-283
FAX
055-283-594
E-MAIL
Beacci.Tornabuoni@ italyhotel.com
CREDIT CARDS
AE, DC, MC, V
CLOSED
Never
RATES
Single L190,000–210,000, double L300,000–340,000; extra person L60,000; Continental breakfast included; lunch à la carte, set dinner (L45,000)

"Just what we have been looking for," "It is nice to feel at home so far away from home," are only two of the comments written by enthusiastic visitors in the guest book, which dates back to 1917, when Sra. Beacci's parents opened this Florentine hotel. One of my favorites was written on November 29, 1928; it says, "We the undersigned guests of the Hotel Tornabuoni Beacci deem it to be in the interests of future American visitors to Florence to know of the perfection of the cuisine, the rare courtesy and the refinement of this hotel." The praiseworthy comment was followed by nine signatures. Over the years, the devoted clientele of writers (including John Steinbeck), actors, models, heads-of-state, and just plain tourists have returned time and again, largely because of the warm personality of Sra. Beacci and the way she makes everyone feel right at home. But no one can keep working forever and nothing ever stays the same: A few years ago, Sra. Beacci stepped down and turned over the running of her hotel to her associate, Francesco Bechi, who told me he considers her to be "like my mother." Along with the help of longtime manager Angelo and his delightful wife, Patricia, the hotel has maintained Sra. Beacci's standards of excellence while at the same time breathing new life into the thirty rooms so perfectly located in the heart of Florence.

Everything about the hotel, which is on the third and fourth floors of an old *palazzo,* is still gracious and discerning without being pretentious. The sitting room, with its wood-burning fireplace, is comfortable and classically furnished with antiques, big sofas, easy chairs, and wall tapestries. Everywhere you look there are beautiful fresh flower arrangements and lush green indoor plants. The large, refreshed bedrooms, done in pastels, with painted furniture mixed with vintage wood, are so inviting that you may want to settle in and stay forever . . . or at least longer than intended. They are all fitted with comfortable reading chairs, dressers with a mirror, good beds with extra pillows, and large, sunny windows, some with a view of Il Duomo or San Miniato al Monte Church, which dates from 1127 and is the oldest in Florence. The bathrooms are slowly being done in a more modern mode, but even those that are vintage are wonderful.

A jasmine-filled rooftop terrace for afternoon drinks or a leisurely breakfast offers splendid views of neighboring rooftops and churches. In addition to breakfast, guests can eat lunch or dinner at the hotel. Snacks at the bar or in the garden are available at lunchtime, but for dinner there is both a set three-course menu and à la carte choices.

ENGLISH SPOKEN Yes

FACILITIES AND SERVICES Air-conditioning, bar, direct-dial phones, minibars, satellite TVs, office safe, elevator

NEAREST TOURIST ATTRACTIONS Everything!

Other Options

Apartment Rentals, Rental Agencies, and Residence Hotels

Those of you who have done it know—in a flat you will save money on meals, have more room, and get to know your neighborhood from a perspective never gained in a hotel stay. In addition to the Florence listings in this book, several of the agencies listed here can also find you an apartment in Rome or Venice. But before deciding on renting a flat in Florence, you should refer to "Tips on Renting an Italian Apartment," page 13.

Apartment Rentals

CONTESSA MARIA VITTORIA RIMBOTTI (central Florence)

TELEPHONE
(805) 987-5278,
(800) 726-6702

FAX
(805) 482-7976

E-MAIL
mail@rentvillas.com

INTERNET
www.rentvillas.com

CREDIT CARDS
MC, V

RATES
Studio and loft apartments start at $820 per month (one-month minimum); one-bedroom apartments start at $1,200 per week (two-week minimum); large two-bedroom apartments start at $1500 per week (two-week minimum). Lower rates for longer stays. Telephone and all utilities are extra.

The Contessa Rimbotti's Florentine apartments top my worldwide list. Nothing else even comes close. I could move into any one of them and feel as though I was in absolute heaven. In fact, I did . . . and I can't wait to go back. One look will tell you that a person of distinguished elegance is in charge here, and that describes Contessa Rimbotti to a T. Her lovely flats, located in two buildings she owns in the middle of Florence, reflect her own refined artistic taste and judgment, as she has personally designed and selected everything you see, employing imagination and creativity at every turn. She once told me, "I always try to put myself in the guests' shoes and provide the best that I can for them." She has succeeded beyond measure. From the smallest tower studio to a large impressive penthouse with wraparound terraces, or one with dreamlike views across the Arno to the Uffizi Gallery and the sparkling lights of the Ponte Vecchio, she has created beautiful living spaces furnished with lovely antiques, rich Italian fabrics, and interesting paintings.

Closet and drawer space abound. The linens are embroidered, the towels are thick and fluffy, and everything is color-coordinated. You will love her bathrooms and kitchens. The marble and tiled bathrooms all have a tub with a shower over it or an enclosed stall shower. Larger ones have double sinks; all have big mirrors and loads of space. In the kitchen there will be Richard Ginori china, quality cooking equipment, and beautiful marble workspaces. Of course, there will also be a dishwasher, a full-size refrigerator, and a complete stove with oven. Upon arrival, you will find water and perhaps a bottle of wine, a small jar of coffee, a few tea bags, and some crackers or cookies to tide you over until you can go food shopping. To help you do that, there will be a packet of information in each apartment listing the best shops and restaurants in the neighborhood as well as the major sites in Florence.

The Contessa maintains an office in Florence with an English-speaking staff able to handle any problems that may arise. Absolutely no details are left to chance. I wondered after my last stay how the Contessa could improve on the perfection of her apartments. I know that by my next visit she will have thought of many beautiful ways.

I am saving the best for last. These apartments are affordable! With a little planning and organization, they are within the reach of many Cheap Sleepers. There is a two-week minimum for the one- and two-bedroom apartments and a one-month minimum for the studios and lofts. To make reservations, there is no direct dealing with Contessa Rimbotti. Booking is handled exclusively through Suzanne Pidduck's Rentals in Italy (and Elsewhere!) at the addresses and numbers given below. For more information on this very well run California-based rental agency, please see page 115 or use the information below for reserving one of Contessa Rimbotti's apartments.

(24) PALAZZO ANTELLESI
Piazza Santa Croce, 21–22
12 apartments, all with shower or bath and toilet

The Palazzo Antellesi was created in the second half of the sixteenth century by joining several medieval towers. The facade was painted in allegorical themes by Giovanni da San Giovanni, the foremost fresco painter of his time. Today it is considered to be the most famous and authentic Renaissance palace on the dramatic Piazza Santa Croce, the ancient site of colorful fooball games with costumed players. The palace has been completely restored and refitted into flats accommodating up to six people.

Aside from their historical significance and original architectural designs, the easy-to-live-in, comfortable flats are furnished with a combination of modern pieces and antiques. The kitchens are equipped with dishwashers and washing machines in addition to all the pots, pans, and crockery you will need to set up any level of housekeeping. Some of the apartments have working fireplaces and sweeping views, not only of the traffic-free piazza below but of the famous sites of Florence and the surrounding rolling hills. Several of the apartments have their own terrace or open onto a private garden. All have American-style bathrooms. Maid service is available, and all but two are accessible by elevator.

The dynamite location puts you within easy range of all that awaits you in Florence. From a practical point of view, excellent markets and food shops are minutes away. So are interesting shops, restaurants, cleaners, and a post office. Many returning international guests consider their favorite flat at the well-managed Palazzo Antellesi to be their second home.

Office hours in Florence are limited by telephone to Monday through Friday from 3 to 6 P.M. Italian time. You can, however, send a fax or e-mail anytime. You can also call the New York number. Finally, you book your stay through Villas International (see page 116).

NEW! APARTMENTS IN SIENA

The owners of the Palazzo Antellesi have created three new apartments in their historic Renaissance *palazzo* in the heart of Siena's old city. This pivotal location allows guests to be within walking distance of the magnificent cathedral, all the necessary shops, and only two hundred yards from the central square, where the city's medieval past comes alive in July and August with the colorful Palio, a horse race in which teams of riders charge bareback around the cobbled Piazza del Campo. Siena is less than one hour's drive from Florence and is an ideal base for exploring the wine regions of Chianti and Montalcino and the historic towns of San Gimigniano, Pienza, Montepulciano, and Monteriggioni.

Because of the nature of the *palazzo* and its historic importance, which prohibits structural changes, some skillful design techniques were necessary to create suitable living spaces, and this means there are very few windows at eye level. The bedrooms of two flats have no

TELEPHONE
Italy: 39-055-244-456 (between 3–6 P.M., Italian time); New York: (212) 932-3480

FAX
Italy: 39-055-234-5552; New York: (212) 932-9039

E-MAIL
manpico@mail.idt.net

CREDIT CARDS
None, cash or personal checks only

CLOSED
Never

RATES
Florence (Palazzo Antellesi): weekly from $1,500–$3,500; Siena: weekly from $950–$1260; 10 percent discount for second month or more and during low season (Jan 15–Mar 15); telephone charges and utilities extra in both locations

windows at all, only skylights. In another, Leocorno, there are no windows to speak of in the sitting area, only little peepholes at the floor level. I only mention it here because for some, the lack of windows might be a problem. The air-conditioned flats are attractively furnished with rustic Tuscan reproduction antiques and display the latest word in pastel-colored kitchen and bathroom designs, complete with good-size dishwashers and washing machines. The closet space is excellent.

ENGLISH SPOKEN Yes

FACILITIES AND SERVICES Florence (Palazzo Antellesi): Fully-equipped kitchens, one apartment with air-conditioning, otherwise portable units available, direct-dial phones, satellite TVs, most have elevators, all with either or both washing machine and dishwasher, maid service extra

Siena: Air-conditioning, fully-equipped kitchens, dishwasher, washing machine, direct-dial phones, elevator, satellite TVs, maid service extra

NEAREST TOURIST ATTRACTIONS Florence (Palazzo Antellesi): Santa Croce Church, Arno, Il Duomo, museums, shopping

Siena: Nearby wine regions, historic towns, base for exploring Tuscany

(71) VILLA IL PODERINO
Via del Giuggiolo, 4 (edge of Florence)
4 flats, all with shower, bath, and toilet

TELEPHONE AND FAX
055-474-473

E-MAIL
poderino@fol.it

CREDIT CARDS
None, cash only

CLOSED
Never

RATES
One-week minimum stay, prices start at $200 per day for one-week stay, which includes all utilities except telephone and heat; rates lower for longer stays; all utilities extra for monthly stays

For a quiet retreat in a country setting just at the edge of Florence, reserve one of the four apartments Andreana Emo has created in her family home, the Villa Il Poderino. The villa, built at the beginning of the fifteenth century, lies in a tranquil four-acre estate surrounded by cedar and olive trees, with beautiful views of Florence and the rolling hills around it. The lovely grounds include several out buildings and a greenhouse.

The villa has an impressive history. It was purchased by Andreana's American great-grandfather, Alfred Parrish, an engineer who also owned homes in Rome, the Veneto, and Lake Como. If you saw the television miniseries *Winds of War* and *War and Remembrance,* you will recognize Villa Il Poderino because all the interiors and many of the garden scenes used for the Italian segments were shot here.

Andreana, whose mother is also American, studied in the United States and attended Stanford University.

When she decided to turn part of her home into apartments, she completely refitted it, but kept the dignified and refined character of the aristocratic mansion intact. The four apartments are all large and done in an eclectic mix of comfortable, well-loved furniture with a sprinkling of family pieces. No, they won't appeal to modernists, but for those seeking quiet refuge . . . perhaps to do some writing, or just to get away from the hustle and bustle of the world for a time, they are ideal.

Surrounding the villa are quiet places to sit and read, watch the sunrise or sunset, or just walk and have enough time to stop and smell the flowers rather than rushing off to deal with the next petty urgency. The kitchens have dishwashers and washing machines, and are fully equipped with all the necessities to set up housekeeping. The bathrooms are great, especially if you love big tubs with claw feet and wonderful old fixtures. There are some stairs to negotiate, and, unfortunately, no elevator.

Central Florence is accessible by bus, which stops about a block from the main gate, or by a thirty-minute walk. For motorists, there is free parking. The villa is also available for short-term study courses, weddings, and receptions.

ENGLISH SPOKEN Yes

FACILITIES AND SERVICES Free parking, TVs

NEAREST TOURIST ATTRACTIONS None, must use car or public transportation or walk thirty minutes

Rental Agencies

In addition to the agencies listed here, please see Rental Directories International (Rome, "Rental Agencies," page 188) for apartments to rent in Florence.

(70) FLORENCE AND ABROAD
Via San Zanobi, 58; second floor

TELEPHONE
055-487-004, 490-143

FAX
055-490-143

E-MAIL
fl_ab@dada.it

CREDIT CARDS
None; will accept U.S. bank checks

CLOSED
Sat, Sun, Aug

Some agencies are from hell. Others, like Florence and Abroad, are pleasant to work with and honestly try to match an apartment with the budgets and needs of their clients. If you decide to go this route, please remember that while the agency *can* and definitely should control the cleanliness and habitability of their rentals, they cannot control views, stairs versus an elevator, the weather during your stay, street noise, or the Italian way of living. Italians have a much higher cost of living than we do; as a result, many have to make do with a great deal less in terms of square footage, modern appliances, and other conveniences many of us take for granted. You will encounter oddities in electricity, plumbing, and even linens. Therefore, it is imperative that you be specific about your needs. Spell out in detail what you absolutely must have: elevator, full bathtub, stall shower with a curtain or door, types of beds, view versus no view, level of noise, and so on. The more specific you are, the better they will be able to serve you. But be reasonable. For $700 a week don't expect a penthouse with a doorman, a washer and dryer operated by a live-in maid, CNN running twenty-four hours a day on the oversize color television, or a modem to keep you in cyberspace.

Florence and Abroad is open to book reservations Monday through Friday 10 A.M. to 12:30 P.M. and 3 to 6:30 P.M.

NOTE: In addition to apartments in Florence, they have villas in the surrounding hills.

ENGLISH SPOKEN Yes; ask to speak with Karen Brennan Piemonte, who is English and very helpful

FACILITIES AND SERVICES Depends on the apartment

NEAREST TOURIST ATTRACTIONS Depends on location of apartment

RATES
Depends on size and type of apartment; security deposit required; studio apartments start at around $675 a week; in short-term rentals, utilities (except telephone) are usually included, some special rates for longer stays

RENTALS IN ITALY (AND ELSEWHERE!)
1742 Calle Corva
Camarillo, CA 93010–8428

Suzanne T. Pidduck has devoted over thirty years to traveling and living in Italy. Her California-based company, which is affiliated with the well-known Cuendet, has now grown into one of the best organizations renting Italian properties—as well as those in other European locations. Through Suzanne you can obtain anything from a studio in Venice to a magnificent Florentine apartment facing the Arno and Ponte Vecchio, a farmhouse in Tuscany, or a panoramic penthouse in Rome. In addition to rentals in Rome, Florence, and Venice, she covers the rest of Italy, as well as the countrysides of Portugal, Spain, and France.

Once you are in your rental, someone who speaks English will be available via toll-free telephone number, or on-site, should the need arise. I used Rentals in Italy (and Elsewhere!) during my last two research trips to Venice and Florence and found them to be competent professionals on every level, and give them all my highest praise.

TELEPHONE
(805) 987-5278, (800) 726-6702

FAX
(805) 482-7976

E-MAIL
mail@rentvillas.com

INTERNET
www.rentvillas.com

CREDIT CARDS
MC, V

RATES
Depends on the apartment, but studios start at around $700 per week for two

NOTE: For an in-depth description of some of the rental properties in Florence, see Contessa Maria Vittoria Rimbotti, page 110.

VILLAS INTERNATIONAL
950 Northgate Drive, Suite 206
San Rafael, CA 94903

TELEPHONE
(415) 499-9490, (800) 221-2260

FAX
(415) 499-9491

E-MAIL
villas@best.com

INTERNET
www.villasintl.com

CREDIT CARDS
None, cash only

RATES
Vary by location, but prices generally start at $675 per week for two in a small studio

From firsthand experience I can say that David Kendall's Villas International Ltd. is a top-rate operation. Through this company I have booked a penthouse in Florence and a modern flat in Vienna. Both were wonderful rental experiences from the moment I arrived until I reluctantly had to leave.

Villas International offers a wide selection of rental properties of all types for the savvy independent traveler who wants more than just a city hotel room. In addition to all major Italian cities, they cover the rest of Europe, Great Britain, Mexico, the Caribbean, and Hawaii. If you want a car, David Kendall will arrange that, too. Properties are well located, and the price ranges will appeal to most budgets. All arrangements can be made through their San Francisco office, which has the added convenience of a toll-free number. There are no charges for membership or the mailing of property descriptions. As with any foreign rental, it is wise to take out cancellation insurance.

Residence Hotels

If you plan to be in Florence for longer than a few days and don't want to rent an apartment, a good way to cut costs is to stay in a residence hotel. Most of the residence hotels are of at least three-star quality and provide the services and amenities found in good hotels. Other advantages include more space, a kitchen in which you can cook a few meals and save on restaurant costs (a big factor with families), and, finally, the feeling of being more at home than you would be in a hotel room.

(27) PALAZZO MANNAIONI RESIDENCE
Via Maffia, 9
19 apartments, all with shower or bath and toilet

TELEPHONE
055-271-091

FAX
055-271-0902

CREDIT CARDS
MC, V

The Palazzo Mannaioni is a moderately priced apartment/residence not far from the Santo Spirito Church. The best rooms, on the third, fourth, and fifth floors, face the cloisters of the church and the bell tower. I like

Nos. 17 and 19 in summer, when you can sit on the terrace, or No. 11, with its wood ceiling, bookcase, and ample closet space. The fourteen studios have a cooking corner, bathroom (get one with a tub, they are better), telephone, television, modern furniture, and elevator service to four of the five floors. Everything from dishes, pots and pans, linens, and twice-weekly maid service with linen change is provided. The maid won't do your laundry, but there is a laundromat within a five-minute walk. Utilities are included; telephone charges are not. The neighborhood is interesting, filled with narrow streets and many old artisans' shops. On the second Sunday of every month a small flea market sets up in front of the church, and on weekday mornings, a vegetable and fruit market. Office hours: Mon–Sat 9 A.M.–12:30 P.M., 4–7:15 P.M., Sun 9 A.M.–noon.

ENGLISH SPOKEN Yes

FACILITIES AND SERVICES Direct-dial phones, elevator to all but the fifth floor, fans, TVs, office safe, maid service

NEAREST TOURIST ATTRACTIONS Santo Spirito, Pitti Palace, Ponte Vecchio

CLOSED
Never

RATES
Small single units from
L130,000 per day, double
L170,000 per day, triple
L210,000 per day, quad
L250,000 per day; better rates
for stays of a week of more

Camping

For the rough and ready, camping in Florence can provide some very Cheap Sleeps. Some of the campgrounds are open year-round, and all are at least a thirty-minute trip from Florence proper. They are jam-packed in summer. It is possible to rent almost everything you will need to set up rural housekeeping. Prices quoted here are per person and include water and electricity hookups. There is often a small convenience store on the premises, but due to the captive audience, prices will be high.

The Federazione Italiana del Campeggio, also called Federcampeggio, issues a free list of campgrounds in Italy and a map. Write to them at Calenzano, Florence 50041, or call 055-882-391.

CAMPING ITALIANI E STRANIERI
Viale Michelangelo, 80 (outside Florence)

Beautiful views, but very crowded and hot in summer. Must arrive early to get a good spot. Crowded. Office is open 6 A.M. to midnight.

ENGLISH SPOKEN Limited

FACILITIES AND SERVICES Bar, market, free showers

NEAREST TOURIST ATTRACTIONS Twenty to thirty minutes to Florence by car or bus

TELEPHONE 055-681-1977

CREDIT CARDS None, cash only

CLOSED Nov–Mar

RATES Tent L9,000; each person in it L12,000

CAMPING PANORAMICO
Via Peramonda, 1 (outside Florence)

ENGLISH SPOKEN Yes

FACILITIES AND SERVICES Convenience store and snack bar (closed in February), free showers

NEAREST TOURIST ATTRACTIONS None; thirty minutes to Florence by car or bus

TELEPHONE 055-599-069

CREDIT CARDS AE, MC, V

CLOSED Never

RATES Tent L18,000 for one person, L1,100 each additional person; camper L9,000 per person

VILLA CAMERATA
Viale Augusto Righi, 2–4 (outside Florence)

The country setting of this campground beside a villa is not only pretty, it is cooler than most. Reservations are accepted by phone or fax, and can be made several months in advance. The campsite is also a hostel, with a computer link to hostels in other Italian cities, so you can make reservations at one of them once you are here (see page 120 for the hostel details). The office opens at 2 P.M. (3 P.M. in winter).

ENGLISH SPOKEN Yes

FACILITIES AND SERVICES Affiliated with International Youth Hostel, showers included, bar

NEAREST TOURIST ATTRACTIONS None; at least thirty minutes to Florence by car or bus

TELEPHONE 055-610-1451

FAX 055-610-300

CREDIT CARDS None, cash only

CLOSED Never

RATES Tent L9,000–11,000, L7,000 for each person in a tent, camper L14,000, each person L7,000

Student Accommodations

Student accommodations vary widely, from rooms for two or three to dormitories housing up to twenty sleepers a night. Most of the sites impose a lockout during the day (i.e., you cannot stay in your room during this period) and a curfew at night. There is nothing elaborate about any of them; they are strictly places to lay a weary head. If possible, try to look at the room before you decide to stay. Another point to remember is that often these accommodations are far from the center of Florence, entailing long bus commutes. It could be cheaper in the long run to find a small hotel closer in and apply the bus fares to the room rates. Also consider, these long rides waste time, and the buses may run infrequently at night or on weekends, further complicating your bargain Cheap Sleep . . . which ultimately it is not.

(25) ISTITUTO ARTIGIANELLI PENSIONATO PIO X
Via dei Serragli, 106
19 rooms, 3 with shower or bath and toilet

TELEPHONE
055-225-044

FAX
055-225-004

CREDIT CARDS
None, cash only

CLOSED
Never

RATES
Single L25,000, double L22,000 per person

The quiet location and the policies of no daytime lockout and no more than four persons to a room make this an attractive hostel choice for groups and/or individuals needing mighty Cheap Sleeps. Originally the building was a convent, with two schools and a marble workshop. The ground floor is still made up of artists' studios, above which is the hostel. The white dormitory-style rooms are bare-bones basic, with thin mattresses and matching bedspreads on army-style cots. Hall showers and toilets are above average. There are no kitchen privileges, but you can bring food and eat it in the dining room. Breakfast is not served. There is a midnight curfew. The management, consisting of a mother, her son, and an aunt, has been on board for thirty years and is serious, but there are no draconian rules posted all over the place. The money made from the hostel goes to help a school for poor children and to the artists in the studios below.

To find the building, look for the sign "Interno 104-110" at the address, and go into the courtyard; the door is straight ahead on the right and up a few stairs.

ENGLISH SPOKEN Some

FACILITIES AND SERVICES Office safe

NEAREST TOURIST ATTRACTIONS Piazza Santo Spirito

(65) OSTELLO ARCHI ROSSI
Via Faenza, 94
96 beds, 10 rooms with shower or bath and toilet

TELEPHONE
055-290-804
FAX
055-230-2601
CREDIT CARDS
None, cash only
CLOSED
Never
RATES
L23,000–25,000 per person,
family rooms for three to six
L26,000–30,000 per person;
towels L1,500;
breakfast L3,000–5,000,
à la carte dinner L5,000–9,500

This strictly youth-oriented Cheap Sleep benefits from its location near the train station. There are ninety-six beds in rooms set up for three to nine. Many of these rooms have their own bathrooms. Sheets, blankets, and pillows are included; towels cost an additional L1,500. The rooms have lockers, and hot showers are free. Breakfast and dinner are served in a university-style dining room with a huge television at one end and windows along a garden badly in need of a caretaker. The walls of the hostel are covered with an international tapestry of graffiti drawn by the guests. There was a time when chalk would have been available for you to add your own touches, but no longer—the walls are full. Reservations are not accepted in the high season, and there is no age limit. Hostel hours are as follows: at 6:30 A.M. it opens; at 9:30 A.M. guests must leave their rooms but can stay in common areas; at 11 A.M. the entire hostel closes; at 2:30 P.M. it reopens, and guests may return to their rooms. The curfew is 12:30 A.M.

ENGLISH SPOKEN Yes

FACILITIES AND SERVICES Elevator, coin laundry, luggage storage, restaurant for breakfast and dinner, office safe

NEAREST TOURIST ATTRACTIONS Train station, Central Market, walking distance to almost everything

OSTELLO VILLA CAMERATA
Viale Augusto Righi, 2–4 (outside Florence)
320 beds, no private facilities

TELEPHONE
055-601-1451
FAX
055-600-315
CREDIT CARDS
None, cash only
CLOSED
Never
RATES
L23,000 with an IYH card,
L27,000 without card;
breakfast included

The beauty of this hostel is its countryside setting; in addition, you can make reservations by telephone or fax several weeks ahead or by writing months in advance. The hostel has a computer link to hostels in other Italian cities, and you can reserve at one of them once you are here. It is not close to Florence, requiring train, bus, and foot to get to it. There is also a campsite here (see page 118). Breakfast is included in the price; dinner is extra. The office is open for check-in from 2 P.M. in summer and 3 P.M. in winter. Room lockout is from 9 A.M. to 2 P.M. in summer, and 9 A.M. to 3 P.M. in winter; curfew is at midnight.

ENGLISH SPOKEN Yes

FACILITIES AND SERVICES Office safe, dinner served (L15,000), midnight curfew

NEAREST TOURIST ATTRACTIONS None; at least thirty minutes to Florence by car or bus

(29) SANTA MONACA HOSTEL
Via Santa Monaca, 6
115 beds, no private facilities

The Santa Monaca Hostel, once a convent for Santa Monaca nuns, is across the river from Piazza Goldoni. It is popular, spacious, and clean, and offers kitchen privileges, a safe for valuables, laundry facilities, lockers, and a list of rules set in concrete. You must be out of your room *for the day* from 9:30 A.M. to 2 P.M. Lights are turned out at midnight and the door is locked at 1 A.M. The hostel office is open from 6 A.M., and for reservations from 9:30 A.M. to 1 P.M. Advance reservations may be made by fax, not telephone, but you can also show up and hope. Three meals a day are served Monday to Saturday and cost extra. The maximum stay is seven days in high season; longer stays are allowed the rest of the year.

The rooms range in size from four to ten beds and are segregated into men's and women's sections. Sheets are provided, and you must use them, not yours. You pay for your entire stay in advance and no luggage will be stored. The kitchen is open from 7 to 9:15 A.M. and from 5 to 10 P.M., but you will have to BYO utensils and cooking pots. The hot shower is free, but the towel is L1,000 extra.

NOTE: To stay here you do not have to belong to a hostel organization, but you must show your passport.

ENGLISH SPOKEN Yes

FACILITIES AND SERVICES Coin-operated laundry, lockers, kitchen (not equipped), restaurant, office safe

NEAREST TOURIST ATTRACTIONS Santo Spirito area

TELEPHONE
055-268-338, 239-6704

FAX
055-280-185

E-MAIL
info@ostello.it

INTERNET
www.ostello.it

CREDIT CARDS
None, cash only and in advance

CLOSED
Never

RATES
L23,000 per person, seven-night maximum stay in high season, longer stays otherwise; breakfast L3,500–6,000 per person, lunch or dinner L15,000

ROME

Everyone sooner or later comes by Rome.
—*Robert Browning, 1868*

In Rome you have to do as the Romans do, or get arrested.
—*Geoffrey Harmsworth,*
Abbyssinian Adventure, *1935*

The Romans take their city for granted, nonchalantly sipping espressos or cool drinks in a sidewalk *caffè* next to a piazza used by gladiators centuries ago. Ruined temples, triumphal arches, and Baroque fountains are everywhere, yet this vibrant city of over three million people refuses to be just a museum of history, art, and legend. The historic center includes the seven hills of the ancient walled city and contains 300 palaces, 280 churches, the ruins of imperial Rome, numerous parks and gardens, the residence of the Italian president, the houses of parliament, and government offices, as well as banks, businesses, hotels, shops, and restaurants. Yes, it is crowded and the traffic jams are legion, with progress gauged by centimeters, not kilometers. Julius Caesar banned traffic during daylight, and in parts of Rome today, cars are banned both night *and* day. But it is often faster, and always more interesting, to walk.

History proves that Rome invented the tourist industry. Once Christianity was declared the Empire's official religion in the fourth century, Rome became the center for massive groups of religious pilgrims, who arrived and had to be housed, fed, impressed, and amused. Developed at the same time as tourism was Rome's other classic industry: bureaucracy. Both are still going strong and show no signs of slowing down.

Rome was not built in a day, and should not be visited in one. Rome can be like a good pizzeria: hot, noisy, smoke-filled, overflowing with people, and offering more choices than you can handle. When you go, take your time and allow it to grow on you gradually.

La dolce vita? Yes, it exists, but it will cost you plenty. There are very few inexpensive *and* acceptable hotels in the center of Rome. Many that did exist a few years ago have upgraded and crossed over the line to moderate and expensive. Unless you are willing to live very, very simply, plan on spending at least $100 a night, and more realistically about $135 to $165, for a decent double in a well-located hotel that may or may not have an elevator and will probably not have air-conditioning.

Hotel prices depend first on the season, then on the type of hotel, the location of the room, and its size. Government star ratings do not reflect decor, the grandeur of the building, how clean it is, or the attitude of the owner; they depend *only* on the facilities offered. Thus, it is important never to judge a hotel by its stars. Many one-star hotels in Rome offer more value for money than big three-stars, which can be cold, ugly, and impersonal, never mind terribly expensive.

The best-priced hotels always fill up fast, therefore it is essential to reserve your room in advance. While prices vary with the time of year, it always pays to try to bargain down the rate. The willingness of management to bargain increases with the length of your stay, the number of vacancies, and the size of your party. Cash is also the hallmark when you care enough to spend the very least.

If you are looking for a wild time in Rome but are strapped for cash, institutional accommodations may *not* be the way to go. Religious institutions, convents, and monasteries welcome boarders of all faiths throughout the year, but their strict curfews and set-in-stone rules will put a damper on frivolity. Many lock up tight and turn off the lights at the main switch at 11 P.M., just when Rome's nightlife is warming up. (If this sort of accommodation interests you, see "Holy Hotels," page 200.)

The year 2000 has been designated the Grand Jubilee by the Roman Catholic Church. In 1300, Pope Bonifacio VIII established the first Jubilee Year, calling Catholic pilgrims to visit Rome. The traditional event was celebrated every fifty years until Pope Paul II designated the celebration to take place every twenty-five years. The Jubilee Year will begin on December 24, 1999, when the pope opens the Holy Door of St. Peter's Basilica, and ends fifty-four weeks later on Epiphany, January 6, 2001, when the Holy Door is closed for another twenty-five years. While the celebration will be worldwide for Catholics, fifteen million of them are expected to make pilgrimages to Rome during this time to renew their faith. When Rome tourist industry leaders start discussing housing options such as tent cities and accommodations outside of Rome that require two- or three-hour shuttle commutes, you know there is going to be a hotel shortage of tremendous proportions. Another looming crisis is parking. To cope with the expected throngs, vast parking lots are planned, but when pressed for locations, no one seems to have an answer. Some hoteliers will take advantage of the situation and hike prices to the heavens; others, who run small and exclusive hotels not geared to groups, do not feel threatened by the influx. The hardest hit for bookings will be the Holy Hotels, followed by the tour-bus chain types. If Rome is in your travel future for the year 2000 and you are interested in a Holy Hotel, today is not too early to begin making arrangements.

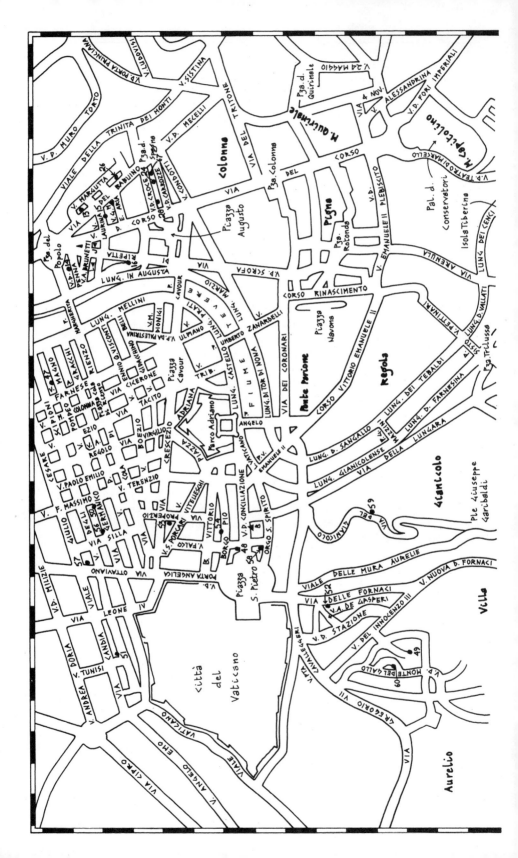

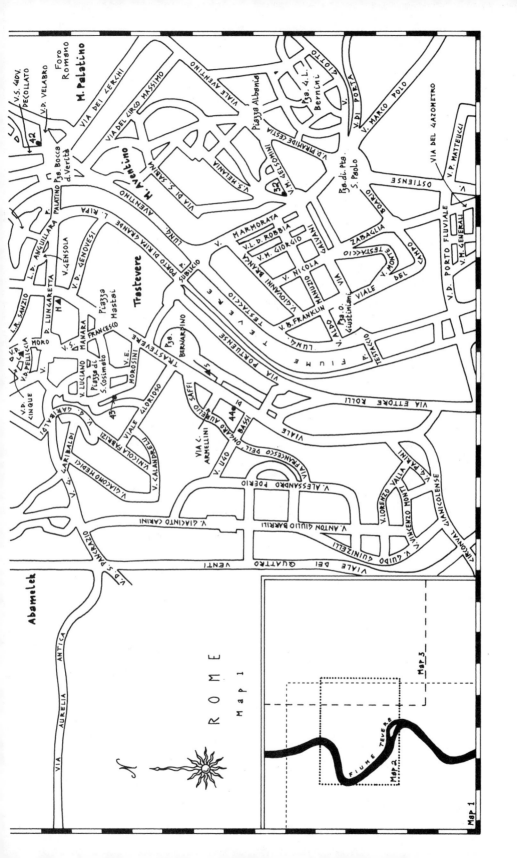

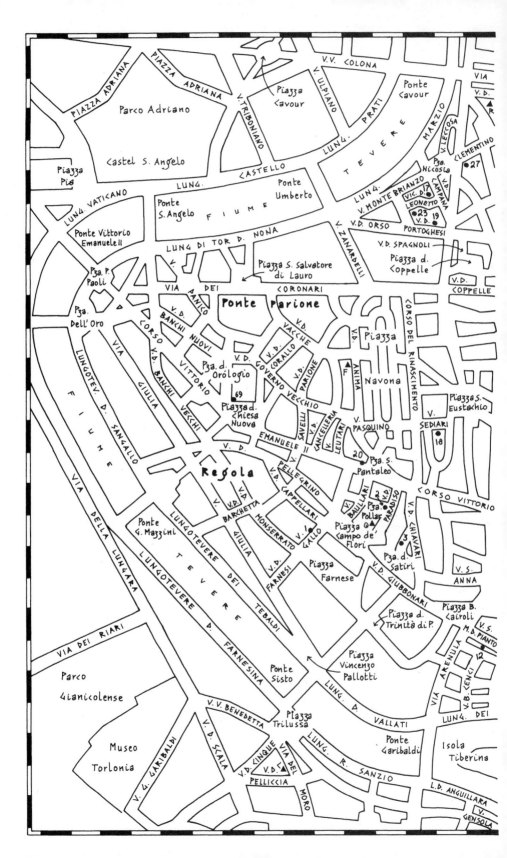

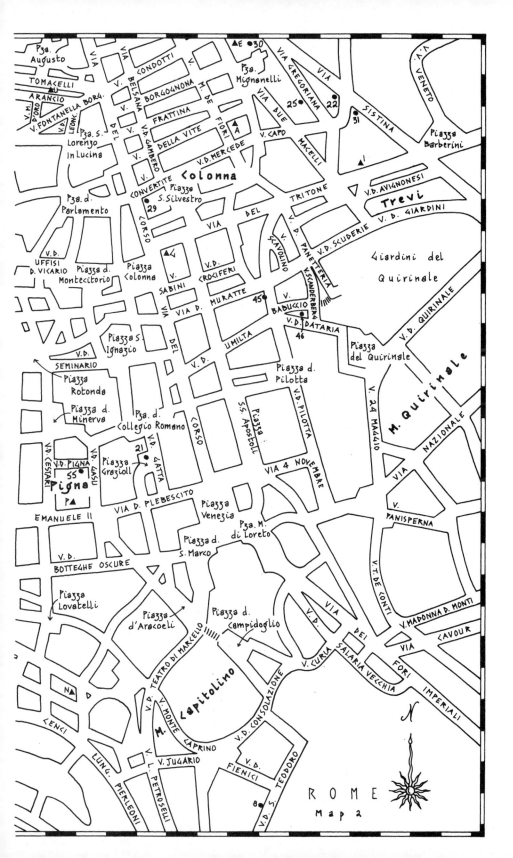

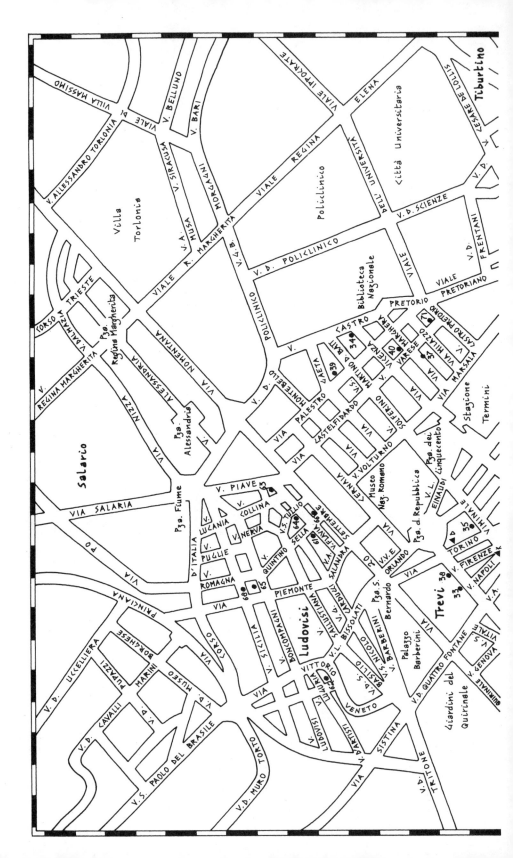

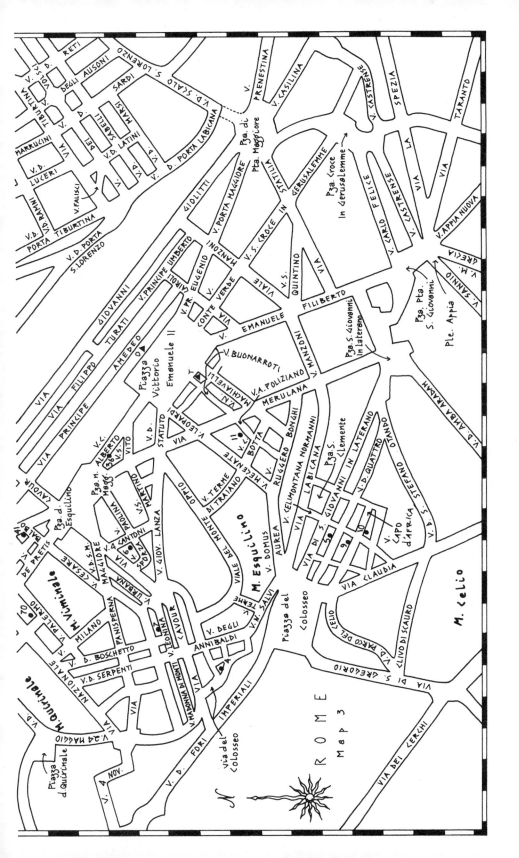

ROME
Map 3

Useful Information

Emergencies

Police, Fire, Ambulance   113

Dentist

George Eastman Clinic
  (American-run dental clinic)   Viale Regina Elena, 287, 06-445-4851, Mon–Sat 7:30 A.M.–1:30 P.M.; 491-949 (24-hour emergency number)

Doctor

American Embassy Health Unit   Via Veneto, 121, 06-467-42150 (they also provide a list of English-speaking dentists and physicians)

American Hospital   Via Emilio Longoni, 69, 06-225-5400; they also have a list of English-speaking dentists and physicians

Homeopathic Doctor   Ambulatoiro Samo (English-speaking doctor), Piazza Navona, 49, Mon–Fri 9 A.M.–12:30 P.M., 3:30–7 P.M., 06-683-0703, 06-683-08379

Pharmacies (dial 1921 for a recorded listing)

Farmacia Internazionale
  Barberini (24-hour pharmacy;
  English-speaking pharmacist) Piazza Barberini, 49, 06-482-5456

Farmacia del Vaticano (Vatican
  Pharmacy; English-speaking
  staff and best-stocked
  pharmacy in Rome)   Porta Sant' Ana entrance, Vatican City, Mon–Fri 7:30 A.M.–noon, 3:30–7 P.M., Sat 7:30 A.M.–noon, 06-698-83422

Embassies

American Embassy   Via Veneto, 121, 06-467-41

British Embassy   Venti Settembre, 80–A, 06-482-5441

Canadian Embassy   Via G. B. de Rossi, 27, 06-841-5341

Currency Exchange

American Express	Spanish Steps/Piazza di Spagna, 38, Mon–Fri 9 A.M.–5:30 P.M., Sat 9 A.M.–12:30 P.M., 06-676-42413; no commission for their traveler's checks
Deutsch Bank	Largo del Tritone, 161, 06-67-181, and Laradg di Torre Argentian, 4, 06-689-2955. Visa and MasterCard holders can withdraw money without a PIN, and cash and traveler's checks of any type can be changed for a 1 percent commission.
Main Post Offices	Via delle Mercede, Via Terme Diocleziano, 30, Mon–Fri 8:30 A.M.–1:30 P.M., Sat–Sun 8:30 A.M.–12:30 P.M. These two post offices have exchange offices; the commission is L1,000 for cash transactions and L2,000 for traveler's checks. They only accept American Express traveler's checks. A third post office, at Piazza S. Silvestro, Mon–Fri 8:30 A.M.–1:50 P.M., Sat 8:30 A.M.–12:50 P.M., 06-672-225, also has a currency exchange, 1 percent commission.

Getting Around

Airport	Leonardo da Vinci, 06-65-951, 06-65-95364, 06-659-5308 (all 24 hours a day)
Bus	Piazza dei Cinquecento, 06-469-54444, daily 7:30 A.M.–7 P.M.
Metro	Via Ostiense, 131-L, 06-659-54552, Mon–Fri 8 A.M.–1:30 P.M., 2–4:30 P.M., Sat 8 A.M.–1:30 P.M. (no English-speaking clerks)
Taxi	3870, 4994, 3570, 88-177
Train Station (Stazione Termini)	4775, or 06-473-07089 (for travel delays)

Lost Property

For items lost on a city bus or tram	ATAC, Via Nicola Bettoni, 1, daily 9 A.M.–noon, 06-581-6040
For items lost on the train	Via Giovanni Giolitti, 24, Mon–Fri 7 A.M.–10 P.M., 06-473-06682

Post Offices

Main Office	Piazza S. Silvestro, Mon–Fri 8:30 A.M.–1:50 P.M., Sat 8:30 A.M.–12:50 P.M., 06-672-225. Also a currency exchange, 1 percent commission
Vatican Post Office (mail sent from here goes the fastest)	Piazza San Pietro, Mon–Fri 8:30 A.M.–7 P.M., Sat 8:30 A.M.– 6 P.M.

Telephones

All numbers have six or seven digits, plus the 06 at the beginning.

Code for Rome	06
Code for United States	001
Operator Assistance and Local Directory Assistance	12
Time	161
Tourist Information	110
Vatican	06-6982

Tourist Information Office

Ente Provinciale per il Turismo (EPT)	Via Parigi, 5, Mon–Sat 8:15 A.M.– 7:15 P.M., 06-488-991
Stazione Termini	daily 8:30 A.M.–7 P.M., 06-487-1270
Ufficio Informazioni Pellegrini e Turisti (Vatican Tourist Office)	Piazza San Sietro, Mon–Sat 8:30 A.M.–7 P.M., 06-698-8-4466

Vatican Visits with the Pope

Held on Wednesdays	Apply no later than two days before to Prefettura della Casa Pontifica; 00120 Citta del Vaticano 6982. You cannot apply sooner than one month before you want to attend.

Special Tour Guide in Rome

"We're not tour guides and we don't just show you the sights."
—Tom Rankin, Scala Reale

For enlightened walking tours and excursions in and around Rome, look no further than Tom Rankin's Scala Reale. Tom is a Princeton graduate with a masters in architecture from Harvard. He came to Rome in 1986, and again on a Fulbright Fellowship in 1991, fell in love with it and the people, stayed, and is now a permanent resident with a lovely Italian wife, Lucia, their son, John, and a business named Scala Reale.

Tom and his highly qualified staff, who are architects, historians, and longtime residents of Rome, lead small private or semiprivate full- and half-day walking tours in Rome, and excursions by car or minivan outside Rome. These tours, consisting of no more than six people, are both fascinating and fun, and enable you to see Rome as you never would on you own, or with a big commercial tour of the city.

As Tom says, "After your Scala Reale experience, Rome will never again seem the chaotic metropolis it might appear at first glance." He is right, and I can promise you his tours will be a highlight of your Roman holiday.

TELEPHONE (888) 467-1986
FAX (617) 249-0186
TELEPHONE AND FAX (ITALY) 39-06-44-700-898
E-MAIL scalareale@mail.nexus.it
INTERNET www.scalareale.org
CREDIT CARDS None, cash only, but credit cards are planned, so ask
RATES Semiprivate half-day walking tours for six start around L200,000 for two; semiprivate full-day excursions for six start around L460,000 for two; private itineraries in Rome start around L340,000 for a half-day, L500,000 for a full day for two; private excursions L500,000–700,000 for two; discounts for multiple tours

Hotels in Rome by Area

The number in parentheses before each hotel corresponds to a number that marks the hotel's location on the Rome map (an entry with no number before it is located outside the parameters of the map); a dollar sign ($) indicates hotels in the Big Splurge category.

HOTELS

Campo de' Fiori

Colosseum/Forum

Jewish Quarter

Piazza del Popolo

Piazza Navona

Piazza Venezia

Spanish Steps (Piazza di Spagna)

Holy Hotels

Campo de' Fiori

The Campo de' Fiori, which means "field of flowers," has been considered a central point of Roman life for centuries. Today along the cobblestone streets are many hotels and houses with ancient, ocre-colored walls, tiny rooms, and innate charm. The square is filled Monday through Saturday mornings with the colorful stalls of market vendors.

(2) HOTEL CAMPO DE' FIORI ★★
Via del Biscione, 6

27 rooms, 9 with shower or bath and toilet, plus 7 apartments scattered in the Campo de' Fiori/ Piazza Navona areas of Rome

TELEPHONE
06-688-06865, 687-4886, 683-09036

FAX
06-687-6003

CREDIT CARDS
MC, V

CLOSED
Never

RATES
Hotel: one to two people L150,000–210,000, triple L185,000–260,000; Continental breakfast included Apartments: rates start at L210,000 for two; Continental breakfast included

Young-at-heart romantics with good backs and strong legs continue to keep the Campo de' Fiori booked solid year-round. They are willing to scale the six flights of steep and winding stairs necessary to reach their room and the fabulous two-tiered roof terraces, where the payoff is the thrilling day or romantic night views over all of Rome.

The clever, artistic rooms offer a grab bag of comforts and not much in terms of amenities . . . but never mind. Adoring guests love them and are willing to overlook not only the stairs, but the lines for the sparse hall facilities. If queuing for your turn in the bathroom is not your idea of a vacation activity, then ask for a room on the first floor, all of which have private bathrooms, or, if you are willing to climb the distance, No. 602 on the top. Three first-floor rooms (Nos. 104, 105, and 106) have exposed brick walls covered by huge arched mirrors facing the bed. Room No. 102 is a minuscule nest, with clouds painted on the ceiling and mirrors flanking two sides of the bed. Don't look for a table, chair, bedside tables, or lamps, but you can expect to have a black-tiled bathroom with blue accents. Higher up, in No. 503, the space is larger, with frescoes, windows facing the front of the hotel, and Art Deco furniture. You will have a dresser and two stools, but no chair or private facilities. The rooms on the second through the sixth floors are similar in decor and amenities. They are characterized by a combination of blue, white, or yellow textured walls, hand-painted ceilings, wood beams, and a balcony or two. Some have a basin only; others a shower. On the second floor, five rooms share one toilet and four share the lone bath. The most requested room is the top-floor perch, No. 602, otherwise known as the "Honeymoon Room," maybe because you can lie in bed under a ceiling of fluffy clouds and look out over Rome, or perhaps it is the statues of naked lovers, or the fact that there is no place to sit other than on the bed.

The seven fully equipped apartments are quite something, running the gamut from modern to traditional to funky. The biggest, G-4, is a sleek choice, with enough space to entertain thirty of your closest friends. The large corner kitchen has an eating bar, good counter room, and a full refrigerator and freezer. In the living room is a huge worktable and one entire wall of shelves and cupboards. The bedroom has more closets behind mirrored doors, ample drawer space, and a black-tiled bathroom with a map of Rome on one wall and mirrors on the other.

For apartments G-1 and G-2, you had better be athletic enough to tackle the stairs. G-1 requires a climb of fourteen steep steps, while the hike in G-2 is along an exhausting, bilious glowing yellow stairwell. G-1 is basically a bedroom and a nice kitchen with a narrow bathroom. G-2 is better, provided you don't need resuscitating on your way to it! The wood-floor living room has sofa beds and a dining area. The small kitchen under the stairway leading to the marble bathroom has enough room for a four-burner stove. One of the best features of the master bedroom, aside from the fan over the bed, is the outdoor terrace, which is where you will spend most of your time in warm weather.

Facilities and services in the apartments vary. There are no phones, but messages may be left for residents at the hotel. Plan on lots of steps in all but G-4, which is the only one with an elevator. Maid service and breakfast at the hotel are included. There are television sets in almost all. More apartments are planned.

ENGLISH SPOKEN Yes

FACILITIES AND SERVICES Hotel: direct-dial phones, no elevator, office safe

NEAREST TOURIST ATTRACTIONS Campo de' Fiori, Piazza Navona

(3) HOTEL TEATRO DI POMPEO ★★★ ($)
Largo del Pallaro, 8
12 rooms, all with shower or bath and toilet

TELEPHONE
06-687-2812, 683-00170

FAX
06-688-05531

CREDIT CARDS
AE, DC, MC, V

CLOSED
Never

RATES
Single L235,000, double L305,000, triple L375,000; lower off-season rates; buffet breakfast included

This attractive hotel was built around the ruins of the Roman Pompeius Theater, where Julius Caesar was assassinated. Breakfast is served in the excavated cavelike ruins of this ancient arena, and a sitting room is carved out of the cellars of the former theater. Some of the original stone walls are still intact. The Pompeo's bright and pleasant rooms rate high for charm, efficiency, and comfort. All twelve are basically the same: authentic beams, polished terra-cotta floors, luggage racks, a cushioned armchair, and a nice armoire with drawers and a mirror. The rustic decor, combined with blue cotton paisley bedspreads on firm mattresses, creates a pleasant, welcoming air. A breakfast buffet and CNN will increase the appeal for many. The management is courteous, and the location near the Campo de' Fiori, Pantheon, and Piazza Navona, along with good transportation to the train station and the Vatican, make this hotel hard to top.

ENGLISH SPOKEN Yes

FACILITIES AND SERVICES Air-conditioning, bar, direct-dial phones, hair dryers, elevator, minibars, radio, satellite TVs, in-room safes

NEAREST TOURIST ATTRACTIONS Campo de' Fiori, Piazza Navona, Pantheon

Colosseum/Forum

The Colosseum, built between A.D. 72 and 80 for animal and gladiatorial contests and public entertainments, is the vivid and enduring symbol of Rome. The Forum was the heart of ancient Rome and a place where people gathered, justice was handed out, and religious ceremonies, banquets, and dances were held.

(4) ALBERGO PERUGIA ★
Via del Colosseo, 7
14 rooms, 10 with shower and toilet

If you are willing to trade style and modern conveniences for a Cheap Sleep in Rome, check into the Albergo Perugia, run for years by Cosimo DiCosta and his old dog Kiko. The rooms are clean, but are mired in one-star tacky taste. Singles roosting in bathless No. 10 will not be able to see out the window. The trade-off for some would be the low price and the fact that the hall bathroom is not shared. Two or three Cheap Sleepers can snooze in No. 12, a quiet room with its own toilet and shower with a curtain. Breakfast is not part of Cosimo's package, so plan to join the locals at the corner *caffè* and jump-start your day with a bracing cappuccino and warm *cornetto* pastry.

ENGLISH SPOKEN Yes

FACILITIES AND SERVICES Direct-dial phones, office safe

NEAREST TOURIST ATTRACTIONS Colosseum, Piazza Venezia

TELEPHONE
06-679-7200

FAX
06-678-4635

CREDIT CARDS
AE, DC, MC, V

CLOSED
Never

RATES
Single L75,000–95,000, double L100,000–130,000; extra bed 35 percent of room rate; no breakfast served

(5) HOTEL CELIO ★★★ ($)
Via dei Santi Quattro, 35-C
10 rooms, all with shower or bath and toilet

Owned by Marcello Quatrini and his brother, Roberto, the Hotel Celio is highly recommended for readers looking for an elegant, small hotel near the Colosseum and all of Rome's most important ancient monuments and treasures. Rich, bold textiles and colors harmoniously blend to create the handsome, dramatic atmosphere that prevails throughout the hotel. Even though the individually decorated bedrooms are basically small, they are well conceived and offer the warmth and comforts one would expect in a lovely Roman home. Each room is named after an Italian master artist, and has a large fresco on the wall behind each gold-and-blue-striped-covered bed. The Michelangelo is the largest

TELEPHONE
06-704-95333

FAX
06-709-6377

INTERNET
www.roma-online.com/ booking/hotel/celio/info.htm

CREDIT CARDS
AE, DC, MC, V

CLOSED
Never

RATES
Single L310,000, double L370,000, suite L445,000; Continental breakfast included and served in the room

room, with two comfortable armchairs and a view over the garden entrance. In the Donatello, a mirror reflects the high ceiling, giving the illusion of more space. The Tintoretto is a room for three, with gold fabric on the walls and a private terrace where you can enjoy alfresco the Continental breakfast that is served to guests in their rooms each morning. Bathrooms have welcome extras such as magnifying mirrors, a radio, and a scale to help you keep a sense of the damage control needed to compensate for those afternoon gelati treats.

If you like the style of the Hotel Celio, and have Venice on your Italian itinerary, you will enjoy Marcello's Hotel San Stefano in Venice (for further details, see page 271).

ENGLISH SPOKEN Yes

FACILITIES AND SERVICES Air-conditioning, bar, direct-dial phones, no elevator (three floors), hair dryers, minibars, parking (L20,000 in hotel driveway, L40,000 in garage), satellite TVs with VCRs (videos L6,000), trouser press, in-room safes, magnifying mirror, radio, and scale in bathroom

NEAREST TOURIST ATTRACTIONS Colosseum, Forum

(6) HOTEL COLOSSEUM ★★★
Via Sforza, 10
50 rooms, all with shower and toilet

TELEPHONE
06-482-7228
FAX
06-482-7285
E-MAIL
colosseum@venere.it
INTERNET
HotelColosseum<albergo-colosseo@flashnet.it>
CREDIT CARDS
AE, DC, MC, V
CLOSED
Never
RATES
Single L182,000, double L245,000, triple L340,000; lower off-season rates; buffet breakfast included

I am always happy to return to the Hotel Colosseum, because it is such a well-run family-owned hotel. As you walk into the hotel from the street, an impressive entryway with an arched wooden ceiling leads to a baronial sitting room furnished in dark, rustic reproductions that look as though they came from an old hunting lodge. Upstairs is a little bar where you can relax after your sightseeing in Rome. When you check in, please be sure to notice the original telephone the Ricci family used when they began this hotel over a quarter-century ago; it is on display to the right of the reception desk.

You can start each day here sitting on carved wooden armchairs placed around a long communal table in the large, medieval-style dining room, with its original hand-painted ceiling. Heavy wooden furniture, wrought-iron sconces, electronic window shades, and parquet or marble floors distinguish the rooms. Some of the twin-bed chambers are small, but if you are traveling light and in search of a room with a view, Nos. 72, 73, 74, and 75 (a single) offer terraces or a balcony overlooking the

Colosseum and Santa Maria Maggiore Church. These rooms also connect, making them ideal for a family stay. Number 63, a large, bright twin, also has a wonderful view of the Colosseum and an old church tower, and in No. 71, the view is of Rome and the dome of St. Peter's. Light snacks are available at the bar, a bonus for families who need to feed children at hours when most Rome restaurants are closed.

ENGLISH SPOKEN Yes

FACILITIES AND SERVICES Air-conditioning in some rooms (L20,000 extra per day), bar, direct-dial phones, elevator, hair dryers, parking can be arranged, TVs (planning to add satellite, now it is available only in the downstairs sitting room), in-room safes (L5,000 per stay), office safe (free), porter

NEAREST TOURIST ATTRACTIONS Colosseum, Forum, Santa Maria Maggiore Church

(7) HOTEL DUCA D'ALBA ★★★ ($)
Via Leonina, 14
24 rooms, all with shower or bath and toilet

For an impeccable stay in the Imperial section of Rome near the Forum and Colosseum, the completely renovated Duca d'Alba is one of my favorite choices. The old Roman neighborhood is dotted with crafts workshops, stores, and interesting restaurants (see *Cheap Eats in Italy*), and public transportation connections are within easy reach.

This outstanding small hotel is owned by the same family that runs the Britannia, near the train station (see page 161). Good taste in furnishings, high-quality materials, and attention to detail extend throughout the hotel. Busts and bas-reliefs adorn the well-lighted hallways, echoing the classic style that characterizes the room interiors. Paneled doors lead to the rooms, which have been designed to appeal to both business travelers and tourists. All are soundproofed and have private safes, electronic door locks, air-conditioning, and, of course, lovely baths. Two singles and two doubles on the fourth floor have terraces. Unless dramatic changes have occurred in No. 110, an inside single with a weird closet, it is the only room I would positively avoid. Tricolored marble floors line the downstairs, which has a large sitting room with a bar and a mirrored breakfast room with black glass-topped tables. A Continental breakfast is served here every morning. The location is a block off

TELEPHONE
06-484-471

FAX
06-488-4840

E-MAIL
duca.d'alba@venere.it

INTERNET
www.italyhotel.com/roma/duca.d'alba

CREDIT CARDS
AE, DC, MC, V

CLOSED
Never

RATES
Single L230,000, double L295,000, suite L450,000; lower off-season rates; buffet breakfast included

the raceway street known as Via Cavour, so while it's close to loads of the action, it is relatively peaceful.

ENGLISH SPOKEN Yes

FACILITIES AND SERVICES Air-conditioning, bar, direct-dial phones, elevator, hair dryers, minibars, satellite TVs, in-room safes

NEAREST TOURIST ATTRACTIONS Colosseum, Forum, Piazza Venezia

(8) HOTEL KOLBE ★★
Via di S. Teodoro, 44
65 rooms, all with shower or bath and toilet

TELEPHONE
06-679-4974/5, 679-8866

FAX
06-699-41550

CREDIT CARDS
AE, MC, V

CLOSED
Never

RATES
Single L110,000, double L145,000, triple L185,000, quad L200,000; breakfast (L8,000 extra)

The Kolbe has been a hotel for twenty-five years, but it is easy to see that it was once a convent. The monks you may catch a glimpse of during your stay are probably occupants of the fourth floor, which is reserved exclusively for them. The quiet rooms have all the ingredients one needs for a restful stay and are well mopped, but they are uninspired in terms of decor. Several that open directly onto the huge garden, which has a fountain, four rose beds, and palm trees, would be ideal choices for anyone with children. A large bar and sitting room with sofas and chairs also faces and opens onto the garden. The dining room serves lunch and dinner. The Kolbe is located between Circus Massimo, the Capitoline, and the Palatino Hills. Bus service is two blocks away.

ENGLISH SPOKEN Yes

FACILITIES AND SERVICES Bar, direct-dial phones, hair dryers available, elevator, office safe, lunch and dinner (prix fixe L25,000, two courses, two side dishes, and fruit; beverage extra)

NEAREST TOURIST ATTRACTIONS Colosseum, Forum, Circus Massimo

(9) LANCELOT HOTEL ★★★
Via Capo d'Africa, 47
57 rooms, all with shower or bath and toilet

TELEPHONE
06-704-50615/6

FAX
06-704-50640

E-MAIL
lancelot@italyhotel.com

CREDIT CARDS
AE, MC, V

CLOSED
Never

Two thumbs up for the Lancelot, a three-star pick just a short sprint from the Colosseum and Forum. It is a comfortable place, run since 1971 by a mother and her attractive daughter and son. They welcome guests as old friends, and indeed, after a stay here, many consider themselves just that. One of the real advantages of the hotel, especially for solo voyagers to Rome, is the dining room, which serves demi-pension or à la carte for dinner only. Seating is at round tables for six or eight, which encourages conversation and a more pleasant experience than dining alone. (Judging from the photos taken during the Christmas holidays, friendships blossomed and a good time was had by all.)

The rooms are large and comfortable, but some do require trade-offs. I like those on the first and sixth floors that open onto a terrace. Number 62 is one of these, with tiled floors and twin beds. The bathroom is where you make the sacrifice: no shelf space. The terrace is shared with the room next door, but a bank of roses divides it into two sections. There is more room and a better bathroom in No. 65, with sink space and a tub with a handheld shower nozzle but, alas, no curtain. You do have terrace access, though. No such trade-offs are required in No. 60, a suite in which you have not only a terrace but a small balcony off the sitting area. The bathroom has a window, a curtain around the combination tub and shower, a shelf, a small table, and heated towel racks. The same goes for No. 6, an especially nice twin, with a white- and beige-tiled floor and an umbrella-shaded terrace. The bathroom has a stall shower and three shelves.

NOTE: Dinner policy. There is a demi-pension rate of L15,000 per dinner, applicable for three consecutive days or more. If less, or the days split, the rate jumps to L35,000 per meal. These three-course meals include dessert, fruit, wine, water, and coffee. Special dietary needs can be accommodated with advance notice.

ENGLISH SPOKEN Yes

FACILITIES AND SERVICES Air-conditioning in ten rooms (L10,000 supplement per day), bar, direct-dial phones, hair dryers, elevator, parking (L15,000 in front of the hotel, which is set in a courtyard off the street), TV in one room, office safe, demi-pension for dinner

NEAREST TOURIST ATTRACTIONS Colosseum, Forum

RATES
Single L145,000, double L220,000, triple L250,000, suite L290,000; inquire about special offers; buffet breakfast included

Jewish Quarter

The Roman Jews have had an important place in Rome for more than two thousand years, making theirs the oldest surviving Jewish community in Europe. Today the central focus of life in the ghetto is along the Via del Portico d'Ottavia.

(12) HOTEL ARENULA ★★
Via Santa Maria de' Calderari, 47; first floor
40 rooms, all with shower and toilet

TELEPHONE
06-687-9454

FAX
06-689-6188

CREDIT CARDS
DC, MC, V

CLOSED
Never

RATES
Single L150,000, double L220,000, triple L265,000, quad L300,000; lower off-season rates; buffet breakfast included

For the Rome Cheap Sleeper who wants a reasonably priced hotel near the heart of old Rome and the Jewish Quarter, the Arenula, just across the Ponte Garibaldi from Trastevere, is a consideration . . . if, that is, you can cope with stairs and then land the right room. Reaching the first-floor lobby requires a climb of only one flight of stairs, and hopefully your room will not be three more flights up to the fourth floor, which would mean 90 more steps from the lobby and 123 from the entrance. The no-nonsense, uniformly austere bedrooms have easy-wipe blond wood furnishings, white walls, tiled floors, and canvas bedspreads. As for the bathrooms, all of the rooms have private facilities, but you will want to make sure that the bidet, shower, and sink are not sitting in the room as pieces of furniture, thus affording absolutely no privacy. You won't have this problem in room 104, which has an enclosed bathroom with lights over the sink and room for a stool. The bathroom situation is okay in No. 402, which has an excellent stall shower with doors, and also in 409, if you don't mind that the hair dryer is in the bedroom. While the red-rooftop view is appealing from this room, the beds are like cement slabs, the bedside lights are poor, and the desk has no light at all.

The combination reception and lobby area has a big-screen television set often turned on, probably to please the desk staff, who display a sign saying "Tell me again how lucky I am to be working here . . . I keep forgetting." *Touché!*

ENGLISH SPOKEN Yes

FACILITIES AND SERVICES Air-conditioning in twenty-five rooms (L20,000 extra per day), bar, direct-dial phones, hair dryers, satellite TVs, office safe

NEAREST TOURIST ATTRACTIONS Tiber River, Trastevere, Jewish Quarter, historic old Rome, Campo de' Fiori

---

Piazza del Popolo

This large square was the first part of Rome pilgrims saw when they arrived through the northern gate, Porta del Popolo. The obelisk in the center was brought from Egypt by Augustus and stood in the Circus Maximus until 1589, when Pope Sixtus V moved it here. The very upmarket neighborhood has many good restaurants, interesting boutiques, and small hotels.

(13) ALBERGO FIORELLA ★
Via del Babuino, 196; first floor
8 rooms, none with shower or bath and toilet

What can you expect at the one-star Albergo Fiorella? Reservations accepted only one day in advance, no entrance after 1 A.M., no lift, no rugs, and no smoking allowed in the cleanest and cheapest Cheap Sleep you will find near the Spanish Steps and the expensive designer boutiques that surround this exclusive corner of Rome. When you arrive, ring the bell on the street and climb up the drab marble staircase to the first-floor door, where Sra. Caterina Antonio Albano will let you in, as she has all of her guests since she opened in 1977. The rooms are far from modern, but they are utterly spotless. The hall facilities follow suit.

Breakfast is served in the family dining room. If you ask Sra. Albano about the family photos in the room, you will be in for a treat. She is very proud of her two sons, her granddaughter, Martha, who is absolutely adorable in her baptismal photos, and her grandson, David. She is a friendly hostess who lives on the premises with her husband, does all the hard work herself, and is sweet and gentle—unless she catches you pulling some sort of hanky-panky, such as washing clothes in your room or having nonpaying overnight visitors. Should these things happen, you will probably be asked to find other accommodations.

ENGLISH SPOKEN Yes

FACILITIES AND SERVICES Lockout at 1 A.M.; advance reservations accepted only one day in advance

NEAREST TOURIST ATTRACTIONS Piazza del Popolo, Spanish Steps, shopping

TELEPHONE
06-361-0597

CREDIT CARDS
None, cash only

CLOSED
Never

RATES
Single L70,000, double L115,000; Continental breakfast included

(14) HOTEL LOCARNO ★★★ ($)
Via della Penna, 22
48 rooms, all with shower or bath and toilet

In my book, the Locarno is a handsome Rome hotel that never fails to please. Since 1925, the family owned establishment, neatly tucked between Piazza del Popolo and the Tiber River, has been drawing a faithful clientele of international guests. The magnificent Belle Epoque lobby and sitting room, with wood-burning

TELEPHONE
06-361-0841

FAX
06-321-5249

E-MAIL
locarno@venere.it

INTERNET
www.venere.it/roma/locarno

CREDIT CARDS
AE, DC, MC, V

CLOSED
Never

RATES
Single L240,000, double
L365,000, triple L400,000,
suite L435,000; Continental
breakfast included

fireplace and a bar to one side, display beveled-glass doors, dark wood paneling, and an impressive collection of Tiffany lamps. A side garden with huge umbrellas is the perfect spot for warm-weather breakfasts or cool afternoon drinks. A summer roof garden adds further to the hotel's charm. Subway and bus stops, good restaurants (see *Cheap Eats in Italy*), and great shopping are all within easy walking distance.

The rooms, all of which face out, vary in size and are nicely appointed with antiques, coordinated fabrics, cable television, and a PC/modem plug. Several have balconies. Even the smallest single has enough space to unpack and stay in comfort. The bathrooms have been revamped in marble, and offer soft towels, a telephone, and a selection of toiletries. For the athletically inclined and *very* brave souls, who are willing to risk life and limb by venturing into Rome traffic, the hotel provides free bicycles for guests to use during their stay.

ENGLISH SPOKEN Yes

FACILITIES AND SERVICES Air-conditioning, bar, direct-dial phones, hair dryers, minibars, radios, satellite TVs, PC/modem plugs, in-room safes, parking, free bicycles, meeting facilities, room service for light snacks

NEAREST TOURIST ATTRACTIONS Piazza del Popolo, Tiber River, shopping

(15) HOTEL MARGUTTA ★★
Via Laurina, 34
21 rooms, all with shower or bath and toilet

TELEPHONE
06-322-3674

FAX
06-320-0395

CREDIT CARDS
AE, DC, MC, V

CLOSED
Never

RATES
One or two persons L175,000,
triple L235,000, quad
L265,000; Continental
breakfast included

Nothing is frilly, fancy, or fantastic at Sr. Rosatti's Hotel Margutta, which is on a quiet street in a good location near the Piazza del Popolo. There is no way I can describe the small lobby other than to call it dull. The breakfast area is equally uninteresting. The good news, however, is that the rooms continue to be *much* better than the dark halls and uninspired lobby would suggest, and the prices are Cheap Sleeping friendly for this rich patch of Rome. Despite some awkward mixes of fabric, patterns, and colors, the spotless rooms, with sound-proofed windows and good lighting, can be recommended. Even though the elevator does not go this high, the best rooms are the three on the top floor; they share a terrace that has blooming rosebushes in spring. Number 52 is a good choice, with white walls, a scrolled metal bed, a tiled bath, and a terrace shared with the room next door. Room 54 is big enough to accommodate a writing desk and a sofa bed. All the rooms have private bathrooms. No, they are not large, nor do they have the latest word in design technology, but most have shower curtains or shields so you won't drench yourself and the entire room at the same time, and you don't have to shuffle down the hall in search of the shower and toilet, or stand in line to wait your turn once you get there.

ENGLISH SPOKEN Yes

FACILITIES AND SERVICES Direct-dial phones, elevator, hair dryers, TVs, office safe

NEAREST TOURIST ATTRACTIONS Piazza del Popolo, Tiber River, Spanish Steps, shopping

Piazza Navona

This piazza has the exact shape of the original, built by Emperor Domitian in A.D. 86. Today the piazza serves as a popular Baroque center stage for the theater of Roman life. Sitting at one of the sidewalk *caffès* that surround the square, or walking through it, serves as the perfect venue for unsurpassed people-watching any hour of the day or night. The neighborhood around it is also known as one of the most expensive patches of real estate in the city.

(17) HOTEL DUE TORRI ★★★ ($)
Vicolo del Leonetto, 23
26 rooms, all with shower or bath and toilet

There is a feeling of reassurance when one returns to a hotel and the same staff is on duty. Continuity of this type tells me that management has a caring attitude toward the staff and the guests. You will experience this at the Due Torri, and more. On top of being attractively decorated, it is well positioned between the Piazza del Popolo and Piazza Navona in a neighborhood with winding streets and ancient buildings. Good shopping and restaurants are within an easy walk (see *Cheap Eats in Italy*). You are also close to the Tiber River and not too far from the Vatican.

The entrance of the hotel leads to a small sitting room with velvet sofas, an unusual hand-painted black chest, and a massive floor-to-ceiling mirror. To one side is the breakfast room, done in green with lattice wallpaper and yellow tablecloths, which gives the illusion of being in a garden. The blackboard greeting wishes you a "good morning" in four languages. The hallways are well

TELEPHONE
06-687-6983, 687-5765, 688-06956

FAX
06-686-5442

CREDIT CARDS
AE, DC, M, V

CLOSED
Never

RATES
Single L200,000, double L285,000, triple L350,000, suite L375,000; Continental breakfast included

lighted and hung throughout with nicely framed prints. You will enjoy a view if you are on the fifth floor, but will have to sacrifice some space because the rooms, a single and three doubles, are smaller here. The advantage is that they cost the same as the other hotel rooms. If you are not on the fifth floor, No. 202 is a large double with its own entry, a desk, and two armchairs. The color scheme is beige, with floral headboards and matching window valances. If you are traveling with young ones, No. 205 is a small two-room suite with a single room suitable for a child, plus a larger bedroom with a four-drawer dresser and matching side tables. Hanging space is limited in this room. Room 404 is a narrow single with its bathroom squeezed behind a sliding door. A better one-person room is No. 407, which has a double bed and reproduction furniture.

ENGLISH SPOKEN Yes

FACILITIES AND SERVICES Air-conditioning, direct-dial phones in rooms and bathrooms, elevator, hair dryers, minibars, radios, satellite TVs, office safe

NEAREST TOURIST ATTRACTIONS Piazza Navona, Piazza del Popolo, Tiber River, Vatican, shopping

(18) HOTEL NAVONA ★
Via dei Sediari, 8
30 rooms, 15 with shower or bath and toilet

TELEPHONE
06-686-4203
FAX
06-688-03802
CREDIT CARDS
AE, MC, V
CLOSED
Never
RATES
Single L100,000–130,000, double L130,000–160,000, triple L195,000–225,000; Continental breakfast included

Historians will be interested to note that this hotel was built on the ruins of the Baths of Agrippa in the first century. The building was redone in the fifteenth century by Borromini, and is now run by an affable Australian, Corry Natale, a graduate of Notre Dame. Corry came to Rome twenty-five years ago to study architecture and never left. Now he and his family own and operate this popular spot geared to student groups from Iowa, California, Florida, and Arizona. Corry runs a tight ship, with a posted list of rules that guests must follow: payment in advance; you must leave your room each day by 10 A.M.; and no visitors, candles, or washing laundry in the rooms.

Recent improvements include a handsome entry with a beautiful new door, double-glazed windows to help keep out the incessant noise one contends with throughout the city, and ten new rooms—one with a kitchenette but all with balconies—custom-designed Murano glass lights, terra-cotta tile floors, and prints of old Rome warming the soft green walls. One benefit many like is that if you stay here you can hire the family Mercedes to transport you to and from the airport for L90,000 each way. Since most taxis cost more than L100,000 for the same ride, this deal is worth consideration, especially if your party consists of several people with bulky luggage.

ENGLISH SPOKEN Yes

FACILITIES AND SERVICES Air-conditioning in eight rooms (L25,000 per day), office safe

NEAREST TOURIST ATTRACTIONS Piazza Navona, Piazza di S. Eustachio, Pantheon

(19) HOTEL PORTOGHESI ★★★ ($)
Via dei Portoghesi, 1
27 rooms, all with shower or bath and toilet

The Portoghesi is refitted, redecorated, and still recommendable, even though the funky charm of the rumpled rooms and old bathrooms gave way to marble, air-conditioning, built-ins, and, unfortunately, higher prices. The setting is marvelous, right in the heart of historic old Rome near Piazza Navona and the Pantheon. The hotel and the street it is on take their name from the neighboring fifteenth-century National Portuguese Church of St. Anthony. Opposite the hotel stands the *Torre dei Frangipane* (Tower of the Monkey), which has a lamp on top given by a grateful family who believed their child was saved by a monkey.

A tiny lobby with a minuscule lift provides guests with what is perhaps an unfair first impression of this 155-year-old hotel in which no two rooms are alike. The best choice, unquestionably, is La Torre, which has a tiled floor, a small sitting area, a walk-in closet, and a light beige marble bathroom with a stall shower and window. Its crowning glory is a beautiful private terrace where you can almost reach out and touch the sculpture on the church next door. Number 44 is a new junior suite. I like the two-tone pink and Roman red colors, the view from both windows, and the ample sink space in the bathroom. Rooms 46 and 28 are standard doubles with soft peach suede-covered walls, green carpeting, and views of the street. The closet space is good. Number 48 is a single with a closet that could be a bit bigger, but there is a luggage rack and a gray-tiled bath with a chrome ceiling and a window for ventilation. The beautiful enclosed rooftop terrace, with wonderful vistas, is a

TELEPHONE
06-686-4231

FAX
06-687-6976

E-MAIL
portoghesi@venere.it

CREDIT CARDS
MC, V

CLOSED
Never

RATES
Single L210,000, double L295,000, junior suite L315,000, suite L350,000–490,000; extra person L55,000; lower off-season rates; buffet breakfast included

romantic place to have breakfast or sip a glass of wine while watching the sun set over this part of ancient Rome.

ENGLISH SPOKEN Yes

FACILITIES AND SERVICES Air-conditioning, small bar, direct-dial phones, hair dryers, satellite TVs, elevator, office safe

NEAREST TOURIST ATTRACTIONS Piazza Navona, Campo de' Fiori, Tiber River, Pantheon

(20) HOTEL PRIMAVERA ★★
Piazza San Pantaleo, 3; first floor
16 rooms, 14 with shower and toilet

TELEPHONE
06-688-13109

FAX
06-688-03109

CREDIT CARDS
None, cash only (this should be temporary)

CLOSED
Never

RATES
Single L120,000, double L130,000–160,000, triple L195,000–210,000; extra bed L60,000; lower off-season rates; Continental breakfast included

Maria Sena is the owner, and Victorio Celentano the ever-present manager of this first-floor choice at Via Vittorio Emanuele Corso, just south of Piazza Navona. The rooms are up a flight of marble stairs in a grand building with a view of Palazzo Braschi. A top-floor remodeling project put the hotel into the two-star category, with two-star prices in the high season to match. The new rooms on the fifth floor have air-conditioning (with a supplemental charge). Attractive wooden doors with brass handles open onto the streamlined rooms with built-in headboards and coordinated neutral materials. Double windows buffer the noise in the rooms facing the square. From No. 11 you will have an illuminated view of St. Andrea della Valle, the second most important church dome in Rome (St. Peter's, of course, being the most important). If No. 11 is booked, you will enjoy the same view from the fifth-floor dining room. The stall showers have curtains, but if you select a room without a private bath, you will save enough over a two- or three-day stay to treat yourself to a special meal.

ENGLISH SPOKEN Yes

FACILITIES AND SERVICES Air-conditioning in rooms on the fifth floor (L20,000 extra per day), direct-dial phones, elevator, hair dryers in fifth-floor rooms, TVs, office safe

NEAREST TOURIST ATTRACTIONS Piazza Navona, Campo de' Fiori, shopping, Forum, Colosseum

Piazza Venezia

Named after its monolithic white palace, this square is a crossroads for Rome traffic, with a mad rush hour that goes at breakneck speed twenty-four hours a day.

Until the Allied troops liberated Rome in 1944, the palace remained closed to the public. Now it serves as a museum for tapestries, ceramics, silver, and medieval sculpture.

(21) HOTEL CORONET ★★
Piazza Grazioli, 5; third floor
13 rooms, 10 with shower or bath and toilet

Big, old-fashioned rooms with high wood-beamed ceilings, a few exposed pipes, and a red-carpeted entry characterize this Cheap Sleep on the third floor of a seventeenth-century *palazzo* that belongs to the aristocratic Doria Pamphili family. Seven of the rooms overlook the *palazzo*'s lovely courtyard, as does the breakfast room. There are three bathrooms for the three rooms that are without them and keys given to the occupants so they really do have their own bath, just outside their room. Overall, this is not a place for uptight types, but for a young-at-heart group of three or four traveling together, it is a good bet in a safe, central location with prices that will not max out a credit card.

ENGLISH SPOKEN Most of the time

FACILITIES AND SERVICES Direct-dial phones, elevator to reception, office safe

NEAREST TOURIST ATTRACTIONS Piazza Venezia, Piazza Navona

TELEPHONE
06-679-2341, 699-22705

FAX
06-699-22705

CREDIT CARDS
AE, MC, V

CLOSED
Never

RATES
Single L120,000–160,000, double L150,000–190,000, triple L180,000–225,000; lower off-season rates; Continental breakfast included

Spanish Steps (Piazza di Spagna)

Keats, Mendelssohn, Baudelaire, and Wagner were only a few of the visitors to Rome who stayed near this famous piazza, named after the Spanish Embassy, which was located here for hundreds of years. It is better known, however, for the sweeping Spanish Steps that lead up to the Trinità dei Monti Church and for the many famous-name boutiques lining the streets that lead to the piazza. The steps are always massed with tourists, pickup artists, regular artists, and anyone else looking for some action. At Christmas there is a nativity scene halfway up, and in May, brilliant pink azaleas frame the steps. The piazza is now home to one of the better places on the planet to consume a Big Mac, plus an American Express office, the famous Babington's Tea Room, and horse-drawn carriages ready to take you anywhere you want to go . . . for quite a price.

(22) ALBERGO INTERNAZIONALE ★★★ ($)
Via Sistina, 79
42 rooms, all with shower or bath and toilet

TELEPHONE
06-678-4686, 679-3047,
699-41823

FAX
06-678-4764

E-MAIL
romint@flashnet.it

CREDIT CARDS
AE, MC, V

CLOSED
Never

RATES
Single L225,000, double
L325,000; lower rates in Aug;
buffet breakfast included

Occupying a prime patch of real estate near the Spanish Steps, the Internazionale is one of Rome's best-located hotels. The modern reception and street-level sitting area give no hint of the real spirit of the hotel, which is captured in the well-done rooms and upstairs eating and sitting spaces. The dining room, with glass chandeliers and an inlaid terra-cotta floor, adjoins a massive sitting room with an impressive carved-wood ceiling, groupings of tufted leather chairs and couches, a glass-topped coffee table with a display of silver, and a huge wood-burning fireplace. The third-floor lounge resembles an old hunting lodge, with its displays of armor, spears, and other antique paraphernalia.

The spacious, pastel-toned rooms have double-glazed windows to buffer the traffic noise, color televisions with CNN, air-conditioning, and private safes. Almost all have turn-of-the-century furnishings, fabric-covered walls, double wardrobes, and luggage space. In the tiled baths, you will use terry towels and have assorted toiletries and a drying line for quick laundry needs. The rooms on the fourth floor come with their own private terrace and views over the nearby rooftops. The management is crisply professional and to the point, and Vincent, the outgoing concierge, is always friendly and ready to ensure that your stay in Rome is smooth.

ENGLISH SPOKEN Yes

FACILITIES AND SERVICES Air-conditioning, direct-dial phones, elevator, hair dryers, minibars, radios, satellite TVs, in-room safes

NEAREST TOURIST ATTRACTIONS Spanish Steps, Via Veneto, Trevi Fountain, shopping

(24) HOTEL CARRIAGE ★★★ ($)
Via delle Carrozze, 36
27 rooms, all with shower or bath and toilet

TELEPHONE
06-699-0124

FAX
06-678-8279

CREDIT CARDS
AE, DC, MC, V

CLOSED
Never

The Carriage is one of my favorite hotels near the Spanish Steps. Classically furnished with lovely antiques and pale blue and gold colors, the hotel offers a soothing, elegant air that appeals to many. The rooms are beautifully coordinated, with antique furnishings, ample closet space, and way-above-average bathrooms, and many have private terraces with picturesque views of Rome and the

Spanish Steps. Two top-floor rooms open directly onto the hotel's rooftop garden, where guests gather at the American Bar for alfresco breakfasts and sunset views. To make your stay here even more special, reserve one of the suites with separate sitting and sleeping areas, each with their own televisions, extra-large bathrooms with deep tubs, stall shower, and lots of hooks and shelf space. Long a favorite with French Embassy personnel and an occasional European film star, the rooms here are in high demand year-round, making reservations essential as far in advance as possible.

ENGLISH SPOKEN Yes

FACILITIES AND SERVICES Air-conditioning, direct-dial phones, elevator to third floor, hair dryers, minibars, radios, TVs, elevator, office safe, room service for snacks

NEAREST TOURIST ATTRACTIONS Spanish Steps, Tiber River, shopping

RATES
Single L285,000–320,000, double L320,000–375,000, triple 475,000, suite 605,000; breakfast included

(25) HOTEL GREGORIANA ★★★ ($)
Via Gregoriana, 18
19 rooms, all with shower or bath and toilet

Very friendly and personalized service along with a great deal of charm are the keynotes at the Gregoriana, which is set in a dynamite location only a whisper away from the famed Hotel Hassler and the top of the Spanish Steps. The nineteenth-century Art Deco–style building was originally occupied by an order of nuns, and Room C still has the ceiling and an archway from the old chapel. A black-and-gold birdcage elevator carries guests from the tiny lobby area to their floors, which are covered in leopard-print or English Liberty wallpaper or in bamboo. There are no public rooms, thus breakfast is served in your room or on your terrace, if you have one. Fanciful Erté letter prints on the doors identify the quiet rooms, which are decorated in a Chinese motif with red lacquer furniture set against stark white walls. The bathrooms have all of the required upgrades. Balconies wrapped in wisteria vines offer pretty cityscape views. For the best of these, ask for Rooms F, R, or S.

ENGLISH SPOKEN Yes

FACILITIES AND SERVICES Air-conditioning, direct-dial phones, elevator, hair dryers, satellite TVs, office safe, parking (L40,000 per day)

NEAREST TOURIST ATTRACTIONS Spanish Steps, Trevi Fountain, shopping

TELEPHONE
06-679-4269

FAX
06-678-4258

CREDIT CARDS
None

CLOSED
Never

RATES
Single L220,000, double L380,000, triple L430,000; lower off-season rates; Continental breakfast included

(26) HOTEL MANFREDI ★★★ ($)
Via Margutta, 61
18 rooms, all with shower or bath and toilet

TELEPHONE
06-320-7676, 320-7695

FAX
06-320-7736

CREDIT CARDS
AE, DC, MC, V

CLOSED
Never

RATES
Single L290,000, double L380,000, triple L490,000, suite L550,000; lower off-season rates; buffet breakfast included

If you are looking for contemporary efficiency in a classy location close to fine shops and good restaurants (see *Cheap Eats in Italy*), the Manfredi should suit you perfectly. The three brothers who own and operate the hotel are constantly upgrading it. The latest improvements are computer modems in all the rooms, and the best air-conditioning system on the market. As one brother said, "Don't worry about being in our hotel in August . . . you will be in Alaska in three minutes after turning on the cool air." The small downstairs reception area, bar, and dining area have pink marble floors and bright lights. The rooms upstairs are uniformly turned out with blue fabric wall coverings and coordinating colors on the beds, curtains, and chairs. The floors are either carpeted or wood, an important consideration for those with allergies. Guests in the suite have their own dedicated telephone and fax plus a Jacuzzi. The tiled and marble bathrooms have good lighting and enough space for more than just a razor and a toothbrush. In No. 101, the imaginative bathroom has its tub up a few steps; in No. 103, a single, there is a big shower; and in No. 106, a double, gold accessories and a marble sink highlight the bathroom. For the area, the rooms are quiet. Discounts are given in winter and summer seasons, and the management is helpful.

ENGLISH SPOKEN Yes

FACILITIES AND SERVICES Air-conditioning, bar, computer modems, direct-dial phones, elevator, hair dryers, minibars, radios, satellite TVs, video players in some rooms (with L15,000 deposit), in-room safes

NEAREST TOURIST ATTRACTIONS Spanish Steps, Piazza del Popolo, shopping

(27) HOTEL MARCUS ★★
Via del Clementino, 94
15 rooms, all with shower or bath and toilet

TELEPHONE
06-683-00320, 687-3679

FAX
06-683-00312

CREDIT CARDS
AE, MC, V

CLOSED
Never

For more than thirty years, the same hardworking family has run this hotel near the Tiber River and between the Spanish Steps. Since it's a two-star, expect some mismatching, fraying around the edges, and cost-cutting measures, such as your morning orange juice poured into a plastic cup. The clean rooms display a smattering of almost-antique furniture mixed with

K-Mart specials. Some have nonworking marble fire-places and high ceilings. The bathrooms in too many are stuck in the corner and provide zero shelf space and no shower curtain or window, but it's all yours. Number 6 isn't bad: it's roomy and has a fireplace, but the shower is small and the traffic noise big. The best overall room is No. 9, which sells as either a double or triple. This choice has a ceiling fan, better drawer space, and a bathroom with a window. Breakfast is included in the rate and is served in a nonsmoking room with a large buffet and three marble-topped tables surrounded by cane-seated, bentwood chairs. Air-conditioning will cost you an additional L20,000 per day, but the TV and safe come with the room.

ENGLISH SPOKEN Yes

FACILITIES AND SERVICES Direct-dial phones, elevator, some hair dryers, satellite TVs, in-room safes, air-conditioning (L20,000 per day)

NEAREST TOURIST ATTRACTIONS Spanish Steps, Piazza Navona, shopping, Tiber River, long walk to Vatican

RATES
Single L120,000, double L170,000, triple L220,000; Continental breakfast included

(28) PENSIONE PANDA ★
Via della Croce, 35
20 rooms, 4 with shower and toilet

The Panda keeps pace with its tony surroundings and is a decent one-star Cheap Sleep providing well-scrubbed, whitewashed accommodations. Its location, a colorful shopping street in one of Rome's most desirable neighborhoods, where you can browse through countless boutiques displaying the latest in fashion and dine in many excellent restaurants (see *Cheap Eats in Italy*), is a stone's throw away from the Spanish Steps. The Panda does not try to be more than it is, so don't look for fancy furnishings, air-conditioning, or your own television with CNN. Four rooms do have private bathrooms that include a stall shower, heated towel racks, and two shelves. Several of the rooms have original hand-painted ceilings. Breakfast is not part of the package, but not to worry: lots of *caffès* and tempting bakeries are scattered throughout this part of Rome. Your problem will not be finding a place to eat but selecting from all the choices.

ENGLISH SPOKEN Very limited, but they do speak French

FACILITIES AND SERVICES Office safe

NEAREST TOURIST ATTRACTIONS Spanish Steps, Piazza del Popolo, shopping, Tiber River

TELEPHONE
06-678-0179

FAX
06-699-42151

CREDIT CARDS
AE, MC, V

CLOSED
Never

RATES
Single L60,000–80,000, double L95,000–130,000, triple L120,000–160,000, quad L160,000–200,000

TELEPHONE
06-679-2082, 699-41697,
678-7880
FAX
06-699-21000
CREDIT CARDS
AE, DC, MC, V
CLOSED
Never
RATES
Single L160,000, double
L180,000; lower rates July 15
through Sept 1; Continental
breakfast included

(29) HOTEL PENSIONE PARLAMENTO ★★
Via delle Convertite, 5; third floor
23 rooms, all with shower or bath and toilet

A tailor occupies the first floor of this building, which is owned by INA, the largest insurance company in Italy. The second floor houses Parliament offices, and the third through the fifth floors are home to the Hotel Pensione Parlamento, which is, for my Cheap Sleeping lire, one of the best values in this area of Rome. To reach the hotel in the past you had to climb seventy-seven steps from the ground floor. The hike up was, and still is, worth the aerobic effort, but I am happy to report that this climb is now optional: a beautiful new mirrored elevator awaits to whisk you to the hotel.

In addition to the elevator, the hotel has seen many stunning improvements, starting with the rooms and extending throughout. For maximum pleasure, request one of the newer bedrooms, which are uniformly outfitted in a salmon color scheme and are furnished with attractive reproduction pieces mixed with 1800 Imperial antiques, and perhaps a matching marble-topped dresser, armoire, and side tables. New beds, tiled floors, double windows, and three-star bathrooms finish the picture. Several rooms have a private terrace with a view of the San Silvester Church bell tower or overlooking the flowering roof garden. If you land in No. 82, you will be in a large family room with black-marble-topped furniture and a bathroom with heated towel racks, a three-way mirror, and telephone. The affable owner, Mr. Chini (pronounced KEE-ney) declares the bathroom in No. 94 to be his favorite. You will understand why when you see its green marble sink, stall shower, and window that opens for light and ventilation. Numbers 84 and 92 are quiet courtyard choices. Avoid No. 76 unless the red carpet and old bathroom are gone. On warm mornings, breakfast is served on the terrace at tables with umbrellas.

ENGLISH SPOKEN Yes

FACILITIES AND SERVICES Air-conditioning in fifteen rooms (L20,000 daily supplement), direct-dial phones, elevator, hair dryers, minibars, satellite TVs, in-room and office safes

NEAREST TOURIST ATTRACTIONS Spanish Steps, shopping

(30) HOTEL SCALINATA DI SPAGNA ★★★ ($)
Piazza Trinita dei Monti, 17
15 rooms, all with shower or bath and toilet

The Scalinata di Spagna used to be on everyone's list of small, charming, inexpensive hotels in Rome. It is still small and charming, but it is *not* inexpensive—not after its transformation from a modest pensione to a three-star hotel. I include it here for those with bigger budgets who are seeking a hotel that has kept its standards while providing personalized service. Guests enjoy a spectacular view from the flower-filled roof garden, where breakfast is served on warm days. The top-drawer location, directly across from the Hassler Hotel (where rates *start* at $400 for the plainest room and go to $2,100 for a suite per night before taxes and breakfast), is within easy access to big-name shopping, good restaurants (see *Cheap Eats in Italy*), and strolling or walking in the Villa Borghese Gardens. Cacao, the resident parrot, who was left at the hotel by a Brazilian artist, remains faithfully on his perch by the reception desk, where he loudly welcomes guests.

The rooms are on the small side and no two are alike, but all are nicely accented with antiques and Murano glass light fixtures. The bathrooms come with both a tub and shower. Number 15, opening onto the terrace, is a good selection, as is No. 11, with its peekaboo look at the Spanish Steps. If you are alone, reserve No. 2, also with a view and done in soft grays and pinks. Room No. 16, richly decorated in gold and blue tones, connects to another room and has access to the terrace. I thought the bathroom tiles, colored egg yolk yellow, were a bit much, but maybe you will like them. Guests are served breakfast year-round on one of the most beautiful glass-enclosed open-roof gardens in Rome. Even though prices are no longer low, demand far exceeds supply because the hotel has developed a loyal following, and many guests plot their return visit long before checking out.

ENGLISH SPOKEN Yes

FACILITIES AND SERVICES Air-conditioning, bar, direct-dial phones, hair dryers, minibars, radios, satellite TVs, in-room safes, parking can be arranged

NEAREST TOURIST ATTRACTIONS Spanish Steps, shopping, Villa Borghese Gardens

TELEPHONE
06-679-3006; local calls 699-40896

FAX
06-699-40598

CREDIT CARDS
AE, DC, MC, V

CLOSED
Never

RATES
Single L350,000, double L450,000, triple L550,000; Continental breakfast included

Testaccio

Testaccio is a working-class, very Roman district. Until 1970 the slaughterhouse was here, but now it is considered an "in" area with popular restaurants and a wild nightclub life. The Protestant cemetery is where you can visit the tombs of John Keats Shelley and Richard Henry Dana, who wrote *Two Years Before the Mast.*

(32) HOTEL SANTA PRISCA ★★
Largo Manlio Gelsomini, 35
50 rooms, all with shower or bath and toilet

TELEPHONE
06-574-191-7, 575-04-69, 575-00-09

FAX
06-574-66-58

CREDIT CARDS
AE, DC, MC, V

CLOSED
Never

RATES
Single L165,000, double L225,000, triple L250,000; Continental breakfast included; lunch or dinner L40,000

You will find the quiet and dignified Santa Prisca Hotel in the Testaccio district of Rome. This is definitely not a hub location, but many Rome veterans enjoy getting out of the noisy, traffic-clogged city center and staying, instead, in an area where they can experience more of the city's day-to-day life. This 1960s-style hotel is run by an order of Argentine and Italian nuns, the Sisters of Immaculate Conception. The hotel offers fifty rooms, all with private baths, direct-dial telephones, and, on the third floor, air-conditioning. Other drawing cards are free parking and a pleasant restaurant that serves three meals a day from a daily-changing menu.

The rooms are plain but immaculate. I like the reading lights over the beds, the spacious closets, the pulldown desks, and the showers *with* curtains. For lazy afternoons spent soaking up the sun, there is a pretty garden. On gray days you can settle into one of the sitting room's comfortable armchairs. If you are not into hotel dining, the Testaccio district is known for its earthy restaurants and is considered one of the "in" areas in Rome for drinking and dining (see *Cheap Eats in Italy*).

The Hotel Santa Prisca can be reached by taking trams 13 or 30 or the metro blueline B.

ENGLISH SPOKEN Yes

FACILITIES AND SERVICES Air-conditioning on the third floor, bar, direct-dial phones, elevator, hair dryer available, free parking, office safe

NEAREST TOURIST ATTRACTIONS Aventine, Testaccio, Baths of Caracalla

Train Station

The neighborhood surrounding the train station holds little on anyone's top ten list of tourist must-dos in Rome, but many inexpensive hotels and some very good restaurants are dotted around the area, and the bus transportation is excellent.

(33) HOTEL BRITANNIA ★★★ ($)
Via Napoli, 64
32 rooms, all with shower or bath and toilet

The warmth of the welcome, the careful attention to details, and the personalized service at the Hotel Britannia add up to a winning combination. I like the fact that management recognizes the work of its staff by having an employee-of-the-month award and a photo of the winner proudly displayed in the lobby. The employees repay with years of dedicated service: Mario and Enrico, the two concierges, have a total of fifty years at the hotel.

The hotel, located right off busy Via Nazionale and within walking distance of the train station, has been done in an attractive modern style. Mirrored walls give the downstairs public areas an open and spacious feeling, while soft built-in sofas, masses of pillows, and a new breakfast room with a skylight, parquet floors, and wall murals depicting views from a Roman villa create a sense of overall style and comfort. The faux-finished marble lobby bathroom is without equal. The American-style bar is a nice place for a quiet rendezvous with other guests, comfortably seated in tufted leather armchairs.

Upstairs, each floor is done in a different muted color: gold and burgundy on the first, yellow and green on the second, cream, gold, and green on the third and fourth. While all the rooms are excellent, the best are the renovated ones on the second floor, or any of the four rooms on either the second or fourth floors with private, plant-filled balconies. Room 403 is one of these. It is a beautiful, light room with circular windows, two settees, and plenty of closets. The soft brown and gray marble bathroom has a Jacuzzi and a heated towel rack in addition to all the other extras, which include digital clocks and radios, mirrored ceilings, scales, plenty of toiletries and towels, hair dryers, and sunlamps. The singles tend to run small, but each has a double bed, all the amenities of larger rooms, and wonderful bathrooms. Only a few rooms have interior views, so if you are at all claustrophobic, it is best to avoid these.

TELEPHONE
06-488-3153

FAX
06-488-2343

E-MAIL
britannia@venere.it

INTERNET
www.italy.com/roma/britannia

CREDIT CARDS
AE, DC, MC, V

CLOSED
Never

RATES
Single L300,000, double L360,000–400,000, suite L500,000; extra person L90,000; lower off-season rates; buffet breakfast included

In the morning, complimentary newspapers and a Rome weather report are placed by each door. The breakfast, which is included in the room price, is above average in quality and quantity; in addition to the usual coffee, tea, or hot chocolate and roll, it includes a choice of three or four cakes, cheese, and fruit juice.

NOTE: Also under the same ownership is the Duca d'Alba near the Colosseum, see page 143 for a description.

ENGLISH SPOKEN Yes

FACILITIES AND SERVICES Air-conditioning, bar, two bathrooms with Jacuzzis, direct-dial phones, elevator, hair dryers, minibars, free parking for five or six cars on a first-come-first-serve basis, radio, satellite TVs, in-room safes, same-day laundry service

NEAREST TOURIST ATTRACTIONS Opera, Via Veneto, Colosseum (thirty-five-minute walk)

(34) HOTEL CANADA ★★★ ($)
Via Vicenza, 58
85 rooms, all with shower or bath and toilet

TELEPHONE
06-445-7770/1/2; toll-free from the United States: Utell (800) 448-8355 Mon–Fri 7:30 A.M.–7 P.M., Sat 9 A.M.– 2 P.M.; Best Western: (800) 528-1234

FAX
06-445-0749

INTERNET
www.hotelbook.com (Utell Web Page)

CREDIT CARDS
AE, DC, MC, V

CLOSED
Never

RATES
Single L195,000–215,000, double L270,000, suite L300,000; extra person L55,000; lower off-season rates; large buffet breakfast included

The Hotel Canada is a marvelous three-star hotel with five-star personnel and services. "The more you give, the more you get," states Sr. Pucci, the distinguished owner. A graduate of the Cornell School of Hotel Management, he has been at the helm since 1965, although he now shares the responsibilities with his son, who is an architect and is responsible for the stylish appeal and arrangement of the entire operation.

The downstairs areas are exceptional, from the piano lounge and bar with inviting sofas and overstuffed chairs to the well-outfitted meeting rooms and large breakfast room—with tables big enough for a buffet-breakfast place setting and a morning paper. The perfectly maintained bedrooms reflect not only good taste but care and concern for the comfort of guests. Room 104 is a double with a beautiful antique desk, a hand-painted wardrobe, and brass accent lamps. Number 108 has a sitting area with comfortable chairs and a large bath. Both Nos. 114 and 134—with a balcony—are junior suites and especially suitable for long stays or for parties of three. Number 214 is a grand room in every way, from the armchairs and desk in the entry to the canopy over the bed, the spacious armoire, the three-drawer chest, and the rich fabrics. Each floor has one room fitted especially for the handicapped. The rooms and baths have all the usual three-star perks, including double-paned windows, automatic locking doors, and telephones and drying lines in the bathrooms. The generous breakfast includes cheese, three types of meat, a hot dish, fresh fruit, and cereals, along with bread, rolls, and hot or cold drinks.

If there is any drawback to this hotel (which is associated with Best Western and Utell) it might be the location, which is not tourist central. There are, however, two metro stops within easy walking distance, one of which goes directly to the airport (Castro Pretorio on the B line).

ENGLISH SPOKEN Yes

FACILITIES AND SERVICES Air-conditioning, bar, direct-dial phones in rooms and bathrooms, elevator, hair dryers, radios, satellite TVs, in-room safes, parking in nearby garage (10 percent off fee), room service, sunlamps, same-day laundry service, rooms and bathrooms for the handicapped

NEAREST TOURIST ATTRACTIONS None; train station is nearby

(35) HOTEL COLUMBIA ★★★
Via del Viminale, 15
45 rooms, all with shower or bath and toilet

Patrizia Diletti, whose family also owns the popular Hotel Venezia (see page 167), dedicated one year of unbelievable hard work to the ambitious reconstruction project that resulted in the Hotel Columbia. What was once a has-been hotel is now a modern stunner with an air of cosmopolitan dignity that is the hallmark of everything this well-connected family touches. The forty-five bedrooms provide copacetic comforts with white walls, salmon-colored carpeting, creamy white quilted bed coverings, and white-tiled baths with marble sink tops. Several have wood beam or brick arched ceilings and grillwork by a Perugian artist. Those on the first floor will soon have balconies. On the fifth floor, guests are treated to a dazzling glassed-in breakfast room that opens onto an outside roof terrace ringed with boxed flowering plants. The yellow marble tables team well with the upholstered chairs and gold sconces to create a garden setting that carries through to the sitting room, where modern paintings by a friend of the family add bright splashes of color and light. The enthusiastic, multilingual staff works hard to please, but no one is more ambitious or single-minded in purpose (to create a marvelous hotel) and determination than the owner, Patrizia Diletti.

TELEPHONE
06-474-4289, 488-3509, 488-3707

FAX
06-474-0209

E-MAIL
columbia@flashnet.it

CREDIT CARDS
AE, DC, MC, V

CLOSED
Never

RATES
Single L185,000, double L250,000, triple L335,000; lower off-season rates; buffet breakfast included

NOTE: For a different Roman holiday, please see Villa Delros on page 194, the exclusive bed-and-breakfast Patrizia's mother has opened in her beautiful country estate on the edge of the city.

ENGLISH SPOKEN Yes

FACILITIES AND SERVICES Air-conditioning, bar, direct-dial phone in the rooms and bathrooms, elevator, hair dryers, minibars, satellite TVs, PC modems, dedicated line for Internet hookup, in-room safes, one nonsmoking bedroom

NEAREST TOURIST ATTRACTIONS Opera, train station

(36) HOTEL D'ESTE ★★★ ($)
Via Carlo Alberto, 4-B
40 rooms, all with shower or bath and toilet

TELEPHONE
06-446-5607

FAX
06-446-5601

INTERNET
www.venere.it/roma/d.este

CREDIT CARDS
AE, DC, MC, V

CLOSED
Never

RATES
Single L235,000, double L320,000, triple L420,000; lower off-season rates; buffet breakfast included

Five blocks from the Termini Station is the Hotel d'Este, a completely up-to-date establishment offering comfort and convenience for the traveler with an expandable budget. Besides a private garage, the hotel has laundry and dry-cleaning services, a full bar, and an umbrella-shaded roof garden for summertime dining.

The public areas of the hotel are exceptionally nice. A brick walkway leads to a sitting room with an inlaid ceiling, furnished with soft, overstuffed chairs. To one side is a smaller room where you can write notes and postcards, and a small bar with slanted beams. Gray and white halls cushioned with Oriental runners lead to the large guest rooms, all outfitted with matching mahogany furniture. Five of the rooms have balconies. Room 440 has the added luxury of a sofa, a writing desk with drawers, and a brass bed. The bathroom has a tub with a handheld shower nozzle, shelf space, and plenty of linen and terry towels. Number 438, also with a balcony, can sleep three in its beds, which are covered with cream-colored spreads. A quiet single with its own entry and very nice bath is No. 112. Number 114, on the other hand, is a small backside single in which the minibar takes up too much closet space, while the bad corner shower with a wood-slat floor nixes Room 218.

ENGLISH SPOKEN Yes

FACILITIES AND SERVICES Air-conditioning, bar, direct-dial phones, elevator, hair dryers, minibars, satellite TVs, in-room safes, porters

NEAREST TOURIST ATTRACTIONS Not much; train station is nearby

(37) HOTEL MARGHERA ★★★
Via Marghera, 29
20 rooms, all with showers only and toilets

TELEPHONE
06-445-7184, 445-7679,
445-0769

FAX
06-446-2539

CREDIT CARDS
MC, V

CLOSED
Never

RATES
Single L210,000, double
L300,000; lower off-season
rates; buffet breakfast included

The lavish foldout brochure printed on heavy, colorful, cotton-weave paper is your first indication that this is a hotel in which the owner is willing to spend money on pleasing guests. That impression is further enhanced by the fresh flowers near the entrance, the public areas, and every bedroom. There just are not many hotels that have seasonal floral arrangements in this abundance. I find it hard to believe this alluring hotel is so close to the train station, which is not an area overflowing with tastefully done establishments.

Though the hotel has aged beautifully, it received a wrinkle-free face-lift several years ago. The owner is a musician and so are many of the guests, who appreciate the attention to detail. In addition to fresh flowers, the rooms have attractive prints on the walls and a padded chair, inviting you to linger. Crisp white linens, puffy comforters, and big, fat pillows ensure a dreamy night's sleep. Tiled bathrooms (none with tubs), writing desks, and wardrobes with shelves provide further comfort. Naturally, everything is coordinated and nicely matched. While every room is a winner, No. 311 hits the jackpot. Not only will you sleep under a canopied bed and enjoy a Jacuzzi and double sink in the mirrored bathroom, you will be able to send faxes from your room.

A buffet breakfast is served in the first-floor dining room, set with round tables covered with linen cloths and surrounded by dainty red-and-white slipcovered chairs with skirts. On each table will be a potted plant and silver sugar bowl. Additional polished silver serving dishes on the buffet and Oriental rugs tossed on the hardwood floor add more style and color to the pleasant surroundings. Also on the first floor is the cozy, Laura Ashley–inspired sitting room with a fireplace. Should you need information on what to do in Rome, the Italian National Tourist Office is right across the street.

ENGLISH SPOKEN Yes

FACILITIES AND SERVICES Air-conditioning, bar, direct-dial phones, elevator, hair dryers, trouser press, satellite TVs, parking can be arranged, office safe

NEAREST TOURIST ATTRACTIONS Near train station; across the street from the Italian National Tourist Office

(38) HOTEL NARDIZZI AMERICANA ★★

Via Firenze, 38

19 rooms, all with shower or bath and toilet

TELEPHONE
06-488-0368

FAX
06-488-0035

CREDIT CARDS
AE, DC, MC, V

CLOSED
Never

RATES
Single L110,000, double L160,000, triple L190,000; good discounts for *Cheap Sleeps* readers; Continental breakfast included

A stay at the Nardizzi Americana guarantees guests twenty-four-hour security: right across the street, surrounded by armed guards, is the Ministry of Defense. You are also only a block or so away from a metro stop, or, if you're trying to keep fit, you can either walk to the Trevi Fountain or keep up your jogging routine in the Villa Borghese. The manager, Nick, is a friendly guy who loves Americans. He brags that he serves the best cup of American coffee in Rome.

The rooms are old but functional, with the odd good piece of furniture stuck here and there. They reflect zip in the style and charm departments, but they are clean and serviceable without being dark and claustrophobic. Breakfast includes Nick's famous coffee, yogurt, juice, and a piece of cheese to go with your bread, butter, and jam, served in a dining room with a vase of fake flowers on each table. Best news of all: If you mention *Cheap Sleeps in Italy* when reserving and show a copy when you arrive, you will receive a discount.

On my last visit, Nick told me big plans were in the works to add a roof garden and to equip all the rooms with private bathrooms, a TV, and in-room safes. If you see this happen, let me know.

ENGLISH SPOKEN Yes

FACILITIES AND SERVICES Direct-dial phones, elevator, office safe, TV (on request, L10,000 per day)

NEAREST TOURIST ATTRACTIONS Trevi Fountain, Via Veneto, train station is not far

(39) HOTEL ROMAE ★★

Via Palestro, 49

22 rooms, all with shower or bath and toilet

TELEPHONE
06-446-3554

FAX
06-446-3914

E-MAIL
htlromae@flashnet.it

CREDIT CARDS
AE, MC, V

CLOSED
Never

"Some of the nicest guests we have come from your book," quotes Lucy Boccaforno, who along with her husband, Francesco, owns this hotel. The young and attractive Boccafornos take great pride in their establishment. They live at the hotel along with his mother and their children: Denise, Luigi, and Francesca. Lucy and Francesco are on board every day to see that everything runs as it should. In addition, they will book tours for you, obtain tickets, and make sightseeing suggestions. Their English is perfect, and they make everyone feel at home.

The functional bedrooms, with tiled floors, lacy white window curtains, and pastel-colored walls are way ahead of the two-star competition in the area. Those on the first and fourth floors are new and, in my opinion, the best. Lucy told me that the mistakes they made in the other rooms have been corrected in these. In addition to ceiling fans, firm mattresses, CNN television, and simple yet sweet decor, Lucy has compiled an information booklet on Rome and placed it in each room.

Downstairs, there is a modern reception area with a fountain and a mural along one wall of the breakfast room, which has black cane chairs around square tables and a small bar to one side. In the afternoons you may find the Boccafornos' children quietly doing their homework here or eating an after-school snack.

ENGLISH SPOKEN Yes

FACILITIES AND SERVICES Bar, direct-dial phones, elevator, fans, hair dryers, satellite TVs, in-room safes

NEAREST TOURIST ATTRACTIONS Museo Nazionale in the Diocletian Bath, train station

RATES
Single L170,000, double L220,000; extra person 35 percent of rate; discount for *Cheap Sleeps* readers; children under twelve free; Continental breakfast included

(40) HOTEL VENEZIA ★★★
Via Varese, 18
61 rooms, all with shower or bath and toilet

On a scale of one to ten, the Hotel Venezia is a ten-plus and climbing. Frankly, I cannot say enough about it: it's a beautiful selection in a business and residential neighborhood a few minutes from the train station. Owner Rosmarie Diletti has turned over the reins to her capable daughter, Patrizia, who continues to truly care about each of her guests, taking a personal interest in their well-being. This kindness extends to the loyal staff, like the porter, who has been with the hotel since 1964.

The hotel is stunning throughout with a museum-worthy collection of fifteenth-, sixteenth-, and seventeenth-century antiques. Most of the paintings are by local artists, or part of the family's own collection. Everywhere you look something interesting catches your eye, including the beautiful fresh-flower arrangements that Sra. Diletti brings in weekly from her country garden. When checking in, notice the picture of the bride and groom hanging over the desk. This is a painting of Sra. Diletti's in-laws, taken at the turn of the century.

A breakfast buffet is laid out on a fifteenth-century altar and served on authentic Italian farm tables. Some of

TELEPHONE
06-445-7101, 446-3687

FAX
06-495-7687; toll-free from the United States: (800) 526-5497

E-MAIL
venezia@flashnet.it

CREDIT CARDS
AE, DC, MC, V

CLOSED
Never

RATES
Single L183,000, double L250,000, triple L335,000; discounts for *Cheap Sleeps* readers; buffet breakfast included

the doors leading from the lounge area are from the sixteenth century, and the glass-topped table base in the sitting room was used to carry saints into villages during the same era. The rooms are done in lovely reproduction and antique furnishings befitting the style and feel of the rest of the hotel. Each room has a Murano chandelier, heavy white curtains, crocheted covers over the bedside tables, and interesting framed prints hanging on the walls. In addition, the closet space is ample and the bathrooms have pretty floral-tiled inserts to give them interest. The best rooms are on the higher floors, where they are flooded with light, and many have balconies that are perfect observation stations for watching the neighborhood life below. Special rates are available if you mention *Cheap Sleeps in Italy* when reserving and show the book when checking in.

TWO VERY SPECIAL NOTES: Rosmarie Diletti has opened her magnificent home on the edge of Rome for visitors at selected times during the year. It is in a garden setting, complete with swimming pool and her own cultivated flower beds. If this exclusive type of Roman bed-and-breakfast appeals to you, please turn to page 194 for further details.

Her daughter, Patrizia, has opened a second hotel, the Hotel Columbia, which is close to and equal in its own way to the Venezia. For details, please see page 163.

ENGLISH SPOKEN Yes

FACILITIES AND SERVICES Air-conditioning, bar, direct-dial phones, elevators, hair dryers, magnifying mirrors in the bathrooms, minibars, radios, satellite TVs, elevator, in-room safes, twenty-four-hour laundry service, complimentary newspapers

NEAREST TOURIST ATTRACTIONS Not much, near the train station

Trastevere

Translated, it means "across the Tiber," and that is just what it is . . . across the Tiber from the Jewish Ghetto. If there is a picturesque bohemian section of Rome, this is it. The center is the Piazza Santa Maria, while the Piazza San Cosimato offers an open food market. Throughout, the narrow streets are full of flapping laundry lines stretched between windows of ancient pink-stuccoed buildings, elderly black-garbed widows gossiping on corners, funky boutiques displaying the latest trends in art and fashion, and one pizza restaurant after another. In the evening, a lively nightlife keeps the action in full force until the wee hours.

(43) PENSIONE CARMEL ★
Via Goffredo Mameli, 11
9 rooms, 8 with shower or bath and toilet

Trastevere is the artistic section of Rome, attracting bohemians during the day and night owls on the prowl until the early morning hours. People are drawn to the picturesque, hippielike atmosphere, a kicked-back respite from the rest of fast-track Rome.

This brings me to Pensione Carmel. While Trastevere is a great place to visit, not everyone wants to actually stay here. If you do, and are down and out and needing a Cheap Sleep, Pensione Carmel is on a tree-lined street about a five- or ten-minute walk from "action central." David Bahbout took over the nine-room pensione from his mother, who had it for twenty years and practiced deferred maintenance. He is always planning to redo much of it, but don't hold your breath (or look for it to be featured on *Lifestyles of the Rich and Famous*). The furniture is not too gruesome—although the bathroom tiles with the butterfly motif do get to me. Rooms 10 and 11 have air-conditioning (at no extra charge) and open onto the hotel terrace. A rabbi-controlled kosher breakfast is served in the rooms. But the pièce de résistance is the glassed-in sunroom and vine-covered summer terrace, which are welcoming places to curl up and write postcards to friends back home or to meet other guests and exchange travel stories and tips.

To reach Pensione Carmel, take bus 75 or 170 from the Termini train station or bus 170 from Trastevere.

ENGLISH SPOKEN Yes

FACILITIES AND SERVICES Air-conditioning in two rooms (no extra charge)

NEAREST TOURIST ATTRACTIONS Trastevere

TELEPHONE AND FAX
06-580-9921

CREDIT CARDS
None, cash only

CLOSED
Never

RATES
Single L70,000, double L120,000; Continental kosher breakfast included

(44) PENSIONE ESTY ★
Viale di Trastevere, 108; third floor
10 rooms, none with shower or bath and toilet

Some of the lowest-priced Cheap Sleeps in Rome are found at this unpretentious, functional pensione slightly removed from the boisterous heart of Trastevere. You will, however, still be within walking distance of all the

TELEPHONE
06-588-1201

CREDIT CARDS
None

CLOSED
Never

restaurants and nonstop nighttime activities Trastevere is famous for. While the rooms lack character (or private facilities other than a basin and running water), they are clean and the mattresses are generally lump-free. A few have balconies facing the street, but unless you can sleep and dream through noise, either bring industrial-strength earplugs or get a room on the back. There are two public bathrooms for all ten rooms. The one tiled in yellow and green is acceptable, but the other needs paint, which hopefully has happened by now. Don't worry about high hotel breakfast charges . . . here you will be forced to go to a neighborhood *caffè* because morning coffee and rolls are not served.

To find the Pensione Esty, ring the bell on the right by the gate, turn up the driveway, and go to the first doorway on the left, which is stairway A (or Scala A). The Pensione Esty is on the third floor.

ENGLISH SPOKEN None

FACILITIES AND SERVICES Elevator to reception

NEAREST TOURIST ATTRACTIONS Trastevere

Trevi Fountain

The movie *Three Coins in the Fountain* and the Frank Sinatra song by the same name ensured that no traveler to Rome would leave without tossing a coin into the magnificent Trevi Fountain. It is clear that every tourist comes here, and when you visit, you will probably think everyone in the city is standing in front of you trying to toss a coin. The fountain, designed by Nicolò Salvi for Pope Clement XII, is magnificent. Don't miss it.

(45) FONTANA HOTEL ★★★ ($)
Piazza di Trevi, 96
24 rooms, all with shower or bath and toilet

TELEPHONE
06-678-6113, 679-1056

FAX
06-679-0024

CREDIT CARDS
AE, DC, MC, V

CLOSED
Never

RATES
Single L300,000–320,000, double L350,000–385,000, triple L435,000; lower off-season rates; Continental breakfast included

If you want to toss your three coins into the Trevi Fountain from the comfort of your own room, check into the top floor at the Fontana. I must be honest with you . . . when I first saw the hotel several years ago, I thought the rooms were not only very small but depressing. *Not anymore!* Elena Daneo, the stylish owner, has transformed the rooms on the first and third floors into imaginative and unusual choices that will have definite appeal for those who don't want to forget for a minute that they are in Rome. For those who value quiet in uniformly predictable surroundings, however, this hotel will have limited appeal.

There wasn't much Sra. Daneo could do about the size of the rooms, but she certainly transformed the atmosphere of each one. No two rooms match (aside from their black enamel doors), and therein lies their charm. Even though it is on the back, people clamor for No. 303—and no wonder. Suitable for up to four sleeping in two double beds with white covers, it has heavy wood beams, bleached pine floors, a mirrored armoire, and a step-down bathroom with a skylight. I think you will like sunny and romantic No. 302, which has the same great bathroom, a king-size bed, and a wall of windows looking at a tiled roof so close you could almost reach out and touch it. The BBC has used room 105, facing the fountain, as the setting for several shows . . . need I say more? In No. 109 you will also have a wonderful Trevi Fountain view. The high ceilings, hardwood floors, attractive furnishings, and light bathroom are further plus points.

The rooftop dining room with a grand piano and terrace has universal appeal, especially if you get there early enough in the morning to nab a windowside table overlooking Rome's most famous fountain. If you select this hotel, bear in mind that it can be very noisy—not only does the fountain spout day and night, but every tourist in Rome has to come and toss a coin into the waters to ensure they will return to the Eternal City. To be sure *her* guests will return, Sra. Daneo gives them all a special coin to toss into the fountain.

ENGLISH SPOKEN Yes

FACILITIES AND SERVICES Air-conditioning in the back rooms (L20,000 daily supplement), fans in the other rooms, direct-dial phones, elevator, hair dryers, TVs, office safe, room service for drinks

NEAREST TOURIST ATTRACTIONS Trevi Fountain, shopping

(46) HOTEL TREVI ★★★ ($)
Vicolo del Babuccio, 20–21
28 rooms, all with shower or bath and toilet

The value is here and the recommendation is high for this excellent choice in the heart of Rome, close to the Trevi Fountain. If you like to walk, you can find something interesting or a photo opportunity in almost any direction. Restaurants and shops are close (see *Cheap Eats*

TELEPHONE
06-678-9563, 678-5894, 699-41406, 699-41876

FAX
06-699-41497

CREDIT CARDS
AE, DC, MC, V

CLOSED
Never

RATES
Single L270,000, double
L350,000, triple L470,000;
very good discounts for *Cheap
Sleeps* readers; buffet breakfast
included

in Italy and "Cheap Chic," beginning on page 291), as are taxis and buses for trips farther afield.

When I first saw the hotel several years ago, it was in the process of renovation and I was not able to include it. After hearing about its new look from several friends, I put it on my "hot" list of hotels in Rome. I can report that the first transformation was impressive. When I returned again to review it for this edition, it had been completely redone again, with even more handsome results.

These user-friendly rooms have the works: space, mirrors, in-room safes, minibars, air-conditioning, good bathrooms, showers with doors, light, and color-coordination. A few have balconies; others have beamed ceilings. Room 109 is a romantic double in soft rose with burgundy carpets and a terrace. The white-tiled bathroom is accented with green and has shelf space and big towels. The top-floor garden offers sketchbook views of Rome. In summer, the buffet breakfast is served here, while in cooler months, it's served in an underground grotto with stone ceilings. The service is always polite, and discounts are extended to *Cheap Sleeps in Italy* readers—two more good reasons to select this exceptionally nice hotel.

ENGLISH SPOKEN Yes

FACILITIES AND SERVICES Air-conditioning, direct-dial phones, elevator (but not to roof garden), hair dryers, minibars, TVs, in-room safes

NEAREST TOURIST ATTRACTIONS Trevi Fountain, Quirinale Palace Via Veneto, shopping

Vatican

No visitor to Rome can leave without a pilgrimage to the most holy place in Christendom, the Vatican and Vatican City. The tiny city state covers about 108 acres, which is the size of most golf courses, but it is full of glorious treasures in the Vatican Museums and Gardens, the Sistine Chapel, and St. Peter's Basilica, all of which deserve as much time as you can afford to give them. If you are mailing things, the Vatican Post Office sells its own stamps and has faster service than the Rome post offices.

(47) CASA VALDESE ★★
Via Alessandro Farnese, 18
35 rooms, 34 with shower and toilet

Whether you are traveling alone, with your significant other, or as a family, one of the best two-star Cheap Sleeping values in Rome is the Casa Valdese. Located in Prati, one of Rome's more exclusive neighborhoods, the hotel gives guests the advantage of being about a thirty-minute walk from St. Peter's Square on this side of the Tiber River, or crossing one of the bridges and being at the Spanish Steps in the same length of time. Walking to Castel Sant' Angelo or Piazza Navona takes a few minutes less. For trips further afield, take the 81 or 78 buses or head for the Lepanto Metro Station, where in ten minutes you can get to the railway station and its shuttle service to Fiumicino Airport.

The hotel is part of a group of a Christian Protestant–run organization that has similar properties throughout Italy (in Florence there is the Istituto Gould, see page 71, and in Venice, Foresteria Valdese, see page 288). The Casa Valdese, a former hostel, opened in 1989 after a complete refurbishing and upgrading. In addition to the simple yet ample and coordinated bedrooms, all with good showers and decent towels, and three with private terraces, there is a wonderful rooftop garden and a restaurant open to the public that serves a moderately priced lunch and dinner. The daily menus are posted at the reception desk and you can reserve your place on a day-to-day basis.

ENGLISH SPOKEN Yes

FACILITIES AND SERVICES Air-conditioning (L6,000 daily supplement), direct-dial phones in most rooms, elevator, two parking places (L25,000 per night), TVs on request, office safe, restaurant for lunch and dinner (L25,000 for three-course meal, L45,000 for both meals, beverages extra, no à la carte)

NEAREST TOURIST ATTRACTIONS Castel Sant' Angelo, Vatican, Spanish Steps, and Piazza Navona within a twenty- to thirty-minute walk

TELEPHONE
06-321-8222, 321-5362

FAX
06-321-1843

CREDIT CARDS
None, cash only

CLOSED
Never

RATES
Single L128,000–180,000, double L90,000–160,000 per person, triple L245,000 for room; breakfast included; children under three stay free, those four to ten get a 50 percent discount; lower rates for stays of three nights or more; half-pension for individuals L25,000, full pension L45,000 (three courses, beverages extra)

(50) GIUGGIOLI HOTEL ★
Via Germanico, 198
5 rooms, 1 with shower and toilet

The Giuggioli is as old-fashioned as the lady who runs it. Located in a large building with several other competitors, it is the *only* one to consider, because it is

TELEPHONE
06-324-3697

CREDIT CARDS
None

CLOSED
Never

RATES
One or two persons L130,000–
150,000; no breakfast served

one of Rome's crown jewels of clean, safe, and inexpensive Cheap Sleep lodging. All five rooms are overseen by a sweet Italian grandmother, Sra. Giuggioli, who has been opening her home for almost fifty years to Cheap Sleepers in Rome. She doesn't speak much English, but that won't matter . . . she has an artful way of communicating in a way that you will understand.

As I approached the front door for the first time I had my doubts. But once I saw the big, clean rooms, each with at least one or two pieces of interesting furniture (I chose to ignore the print mismatches, a vacuum sitting in one corner, and hotel laundry blowing in the breeze from the balcony), I was duly impressed. The most expensive double is Room 4, the expansive matrimonial suite, which has two fabulous marble-topped dressers and a massive mirrored armoire that would not be out of place at the Hotel Hassler. This is the only choice with a private bathroom; the other four share one large communal hall bath. There are no public areas, but if you ask, you will probably be able to use her sitting room, which has mementos and bric-a-brac gathered over decades of living here and her cat, Mattia, moving and snoozing from one sunny spot to another.

ENGLISH SPOKEN None

FACILITIES AND SERVICES None

NEAREST TOURIST ATTRACTIONS Vatican, Vatican Museums

(51) HOTEL ALIMANDI ★★★
Via Tunisi, 8
33 rooms, 29 with shower or bath and toilet

TELEPHONE
06-397-23941

FAX
06-397-23943

E-MAIL
alimandi@tin.it

INTERNET
www.travel.iol.it/alberghi/
alimandi

CREDIT CARDS
AE, DC, MC, V

CLOSED
Never

RATES
Single L143,000, double
L195,000, triple L230,000;
buffet breakfast (L16,000 extra
per person, per day)

The Alimandi is better than ever. Brothers Paolo, Enrico, and Luigi Alimandi own not only the hotel but the entire building, which is unusual in Rome. This means that provided they can cut through the Roman red tape that unfurls the minute a building change is suggested, they are free to do what they want to improve their hotel and not have to heel to the demands of a cheapskate owner. And improve it they have . . . *transformed* would be a better word.

The hotel has now been redone from top to bottom and, as a result, added a star. On the fourth floor is an inviting garden, and on the roof, an awning-shaded terrace with a view to the Vatican, its gardens, and the Sistine Chapel. Downstairs has a beautiful new entry and reception with a bas-relief done by their nephew (who is also responsible for the thirty-five other bas-reliefs in the hotel). His wife painted the mural of Rome that highlights one breakfast room, while a skylight serves as the focal point of the other. Also new is the Spanish-style bar with windows made of colored glass, a TV and game room, and a self-service laundry. The rooms come with a built-in wardrobe, a desk and chair, some luggage space, and a tile floor. The showers have curtains, a simple feature missing in all too many Italian hotels. One room is suitable for handicapped visitors.

The brothers are committed to offering the best service possible to their guests. To make sure of this, they are on the job daily, checking up on the maids, answering guests' questions, and providing helpful advice. There is a minivan available to provide airport transfers, which must be booked when reserving and costs L70,000 per trip.

ENGLISH SPOKEN Yes

FACILITIES AND SERVICES Air-conditioning in some rooms, fans in the others, bar, direct-dial phones, two elevators (one glass-enclosed), hair dryers, radios, satellite TVs, in-room safes, parking (L30,000 per day), coin-operated self-service laundry, magnifying mirrors in bathrooms, airport transfers (L70,000)

NEAREST TOURIST ATTRACTIONS Vatican, Vatican Museums

(52) HOTEL EMMAUS ★★
Via delle Fornaci, 23–25
29 rooms, all with shower and toilet

It will be hard to get much closer to Vatican City than you will be at the newly revived Hotel Emmaus. Because of its A-plus location, it is a popular choice, and has already been booked by the Vatican Offices for Easter in 1999 and 2000. Enzo De Santis and his two brothers and a sister bought the old hotel in 1991 and have since fluffed and dusted it, turning it into a modern, comfortable choice just a heartbeat from St. Peter's. The rooms are not intended for long, leisurely stays, but certainly provide Cheap Sleepers with a dependable place for a short Rome visit. Enzo and his siblings are good hosts, proving true their statement to me, "We really care and we try to do our best." Enzo speaks perfect English, which he polished in his younger days when he

TELEPHONE AND FAX
06-638-0370, 635-658, 635-331, 635-371

CREDIT CARDS
AE, DC, MC, V

CLOSED
Never

RATES
Single L130,000, double L200,000, triple, L230,000, quad L270,000, lower off-season rates; buffet breakfast included

drove 17,000 miles throughout the United States, seeing more of it than most of us ever will.

ENGLISH SPOKEN Yes

FACILITIES AND SERVICES Air-conditioning in one room, fans in others, bar, direct-dial phones, elevator, hair dryers, minibars, TVs, office safe, two bathrooms for handicapped guests

NEAREST TOURIST ATTRACTIONS Vatican, Vatican Museums

(53) HOTEL OLYMPIC ★★★ ($)
Via Properzio, 2-A
55 rooms, all with shower or bath and toilet

TELEPHONE
06-689-6650, 689-6652, 689-6653
FAX
06-683-08255
E-MAIL
olympic@venere.it
CREDIT CARDS
AE, DC, MC, V
CLOSED
Never
RATES
Single L235,000, double L320,000, triple L355,000, suite for four L600,000; lower off-season rates; Continental breakfast included

The Hotel Olympic, one of the best three-star hotels in the Vatican section of Rome, is appealing and formal, with all the services and facilities one expects in a well-managed hotel. From top to bottom, the hotel is done with style and verve, while keeping the comfort of its guests the number-one priority.

The rooms have a personalized decorator look, with crisp linen bed coverings, built-in desks, and fabric-covered walls. The bathrooms have good natural light, shelf space, and absorbent towels. Number 302, with soft charcoal-gray walls, is an exceptionally good choice. It is a corner room with two double-glazed windows, a curved burled-wood desk, matching curtains and bedspreads, and ginger-jar lamps. The modern bathroom has marble and tile, Lucite towel racks, and a rolling cart for extra storage. If you want a glimpse of St. Peter's, ask for Nos. 501 or 502. They are small and compact, and the view is from the bathroom window. Room 205 is nice for two and has a bathroom featuring a large tub and mirror.

The refined downstairs lobby and sitting rooms have gilt mirrors, a massive marble table, and large paintings that work together to create a pleasing elegance. Adding to the look are large sofas, Directoire chairs, and a full-service bar outfitted in a leopard-skin print. The two breakfast rooms have green-and-white-striped chairs arranged around tables draped in botanical prints. An interesting nontouristy market operates on Via Cola Rienzo, just a few minutes away. While the walk to the Vatican is not too far, it should help to build your appetite for a nice lunch or dinner (see *Cheap Eats in Italy*).

ENGLISH SPOKEN Yes

FACILITIES AND SERVICES Air-conditioning, bar, direct-dial phones, elevator, hair dryers, minibars, radios, satellite TVs, some trouser presses, office safe

NEAREST TOURIST ATTRACTIONS Vatican, Tiber River

(54) HOTEL SANT'ANNA ★★★ ($)
Borgo Pio, 133
20 rooms, all with shower or bath and toilet

The Hotel Sant'Anna scores high for location, only a few blocks from St. Peter's, and always as one of the better choices in this area. When I visited the hotel to check on it for this edition, I found Viscardo, the owner, in overalls working right alongside thirty-five other workmen, all racing against the clock to finish a remodeling project to refresh the rooms (now they will have either wallpaper or hand-painted murals depicting various Roman scenes) and add a much needed elevator. The hotel was closed for the duration of the work, but I was able to look at some of the new rooms to verify that they were testimonies to the artistic spirit of the hotel. Those on the top floors retain their own private terraces. On the third floor, the hand-detailed rooms have slanting roofs and built-in furniture, which allows for more living space. The baths continue to pamper guests with marble showers, terry towels, good lighting, and up-to-date fixtures. The frescoed lobby with a small sitting room leading to a garden and the basement breakfast room where the buffet is served are still in place, and, obviously, so is the very hardworking owner.

ENGLISH SPOKEN Yes

FACILITIES AND SERVICES Air-conditioning, direct-dial phones, elevator, hair dryers, minibars, radios, satellite TVs, in-room safes, parking (L40,000 per day), two rooms for the handicapped

NEAREST TOURIST ATTRACTIONS Vatican, Vatican Museums, Tiber River

TELEPHONE
06-688-01602

FAX
06-683-08717

E-MAIL
santanna@travel.it

CREDIT CARDS
AE, DC, MC, V

CLOSED
Never

RATES
Single L230,000, double L300,000, lower off-season rates; buffet breakfast included

(56) PENSIONE LADY ★★
Via Germanico, 198; fourth floor
7 rooms, 2 with shower and toilet

Dario and Angela Venneri, who have been here for thirty-five years, run a tight ship, and their sweet rooms remind me of stays in homes of maiden aunties. Number 6 and its furnishings hearken back to the thirties. The inside courtyard view is uninspiring, but the vista is better in No. 5, as is the tiled floor. Cheap Sleepers on a

TELEPHONE
06-324-2112

FAX
06-324-3446

CREDIT CARDS
V

CLOSED
Never

RATES
Single L110,000, double
L130,000–150,000; extra bed
35 percent of room rate

real economy kick should reserve a room with only a sink and use the clean hall facilities at this budget entry. Your cost for a Cheap Sleep is further reduced because the Venneris don't serve breakfast. Consider that not only a money-saver for you but a chance to mingle with the neighborhood regulars over a foamy latte at the corner cafe.

ENGLISH SPOKEN Yes, and French

FACILITIES AND SERVICES Direct-dial phones, elevator, TV on request

NEAREST TOURIST ATTRACTIONS Vatican, Vatican Museums

(57) PENSIONE OTTAVIANO ★
Via Ottaviano, 6
7 communal rooms, no private facilities

TELEPHONE
06-397-38138

FAX
06-397-37253

INTERNET
www.enjoyrome.it/ottavhtl.htm

CREDIT CARDS
None, cash only

CLOSED
Never

RATES
Double L40,000 per person, triple L35,000 per person; dorm bed L25,000 per person; showers included

Check in here for a Cheap Sleep on a cotlike bed in a shared room with no heat or air-conditioning, no curfew, and no refunds of the cash-only, pay-in-advance rates. Sheets and blankets are provided and so are free showers, but towels are not, and neither is breakfast. There is a refrigerator in every room, plus a communal microwave and individual lockers. A list of Vatican dos and don'ts along with stern house rules occupies a prominent position in the reception area. If you stay here, in addition to the refund policy already mentioned, on the day you leave they want you to be gone absolutely no later than 9 A.M., and they will not store your luggage after checking out. Benefits? It is the only hostel-type accommodation in this very safe area of Rome that is literally a block or two from the Vatican. The laid-back management is friendly and willing to shoot the breeze and divulge all sorts of cheap survival tactics, which you will no doubt be interested in if you are staying here.

ENGLISH SPOKEN Yes

FACILITIES AND SERVICES Individual lockers

NEAREST TOURIST ATTRACTIONS Vatican, Vatican Museums

Via Veneto

What was once the famed center of *la dolce vita,* Via Veneto is now a wide stretch where you will find the American Embassy, many hotels, and expensive restaurants patronized by men and women hiding behind dark glasses day and night hoping to rekindle their lost lives and/or wheeling and dealing on their incessantly ringing cell phones. The area around Via Veneto is where many offices, stores, ministries, banks, and airlines have offices, giving it the busy feeling of Rome's business center.

(61) ALBERGO MONACO ★
Via Flavia, 84; first floor
10 rooms, none with shower or bath and toilet

It is bare-bones basic: linoleum or tile floors in simple, spotless rooms with no nicks, tears, or nightmarish colors. There aren't any private showers or toilets either, instead there are four baths and four toilets to serve ten rooms. Two sisters, Maria and Elda, have owned the Monaco since 1963 and care for it well. Maria and her family live here and her daughter, Luisa, speaks English. Everyone pitches in on a daily basis to keep the hotel going. Student groups are welcomed and meals can be prepared if requested when reserving. They take a friendly interest in their guests, but please remember that this is their home, so observe the signs that say "Silence please," and "Drunks are not allowed here." There is a midnight lockout, but since the hotel is close to the nocturnal haunts around Via Veneto, they will open the door for you if you tell them ahead of time you might be late coming back.

ENGLISH SPOKEN Yes

FACILITIES AND SERVICES None

NEAREST TOURIST ATTRACTIONS Via Veneto, Villa Borghese

TELEPHONE
06-474-4335, 481-5649

CREDIT CARDS
None, cash only

CLOSED
Never

RATES
Single L50,000, double L75,000; extra bed L35,000 per person; no breakfast served, except to groups

(62) HOTEL ALEXANDRA ★★★ ($)
Via Vittorio Veneto, 18
45 rooms, all with shower or bath and toilet

The Alexandra has managed to retain some style while yielding to the demand for color television, air-conditioned rooms, and minibars. It is on the busy Via Veneto, just down from the American Embassy. Ear-shattering automobile and motor-scooter traffic and partyers in search of *la dolce vita* surge along this famous street twenty-four hours a day. If undisturbed sleep is a priority, request a room away from the constant noise, or plan to keep the windows closed and the air-conditioning running at all times.

The comfortable rooms have enough space for guests to spread out and stay a while. The five suites, some with

TELEPHONE
06-488-1943/4/5

FAX
06-487-1804

CREDIT CARDS
AE, DC, MC, V

CLOSED
Never

RATES
Single L290,000, double L385,000, triple L475,000, suite rates on request; lower off-season and group rates; buffet breakfast included

Liberty-style furnishings, have nice bathrooms and separate sitting areas. A good choice for these upgraded rooms is No. 444, decorated in salmon and pink with wainscoting detailing the walls. The brass bed is down two steps. Room 219, on the front of the hotel, is in feminine pinks and perfect for a single traveler. There is an armoire for your clothes and a bathroom with a shower, but remember, noise will prevail unless you keep your window shut tight. Room No. 220 is the same story. Number 442 is also a single, but with the advantage of a higher location. I like the view of the tree and the original inlaid furniture. The bathroom has one mirrored wall, a corner sink, and a shower.

Breakfast is served in an interesting room with a glass-domed roof. The polished black floor mirrors it all, and thanks to fresh flowers on the yellow-clad tables, guests have the illusion of dining in an outdoor garden. Plans are afoot for a new reception area, lounge, restaurant, and elevator.

ENGLISH SPOKEN Yes

FACILITIES AND SERVICES Air-conditioning, bar, direct-dial phones, elevator, hair dryer available, minibars, parking by arrangement (L32,000–50,000 per day, depending on size of car), satellite TVs, office safe

NEAREST TOURIST ATTRACTIONS Via Veneto; twenty-minute walk to the Colosseum and Piazza Venezia

(63A) HOTEL ERCOLI ★★
Via Collina, 48
14 rooms, all with shower and toilet

TELEPHONE AND FAX
06-474-5454, 474-4063

INTERNET
www.italmarket.com/hotels/ercoli

CREDIT CARDS
MC, V

CLOSED
Never

RATES
Single L105,000, double L155,000, triple L200,000; Continental breakfast included

For Cheap Sleepers in search of the good life for less, the Hotel Ercoli offers fourteen snappy bedchambers that have been refreshed from A to Z. The color scheme is yellow and blue, the fabric matches on the curtains, headboards, and beds, the mattresses are orthopedic, and the all-new baths have stall showers, a small sink, a shelf, plus a hook. Three or four happy campers can check into No. 11, the only room with a balcony, but one or two of you should have backs strong enough to withstand sleeping on the foldout-chair beds. Breakfast is served in a formal room with round tables covered in white cloths. The desk staff, particularly the manager, Giorgio, is friendly and proud of this hotel. They should be . . . its face-lift is impressive.

ENGLISH SPOKEN Yes

FACILITIES AND SERVICES Bar, direct-dial phones, elevator, fans, hair dryers, TVs, office safe

NEAREST TOURIST ATTRACTIONS Via Veneto, Villa Borghese

(64) HOTEL MARCELLA ★★★ ($)
Via Flavia, 106
75 rooms, all with shower or bath and toilet

A new lobby has replaced the older-style garden setting with a contemporary in Roman red with a bar area to one side and a lounge with comfy sofas and armchairs on the other. Breakfast is served either on a dazzling glass-enclosed seventh-floor terrace with picture-postcard views of Rome, or on the open section to one side of it with shaded tables, attractive plantings, and a corner gazebo.

All but the first-floor rooms have been redone. The new decor is well-coordinated, with smart touches such as Napoleonic draped beds, recessed lighting, and fabric-covered walls. The immediate neighborhood is interesting for its market stalls, which sell everything from meat, cheese, fruits, and vegetables to bread and household items. Good restaurants (see *Cheap Eats in Italy*) are within easy reach. If you need to go to the American Embassy, it is eight hundred meters from the hotel door.

ENGLISH SPOKEN Yes

FACILITIES AND SERVICES Air-conditioning, bar, direct-dial phones, elevator, hair dryers, minibars, radios, satellite TVs, in-room and office safes, laundry facilities

NEAREST TOURIST ATTRACTIONS Close to U.S. Embassy; walking distance to Villa Borghese, Via Veneto

TELEPHONE
06-474-6451, toll-free from the United States (Utell) (800) 448-8355

FAX
06-481-5832

E-MAIL
info@hotelmarcella.com

INTERNET
www.hotelmarcella.com

CREDIT CARDS
AE, DC, MC, V

CLOSED
Never

RATES
Single L230,000–280,000, double L330,000, triple L420,000; lower off-season rates; buffet breakfast included

(65) HOTEL OXFORD ★★★ ($)
Via Boncompagni, 89
58 rooms, all with shower or bath and toilet

For those wanting a well-located hotel with all the amenities, the Hotel Oxford has been filling the bill for years. For night owls, the Via Veneto is close by, and for exercise enthusiasts, the Villa Borghese Gardens provide a good setting for a walk or jog. If you arrive by train, the cab ride will only be ten or fifteen minutes, depending on traffic.

Several public sitting areas and a bar offer comfortable places to relax after a day of fitting in the "must dos" of Rome. The well-lighted dining room serves a

TELEPHONE
06-428-28952

FAX
06-428-15349

E-MAIL
info@hoteloxford.com

INTERNET
www.hoteloxford.com

CREDIT CARDS
AE, DC, MC, V

CLOSED
Never

RATES
Single L210,000, double
L260,000, triple L310,000;
lower off-season rates; buffet
breakfast included

buffet breakfast and dinner. Breakfast is included with the room, but dinner is extra. The food is perfectly adequate but hardly gourmet. It can be a port in a storm, however, if you are traveling with children or are too tired to go out in the evening.

All of the rooms have been renovated in a universal all-purpose manner and provide the basics for a restful stay. The only exceptions are the rooms similar to No. 230, which are done in hideous pea green. The hotel is on the American Embassy list for personnel coming to Rome, so reservations can be tight if you wait until the last minute to make your plans.

ENGLISH SPOKEN Yes

FACILITIES AND SERVICES Air-conditioning, bar, direct-dial phones, elevator, minibars, radios, satellite TVs, office safe, restaurant serves breakfast and dinner only

NEAREST TOURIST ATTRACTIONS Via Veneto, Villa Borghese, close to U.S. Embassy

(66) HOTEL RANIERI ★★★
Via Venti Settembre, 43; second floor
47 rooms, all with shower or bath and toilet

TELEPHONE
06-481-4467
FAX
06-481-8834
E-MAIL
hotel.ranieri@italyhotel.com
INTERNET
www.venere.it/roma/ranieri
CREDIT CARDS
AE, DC, MC, V
CLOSED
Never
RATES
Single L210,000, double
L275,000, triple L330,000;
lower off-season and weekend
rates; Continental breakfast
included

I like the Ranieri, located on the second through the fifth floors of a building facing the Ministry of Defense, because it consistently offers exceptional value for my money and delivers a high standard of personalized service to its contented guests. It is the type of place that once found eliminates the need to shop for any other hotel in Rome.

From the moment you get off the elevator at the second-floor entrance, you will receive an enthusiastic and warm welcome. You are first greeted by Laura, the hospitable, Australian-born assistant manager, who is loaded with tips and suggestions on what to see and do, places to shop, and good local restaurants (see *Cheap Eats in Italy*). Carrying the welcome further are the two bellmen, brothers Carlo and Silverio, who have been with the hotel for over a quarter of a century. They are eager to help with luggage, mix a drink, or do whatever you need to smooth out your visit to Rome. To ensure that all is running well, that the maids are on their toes, and that all is spotless and well-groomed, the owner's eighty-year-old mother visits the hotel daily.

The owner of this outstanding three-star hotel, Mr. Ranieri, must lie awake nights thinking of ways to improve his up-to-the minute quarters. Absolutely no detail escapes his notice and he is not afraid to spend lavishly to provide his guests with every amenity possible. Slippers are placed next to the beds, which have fine orthopedic mattresses to ensure a good night's rest. Double-glazed windows, acoustical ceilings, and hall insulation buffer traffic and other noises, and hall air-conditioning keeps you cool and refreshed during the sizzling summers. The large-screened television sets are the best brand money can buy. Guests arriving with PCs will be able to hook up directly to the Internet through a separate international plug (which means you can leave the adapter at home) installed just for this purpose. There is abundant closet space, a private safe, and trouser presses for the men. The polished granite bathrooms are equal matches for the rooms and provide plenty of shelf space for toiletries. They even have the latest word in Swedish bidets.

There is more to come. In case you do not want to venture out for lunch or dinner, tell the desk ahead of time and a delicious three- to four-course meal will be freshly prepared and served in the dining room. In addition, hot snacks are always available in the cheerful bar, or brought to your room if you prefer.

Mr. Ranieri told me he feels he has to offer more for his guests because his hotel is on the second floor. I can't imagine what he is going to do for encores next time around—but I know he will always think of something.

ENGLISH SPOKEN Yes

FACILITIES AND SERVICES Air-conditioning, bar, direct-dial phones, elevator, hair dryers, minibars, international PC plugs and telephone line for Internet hookup, radios, satellite TVs, elevator, in-room safes, trouser press, room service for light snacks, dining room for lunch or dinner

NEAREST TOURIST ATTRACTIONS Via Veneto, opera, shopping, train station

(63B) PENSIONE TIZI ★
Via Collina, 48; first floor
18 rooms, 7 with shower or bath and toilet

Sr. Antonio has a good Cheap Sleep going with his eighteen-room abode, spread out on two floors of a building (above the Hotel Ercoli, see page 180) in a safe neighborhood about fifteen or twenty minutes from

TELEPHONE
06-474-3266, 482-0128

FAX
06-474-3266

CREDIT CARDS
None, cash only

Single L50,000 (all without
private toilet and shower),
double L80,000–100,000,
triple L120,000–230,000;
Continental breakfast
(L10,000 extra)

Termini Station. His family lives here, so expect to run into Maria Helena, Tiziana, Rosa, and Antonio over the course of your stay.

The deliberately simple, renovated double rooms feature nice wallpaper, white metal beds on tiled floors, a modern wood-finished desk, one hard chair, a wardrobe, and matching bedside tables. The singles are something else: these cell-like cubicles, facing a blank wall, are budget pads . . . period. Not recommended. If a better bathroom is a must, reserve a renovated room. The older models are okay, the furniture all matches, but the dated bathrooms are showing signs of wear and tear. Because breakfast is extra, my advice is to skip it here and mingle in a neighborhood *caffè.* For groups of twenty or more, lunch or dinner can be served if arranged at the time of booking.

ENGLISH SPOKEN Limited

FACILITIES AND SERVICES Elevator to reception, office safe

NEAREST TOURIST ATTRACTIONS Twenty-minute walk to train station, Via Veneto

Edge of Rome

It is just that, the edge of the city, appealing to those who might be driving and do not want to fight the crazy Rome traffic, and to those who don't mind a commute of at least thirty or forty minutes to most tourist attractions.

HOTEL VILLA DEL PARCO ★★★ ($)
Via Nomentana, 110
23 rooms, all with shower or bath and toilet

TELEPHONE
06-442-37773
FAX
06-442-37572
CREDIT CARDS
AE, DC, MC, V
CLOSED
Never
RATES
Single L210,000, double
L270,000, triple L360,000; 25
percent reduction on weekends
and in August; buffet breakfast
included

If you are looking for something out of the ordinary or have a car, this beautiful tranquil retreat at the edge of Rome proper is a marvelous choice. The Bernardini family villa and gardens date from 1910, and since 1958, they have been operating their home as a gracious hotel.

The hotel is lovingly appointed with tasteful, coordinated fabrics that work to enhance the mixture of family antiques with comfortable furniture. The sitting room has an heirloom grandfather clock and old-style sofas and inviting wing chairs set in cozy conversational clusters. From June through September, breakfast is served on a shaded terrace that wraps around the front and side of the hotel. In winter months, mornings begin around five nicely set tables standing on polished hardwood floors.

A winding staircase with a burnished handrail leads to the individually decorated bedrooms. Number 10, a double with a balcony, has an inlaid wooden floor complementing a handmade armoire. Number 1, another double, has pink wallpaper and a small entryway lined with prints. The pink-and-white-tiled bath has a tub with handrails and a three-tiered table for toiletries. I like No. 7 on the back for its good light, soft sofa, and stall shower. My favorite single, or small double, is No. 11, with carpet, curtains, and bedspread done in soft shades of tangerine.

Buses to the center of Rome stop by the hotel; number 62 will have you at the Vatican in thirty minutes. For motorists there is off-street parking in front of the hotel. Weekend stays mean a 25 percent reduction in the regular rates, and in August, this discount is given every day.

ENGLISH SPOKEN Yes

FACILITIES AND SERVICES Air-conditioning, bar, direct-dial phones, elevator, hair dryers, minibars, parking (L10,000 per day), radios, satellite TVs, office safe, twenty-four-hour room service for light stays, dogs accepted

NEAREST TOURIST ATTRACTIONS Nothing; must have car or use public transportation

Other Options

Apartment Rentals and Residence Hotels

Some lucky travelers require a home base for a month or more, but hotel rooms can grow very small and impersonal over a long stay. Private rentals (almost) require a legal team in back of you to deal with all the red tape, nonfunctioning plumbing, and escalating costs you are guaranteed to encounter if you rent from an individual without an organization to back you up. To circumvent these potential stress-filled pitfalls, the best choices for a long-term stay, in my opinion, is a residence hotel or a U.S.-based rental agency.

At first glance they might seem expensive, but when you consider that you have the space and comfort of an apartment, plus maid and linen service (often an extra option in a private apartment), a kitchen, parking, and other perks, it is worth the extra outlay, especially if a family or a group of three or four are involved. When you cost it out per person, it is not much more than a good hotel, and, in most cases, the longer the stay, the lower the price. In addition, if you stay a while, you will soon be living like a local, shopping with your neighbors and having your morning cappuccino at the same bar with the other regulars. You will know the butcher, the baker, and the produce man, as well as the newspaper dealer on the corner, who will save your favorite periodicals when they are running low. All in all, it gives one a real feel for the city, one you never experience from the vantage of a hotel room.

Rental Agencies

I have said many times that staying in an apartment can result in a vacation experience you will always remember, most often with great pleasure. Occasionally it can become an expensive burlesque filled with enough frustration to dampen all aspects of a pleasurable vacation. Such a situation is described below under International Services. Who needs this? No one, and certainly not the readers of these pages. On the other hand, there are wonderful exceptions I can vouch for and recommend to you. The agencies and individuals listed here have proven to deliver on their promises, keeping the care and comfort of their clients uppermost in their minds. Also see Rentals in Italy (and Elsewhere!) and Villas International (Florence, "Rental Agencies," pages 115 and 116) for apartments to rent in Rome, and before reserving any flat, please refer to "Tips on Renting an Italian Apartment," page 13.

GIRO D'ITALIA
7458 Devon Street
Philadelphia, PA 19119

The *Philadelphia Inquirer* described James Dominic of Giro d'Italia, a personalized travel counseling service designed to customize your visit to Italy, as follows, "Using a travel counselor is like hiring a personal tailor. You won't go naked without one, but if you want the vacation to fit like a fine Italian suit, he is worth the money." James begins his service with a one-hour in-depth telephone interview to assess your travel dreams and desires. Once you decide to have him plan your trip, the cost will be $75 per hour. When you figure this against the cost of the entire trip and the benefits you will have . . . you will probably echo the sentiments of the *Philadelphia Inquirer.*

TELEPHONE
(215) 248-2570

FAX
(215) 248-1919

E-MAIL
ciaociro@aol.com

CREDIT CARDS
None, cash or check only

RATES
First hour telephone interview to assess client's needs and wishes is free. Every hour thereafter is $75. Average trip planning is around $375.

(67) INTERNATIONAL SERVICES USA, INC
Via del Babuino, 79 (Spanish Steps)

The advertisement for International Services in the English Yellow Pages for Rome promises "castles in the sky or villas in the vineyard." It should say "pie in the sky and clients in the lurch." Amazing, but true, this outfit continues to be open for business, but it is hard to understand how or why.

TELEPHONE
06-360-00018/9

FAX
06-360-00037

CREDIT CARDS
None, cash in advance

RATES
Vary with each rental

When planning a trip, often it is more important to know ahead of time about the pitfalls and problems that can otherwise ruin a dream vacation. If you only get one valuable piece of information from *Cheap Sleeps in Italy,* let it be this: *Absolutely NEVER use International Services to lease an apartment or villa anyplace on this planet.*

I dealt with this company exclusively over a four-month trip to Italy and it was a total disaster. Up front they are helpful, making all kinds of promises. In reality they deliver very little other than massive headaches for their clients. Upon the client's arrival, they exit the job and leave the client alone to deal with problems, which *will* occur. The Italian landlords, provided you can even find them, seldom speak English, and certainly not when you need help with something that is malfunctioning in their rental. They seem to be unavailable for anything but collecting your money and deposit in advance. You could be faced with freezing cold or blistering hot flats located up shadowy stairways and behind creaking doors, where nothing works except you, trying to open and shut the windows, operate ancient plumbing, and keep the wiring from blowing up. In addition, you may find no sheets, towels, or maid service as agreed upon and paid for in advance, as well as filthy quarters with the owner's dirty clothes, trash, and spoiled food sitting around. It only gets worse. On top of all this you will be charged hefty deposits and then, should you dare ask about the return of your deposit after the agreed-upon waiting period, expect nothing but returned letters and refused phone calls, until you're finally forced to take legal action. This is an international service creating a nightmare from travel hell that no one needs, least of all you. Avoid them, please!

RENTAL DIRECTORIES INTERNATIONAL
2044 Rittenhouse Square
Philadelphia, PA 19103

TELEPHONE
(215) 985-4001

FAX
(215) 985-0302

E-MAIL
Rentdirect@aol.com

CREDIT CARDS
MC, V accepted for the purchase of the directory only ($40 plus $3 shipping); all rentals in cash only

RATES
Depends on the owner; when renting payment is requested in the currency indicated in the property listing

Many people are now arranging their vacations to include renting apartments or homes abroad for stays that range from a week to a year or more. Sometimes trying to arrange this through foreign real estate agents takes red tape and confusion with Byzantine Italian landlord rights and laws to new levels. If you are interested in a home rental abroad for stays of a week or more and want to avoid the middleman, consider handling it yourself. This is *not* a house-exchange program, but one in which you thumb through a directory, select a property, and get in touch directly with the owner to make all the arrangements for your stay. The only additional cost to you is the directory for the area you wish to visit. Directories are updated yearly and come out in the fall. Rates for the properties depend on individual owners and what they offer. You can generally count on savings of between 30 to 60 percent over what you would pay if you went through an agency.

NOTE: Now working with Helen London and Rental Directories International is James Dominic's Giro d'Italia, a personalized travel counseling service designed to customize your visit to Italy (see page 187).

Residence Hotels

(68) MAYFAIR RESIDENCE
Via Sicilia, 183 (Via Veneto)
41 apartments, all with shower or bath and toilet

Via Veneto is one of Rome's most expensive addresses, and the Mayfair Residence is about a twenty-minute walk from this tree-lined boulevard. Unless you know what to look for, you will pass right by the Mayfair, as it is in a very nondescript building with only a brass plaque noting its name. Once inside, that all changes. This apartment hotel offers attractive, large studios and one-bedroom units for those who are staying longer in Rome and need more space than normal hotel rooms provide. The quarters on the first two floors have their own terraces. All are fully fitted and have maid service, nice furnishings, good bathrooms, and more closet space than many of us have in our own homes. If you are not inspired to get busy early in the morning in the well-stocked kitchen, a Continental breakfast is served.

As with other residence hotels, the longer the stay, the better the rates.

ENGLISH SPOKEN Yes

FACILITIES AND SERVICES Air-conditioning, bar, direct-dial phones, elevator, hair dryers, radios, satellite TVs, fully equipped kitchens, in-room safes, meeting rooms, maid service (Monday through Saturday)

NEAREST TOURIST ATTRACTIONS Via Veneto, Villa Borghese Gardens

TELEPHONE
06-428-20481, 428-14887

FAX
06-428-15753

CREDIT CARDS
AE, DC, MC, V

CLOSED
Never

RATES
Studios for one to two persons start at L275,000 per day including all taxes; breakfast included; discounts for longer stays

(42) PALAZZO AL VELABRO
Via del Velabro, 16 ((Trastevere)
35 rooms, all with shower or bath and toilet

For first-timers it may be difficult to find, but once there, you will agree that the accommodations are exceptional. The Palazzo al Velabro sits on the Piazza Bocca della Verità, facing the Palatino Hill, the Arc of Giano, and the Temple of Vesta.

The spacious, comfortable studios and apartments have modern furnishings, kitchens large enough for some serious cooking, excellent closet space, and enviable bathrooms with sink space, enclosed showers and tubs, and plenty of towels. Maid service is included. The drawback is that the studios on the first three floors face a wall that in some instances is so high you cannot see the sky. Be sure to ask for something on the fourth or

TELEPHONE
06-679-2758, 679-2985, 679-3450 (can also call Villas International, see page 116)

FAX
06-679-3790

E-MAIL
velabro@venere.it

CREDIT CARDS
AE, DC, MC, V

CLOSED
Never

RATES
Studios for one to two persons
L250,000–270,000, doubles
(up to three persons) start at
L330,000; extra bed L50,000;
extra cot L35,000; all taxes
included; minimum seven-
night stay; discounts for month
stays or longer; breakfast
L15,000 extra

fifth floors if you want a view. Number 35, for instance, looks out at the Palatino Hill.

The residence is quite a walk from shops, an important point if you are setting up housekeeping for any length of time. However, if you have a car, this will not be a problem—only the hairy Rome traffic will be. There also is good bus service across the Tiber River to Trastevere, where there are many shopping possibilities. The minimum stay is seven days. This residence can be booked through Villas International (see page 116), which is located in San Francisco.

ENGLISH SPOKEN Yes

FACILITIES AND SERVICES Air-conditioning, bar, direct-dial phones, elevator, hair dryers, radios, satellite TVs, fully equipped kitchens, free parking, office safe, trouser press, laundry service, maid service

NEAREST TOURIST ATTRACTIONS Trastevere, Colosseum, Forum

(16) RESIDENZA DI RIPETTA
Via di Ripetta, 231 (Piazza del Popolo)
70 studios and apartments, all with shower or bath and toilet

TELEPHONE
06-323-1144
FAX
06-320-3959
E-MAIL
info@ripetta.it
CREDIT CARDS
AE, DC, MC, V
CLOSED
Never
RATES
Studios for one or two start at
L4,200,000 per month, plus 10
percent tax; lower rates for
longer stays

The Residenza di Ripetta has been my home away from home during my Rome visits, and, as always, from beginning to end, my stays have been wonderful. I like returning year after year to greet the same reception and office staff and saying hello to the hardworking maids. Everyone always goes out of their way to be helpful, not only to me but to every other guest, some of whom came to stay for a short time and have never left.

The Residenza is housed in a seventeenth-century former convent a block or so down from the Piazza del Popolo. Its exceptional apartments vary in size from large studios to two-level units. Every extra imaginable is offered, including a coffee and cocktail bar, twenty-four-hour concierge, roof garden, garage, and meeting rooms. The furnishings are modern, the closets tremendous, the kitchens fully equipped, and the marble, mirrored bathrooms well lighted, with shelf space and good towels. Taxis are a whistle away, there is a metro stop at the Piazza del Popolo, and excellent bus service zips right by the front door. Many outstanding restaurants are close by (see *Cheap Eats in Italy*), and you will be a short walk away from the best shopping in Rome.

ENGLISH SPOKEN Yes

FACILITIES AND SERVICES Air-conditioning, bar, direct-dial phones, elevator, fully equipped kitchens, hair dryers, locked garage parking, in-room safes, satellite TVs, roof garden, maid service, laundry and cleaning service, meeting rooms

NEAREST TOURIST ATTRACTIONS Piazza del Popolo, shopping, Spanish Steps, Tiber River

(10) RESIDENCE VIALE
Via Capo d'Africa, 7 (Colosseum/Forum)
6 apartments, fully equipped

The six apartments are new and modern in tone. The largest two come with their own terrace, but all six have white walls, hardwood floors, glass-topped tables, excellent closets, and tiled bathrooms with a shower. They also both have a separate fully equipped kitchen and bedroom—a real bonus if you have children and need to put them to bed early. Down the street is a morning vegetable market, and for other housekeeping needs, small shops close by where you can buy whatever you need. If you are not cooking, there are neighborhood restaurants (see *Cheap Eats in Italy*). The underground stop is less than fifteen minutes away and bus connections are even closer. Convenience extras for most guests are the laundry facilities, fax, daily maid service during the week, and twice-weekly linen changes.

ENGLISH SPOKEN Yes

FACILITIES AND SERVICES Air-conditioning, direct-dial phones, fax service, elevator, fax, satellite TVs, maid service Monday through Friday, laundry

NEAREST TOURIST ATTRACTIONS Colosseum, Forum

TELEPHONE
06-704-52089

FAX
06-700-5897

CREDIT CARDS
AE, MC, V

CLOSED
Never

RATES
All rates include taxes and are calculated based on the size of the apartment; one bedroom L220,000 per night, larger one bedroom with terrace L285,000 per night; lower rates after one month

---

Bed-and-Breakfasts

(69) BED & BREAKFAST ITALIA
Palazzo Sforza Cesarini, Corso Vittorio Emanuele II, 282

Bed & Breakfast Italia has jumped onto the rapidly growing bandwagon of homestay—or bed-and-breakfast—accommodations. With more than 1,000 different apartments or houses in Italy offering 2,500 housing options that range from a simple room with a shared family bathroom to your own castle, chances are excellent they will have something for you, whatever your budget or needs may be. In Rome, their offerings run the

TELEPHONE
06-687-8618

FAX
06-687-8619

E-MAIL
md4095@mclink.it

INTERNET
www.bbitalia.it

CREDIT CARDS
AE, MC, V

CLOSED
Never

RATES
Single from L105,000, double
from L175,000 (two-night
minimum)

gamut from a big room in a suburban apartment to a great loft in Trastevere or a Scandinavian modern penthouse flat with a wraparound terrace and views that never end. All the accommodations are graded from two to four crowns. A two-crown site will be a room and shared bath with your host, three crowns means you will have your own bathroom, and four means luxury. The host has to meet certain standards laid out in a "Hospitality Charter" that ensure each guest will receive the best service possible. The charter includes, among other things, being treated as a friend of the host and having a cup of coffee or tea offered upon arrival. To be assured of the best experience in this type of Cheap Sleep, be sure to state your needs (such as no smoking) and requirements very clearly before booking. The minimum stay is two days, but you can stretch that to forever if you wish. English is spoken in the booking office, but otherwise it depends on your host.

CASA STEFAZIO
Via della Marcigliana, 553 (outside Rome)
4 rooms, 1 suite, all with shower or bath and toilet

TELEPHONE
06-8712-0042

FAX
06-8712-0012

CREDIT CARDS
None, cash only

CLOSED
Jan–Mar

RATES
Single $140, double $180, suite
$220; breakfast included; one-
half total payment required as
deposit, balance due upon
arrival

A reader writes: "The minute we walked into the house we felt we were visiting family (except that they won't let you do any work) and I will always consider this to be my home in Italy. Stefania was wonderful regarding ideas for sightseeing and Orazio's cooking was magnificent. Leaving to come home was very difficult indeed."

This *Cheap Sleeps in Italy* reader shares my enthusiasm: Casa Stefazio is not only absolutely wonderful, but it ranks as the best one I have seen abroad . . . period. Even if this sort of accommodation has never appealed to you before, Casa Stefazio will change your mind, because a stay here is truly a special experience you will always treasure. As you can see, every guest who walks in for the first time feels immediately at home and leaves as a friend.

Several years ago when the last of their children left the nest, Orazio and Stefania Azzola decided to sell their beautiful Tuscan-style home. But when it came right down to doing it, they realized they loved living here and hated the thought of leaving. Many American friends encouraged them to stay and open their home as a bed-and-breakfast. They did. The result is Casa Stefazio, which bears as much resemblance to a normal bed-and-breakfast as a Rolls Royce does to a bicycle. Come once and you will not consider vacationing anywhere else in Italy.

The home is located about thirty minutes from central Rome in a quiet compound of private residences surrounded by rolling countryside and beautiful gardens. Tennis courts and a swimming pool at a private club are within walking distance. A horseback-riding stable is across the road. If you do not have your own car (which you should seriously consider renting if you stay here), there is local bus service and taxis can be called. The spacious guest rooms are as attractively furnished and appointed as the rest of the house. Each has a private bathroom and is air-conditioned. One is a two-room suite with a private living room, its own sauna, and a separate entrance. If you do not like steps, ask for the Pink Room on the ground floor. The Blue Room is just right for one, and if you want a television set, ask Stefania and she will have it for you.

Both Orazio and Stefania speak perfect English and love people. They have traveled extensively and spend part of each year in the United States. Naturally, they have many, many friends. Orazio is a Cordon Bleu chef and Stefania, a native-born Roman, is a virtual encyclopedia of knowledge about her city. They both do everything possible to make their guests feel at home by serving breakfast either in your own room or in their kitchen. At sunset, you will be invited to join them on the terrace, or beside the roaring fire, for a glass of wine and Orazio's delicious appetizers. If you want him to prepare dinner, just say so the night before and they will set a place for you at their table. Orazio will conduct cooking classes if there are enough requests.

They go even further by personally conducting deluxe six- and ten-day guided tours starting in Rome and continuing along the Amalfi Coast to Positano, Capri, Pompeii, and Tuscany—including Florence and Siena. The ten-day trip starts along the Appian Way, goes on to Florence, Siena, and Venice, then heads back to Villa d'Este and Tivoli. These tours are so popular that reservations are required at least three months in advance. The tours are for a maximum of seven or eight persons and everything but airfare to Italy, hotel extras, and a few lunches is included (six-day trip: $2,800 per person; ten-day: $4,500 for person). They can also customize their tours to the needs and interests of a group of friends traveling together. In my opinion, the tours are knock-outs, even if you have already been to these places before. With Orazio and Stefania as your guides, you will see them anew.

The Azzolas state on their brochure, "Please allow us to exceed your expectations." I can assure you, they will . . . by far.

ENGLISH SPOKEN Yes

FACILITIES AND SERVICES Air-conditioning, bar, minibars, free parking, satellite TVs, dinner available ($35 per person, including wine), airport transfers ($100, minimum of three persons), no smoking allowed, no pets

NEAREST TOURIST ATTRACTIONS None within walking distance

VILLA DELROS
(outside Rome)
2 suites and 2 singles

TELEPHONE AND FAX
06-336-78402

CREDIT CARDS
AE, MC, V accepted, but cash preferred

CLOSED
Jan–Mar

RATES
Single $50, double $150; large breakfast included; dinner on request ($30 per person, includes wine)

Readers of *Cheap Sleeps in Italy* who have stayed at Rosmarie Diletti's lovely Hotel Venezia (see page 167) will be pleased to know that after turning over the reins of the hotel to her son and daughter, she found retirement did not suit her. Always the consummate business-woman eager for a new challenge, she decided to turn part of her country estate on the edge of Rome into a very exclusive bed-and-breakfast.

Welcome to Villa Delros, *un mondo di sojni* (a world of dreams).

Discerning guests who appreciate the beauty of stay-ing in a peaceful country villa not far from the center of Rome will never forget their sojourn at Villa Delros, and will probably spend a good portion of their stay plotting their return. Set amongst the rolling hills surrounding Rome, the magnificent villa provides guests with a rare look inside the art-filled home Sra. Diletti built a quar-ter of a century ago. Over the years she has collected priceless pieces of museum-quality furniture, paintings, and artifacts. The expansive grounds serve as the perfect backdrop for her beautiful plants and flowers. Guests are invited to enjoy the terraces, the swimming pool, or strolling through the grounds.

The two suites and two single rooms in the main house are all lavishly furnished with Rosmarie's beauti-ful antiques and paintings. The air-conditioned suites have a bedroom with one large bed that can be divided into twins, a sitting room with a comfortable sofa, chairs, and worktable, and a dressing room. The beautiful baths have both a tub and shower and are fully stocked with toiletries. The single rooms are without air-conditioning, but have the added advantage of a small kitchen corner. The bathrooms are lovely, one with a shower, the other with hand-painted ceramics and a tub. A wonderful breakfast is, of course, included, and upon request, Rosmarie will prepare dinner for her guests, probably using whatever herbs and vegetables she can from her gardens. For motorists, there is free parking. Public transportation is about a ten-minute trip by car, and can be provided for guests without their own cars.

ENGLISH SPOKEN Yes

FACILITIES AND SERVICES Air-conditioned suites, direct-dial phones, hair dryers, free parking, satellite TVs, safe in the house, swimming pool, free transport from the villa to public transportation, dinner on request

NEAREST TOURIST ATTRACTIONS None, must use public transportation

Camping

Yes, you can camp in Rome. You can rent tents or cabins, but in the tents, you will have to bring your own camp stove. The locations require long bus rides with transfers to get into central Rome, but the prices are cheap, so for some, the savings may be worth the trek back and forth to civilization.

The Federazione Italiana del Campeggio, also called Federcampeggio, issues a free list of campgrounds in Italy and a map. Write to them at Calenzano, Florence 50041, or call 055-882-391.

CAPITOL CAMPGROUND
Via Castel Fusano, 195 (outside Rome)

The Capitol has its own swimming pool and tennis courts and is a few train stops from the beach at Ostia and near the ancient ruins of the Roman seaport Ostia Antica. To get to central Rome, allow an hour via train and metro or bus. It is open year-round. The reception desk is open daily from 7 A.M. to 11 P.M.

ENGLISH SPOKEN Limited
TELEPHONE 06-565-7344
FAX 06-565-2143
CREDIT CARDS None, cash only

CLOSED Never

RATES L12,500 per person; L12,000 per tent, L7,000 per car, L14,000 per person in a caravan; showers L1,000

FABULOUS
Via C. Colombo (outside Rome)

The eighteen-kilometer distance from Rome is not fabulous, but in the dog days of August, the three swimming pools (open June to September) might be. This campground is open year-round, and a bus that will take you to the Eurfermi metro stop comes by every fifteen minutes. There is a bar and market, and the showers will cost you L800.

ENGLISH SPOKEN Limited

FACILITIES AND SERVICES One pool for children, two for adults, tennis courts, pizzeria for dinner, convenience market

TELEPHONE 06-525-9354

FAX 06-525-9854

CREDIT CARDS AE, DC, MC, V

CLOSED Never

RATES Campers L12,000 for the camper and L12,000 per person, tents L8,000 for the tent, L12,000 per person (includes electricity), car L8,000, L800 for a shower

FLAMINIA
Via Flaminia Nuova, 821 (outside Rome)

This campsite has cabins with private showers and a swimming pool, plus a market, a restaurant, a disco, a bar, and coin-operated washers. It's open from March to October, with twenty-four-hour reception. To get here (about eight kilometers from Rome), take bus 910 from the train station to Piazza Mancini, then transfer to 200. Get off on Via Flaminia Nuova when you see the Philips building.

ENGLISH SPOKEN Sometimes

TELEPHONE 06-333-2604

CREDIT CARDS MC, V

CLOSED Nov–Feb

RATES Tents L7,000, plus L12,000 per person; cabins L60,000 per night for two people

NOMENTANO
Via della Cesarina (outside Rome)

Located eight kilometers from Rome, it is open from Easter until the end of October. Advance reservations are not necessary. On-site is a bar, a cafeteria, and a market. Campers also have access to a pool and tennis courts.

To get there, from the train station take bus 36 to Piazza Sempoine, where you catch bus 337. Ask the driver to let you off on Via Nomentano.

ENGLISH SPOKEN Limited
TELEPHONE AND FAX 06-41-40-02-96
CREDIT CARDS AE, MC, V
CLOSED Oct–Easter
RATES Tents L5,000, plus L9,500 per person; cabins L25,000 per person

ROMA CAMPING
Via Aurelia, 831 (outside Rome)

The advantage here is that it is open year-round and is as close as camping gets to the Vatican. Showers, a bar and snack bar (from March to November), and sightseeing tours are part of the package. A swimming pool is not. Someone is at the desk twenty-four hours a day, but they take cash only; plastic is out. Prices start at L12,000 per person, electricity included, with spaces for vans, trailers, and cars as well as basic tents.

ENGLISH SPOKEN Yes
TELEPHONE 06-662-8863
FAX 06-664-18147
CREDIT CARDS None, cash only
CLOSED Never
RATES L14,000 per person in a tent, electricity included; cars L7,000, vans L11,000, caravans L12,000

SEVEN HILLS
Via Cassia, 1216 (outside Rome)

This campsite has the most going for it: beautiful grounds with peacocks, swans, goats, deer, and rabbits, and creature comfort extras that include a swimming pool, disco, bar, market, and pizzeria. A daily shuttle bus goes to central Rome at 9:30 A.M. and returns at either 1:30 or 5:30 P.M. (L6,000). After a five-day stay, there is a 10 percent discount, showers are free, and so are children up to age five. There are no credit cards accepted, but they do have a money-changing office. If your idea of camping is a hotel without room service, they have bungalows with kitchens, and you can provide your own room service.

ENGLISH SPOKEN Yes
FACILITIES AND SERVICES Bar, supermarket, pizzeria,

pool, barbecue, laundry, medical service, disco, money exchange, free showers

TELEPHONE 06-303-62751, 303-10826

FAX 06-303-10039

CREDIT CARDS None, cash only

CLOSED Never

RATES Per person charge per day, L12,500, children under four free; tent L9,000; motorcycle L4,000, car 7,000, caravan L14,000, camper L16,000, mobile homes for two without toilet or kitchen L80,000, for 4 persons with toilet and kitchen L120,000; bungalows for two with kitchen and toilet L110,000; extra person L40,000; bus service to Rome L6,000 per person round-trip. Sheets, blankets, hot showers, and electricity are free.

TIBER
Via Tiberina (outside Rome)

They have high- and low-season rates, and are open for campers from March until the end of November. Here you can drink at the bar, shop at their market, swim in the pool, and eat in the restaurant-pizzeria. A shuttle will transport you 1½ kilometers to the metro, which will take you to Rome, another fifteen kilometers away.

ENGLISH SPOKEN Yes

TELEPHONE 06-336-12314, 336-10733

FAX 06-336-12314

CREDIT CARDS MC, V

CLOSED Nov–Feb

RATES All rates are per person, per day: tent L6,000–8,000, car L6,000, caravan L9,500, camper van L10,000, mobile home L14,000; lower off-season rates

---

Jubilee Year 2000 Pilgrimage to Rome

CENTRAL OFFICES TO HANDLE THE PILGRIMAGES–JUBILEE YEAR 2000

The year 2000 not only marks the beginning of the twenty-first century, but the Jubilee Year in Rome, when the Holy Door is opened to pilgrims around the world. This very revered event happens every twenty-five years and draws millions of pilgrims who come to pray, take part in the year-long series of events, and hope to find accommodations. Reservations are made years in advance. To deal with the tidal wave of visitors, Rome officials are not only relaxing some of the excruciatingly involved hoops hotel owners need to jump through to expand, but talking tent cities, and predicting that people will be housed hundreds of miles outside of Rome and bussed in. It has the potential of becoming a zoo. I asked several hotel owners what they were going to do, and most of them said, "Nothing. We are not anxious to house these pilgrims because many of them are very poor and cannot pay Rome hotel prices." Others were taking advantage of the low-cost loans and spiffing up their properties with the idea of charging whatever the market will bear. If you are part of a group, or an individual planning on a Holy Roman pilgrimage in the year 2000, these two offices can provide you with information to help you plan your trip. They also have a list of convents both near and far from the Vatican that will be able to accommodate pilgrims.

(48) CENTRO ASSISTENZA PASTORALE
St. Peter's Square, Piazza Pio XII, 4 (Vatican)

This office, also known as the Vatican Office in Charge of Pilgrims Staying in Religious Homes, is a good place to begin your search for a Holy Hotel anytime, not only for 2000. Open year-round Monday to Friday from 9 A.M. to 6 P.M., and Saturday until 1 P.M., it provides assistance in booking guides, excursions, hotels, and restaurants. They prefer to do packages for church groups, but will consider lone pilgrims if you come through your church. The fee depends on how much the office does for you.

ENGLISH SPOKEN Yes

TELEPHONE
06-698-84896
FAX
06-698-85617
CREDIT CARDS
None, cash only
CLOSED
Sun
RATES
Depends on services rendered and site selected

(55) OPERA ROMANA PELLEGRIMAGGI
Via della Pigna, 13-A (Vatican)

This organization publishes a list of convents in Rome for pilgrims, and someone in the office usually speaks English, but you can't count on that with the nuns in the convents. Send a fax for information and state where in Rome you would like to be housed. Close in, they have accommodations near the Vatican and the Spanish Steps.

TELEPHONE
06-69-501
FAX
06-699-40717

Holy Hotels

Convents, monasteries, and religious institutions provide spartan accommodations to travelers who do not mind austere surroundings (with a few exceptions), out-of-the-way locations (again with exceptions), and lockouts by 11 P.M. Prices are not always as low as the surroundings suggest, but these are very safe places to stay and many provide meals at nominal cost. Making arrangements by mail can be very frustrating. Many places simply do not answer because they are too busy, and showing up on the spot is risky. Your best bet is to telephone or fax for your reservations as far in advance as possible. Some English is usually spoken, but of course Italian will get you much further. Mentioning your priest or bishop will not hurt either. Note: Also see Centro Assistenza Pastorale and Opera Romana Pellegrimaggi, under "Jubilee Year," page 199.

The following list is by no means exhaustive, but it should get you started.

(1) CASA DI SANTA BRIGIDA
Piazza Farnese, 96 (Campo de' Fiori)
22 rooms, all with shower or bath and toilet

TELEPHONE
06-688-92596, 688-92497

FAX
06-688-91573

E-MAIL
brigida@mclinik.it

INTERNET
www.brigidine.org

CREDIT CARDS
None, cash only

CLOSED
Never

RATES
Single L150,000, double L250,000; breakfast included; lunch or dinner around L30,000 per person, per meal

Definitely one of the most central and most expensive of the Holy Hotels, Santa Brigida is just next to Campo de' Fiori, which puts you in the center of tourist Rome. Inside, it has the atmosphere of an elegant and aristocratic home filled with lovely furniture. Santa Brigida takes guests of every age, nationality, and creed. There is a small church for those who wish to attend the Sisters' liturgical worships. On the first floor are the three rooms in which St. Bridget lived and where she died in 1373. Full-board, half-board, or just bed-and-breakfast plans are available. Each room has a bath or shower, toilet, central heat, and a direct-dial telephone. You can forget about television and CNN broadcasts. This is an extremely popular place and reservations are required as far in advance as possible. To reserve, telephone directly. They told me they do not answer letters because they do not have time. Singles pay more than two people sharing a room, so keep this in mind.

NOTE: Rome has two other residential guest homes run by the same order of nuns. Both are far from the center, I've included them here just in case that does not matter to you: Suore di S. Brigida, Via delle Isole, 34, tel: 06-841-4393, 841-7251; Suore di S. Brigida, Via Cassia, 2040, tel: 06-378-0272.

ENGLISH SPOKEN Yes

FACILITIES AND SERVICES Direct-dial phones, elevator, full- and half-board available

NEAREST TOURIST ATTRACTIONS Campo de' Fiori, Piazza Navona, Pantheon, Piazza Venezia

(49) FRANCISCAN SISTERS OF THE ATONEMENT
Via Monte del Gallo, 105 (Vatican)
25 rooms, all with private shower and toilet

This is near Vatican City, and there will be some walking up and down hills required to get to where you are going and then back again. There is an 11 P.M. lockout.

ENGLISH SPOKEN Yes

FACILITIES AND SERVICES Air-conditioning in three loft rooms that are up ten steps; elevator to the third floor

NEAREST TOURIST ATTRACTIONS Vatican, Vatican Museum

TELEPHONE
06-630-7820

FAX
06-638-6149

CREDIT CARDS
None, cash only

CLOSED
Dec 15–Jan 7

RATES
Single L65,000, double L55,000 per person; breakfast included; dinner L20,000 per person

(23) FRATERNA DOMUS
Via dell' Cancello, 9 (at Via di Monte Brianzo, 62)
(Spanish Steps)
15 rooms, all with shower or bath and toilet

If the Holy Hotel route appeals to you, this is a great choice, and frankly my favorite. The smoke-free rooms are simple, fitted with a table, an armoire, a religious picture, and twin (no double) beds. The food is wonderful, and the Sisters warm-spirited, friendly, and welcoming. It is located close to the Tiber River, near Piazza Nicosia and the Spanish Steps. The small church, St. Lucia, is beautiful, inspired by St. Francis d'Assisi, with original mosaic floors that date from the Middle Ages. The ceiling was done in the 1800s by a Polish painter, and the original stained-glass backdrop by the altar dates from the 1400s. The church is run by the Sisters and Mass is held on Sundays at 11 A.M. Even if you do not want to stay with the Sisters, please consider coming for lunch or dinner (see *Cheap Eats in Italy*). Lunch is served at 1 P.M. and costs in the neighborhood of L30,000 per person, wine extra, and dinner is at 7:30 P.M., same price. The food is served family style and there is no choice of dishes. They are closed on Thursdays. Please call ahead to reserve. There is no smoking allowed in the rooms and the lockout is at 11 P.M.

TELEPHONE
06-688-02727, 688-05475

FAX
06-683-2691

CREDIT CARDS
None, cash only

CLOSED
Never

RATES
Single L70,000, double L95,000; breakfast included; lunch or dinner L30,000 per person

ENGLISH SPOKEN Yes

FACILITIES AND SERVICES Lunch and dinner served, office safe

NEAREST TOURIST ATTRACTIONS Tiber River, Spanish Steps, excellent shopping

(31) SUORE DI NOSTRA SIGNORA DI LOURDES
Via Sistina, 113 (Spanish Steps)
17 rooms, 11 with shower and toilet

TELEPHONE
06-474-5324
FAX
06-474-1422
CREDIT CARDS
None, cash only
CLOSED
Never
RATES
Single L60,000–70,000, double L60,000–65,000 per person

There is no English spoken, period, at this Holy Hotel in the shadow of the Spanish Steps. The curfew is 10:30 P.M. In theory, office hours are from about 9 A.M. to 6 P.M., but the office is shut tightly between 12:30 to 1:30 P.M. while the Sisters have lunch, and at other times it is difficult to get anyone's attention. The singles share baths, but some of the doubles and triples have their own.

ENGLISH SPOKEN None

FACILITIES AND SERVICES None

NEAREST TOURIST ATTRACTIONS Spanish Steps, Via Veneto, shopping

(11) SUORE DI SAN GIUSEPPE DI CLUNY
Via Angelo Poliziano, 38 (Colosseum/Forum)
20 rooms, 9 with shower and toilet

TELEPHONE AND FAX
06-487-2837/8
CREDIT CARDS
None, cash only
CLOSED
Never
RATES
Single L65,000–74,000, double L120,000–135,000; group rates L70,000 per person, half-pension, L80,000 per person full-pension; all rates include breakfast; meals L25,000 extra per person, per meal; children under three are free, from three to ten, 50 percent off

If you want to brush up on your French during your stay in Rome, here is a good place to do it, as most of the Sisters speak French but virtually no English. There is a pretty chapel here and a garden. No single men are allowed, but women, couples, and families are welcomed. It is a popular Holy Hotel, so get your request in for a bed at least three to four months in advance. Three meals a day are served, but only breakfast (served Monday to Saturday, never on Sunday or holidays) is included in the rate.

ENGLISH SPOKEN Limited, but the Sisters speak French

FACILITIES AND SERVICES None

NEAREST TOURIST ATTRACTIONS Colosseum, Forum

(59) SUORE DOROTEE
Via del Gianicolo, 4 (Vatican)

TELEPHONE
06-688-03349
FAX
06-688-03311
CREDIT CARDS
None, cash only

Halfway up Janiculum Hill above Vatican City, the Suore Dorotee is in a quiet spot with a pretty garden near the North American College, where many Americans study for the priesthood. Climbing up and down some hills will be required. Curfew is at 10:30 P.M., only some of the rooms have private bathrooms, and a few of the Sisters speak English. They do not answer written requests for accommodations.

ENGLISH SPOKEN Limited

RATES
Prices start at L80,000 per person with breakfast and either lunch or dinner

(60) SUORE TEATINE
Salita Monte del Gallo, 25 (Vatican)

As with the other Vatican Holy Hotels, be sure you can climb a hill if you stay here.

TELEPHONE 06-637-4084, 637-4653

FAX 06-393-79050

RATES L75,000 per person for bed and breakfast; L20,000 extra per meal for pensione plan

Student Accommodations

Low-cost short-term (i.e., tourist) student housing does exist in theory in Rome, but nailing it down may take some doing. It is important to know that these facilities are open to visiting students only when the regular Italian students are away on summer vacation or during other vacation periods of the year. The accommodations are far from luxurious. Most are beds in dorms that sleep anywhere from two to ten people. Plan on bringing your own soap and towels, although sheets and blankets are usually available at a nominal cost. Many sites are far from the action in Rome, but the prices are right. Always call ahead to see if you qualify and if there is space before making the long trek. Bring cash; credit cards are never accepted. English is not a problem— someone always knows enough to help you.

NOTE: A membership in the International Youth Hostel Federation (IYHF) opens the door to many inexpensive dormitory accommodations in youth hostels and other student lodgings. It is possible to buy the card onsite at some places, but it is much more convenient to have it already. The IYHF membership is available from American Youth Hostels, P.O. Box 37613, Washington, D.C., 20013-7613; tel: (202) 783-6161.

(70) CENTRO TURISTICO STUDENTESCOE
GIOVANILE (CTS)
Via Genova, 16 (central Rome)

This Italian student organization helps student tourists find dorm lodgings, book transportation, hook up with inexpensive tours, and generally get plugged into the student Cheap Sleeping and traveling groove.

TELEPHONE 06-462-0431
FAX 06-46-204326
E-MAIL ctsinfo@cts.it
INTERNET www.cts.it
RATES Vary according to the establishment

CENTRO UNIVERSITARIO MARIANUM
Via Matteo Boiardo, 30 (outskirts of Rome)
96 rooms, 4 with shower and toilet, around 45 with shower only

These lodgings are oriented toward student travelers.

FACILITIES AND SERVICES Lift, chapel, open 6:30 A.M. to midnight, lockout at midnight, TV and VCR in lounge, dining room for meals, thirty minutes by bus to central Rome
TELEPHONE 06-700-5453
FAX 06-772-09466
CLOSED Aug
RATES Single L50,000; lunch or dinner L20,000 extra per meal

(71) ENJOY ROME
Via Varese, 39 (central Rome)

This student company has many services, including accommodation help.

TELEPHONE 06-445-1843
FAX 06-445 0734

INTERNATIONAL YOUTH HOSTEL (OSTELLO DE LA GIOVENTIA FORO ITALICO)
Via delle Olimpiadi, 61 (outskirts of Rome)

Because this hostel is part of IYHF, it can offer better value and consistent, safe, accommodations.

FACILITIES AND SERVICES Three-day minimum stay in 334 beds, some with wheelchair access; dorm rooms; no showers, but hall shower included in price; open 7 to 9 A.M. and 2 to 11 P.M.; lockout at midnight with no use of rooms during day
TELEPHONE 06-323-6267
FAX 06-324-2613
RATES L30,000 per person with an International Youth Hostel Federation (IYHF) card

(58) SAN LORENZO YOUTH CENTER
Via Pfeiffer, 24 (Vatican)

TELEPHONE
06-698-85332
FAX
06-698-85095

First you have to find it! Face the Vatican and walk up the left side of Via della Conciliazione. When you come to Via Pfeiffer, turn left and go to the end, about a block. The San Lorenzo Youth Center is on your right. That said, there were whispers during my last check that a change could be possible. To avoid a trip for nothing, call before you go and double-check on the address.

The purpose of this Catholic youth center, founded by a German bishop in 1983, is to enable young people from around the world to meet, talk about their faith, and participate in Catholic services in the chapel. In addition to the religious aspect of the organization, the center provides information about tourist Rome, can get tickets for papal audiences, and helps with places to stay—chiefly in pensiones and religious retreats. There is no charge for any of their services. The young, multilingual international staff is friendly and delightful. They are open Monday to Saturday from 11 A.M. to 7 P.M. and Sunday from 3 to 7 P.M. Mass is offered at 6 P.M. daily, and a Time of Adoration is held from 4:30 to 5:30 P.M.

(41) YWCA
Via Cesare Balbo, 4 (Train Station)

TELEPHONE
06-488-0460, 488-83917
FAX
06-487-1028
RATES
From L35,000–70,000 per person, depending on number of roommates and plumbing. A Continental breakfast is included Monday through Saturday, but never on Sunday, holidays, or in August

The YWCA, off Via Torino, is open to women, couples and families . . . no single men. Guests sleep in seventy-four beds, in rooms with either a private shower and toilet, or with neither. The shower in the hall is included in the price. Lunch is the only meal besides breakfast that is served, and costs L20,000 per person. There is a lockout at midnight, no refunds, no showers between 10 P.M. and 7 A.M., and, of course, no credit cards. But you will have all-day access to the rooms. The welcome can range from pleasant to frozen stiff and, in both of my visits, I got the picture that this is hardly "fun city."

VENICE

A wonderful piece of world. Rather itself a world.
—*John Ruskin*

I loved her from my boyhood; she to me was a fairy city of the heart, rising like water-columns from the sea.
—*Lord Byron*

Visitors are caught by the spell of Venice for many reasons: few cities have produced so much literature and art, so many photos, as much history, or so many proposals of marriage. Venice reflects lives and loves lived with an intensity and magnificence that has never been duplicated. This same grandeur that inspired Byron, Goethe, Shelley, and Wagner is visible to the millions of people who visit Venice each year. The Doge's Palace, St. Mark's Square, the Basilica, and the Bridge of Sighs recall the golden age of Venice, when Marco Polo sailed from the harbor to open trade routes to the East. Venice then rose to become Europe's main trading post between East and West. At its height, more than 200,000 people lived in Venice, more than three times its present population. Today, tourism is the biggest industry, and ten million visitors routinely spend more than $100 million a year to gaze at her beauty.

Venice was officially founded on March 25, A.D. 421. There are three thousand *calli* (narrow alleyways and streets), the same number as there are wooden stakes under each of the two bridgeheads at Rialto Bridge. Venice is made up of 100 islands separated by more than 150 canals and joined by 428 bridges, 50 of them private. It is divided into six districts, or *sestieri:* Castello, San Marco, and Cannaregio on one side of the Grand Canal, and San Polo, Dorsoduro, and Santa Croce on the other. To begin to know and understand Venice, it is essential that you arm yourself with the best street map money can buy. This will not help much, other than to give an overall picture, because as those who love the city will tell you: Venice cannot be learned by rote; it is absorbed through the pores. Part of being in Venice is becoming hopelessly lost in the magical beauty of this fairy-tale city of gondolas and crumbling ornate palaces. Within each *sestiere* there is one long series of addresses, which are usually given by the name of the *sestiere* and the number of the address (San Marco, 2207). Unless you are a native and a postal official, chances are you will have no idea where that number is in the district of San Marco. This makes looking for places desperately frustrating. (San Polo, the smallest district, has *only* 3,144 addresses; Castello, the largest, has 6,828.)

There is no use pretending that one of the world's most romantic cities is anything but *very* expensive. However, time spent here does not necessarily call for dipping into retirement funds or mortgaging the ranch, although you will have to use a degree of self-restraint and, at the same time, plan on spending more for everything here than you will elsewhere in Italy. Consider your trip to Venice a gift to yourself—you worked hard and deserve it and, as the old saying goes, you can't take it with you.

The best time to go is from March through June, and from September until December. From the beginning of January until Carnivale, many hotels and shops close completely. However, during this off-season (which many hotels consider to be November to March, not including Christmas or Carnivale, and then again during all of July and August, when the heat and the mosquitoes drive the natives away), the pace is slower, crowds thinner, and hotel prices *much* less. During Carnivale, which is roughly the two weeks before Lent, and again between Christmas and New Year's, the "Great Tourist Hordes" descend in unbelievable numbers. You will need a miracle to find a reasonable hotel room without a long-range, advance reservation. If you come during this time, prices are ridiculously high. If you decide to brave the masses and the price gouging . . . pray to St. Christopher, the patron saint of travelers, and to St. Anthony, the patron saint of finding things; cross your fingers; bow to Mecca; rub a Buddha; and hope you won't get completely soaked. Of these prime times in Venice, Carnivale is positively the worst crush of humanity imaginable. As one wag put it, "During the height of Carnivale, you could drop dead on St. Mark's Square and still be standing upright five hours later." It is true. You simply cannot move more than one centimeter every five minutes! Avoid this period at all costs unless claustrophobic crowds are your passion.

It is important for visitors to adopt a philosophical attitude about Venetian hotels. First of all, you will not get the values you will in other places. Some hotels could have a higher rating, except that they are in a historic building that cannot be altered, preventing such improvements as an elevator, modern plumbing, air-conditioning, or just simply more space. While you probably will sacrifice comfort in small quarters that will *never* be modernized, you will be compensated by the frescoed ceilings and the age-old beauty of the building surrounding you—and, perhaps, by the final payoff of a view onto the Grand Canal, causing you to fall in love all over again. Who could ask for anything more?

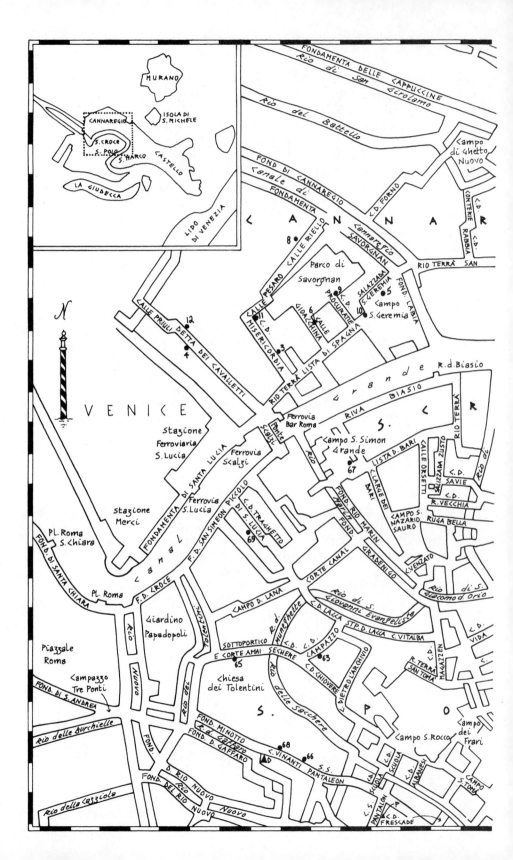

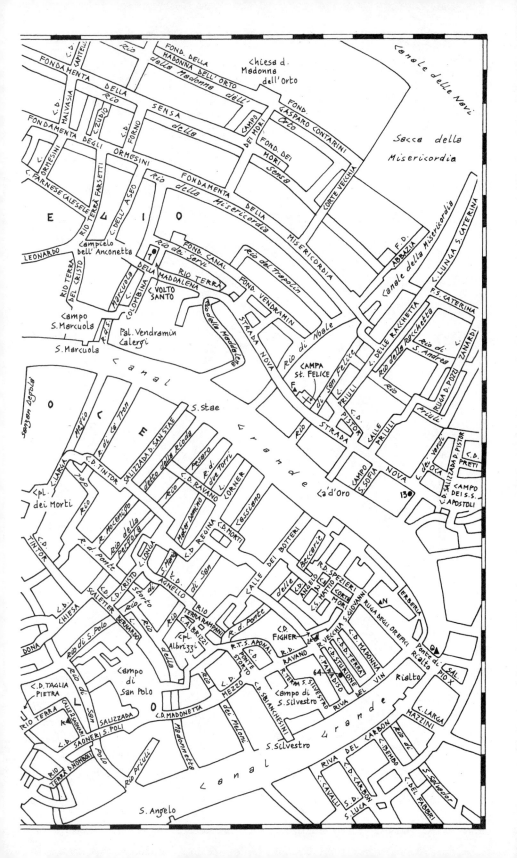

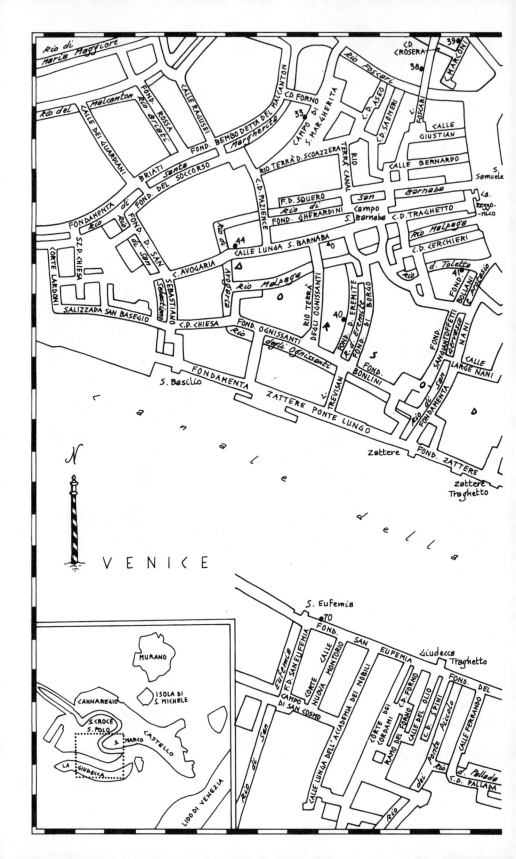

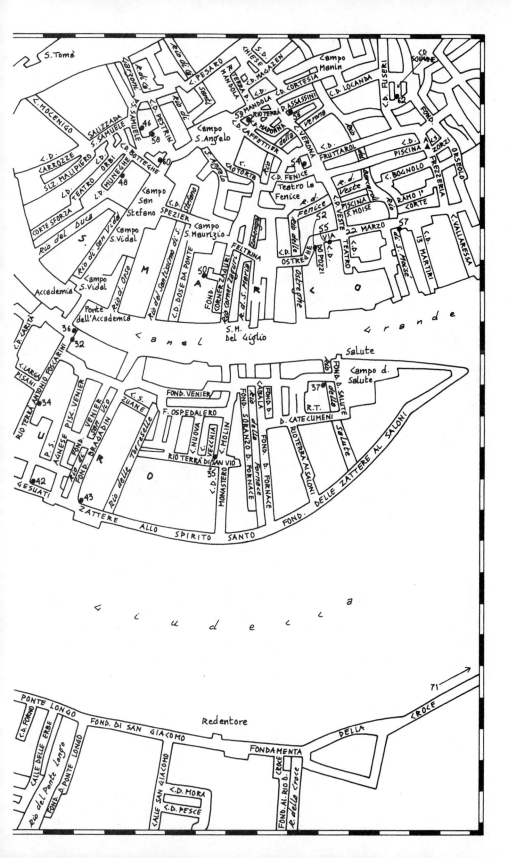

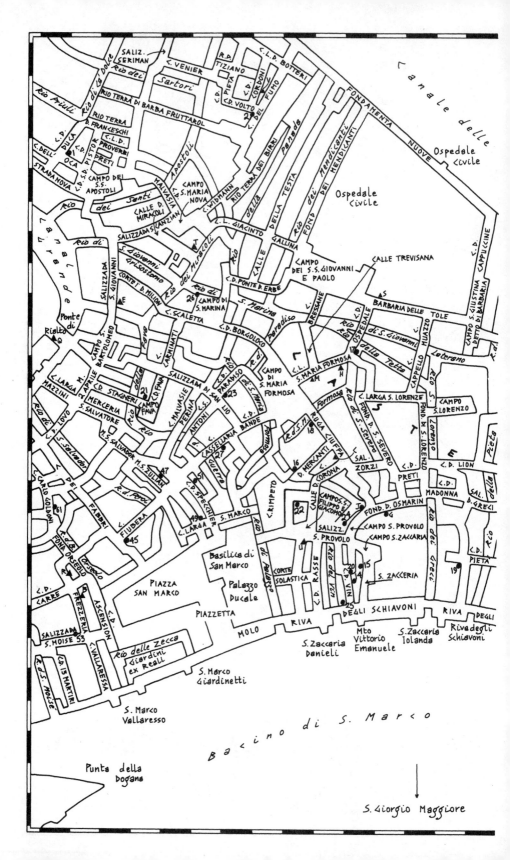

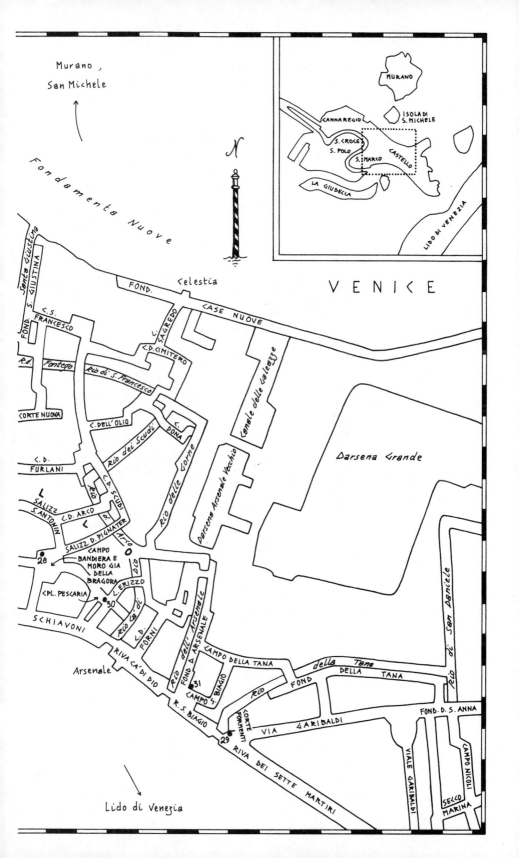

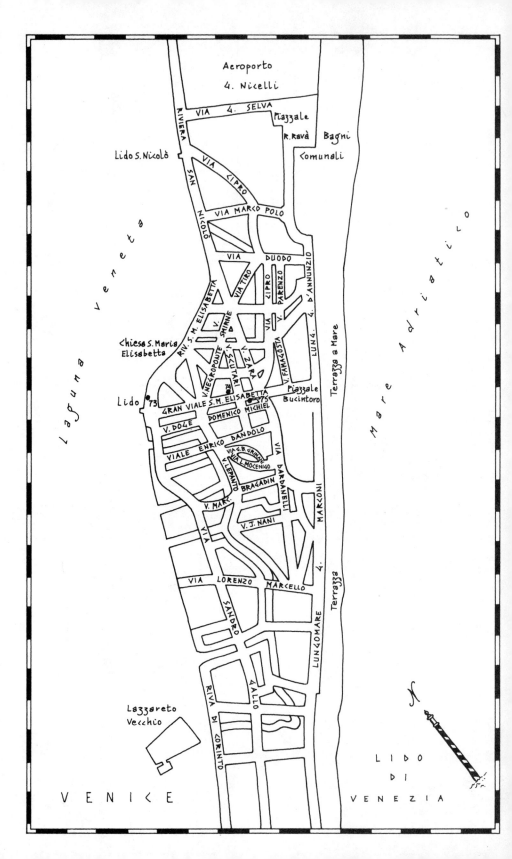

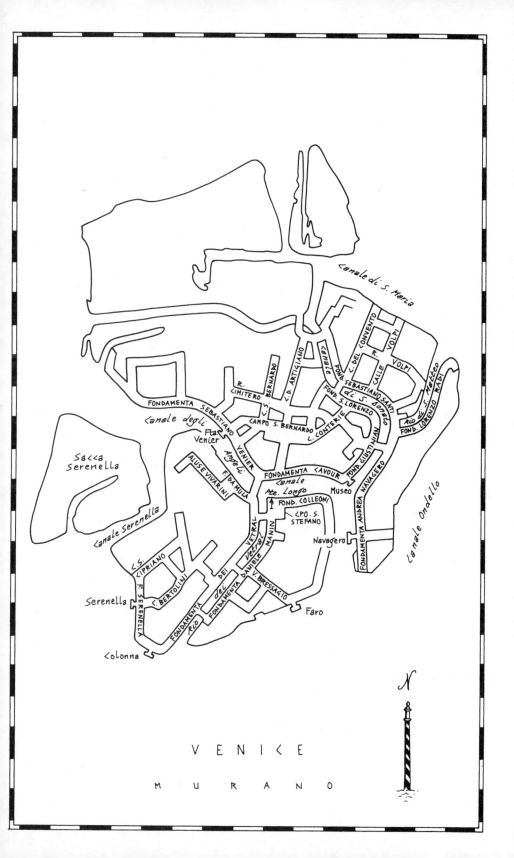

Canale di S. Maria

V. DEL CONVENTO
R. VOLPI
CALLE VOLPI

FOND. SEBASTIANO SANTI
di S. DONATO
FOND. S. LORENZO

Rio di S. Matteo
FOND. LORENZO RATI

R. ARTIGIANO
ZECCHE
R. BERNARDO
R. CIMITERO
C. D. ARTIGIANO

FONDAMENTA SEBASTIANO
Canale degli
CAMPO S. BERNARDO
L. CONTERIE
FOND. GIUSTINIAN

Fta
Venier
Angeli
VENIER
FONDAMENTA ANDREA NAVAGERO

Sacca
Serenella
FIDAMULA
ALUSE VIVARINI

FONDAMENTA CAVOUR
Canale
Pte. Longo
Museo
FOND. COLLEONI
CPO. S. STEFANO

Canale Serenella
Navagero
Canale Ondello

C. S. CIPRIANO
C. BERTOLINI
VETRAI
DEI
FONDAMENTA DANIELE MANIN
V. BRESSAGIO

Serenella
F. SERENELLA
FONDAMENTA
Rio
dei
Faro

Colonna

V E N I C E

M U R A N O

N

Useful Information

Emergencies

Police and Fire	113
Ambulance	041-523-0000

Medical Help

Hospital with Emergency Room	Santi Giovanni & Paolo, 041-529-4516/7
Medical Assistance	041-520-3222 (daytime), 531-4481 (evenings and weekends)
Late-night Pharmacy Information	192, or 041-522-4196

Getting Around

Airport	041-260-6611, 260-9260 (general inquiries), 260-6436 (lost and found)
Train	041-1478-88-088 (general inquiries), 785-238 (lost and found)

Consulates

Great Britain	Palazzo Querini, 1051, (Dorsoduro), 041-522-7207, Mon–Fri 9 A.M.–noon, 2–4 P.M.
United States	The closest U.S representative is in Trieste at Via dei Pellegrini, 42, 041-191-780

Currency Exchange

Güetta Viaggi	1289 (San Marco), 041-520-8711
American Express	Salizzada S. Moisè, 1471 (San Marco), 041-520-0844

Post Office

Post Office	Fondeggio Dei Tedeschi, Campo San Bartolomeo, near Rialto Bridge, Mon–Sat 8:30 A.M.–7:30 P.M.

Telephones

Code for Venice	041
Code for United States	001
Time	161
Weather	191

Tourist Office

Tourist Office   Calle dell' Ascensione, 71-C, off Piazza San Marco, 041-522-6356, 529-8730, Winter (Nov–March): Mon–Sat 8:30 A.M.–1:30 P.M.; summer (Apr–Oct): 8:30 A.M.–7:30 P.M.

Rolling Venice Card

For young people between the ages of fourteen and twenty-nine, one of the best ways to save money in Venice is to buy a Rolling Venice Card. As their brochure says, it "makes the city more accessible and fun to see, stay in and revisit . . ." Cardholders are entitled to a lower rate on the *vaporéttos* (water bus), at least a 10 percent discount on participating restaurants and food establishments, hotels, admissions to various museums (except Accademia), theaters, cinemas, sports facilities, tourist sites, and shops. These places will be listed on a map you will receive when you get your card. The cost is L7,000, and you will need your passport and a passport-size photo when you buy it. You can purchase the card at the train station at the Rolling Venice Box in summer (July–September) daily between 8 A.M. and 8 P.M., tel: 041-534-2852, 524-2904, and during the year from Monday through Friday 8:30 A.M.–12:30 P.M., 3–7 P.M., Saturday 8:30 A.M.–12:30 P.M., tel: 041-524-1334, fax: 041-716-600. The card is also for sale at the following locations:

Comune di Venezia
Assessorato alla Gioventù
Corte Contarina, 1529, San Marco
Tel: 041-274-7651
Fax: 041-274-7642
Hours: Mon–Fri 9 A.M.–1 P.M., Tues, Thur 3–5 P.M.

Ital Travel
Piazza San Marco, 71-G
Tel: 041-522-9111
Hours: Mon–Fri 9 A.M.–1 P.M., 3–6:30 P.M.

Transportation

Hiring a gondola to take you from points A to B in Venice is a very expensive way to commute. A thirty-minute gondola ride starts at around L60,000. Water-taxis are also very expensive and not worth the money unless there are several in your party and you are coming or going to the train station with mounds of luggage. Using the *vaporéttos* is the most economical and efficient way to go any distance in Venice. However, there is another water-taxi service, largely unknown to visitors—the Traghetto. Years ago there used to be hundreds of these gondolas crossing the Grand Canal, but now their number has been reduced to seven.

The gondoliers go back and forth with three or four people. The fare is around L1,000, which you pay when you get in. The natives stand, but it's okay if you want to sit. It is an inexpensive way to ride in a gondola, and it can save you extra miles of walking from one bridge to another in an attempt to cross the Grand Canal. The seven crossing points are between Sant'Angelo and San Tomà, San Marcuola and Fondeco dei Turchi, Riva del Carbon and Rive del Vin, Santa Sofia and the Pecheria at Rialto Bridge, San Barnaba and San Samuele, Santa Maria del Giglio and San Gregorio, and the Ferrovia and San Simeone Piccolo.

Special Venetian Travel Tip: Don't Miss Samantha!

For a memorable private tour through the back streets of Venice and an inside peek into how the Venetians live, work, play, and even die, please call Samantha Durell at her Venetian Travel Advisory Service. Samantha is from New York, but years ago she fell in love with Venice, and despite the cries from family and friends, she followed her dream and moved here. Besides being delightful, she knows and understands Venice better than most natives, and seems to know them all. You cannot walk more than a block without someone rushing up to her with everything from a "Ciao, Samantha" to a huge bear hug. It is clear, everyone adores Samantha, and after one day spent with her, you will too. In addition, I don't think there is anything she cannot do or arrange to have done . . . from meeting planes, digging out special shopping finds, arranging weddings, or helping you to order, and have sent, your personal gondola. Her talents do not stop here. She is also a world-recognized photographer of Venetian landscapes that have been purchased by both Venetian and American collectors and is represented by an art gallery in Venice and has regular showings in other Italian galleries. The Bloomingdale stores in the United States purchased many of her hauntingly beautiful Venetian photographs and featured them throughout fourteen of their stores during their nationwide salute to the preservation of Venice.

Finally, I know who is going to plan all my weddings from now on! If you or anyone you know is planning to get married, consider having Samantha arrange everything, from the moment the bridal party and friends arrive until the last one leaves Venice. She will do the paperwork (that alone is worth its weight in gold if you have ever tried to make *any* headway with Italian civil servants and their addiction to red tape), see to it that the bride's hair and makeup are done, arrange for your wedding gondola, reserve a romantic restaurant for the bridal luncheon or dinner after the ceremony, hire photographers and videotapers, and gently hold everyone's hand all the way to the end, ensuring that your special day goes along without a hint of a snafu. During my last trip to Venice, I was fortunate enough to attend one of her wedding productions, and it was nothing short of a page of beautiful memories right out of a marvelously romantic fairy tale.

Whatever reason takes you, your family, or friends to Venice, all I can say is—don't miss Samantha!

AVAILABILITY Samantha is in Venice from Carnivale to Thanksgiving.

RATE Depends on type of services and/or tour she does for you. Generally, four- to five-hour tours are $225 for two, $50 for each extra person. She has family rates for parents traveling with their non-adult children. Wedding planning starts at $1,500 and goes up according to the complexity of planning and arrangements you want her to handle. To arrange for her services, please book as far in advance as possible. Call or fax Venetian Travel Advisory Service in New York at (212) 873-1964; or in Venice, call or fax her at 041-523-2379.

Hotels in Venice by Sestiere (District)

The number in parentheses before each hotel corresponds to a number that marks the hotel's location on the Venice map (an entry with no number before it is located outside the parameters of the map); a dollar sign ($) indicates hotels in the Big Splurge category.

HOTELS

Cannaregio

Castello

OTHER OPTIONS

Cannaregio

This is the northern district of Venice, where you will find the train station and one of the most tourist-trod and tacky of streets—Lista di Spagna. At the end of this street is the imposing Palazzo Labia, with frescoes by Tiepolo of the life of Cleopatra, set in the pomp of eighteenth-century Venice rather than in ancient Egypt. Venture a few streets away from all the commercial hustle and you will find the quiet Jewish Ghetto, the first place in the world to use the name of ghetto. There are relatively few tourist attractions here other than the Madonna dell'Orto, with its Tintoretto paintings, and the Ca'd'Oro, a magnificent palace on the Grand Canal with a collection of beautiful paintings and carvings.

(1) ALBERGO BERNARDI-SEMENZATO ★
Calle del Oca, S.S. Apostoli, 4363-66
25 rooms, 9 with shower or bath and toilet

TELEPHONE
041-522-7257

FAX
041-522-2424

CREDIT CARDS
AE, MC, V

CLOSED
Dec 1–10, Jan 15–30 (dates can vary)

RATES
Single L45,000–55,000, double L65,000–85,000, triple L90,000–115,000, quad L110,000–130,000; lower off-season rates; Continental breakfast (L5,000 extra)

Gregarious owner and English teacher Maria Teresa Pepoli and her husband, Leonardo, a pharmacist, had this hotel for a few years before they finally bit the bullet and sunk a tremendous amount of money and two years of their time and labor into redoing the hotel and annex. The face-lift literally transformed a peeling, wilted one-star into a handsome choice for Cheap Sleepers looking to max out on budget value in Venice. Maria designed the Murano glass lights in the reception, as well as most of the renovation project itself; her husband painted the walls.

The rooms are now alike in the hotel—simple, clear-cut, many with original beams and views. Number 7, a double with a nice bathroom featuring handmade decorative tiles, has two windows opening onto a very narrow street. Number 9, a bright double with roofline views, is bathless.

The seven rooms in the annex are preferable to those in the hotel because they feature more antiques and hand-painted beamed ceilings, and overlook a garden or a canal. The down side is that only a few have private facilities. Bathless room 5 compensates with a garden view and features a marble fireplace, inlaid floor, large table, and impressive bureau. The best annex choice is No. 2, with a marble tile bathroom. This garden-view room is large, with nicely detailed walls and ceilings and a Murano chandelier. Number 3, also with a private bath, looks out onto a magnolia tree. For a canal room with a romantic sunset view, book No. 6.—the furniture is modern and there is no toilet . . . but, oh, what a canal view!

More reasons to stay here include private room safes, the location near good, low-cost restaurants (see *Cheap Eats in Italy*), and Maria and Leonardo, who are not only warm and welcoming but full of hints and tips about what to see and do in Venice.

ENGLISH SPOKEN Yes, and French and Russian

FACILITIES AND SERVICES Direct-dial phones, in-room safes, some satellite TVs in the hotel (L5,000 per day), regular Italian TVs in annex on request

NEAREST TOURIST ATTRACTIONS Jewish Ghetto, Grand Canal, Fondamente Nuove for trips to Murano and Burano

(2) ALBERGO CASA BOCCASSINI ★
Calle del Fumo, 5295
13 rooms, 6 with shower or bath and toilet

One damp March day I was walking from my flat to the Fondamenta Nuove to catch the No. 52 boat to go to Murano when I noticed the Albergo Casa Boccassini tucked along a narrow alley. This is a neighborhood composed of working Venetians, one that most visitors barely notice, let alone explore. However, for more than twenty years, Fernanda Bortoluzzi has been running her artistically funky hideaway, which she has filled with family furniture that ranges from the good to the bad to the ugly. Her prices are geared to Cheap Sleepers, she is delightful, and the neighborhood is interesting because it is *real*. If you are a modernist, a computer dependent, or an exacting scientist or engineer, this is probably not your Venice dream hotel. If, on the other hand, you are a poet, a nostalgic romantic, or a pair of cash-strapped lovers . . . read on.

The rooms are not all created equal. Number 6, a double with matching antiques, a garden view, and a manageable bathroom, is the best. Number 9 has been improved. Now it has a polished sea-green-tile floor, white walls, and modern furniture. There is no view or bathroom, but the hall facilities are just fine. The furniture is also modern in No. 11, and you will wake to the singing of birds from the sunny windows facing the narrow street. Number 8 is a large room with a garden view from all three windows. The purple-tiled bath has a half-tub and a shower.

TELEPHONE
041-522-9892

FAX
041-523-6877

CREDIT CARDS
None, cash only

CLOSED
Nov–Jan, but open Dec 27–Jan 1

RATES
Single L70,000 (none with private bathroom), double L110,000–150,000, triple L160,000–200,000, quad L190,000–250,000; lower off-season rates; Continental breakfast included (deduct L5,000 if not taken)

The garden is as eclectic as Fernanda, but it's lighted at night and large enough to accommodate several tables, where breakfast is served in summer.

ENGLISH SPOKEN Very limited, but Fernanda speaks French

FACILITIES AND SERVICES Direct-dial phones, TVs (L5,000 per day, but only in rooms with bathrooms), office safe

NEAREST TOURIST ATTRACTIONS Fondamenta Nuove and boats to Murano and Burano; about a twenty-minute walk to Rialto

(3) ALBERGO S. LUCIA ★
Calle del. Misericordia, 358
15 rooms, 7 with shower or bath and toilet

TELEPHONE
041-715-180, 710-610

FAX
041-715-180

CREDIT CARDS
AE, DC, MC, V

CLOSED
Dec and Jan

RATES
Single L80,000–100,000, double L120,000–160,000, triple L160,000–190,000, quad L230,000; Continental breakfast included (in off-season only deduct L10,000 if not taken)

No carpets, but a pretty, sunny front patio, spotlessly clean rooms (thanks to the head maid, who has been here almost twenty years), and stall showers *with* doors more than make up for the lack of zing in the rooms. The forty-five-year-old hotel, owned by the Parceanello family, is on a peaceful side street just off the "zoo" area along Lista de Spagna, which runs from the train station. The plain, cream-colored rooms with blond wood furniture are all good-sized, light, and quiet, ensuring visitors a peaceful night's rest. Only four of the rooms are on the dull back, the rest either look out over the patio or open onto it. Breakfast can be served inside a tiny room with four tables or on the front patio, which is shielded from the street and pedestrians by an ivy-covered fence bordered by flower beds. The breakfast is mandatory during the high season, but in winter, the cost can be deducted from the room rate.

ENGLISH SPOKEN Yes, also French

FACILITIES AND SERVICES Direct-dial phones, office safe

NEAREST TOURIST ATTRACTIONS Train station, Grand Canal

(4) HOTEL ABBAZIA ★★★ ($)
Calle Priuli, 68
39 rooms, all with shower or bath and toilet

TELEPHONE
041-717-333

FAX
041-717-949

CREDIT CARDS
AE, DC, MC, V

CLOSED
Never

In its golden age, the Abbazia was a monastery housing forty to fifty Carmelite Friars of Venice. Their work included producing a special medicinal water called Melissa Water. Now the main center for this production has been moved to Verona. Eventually, the friars relinquished part of their Venice property, and it has been converted into this tranquil hotel. Today, a few of the monks still live in quarters on the other side of the garden and run the church next to the train station.

The location, in a small alley next to a row of low-cost hotels behind the station, is not spectacular in itself. However, once inside the hotel, you will feel a million miles removed from all the activity surrounding the station. The rooms have been faithfully restored, maintaining the quiet atmosphere and spirit of the original monastery. Scattered throughout the hotel are pieces of furniture the monks used in their daily lives and church services. For example, the lobby, which was once the chapel, has wooden abbey benches around the perimeter and the pulpit along one side. The yellow breakfast room, with a huge skylight, was once the kitchen. Wide hallways are graced with Oriental carpet runners and black-and-white prints of old Venice.

The largest rooms, upstairs, face the garden, which was the central courtyard of the monastery. All have plenty of closet and luggage space, ample light, nice bathrooms, and attractive reproduction furnishings. Favorites include No. 303, a suite, and No. 203, a double overlooking the garden with a larger bathroom than most. The singles are very small, and a few are frankly depressing and must be avoided. These are Nos. 216, which is windowless, and 319, which has opaque glass in its sole window. The good news is that they rent for significantly less lire, yet have all the amenities found in the larger rooms. Number 210, on the other hand, is still small but has a nice salmon-colored bathroom with a tub.

NOTE: The management offers discounts to *Cheap Sleeps* readers who mention the book when reserving and show it upon arrival. Also, the *Cheap Sleeps in Italy* reader discounts change for each of the hotel's low, middle, and high season, which are as follows: low season, January 2 to March 1, November 12 to December 24; midseason, March, June through August; high season, April and May, September through November 11, Christmas, New Year's.

ENGLISH SPOKEN Yes

FACILITIES AND SERVICES Air-conditioning, bar, direct-dial phones, hair dryers, minibars, satellite TVs, office safe

NEAREST TOURIST ATTRACTIONS Grand Canal, train station

RATES
Single or double L290,000–330,000; extra person 30 percent of room rate; excellent seasonal discounts given to *Cheap Sleeps* readers; buffet breakfast included

(5) HOTEL AL GOBBO ★
Campo S. Geremia, 312
120 rooms, 57 with shower or bath and toilet

TELEPHONE
041-715-001
CREDIT CARDS
None, cash only
CLOSED
Dec 15–Feb 1
RATES
Single L75,000–95,000, double L105,000–130,000, triple L170,000; some long-stay discounts; Continental breakfast included

Maria di Vinco fits everyone's picture of the perfect Italian grandmother: regal yet genteel, and with a heart of gold. She does not speak English, but that does not seem to matter to the many Cheap Sleepers who have discovered her one-star jewel. She has been here for years, and has not changed the way she runs things as evidenced by her daily calendar, where she carefully writes in the reservations.

The word *gobbo* means "hunchback." The Italians have a superstition that if you touch the back of someone with a hump, it will bring you good luck. If you stay here, you will feel lucky, for this is a wonderful choice. The neat, clean bedrooms have unadorned wash-and-wipe furniture. A few of the roosts overlook a lovely garden, while others open onto a square (Campo S. Geremia). Number 1, always a favorite, faces the *campo,* and has a bathroom with an enclosed stall shower. For those opting for bathless rooms, the communal bathroom is one of the best in Venice, with a stretch tub and separate stall shower. Breakfast is served on a round table in the sitting room, where you will feel as though you are in someone's nice home, not in a hotel near the train station in Venice.

ENGLISH SPOKEN Not much

FACILITIES AND SERVICES Office safe

NEAREST TOURIST ATTRACTIONS Jewish Ghetto, Grand Canal, train station

(6) HOTEL CAPRERA ★★
Calle Gioacchina, 219
20 rooms, 4 with shower or bath and toilet

TELEPHONE
041-715-271
FAX
041-715-927
E-MAIL
caprera@gpnet.it
CREDIT CARDS
AE, MC, V
CLOSED
Nov 15–Jan 15
RATES
Single L85,000, double L120,000–185,000, triple L150,000–220,000; Continental breakfast (L12,000 extra)

Massimo Bico, his wife, their three young children, his mother, and a friendly golden cocker spaniel named Matisse run the tidy Caprera. In the lobby area, Massimo displays his unusual collection of hundred-year-old wooden Venetian boat miniatures. Be sure to take a few minutes to look at them, each a faithful reproduction of Venetian transport boats, a covered gondola, and a gondola regatta. The frill-free, whitewashed rooms are pillbox modern and neat, with bright bedspreads and easy-wipe Formica furniture. Those with bathrooms have a full-length mirror—a rarity in Venice. You are not stuck for an expensive breakfast, and there is no extra charge for the excellent hall shower, which comes equipped with towels and soap. Five rooms have terraces. For the bathless quarters, guests have the use of a toilet and bath on each floor. On the top floor is a large family room (No. 31), and on the ground floor is a room suitable for a handicapped visitor. The hotel is quiet, situated on a side street off the pulsating Lista di Spagna.

ENGLISH SPOKEN Yes

FACILITIES AND SERVICES Direct-dial phones, office safe

NEAREST TOURIST ATTRACTIONS Train station, Grand Canal

(7) HOTEL EDEN ★★★
Campiello Volto Santo, 2357
12 rooms, all with shower and toilet

For a solid three-star close to the railway station and within betting distance of the casino, check into this twelve-room dollhouse. Half of its nests face a canal, while others overlook the neighboring convent gardens or a quiet cul-de-sac. The *piccolo* doubles and *molto piccolo* twins are tastefully pulled together, with good beds and serviceable bathrooms. The rates are excellent for a three-star, especially in the low season. Plans are on the drawing board to expand to eighteen rooms.

ENGLISH SPOKEN Yes

FACILITIES AND SERVICES Air-conditioning in six rooms (free), bar, direct-dial phones, hair dryers, minibars, TVs, in-room safes, porter

NEAREST TOURIST ATTRACTIONS Casino, railroad station, Piazzale Roma

TELEPHONE
041-524-4403, 524-4405

FAX
041-720-228

CREDIT CARDS
AE, MC, V

CLOSED
Never

RATES
Single L190,000, double L280,000; extra bed 35 percent of room rate; Continental breakfast included (served either in the dining room or in your room)

(8) HOTEL HESPERIA ★★
Calle Riello, 459
20 rooms, 18 with shower or bath and toilet

The Hotel Hesperia is the perfect hideaway for romantics who do not like big, brassy hotels in busy areas. If you are willing to go around the corner from the well-worn tourist track near the train station, you will be rewarded by this two-star that offers many three-star features. The tranquil haven on a quiet little canal is almost fully renovated. Many of the rooms are named after well-known artists, and copies of the artists' works hang inside. The restful bedrooms are not large, but they are nicely equipped and tastefully decorated with

TELEPHONE
041-715-251, 716-001

FAX
041-715-112

CREDIT CARDS
AE, DC, MC, V

CLOSED
Never

RATES
Single L190,000, double L190,000–260,000, triple L350,000; lower off-season rates; Continental breakfast included

Murano glass chandeliers. Four of them face the Cannaregio Canal. The hotel is also in partnership with the adjoining restaurant. I was not able to try it because it was undergoing renovation and a change in chefs when I visited, so if you dine there, please let me know what you think.

ENGLISH SPOKEN Yes

FACILITIES AND SERVICES Bar, direct-dial phones, fans on request (L15,000 per day), hair dryers, minibars, TVs, in-room safes

NEAREST TOURIST ATTRACTIONS Jewish Ghetto, Grand Canal, train station, Piazzale Roma

(9) HOTEL ROSSI ★
Calle delle Procuratie, 262
14 rooms, 10 with shower or bath and toilet

TELEPHONE
041-715-164

FAX
041-717-784

CREDIT CARDS
AE, MC, V

CLOSED
Jan until Carnivale

RATES
Single L75,000–100,000, double L120,000–150,000; extra bed L40,000; lower off-season rates; Continental breakfast included

This hotel has been in the Rossi family since the grandmother of the present owner, Francesco Rossi, started it more than half a century ago. You will see her portrait hanging on the right of the breakfast room entrance. The Rossi continues to be a terrific little Cheap Sleep, but staying here may entail a few minor sacrifices. First of all, there is no elevator, but the climb up three flights of stone stairs is easy if you are in shape or interested in working off all those pasta dishes. Next, you will have to give up charm and character for modern furniture and chenille bedspreads. Music to the ears of most Cheap Sleeping travelers is the 10 percent discount during the off-season, a cheerful hotel staff; rooms that are quiet, clean, and kept up; and plumbing that works. Breakfast is served in a small, no-smoking room with benches and stools arranged around four red-and-white covered tables, or served in your room at no additional charge. Another point in its favor is the location, on a narrow alley off the busy Lista di Spagna, which means you can walk easily to the train station or to the Piazzale Roma parking garages.

ENGLISH SPOKEN Yes

FACILITIES AND SERVICES Direct-dial phones, fans in all rooms (free) office safe

NEAREST TOURIST ATTRACTIONS Jewish Ghetto, Grand Canal, train station, Piazzale Roma

(10) HOTEL SAN GEREMIA ★★
Campo San Geremia, 290-A
21 rooms, 14 with shower or bath and toilet

Affordability is the thrust at the San Geremia, a choice especially well suited to lone travelers, thanks to the small size of most of the rooms. The main sitting room has a large picture window opening onto the Campo San Geremia, offering great people-watching. Next to this is a dollhouse-size breakfast room with a miniature bar, television set, and fireplace. To reach your room, you will have to cope with stairs (sixty-five in all if you land on the top floor). Oddly enough, the one you will probably have to be put on the waiting list for is No. 420, which requires the full hike of sixty-five steps to reach it. It *is* nice, with a small entry landing and its own terrace facing the *campo,* but the bathroom is minute. One floor down is No. 305, also with a terrace view of the tile roofs and treetops. You will want to avoid Nos. 202 and 203, so tiny you can barely get around the bed. You cannot find fault with most of the other rooms, even though they are small, have chenille bedspreads, and have a few skyless vistas along the back. If you live on the front side, you will have noise but also a view of the *campo* in front, which is dotted with children playing, old people gossiping, and strolling couples in love.

ENGLISH SPOKEN Yes

FACILITIES AND SERVICES Bar, direct-dial phones, hair dryers, satellite TVs, in-room safes

NEAREST TOURIST ATTRACTIONS Grand Canal, train station

TELEPHONE
041-716-245, 716-260

FAX
041-524-2342

CREDIT CARDS
AE, DC, MC, V

CLOSED
Usually Dec 1–15

RATES
Single L120,000–190,000, double L150,000–210,000, triple L280,000, quad 360,000; lower rates for *Cheap Sleeps* readers who mention the book when reserving; Continental breakfast included (deduct L5,000 if not taken)

(11) HOTEL VILLA ROSA ★
Calle Pésaro, 389
33 rooms, all with shower or bath and toilet

The Villa Rosa has thirty-three rooms aimed at Cheap Sleepers desiring to roost near the train station in a hotel that delivers value with a capital V. The hotel—which is off Calle del. Misericordia, which is off Lista di Spagna—has recently undergone a face-lift that included a coat of white paint, cleaning the ceiling beams in the dining room and entrance, and redoing the rooms, all of which now have telephones, TVs, fans, and private bathrooms with a few toiletries. Five rooms have balconies; few have views. All are clean and quiet. If you are out of shape when you arrive, that will quickly change, as the hotel

TELEPHONE
041-718-976

FAX
041-716-569

CREDIT CARDS
AE, MC, V

CLOSED
Nov 1–Mar 1

RATES
Single L100,000, double L150,000, triple L190,000; Continental breakfast included

seems to meander all over the place and has lots of stairs—easily replacing your Stairmaster at home. The management is polite and the house cat friendly when not asleep on the sofa in the lobby. Obviously the hotel is doing well . . . it can afford to close from November 1 through February.

ENGLISH SPOKEN Yes

FACILITIES AND SERVICES Direct-dial phones, some hair dryers, TVs, office safe

NEAREST TOURIST ATTRACTIONS Jewish Ghetto, train station, Piazzale Roma

(12) LA LOCANDA DI ORSARIA ★★★ ($)
Calle Priuli, 103
8 rooms, all with shower or bath and toilet

TELEPHONE
041-715-254
FAX
041-715-433
CREDIT CARDS
AE, DC, MC, V
CLOSED
Never
RATES
Single L190,000, double L280,000–310,000, triple L320,000, quad L400,000; discounts for *Cheap Sleeps in Italy* readers who mention the book when reserving; children under seven free; buffet breakfast included

From June until September, Venice is full of tourists and mosquitoes—the man-eating variety who show little mercy and are immune to the most repellent sprays and lotions. You would think window screens would be as normal a requirement as a glass of *vino* with a plate of pasta, but they are not. The exception to this phenomenon is La Locanda di Orsaria. This unique hotel, *with window screens,* is owned and overseen by Pietro Polesel, who tells me that some of his favorite guests are *Cheap Sleeps in Italy* readers. However, window screens are not the only plus they offer. Here you have excellent value, along with air-conditioning and private safes in attractive and clean rooms furnished in dark wood and appointed with full-length mirrors, Murano light fixtures, and spacious wardrobes. All the bathrooms have stall showers. In the morning, a generous breakfast that includes cornflakes, yogurt, cheese, pastries, and fresh croissants is served in a corner of the lobby.

ENGLISH SPOKEN Yes

FACILITIES AND SERVICES Air-conditioning, direct-dial phones, hair dryers, minibars, satellite TVs, in-room safes, and window screens (!)

NEAREST TOURIST ATTRACTIONS Train station, Piazzale Roma, Grand Canal

(13) LOCANDA AI SANTI APOSTOLI ★★★ ($)
Strada Nova, 4391; third floor
10 rooms, all with shower or bath and toilet; 2 apartments with kitchens, shower, bath, and toilet

TELEPHONE
041-521-2612
FAX
041-521-2611

The Locanda ai Santi Apostoli is the perfect address for the discriminating traveler who values beautiful surroundings and wants a very special hotel. Quite simply, there is nothing else remotely like it in Venice for the price.

The hotel, which is on the third floor of a Venetian palace owned by the Bianchi family for five hundred years, was conceived and executed by Stefania Bianchi and an architectural design team consisting of her husband, son, and daughter. After two years of labor, the result is one of the most wonderfully imaginative hotels I have seen in some time. Personally managed by the Bianchis on a daily basis, it offers the warmth and hospitality of a distinguished home and caters to a growing corps of dedicated guests.

The hotel is reached via a ground-floor elevator that takes guests to the third-floor reception desk, which is in front of a smartly turned out lobby. Creamy slipcovered armchairs, soft sofas, and lovely paintings are the backdrop for three windows overlooking the Grand Canal. Breakfast is served in a bright room with yellow-and-white-checked cloths draped over round tables and upholstering the chairs. Fresh and dried flowers are everywhere, including in all of the bedrooms.

No two of the rooms are alike, but in all you will find decor worthy of a glossy magazine feature story, a welcome basket of fresh fruit and candies, comfortable armchairs, and excellent bathrooms fitted with soft monogrammed towels. The best room in the house is No. 9, with views of both the Grand Canal and Rialto Bridge. Sra. Bianchi's sense of good taste and style are evident in the room's burgundy Oriental print fabric used for the upholstery, draperies, and bedspreads. Number 8 is the only other room with such a spectacular view. It has three windows on the Grand Canal and is coordinated with antiques, floral prints, and white linens with deep pink accents. The bathroom is in gray tile. Breakfast in bed is a *must* in either of these rooms! Room No. 7 has two windows and a tiny tiptoe view of the Grand Canal, and can be joined with No. 8 to form a delightful family suite. Other favorites include No. 3, in bright green with blue highlights; No. 4, an unorthodox combination of yellow, eggplant, and pink that really works; No. 11 with pink and green hydrangeas in the bedroom and a pink-and-white-tiled bath; and, finally, Nos. 1 and 2, small bedrooms with bright green and purple accents. These two rooms share a bath and are another excellent family choice. While you cannot see

CREDIT CARDS
AE, DC, MC, V

CLOSED
2 weeks in Aug, Dec 15–end of Jan

RATES
Single L200,000–300,000, double L300,000–450,000; apartments L380,000; discounts for long stays and occasionally on weekends; Continental breakfast included

the Grand Canal from them, you can hear the boats as they travel along it.

New! Two stunning apartments have been added to make the Locanda ai Santi Apostoli even more desirable. Both have fitted kitchens, the same excellent taste in design and furnishings and are highly recommended for those travelers either in Venice for a longer stay, or for those desiring much more living space.

ENGLISH SPOKEN Yes

FACILITIES AND SERVICES Air-conditioning, bar, direct-dial phones, elevator, hair dryers, minibars, equipped kitchens in two apartments, room service, TVs, office safe

NEAREST TOURIST ATTRACTIONS Train station, Piazzale Roma, Rialto Bridge

Castello

The largest district and the only one not touching at some point on the Grand Canal, Castello is divided in two by the Arsenale, the shipyards where Venice built her shipping fleet, which once dominated the Mediterranean. The focal point for this district is the Gothic church Santi Giovanni e Paolo, the pantheon of Venice and considered one of the most monumental squares in the city. One of the prettiest squares is Santa Maria Formosa. The San Zaccaria Church in the south portion of the district played an important if controversial role in the history of Venice, and on the southern waterfront is Riva degli Schiavoni, where everyone in Venice walks, hoping to see and be seen.

(14) ALBERGO DONI ★
Calle del Vin, 4656
12 rooms, 3 with shower and toilet

TELEPHONE AND FAX
041-522-4267

CREDIT CARDS
None, cash only

CLOSED
End of Dec to Carnivale

RATES
Single L85,000, double L120,000–165,000, triple L165,000–210,000; towels L2,000; Continental breakfast included (deduct L15,000 per person, per day if not taken)

In back of St. Mark's Square, as you head toward Campo San Zaccaria and just off Riva degli Schiavoni, is this old-fashioned Cheap Sleep. The rooms either overlook the parked gondolas on the Rio del Vin or a garden with fruit trees. Large and airy bedrooms, the majority of which are outfitted with only a bidet, a basin with hot and cold running water, vintage furniture, and creaking wooden floors, tell you they have not been blessed by renovation. Four have canal views and all are spotless and always booked by an older group of Cheap Sleepers who know a bargain deal when they see one. To make your sleep here even cheaper, ask to have the L15,000 per person, per day cost of breakfast deducted and go instead to a neighborhood *caffè* and do as the Venetians do: have your cappuccino and *cornetto* while standing at the bar.

ENGLISH SPOKEN Yes

FACILITIES AND SERVICES Office safe, 1 A.M. curfew

NEAREST TOURIST ATTRACTIONS St. Mark's Square

(15) ALBERGO PAGANELLI ★★
Riva degli Schiavoni, 4182
20 rooms, all with shower or bath and toilet

Most hotels along this premium stretch of water in Venice charge almost half again as much as the Paganelli. While the prices may seem high for some committed Cheap Sleepers, there is significant value in what you will get. Francesco Paganelli, who was born at the hotel, continues to carry on his family's tradition of hotel-keeping, which began when his grandfather opened the hotel in 1874. Before that, the hotel was part of the San Zaccaria convent, whose claim to fame came in the sixteenth century when the nuns revolted against the bishop and the Church.

The hotel now consists of two sections: the annex on the square (Campo San Zaccaria, 4687) and the older section facing the lagoon. While some may feel the annex rooms have the edge for their modern features and bathrooms, most of those in the older section have lagoon views.

If you select the annex, ask for No. 22, a double on the square with original pitched ceilings with exposed beams, lovely Venetian painted furniture, and Oriental rugs. The bathroom has a shower and a half-tub. Room 24, with a view of the San Zaccaria Church, is the room in which Sr. Paganelli was born, and No. 23, a small double with wood beams, has an excellent bathroom. Views over the lagoon in Rooms 16 and 18 announce, "This is Venice!" The hotel is booked months in advance, so please do not wait until the last minute to reserve.

ENGLISH SPOKEN Yes

FACILITIES AND SERVICES Air-conditioning in all annex rooms and six rooms in main building, direct-dial phones, double windows for noise, hair dryers, satellite TVs, in-room safes

NEAREST TOURIST ATTRACTIONS St. Mark's Square

TELEPHONE
041-522-4324

FAX
041-523-9267

CREDIT CARDS
AE, MC, V

CLOSED
Never

RATES
Single L170,000, double L250,000–280,000; extra bed 35 percent of room rate; large Continental breakfast included

(16) CASA VERARDO ★
Calle Castagna, 4765
11 rooms, 9 with shower and toilet

TELEPHONE
041-528-6127, 528-6138

FAX
041-523-2765

CREDIT CARDS
MC, V

CLOSED
Never

RATES
Single L90,000–130,000, double L170,000–210,000; Continental breakfast included

What a difference new owners with a sense of style and imagination, and armed with paint, simple fabrics, and huge doses of elbow grease can make. Say hello to Massimo and Sandra Filippi, the artistic duo who transformed this eleven-room pensione into the snappy one-star you see today. Sitting on a little canal just after you cross over the Ponte Storto, off Ruga Giuffa, the building is a fourteenth-century *palazzo* that was at one time a school for Jewish students when the ghetto extended this far.

The individually decorated bedrooms have high ceilings and fireproof fabrics and mattresses. Number 6, a large double, looks better than many three-star hotel rooms. It has two windows framed by ruby-red tieback curtains over filmy white sheers and a view to the courtyard fountain. A corner of the ceiling reveals a fresco, and the Oriental rug and antiqued armoire add just the right amount of panache. Room 4 has carpet, a soft green bed with headboard detail, a crystal chandelier, and a gray-blue-tiled bath with a shower and curtain. Number 1, in soft yellow with ceiling detail and a sofa, features a beautiful set of furniture that includes an armoire and a four-drawer dresser. The two-hundred-year-old inlaid floor in No. 3 is the star in this room, but not far behind are the Art Deco–style twin beds with matching marble-topped side tables and a wardrobe with mother-of-pearl detail. The smallest room is No. 8, just off the entry, a sweet, narrow single with lavender floral wallpaper à la Laura Ashley. Before opening the hotel, Massimo was an independent music producer, but now he and Sandra work welcoming their guests to what is rapidly becoming the place to stay for savvy Cheap Sleepers in Venice.

ENGLISH SPOKEN Yes

FACILITIES AND SERVICES Bar, direct-dial phones, fans on request, office safe

NEAREST TOURIST ATTRACTIONS St. Mark's Square

(18) HOTEL AL PIAVE ★★
Ruga Giuffa, 4830
14 rooms, all with shower and toilet; 2 apartments

TELEPHONE
041-528-5174, 522-6468

FAX
041-523-8512

Paolo and his wife, Mirella, are carrying on the tradition set by his father when he opened the doors of the Piave in 1945. If you look above the reception desk, you will see a photo of his mother and father proudly displayed. In the last few years, Paolo has worked slowly but surely on replacing the bizarre color schemes in the rooms with soft, coordinated colors and serviceable reproduction furnishings. He has added six suites, which provide enough extra space to make the difference, and replumbed the baths, putting in heated towel racks, marble tilework, and better lighting.

The apartments are nicely organized and arranged, but in most, views are limited. Guests don't seem to mind, and feel compensated by the well-equipped kitchens, four-star bathrooms, and interesting location, where they can get to know the merchants and quickly sample the day-to-day Venetian life and feel a part of it. A Continental breakfast is included in both the hotel and apartment rates and is served in a breakfast room with cushioned banquette seating.

ENGLISH SPOKEN Yes

FACILITIES AND SERVICES Air-conditioning in the hotel rooms, fans in the apartments, direct-dial phones, hair dryers, TVs, office safe

NEAREST TOURIST ATTRACTIONS San Marco, interesting local neighborhood with great shopping

CREDIT CARDS
AE, DC, MC, V

CLOSED
Jan

RATES
Single L170,000, double L240,000, triple L285,000–395,000; apartments: L245,000–465,000 per day, lower off-season rates and for longer stays in the apartments; Continental breakfast included in both rates

(19) HOTEL BISANZIO ★★★ ($)
Calle della Pietà, 3651
42 rooms, all with shower of bath and toilet

The Bisanzio's brochure states, "Visiting Venice is like falling into an unforgettable atmosphere." That is so true . . . and to enhance your stay in this romantic city, consider this stunning choice in a redone sixteenth-century villa off Riva degli Schiavoni, only a few minutes from St. Mark's Square.

Even though you are close to it all, the rooms are quiet and lovely, impeccably arranged and coordinated in the Venetian antique style, featuring tiled baths, inlaid parquet floors, and eight rooms with private terrace balconies. Room 34 is a wonderful twin with an ancient timbered ceiling and its own balcony displaying green plants. The bathroom is generous, with enough space to unpack your cosmetics and actually see what you have in front of you. Number 80 is a large room with an extra sofa bed and a geranium-lined terrace looking onto San Zaccaria. Number 88 is a single with no terrace but a roofline view of the tip of the cross on the church and its bell tower.

TELEPHONE
041-520-3100, toll-free in the U.S., Best Western (800) 528-1234

FAX
041-520-4114

E-MAIL
email@bisanzio.com

CREDIT CARDS
AE, DC, MC, V

CLOSED
Never

RATES
Single L240,000, double L350,000; extra person L90,000; good off-season discounts; buffet breakfast included

A buffet breakfast is served in a pleasant dining room with a bouquet of dried flowers on each coral-pink-covered table. There is a balcony sunroom, in addition to a large sitting room with overstuffed chairs and sofas. An added benefit is the toll-free number to call in the United States. Be sure to ask for the lowest rate offered during your visit, because the prices vary greatly even within one month.

ENGLISH SPOKEN Yes

FACILITIES AND SERVICES Air-conditioning, bar, direct-dial phones, elevator, hair dryers, minibars, radios, satellite TVs, in-room and office safes

NEAREST TOURIST ATTRACTIONS St. Mark's Square

(20) HOTEL CAMPIELLO ★★
Calle del Vin, 4647
16 rooms, all with shower or bath and toilet

TELEPHONE
041-523-9682, 520-5764

FAX
041-520-5798

E-MAIL
campiello@hcampiello.it

INTERNET
www.hcampiello.it

CREDIT CARDS
AE, DC, MC, V

CLOSED
Jan, dates vary

RATES
Single L165,000, double L265,000, triple L330,000, quad L385,000; lower off-season rates; Continental breakfast included

Airy, crisp, clean, and very desirable—this is the overall atmosphere of the Campiello, which is just off Riva degli Schiavoni. Nicoletta and Monica Bianchini inherited the hotel from their grandfather and parents. When the two sisters took over, they updated the hotel, painted the halls white, polished the wooden parquet floors, and installed simple blond wood furniture and bamboo headboards to offset the white spreads. Gauzy curtains and photos of costumed Carnivale participants finish the simple rooms. The bathrooms are nice and feature terry-cloth towels. Seven of the rooms have beamed ceilings, and the views are either onto the little *campiello* in front or to a square in the back. Some of the singles are viewless, but they have all the perks the other rooms do. Comfortable chairs, gold damask wall coverings, and Murano glass sconces line the sitting area, which has a bar and small breakfast room off of it.

ENGLISH SPOKEN Yes

FACILITIES AND SERVICES Air-conditioning, bar, direct-dial phones, hair dryers, satellite TVs, in-room safes

NEAREST TOURIST ATTRACTIONS St. Mark's Square

(21) HOTEL CANEVA ★
Ramo Dietro la Fava, 5515
23 rooms, 14 with private shower and toilet

TELEPHONE
041-522-8118

FAX
041-520-8676

CREDIT CARDS
AE, MC, V

It is not a fancy Cheap Sleep, but you can't complain about the views. Six rooms have a balcony *and* a canal view, eleven have a canal view but no balcony, and the rest have no view at all—and you absolutely don't want one of these viewless numbers. What for? You will pay the same price for a view room, so why not get it?

Massimo Cagmato's family has been running the hotel since the mid-fifties, and they have certainly saved money by not spending it to upgrade the rooms, spring for better beds, or change the auditorium foldup chairs that provide the only seating in many of the rooms other than a two-inch mattress lying on a metal cot (ouch!). I can assure you, however, that cleanliness is taken seriously: the linoleum hall floors are swabbed daily and the bathrooms don't need an extra dousing of Lysol. The setting, about halfway between San Marco and Rialto Bridge, is another strong point and so are some of the facilities such as hair dryers and televisions in the rooms with baths, and air-conditioning available for a small supplement. So, if you don't mind a taste of the fifties, can sleep on a thin mattress in a room with a great Venetian view, and value the location, this Cheap Sleep in Venice can be yours fifty weeks of the year.

ENGLISH SPOKEN Yes

FACILITIES AND SERVICES Air-conditioning (on request, L10,000 daily supplement), hair dryers and TVs in rooms with private bathroom, office safe

NEAREST TOURIST ATTRACTIONS San Marco, Rialto Bridge

CLOSED
One week in Nov, one week in Jan (dates vary)

RATES
Single L80,000–110,000, double L110,000–150,000, triple L145,000–200,000, quad L180,000–250,000, lower off-season rates; Continental breakfast included

(22) HOTEL CASTELLO ★★★ ($)
Calle Sagrestia, 4365
26 rooms, all with shower or bath and toilet

As you can see from the prices, this is not a slice of Cheap Sleeping heaven. Instead it is a three-star hotel near St. Mark's Square and Campo San Filippo e Giacomo, featuring modern comforts in typical Venetian surroundings. These include the requisite flowery Murano chandeliers, hand-painted pastel furniture, and low ceiling beams. The bar/dining room provides guests with armchairs, a television set, and Oriental rugs on marble floors. The fabric-covered hallways keep exterior noise to a minimum.

The rooms are uniformly arranged and outfitted. Solo voyagers will be happy in No. 119, which can also be a compact double. It has a blue color theme, carried out in the room carpeting and bathroom tiles. In addition to two chairs and a desk, it has a rooftop view. Room 151 is a double with a small entry and lots of space in addition to its view. Number 125, a soft and pretty pink choice,

TELEPHONE
041-523-0217, 523-4545

FAX
041-521-1023

CREDIT CARDS
AE, DC, MC, V

CLOSED
Never

RATES
Single L300,000, double L380,000, triple L490,000; extra bed L40,000; lower off-season rates; Continental breakfast included

also has a view from its two street-facing windows. The hotel has a sister hotel, the Hotel Santa Marina (see page 242).

ENGLISH SPOKEN Yes

FACILITIES AND SERVICES Air-conditioners, bar, direct-dial phones, minibars, TVs, office safe, laundry service

NEAREST TOURIST ATTRACTIONS St. Mark's Square

(23) HOTEL DA BRUNO ★★
Salizzada San Lio, 5726-A
29 rooms, all with shower or bath and toilet

TELEPHONE
041-523-0452, 523-5324
FAX
041-522-1157
CREDIT CARDS
AE, MC, V
CLOSED
Jan 7 to Carnivale
RATES
Single L200,000, double L250,000, triple L330,000; lower off-season rates; Continental breakfast included

My flat in Castello was not far from this two-star hotel, so I had more than six weeks to observe it, and I was impressed. At one point, a Chinese fencing team from Beijing was in residence, while during Carnivale it was filled with French revelers. The management is friendly, the housekeeping good, and the location excellent for shopping (see "Cheap Chic," page 291), eating, and walking either to St. Mark's Square or the Rialto Bridge.

Colorful blooming plants by the door welcome guests to the small lobby, which has a lovely Murano mirror and wall lights and a black tufted settee. The rooms, which are a quantum leap ahead of most two-stars in the area, are all nicely done, with colors that blend together, and offer CNN television, fans, and in-room safes . . . all rare birds in Venice in any two-star hotel. Number 144 is in soft rose, which is carried out on the bedspread and cloth on the bedside table; No. 134 is in shades of green, with wood beams and Oriental rugs. If you want a bathtub, ask for No. 61, which can be a double or a triple. For terrace exposure, you will want to reserve No. 371, a double on the top floor.

ENGLISH SPOKEN Yes

FACILITIES AND SERVICES Bar, direct-dial phones, fans in all rooms, hair dryers, satellite TVs, in-room safes

NEAREST TOURIST ATTRACTIONS Shopping, St. Mark's Square, Rialto Bridge

(24) HOTEL FONTANA ★★
Campo S. Provolo, 4701
16 rooms, all with shower or bath and toilet

TELEPHONE
041-521-0533, 522-0579
FAX
041-523-1040
E-MAIL
htlcasa@gpnet.it

The Hotel Fontana has turned out to be a Cheap Sleeping jewel and remains at the top of my list as one of the best two-stars in Venice, where a family atmosphere prevails from the sitting room and bar to all four floors of the hotel. This is thanks in large to the matriarch of the family, Lina Stainer, a warm and wonderful lady adored by her children, grandchildren, and all who meet her.

Since 1967, the Fontana has been owned by the Stainer family. For four hundred years before that, the building was a convent for Austrian nuns, and their influence is still apparent, especially in the breakfast room, which is more than just a room in which to enjoy a morning meal. The consecrated brick archway means that Mass can be celebrated here, and the stained-glass windows were probably installed long before the Stainers bought the place from the Austrian nuns. Included in the sale were all the books and furnishings from the convent, many of which you still see. Before you leave the room, be sure to look for Mario and his brother Roberto's childhood photos by the door.

Speaking of photographs, when you walk in the hotel, you will notice a museum-quality display of Venetian photos. These stunning photographs, as well as the large posters hanging here and throughout the hotel, are the work of Mario Stainer. Sr. Stainer's magnificent photography is world renowned, especially his work detailing the intricate floors of the Basilica on St. Mark's Square (look for his book *Pavimenti* in Venetian bookshops) and his beautiful photographs of antique Venetian glass beads in *Perle Veneziane.*

The well-lit, well-furnished rooms have shiny bathrooms, pleasing color schemes, and crisp cotton bedspreads. The majority have views over the garden or San Zaccaria Church. I like rooms 11 and 12 on the fourth floor because of their private terraces with views of the church, which are pleasant for a summer breakfast or an afternoon drink. Families should request No. 14, a two-room suite with a skylight and a charming view of the church. Other good choices include No. 4, a triple with a terrace and a view of the garden; No. 6, a double with two windows on the square; and No. 8, a light-filled double on the back with two armchairs and the hotel's usual spotless bathroom. Many *Cheap Sleeps* readers have found the Fontana, making it one of the most requested hotels in this area of Venice . . . so plan accordingly!

ENGLISH SPOKEN Yes

FACILITIES AND SERVICES Bar, direct-dial phones, TVs, office safe

NEAREST TOURIST ATTRACTIONS St. Mark's Square

INTERNET
www.gpnet.it/htlcasa

CREDIT CARDS
AE, DC, MC, V

CLOSED
Never

RATES
Single L150,000, double L250,000, triple L280,000, quad L320,000; lower off-season rates; Continental breakfast included

(25) HOTEL PENSIONE WILDNER ★★
Riva degli Schiavoni, 4161
16 rooms, all with showers only and toilets

TELEPHONE
041-522-7463, 523-0544

FAX
041-526-5615

CREDIT CARDS
AE, DC, MC, V

CLOSED
Never

RATES
One or two persons L210,000–300,000; extra person L60,000; buffet breakfast included

If you stay at the famed Danieli, a magnificent palace built in the fourteenth century by Doge Dandolo, you will be in the company of kings, princes, political greats, artists, and a host of other famous personalities who have stayed here. The prices range from $450 for the littlest single to more than $1,000 for a suite. Breakfast, at $30 a person, is extra. This is hardly a Cheap Sleep in Italy. However, just a minute or two down the way is the Hotel Pensione Wildner, with the same views and exposure from eight of its front windows.

The Wildner is hardly a palace . . . call it a fifties-style pensione complete with leatherette sofas, orange and beige colors, Murphy beds in some rooms, and laminated furniture. Dated it is, but expensive (for the location) it is not. Even though the rooms are past their due date from a decorator's standpoint, they are clean and livable for short or long stays. If you stay here, you want a view room (even though they are more expensive), and No. 16 is a good choice, with three windows offering canal views, twin beds, a sofa bed, and two chairs. The hotel operates a restaurant in front, but it is touristy. If you are interested, however, half-pension for a three-course set meal is L40,000, beverage extra.

ENGLISH SPOKEN Yes

FACILITIES AND SERVICES Air-conditioning, bar, direct-dial phones, satellite TVs, office safe, restaurant for lunch or dinner (L40,000 per person)

NEAREST TOURIST ATTRACTIONS St. Mark's Square

(26) HOTEL SANTA MARINA ★★★ ($)
Campo di Santa Marina, 6068
20 rooms, all with shower or bath and toilet

TELEPHONE
041-523-9202, 520-3994

FAX
041-520-0907

CREDIT CARDS
AE, DC, MC, V

CLOSED
Never

RATES
Single L270,000, double L370,000, triple L420,000; lower off-season rates; Continental breakfast included (deduct L10,000 if not taken)

The Santa Marina is a smartly refurbished candidate on a neighborhood square in the heart of Venice. Guests are served breakfast on the hotel's private terrace, the ideal place to observe Venetian life as you relax and contemplate the day ahead. Otherwise, breakfast is served in the bar, which has moss-green velvet-covered booths. The management is not only accommodating but generous with its time, helping guests maximize their Venetian holiday.

The quiet bedrooms, with floral-painted doors, are tastefully done with reproduction-style painted furniture, modern Murano glass lighting, and soft colors assigned to each floor. For the best views, be sure to request a room looking onto the square. On the first floor, the rooms are coordinated in blue; on the second, everything is in beige, and these are the lightest rooms; and pink rules on the third floor. I like No. 107 because it is the biggest. It has twin beds, a sofa, and two windows overlooking the square. The Hotel Castello (see page 239) is under the same ownership.

ENGLISH SPOKEN Yes

FACILITIES AND SERVICES Air-conditioning, bar, direct-dial phones, hair dryers, minibars, satellite TVs, office safe

NEAREST TOURIST ATTRACTIONS Rialto Bridge

(28) LA RESIDENZA ★★
Campo Bandiera e Moro, 3608
15 rooms, all with shower or bath and toilet

The quiet neighborhood around La Residenza is a world away from the milling hordes near St. Mark's Square and the pedestrian-clogged Riva degli Schiavoni, both of which are only a short walk from the hotel. When you reach the Campo Bandiera e Moro and see the red flag flying in front of the building and the colorful flower boxes under the windows, you will know you have found La Residenza. To enter, press the nose of the lion to the right of the large entrance doors and walk through the inner courtyard, with statues and a coat of arms, and up two flights of stairs to the reception desk.

This fifteenth-century Gothic *palazzo* was the former home of the Gritti family, one of the wealthiest, and certainly the most prestigious, in Venice. The ornate salon, with its magnificent sculpted plaster walls and ceilings, lovely paintings, marble floors, and massive furniture, complete with a grand piano, suggests the type of opulent life the former residents led.

For too long it was run by a grouchy old skinflint who refused to spend one lira to improve or update anything. People were forgiving and came anyway, enamored by the history of the hotel and its location. They don't have to look the other way anymore! I am so happy to report that the hotel has a new owner, who had the foresight and wherewithal to revamp this drooping dowager, turning her into the well-dressed, elegant lady she should be. He kept the beautiful salon with its black lacquered piano, recovered the furniture, and gave seven of the

TELEPHONE
041-528-5315, 588-5042

FAX
041-523-8859

CREDIT CARDS
AE, DC, MC, V

CLOSED
Never

RATES
Single L160,000, double L250,000; extra bed 30 percent of room rate; Continental breakfast included

fifteen rooms new looks. For my Cheap Sleeping lire, these are the ones I want, because they are fresh and have new fabrics and carpeting, nicer bathrooms, and built-in air-conditioning (as opposed to an ugly portable unit on wheels that appears in the older rooms). Besides . . . they cost the same as the vintage rooms, so why not?

ENGLISH SPOKEN Yes

FACILITIES AND SERVICES Air-conditioning in new rooms, portable units in others, direct-dial phones, minibars, satellite TVs, in-room safes in new rooms

NEAREST TOURIST ATTRACTIONS St. Mark's Square

(29) LOCANDA TOSCANA-TOFANELLI ★
Via Giuseppe Garibaldi, 1650
9 rooms, none with shower or bath and toilet

TELEPHONE
041-523-5722

CREDIT CARDS
None, cash only

CLOSED
Jan 4–Feb 15, and when it is very cold

RATES
Single L45,000, double L80,000; Continental breakfast (L5,000 extra)

For a truly spartan, no-frills Cheap Sleep in a hotel that has not been remodeled or upgraded since it opened decades ago, try the Locanda Toscana-Tofanelli. The seaside location is more than a few heartbeats away from the thick of things touristy, but the low prices and sweet sisters who run it more than make up for these "inconveniences." The sisters are Nella and Micole, who is also the cook in their restaurant on the ground floor (see *Cheap Eats in Italy*). Nella and Micole, who wear porch dresses and fuzzy slippers, have been here almost forever. As Nella said to me, "I am older than the street!" Not quite, but close.

While some might consider the location, about a twenty-minute walk along the water to St. Mark's Square, to be fringe, I like it. I enjoy strolling along the nearby narrow canals, whose waters are bordered by buildings with flowers cascading from windows, children and dogs happily playing in the street, and lines of laundry flapping overhead. The area is a photo opportunity if there ever was one.

The rooms are definitely *vecchio*, with exposed pipes, bare floors, and some with no running water. There is no heat either (they shut down the hotel when it gets *too* cold, Nella told me). Two double rooms have sea views and two others (Nos. 8 and 9) look onto a canal. Three have little balconies that are perfect for inspired people-watching. Naturally, all the facilities are of the down-the-hall variety, and the hall bathroom with the tub is better than the pink-tiled one with only a shower. The sisters both have eagle eyes and lock up tight at midnight after closing the restaurant. No keys are provided . . . so if you miss curfew, you won't be sleeping here.

ENGLISH SPOKEN Yes

FACILITIES AND SERVICES Office safe, midnight lockout

NEAREST TOURIST ATTRACTIONS Interesting local area; twenty-minute walk to St. Mark's Square

(30) NUOVO TESON ★★
Ramo Pescaria, 3980
30 rooms, all with shower or bath and toilet; 3 apartments with equipped kitchens

The Nuovo Teson is set back on a pretty square just off the busy Riva degli Schiavoni, a whisper or two away from St. Mark's Square and across the way from one of the best fish restaurants in Venice, Al Covo (see *Cheap Eats in Italy*). The main section of the hotel has a cozy bar with inviting chairs and a sunny breakfast room overlooking the street. The rooms are modestly appointed, yet offer space for daytime living and have Venetian-style reproduction furniture (decorated with hand-painted flowers done by young women studying at art universities in Florence). An annex around the corner from the hotel offers three additional rooms, but I find them somewhat depressing and dark, although as nicely appointed as the main part of the hotel.

In 1998, owner Nicola Caputo was able to purchase the building next to the hotel, and he has turned this space into three very nice apartments with equipped kitchens. The only thing he left from the old building was a door handle to the entry; from there on out, it is all new. They are also furnished in reproductions of Venetian country furniture, and have good bathrooms. There is no minimum stay in the apartments.

ENGLISH SPOKEN Yes

FACILITIES AND SERVICES Air-conditioning in the apartments, bar, direct-dial phones, TVs in annex rooms and apartments, office safe

NEAREST TOURIST ATTRACTIONS St. Mark's Square

TELEPHONE
041-522-9929, 520-5555

FAX
041-528-5335

CREDIT CARDS
AE, DC, MC, V

CLOSED
Dec 1–Christmas

RATES
Single L200,000, double L220,000, triple L260,000, apartments L500,000; lower off-season rates; Continental breakfast included

(31) PENSIONE BUCINTORO ★★
Riva San Biagio, 2135
28 rooms, 23 with shower or bath and toilet

The Pensione Bucintoro is a family-run hotel with a minimum of style and upgrades. The rooms are clean, well maintained, and damage-free, but they are also boring. They are, however, saved from oblivion by the

TELEPHONE
041-522-3240

FAX
041-523-5224

CREDIT CARDS
None, cash only

CLOSED
Dec–Carnivale

RATES
Single L110,000–145,000, double L200,000–260,000, triple L330,000; lower off-season rates; Continental breakfast included

fabulous views from every one—over the San Marco basin with the Lido on one side and Doge's Palace on the other. Primo people-watching is available from an outside terrace facing the walkway along Riva San Biagio. The hotel is an easy walk to St. Mark's Square, the center of all the action in Venice. For trips farther afield, you can walk along the Riva degli Schiavoni and catch one of the *vaporéttos* that depart every few minutes.

ENGLISH SPOKEN Yes

FACILITIES AND SERVICES Bar, direct-dial phones, hair dryers, office safe

NEAREST TOURIST ATTRACTIONS St. Mark's Square, close to *vaporétto* stops

Dorsoduro

Dorsoduro, a long finger of land between the center of the city and the lagoon, constitutes the southern part of Venice. Campo Santa Margherita is its largest open space, with a daily market and a life of its own almost twenty-four hours a day. Standing on the Grand Canal is the seventeenth-century Baroque church of the Salute, one of the most beautiful buildings in Venice. Inside are three Titians on the ceiling and Tintoretto's *Marriage in Cana* on the left of the altar. Also here is the Peggy Guggenheim home, which now holds her collection of contemporary art, and the Accademia, the city's most important art museum.

(32) AGLI ALBORETTI HOTEL ★★
Rio Terrà Antonia Foscarini, 884
25 rooms, all with shower or bath and toilet

TELEPHONE
041-523-0058

FAX
041-521-0158

E-MAIL
alborett@gpnet.it

CREDIT CARDS
AE, DC, MC, V

CLOSED
Sometimes from Jan 6–30

The Agli Alboretti, owned by Dina Linguerri, is close to the Accademia Gallery, which has the world's finest collection of Venetian art. For other sightseeing, the Accademia *vaporétto* stop is only a few steps away.

The entrance off the street leads to an intimate paneled lobby with a collection of attractive oils and watercolors of Venice displayed on the walls. An interesting model of a seventeenth-century ship permanently docked in the window. Beyond the lobby is a little lounge and a garden with a vine-covered arbor, where you can have breakfast on warm mornings or relax in the shade on hot summer afternoons. On the second floor is a comfortable sitting room with CNN television reception. The rooms are very small and so are the bathrooms, many of which have deep half-tubs with handheld shower nozzles and no shower curtains, but this is an old building and one cannot expect spacious quarters or the latest bathrooms. The rooms do, however, have air-conditioning, a big bonus in the sizzling summertime. Number 7, a single, has bright white walls, a heavily beamed ceiling, dark wood furniture, and a view to the street through a set of double windows. Number 9 can be a triple, but it's better for two. The two windows that face the street let in plenty of light. The soft yellow walls tie in with the multicolored floral spread, and the small bathroom has a heated towel rack. Number 5, with one wall papered in light blue, has antique walnut bedside stands, a small writing table, and two attractive chairs. Number 22 is larger than most and is used for two or three persons. I like its walk-in closet and garden view. Avoid No. 19, which is too small and dark for any degree of comfort, and No. 2, which has a poor shower situation.

Sra. Linguerri operates a high-end restaurant next door to the hotel, and guests can take a half- or full-board. Sra. Linguerri is a wine connoisseur, and her wine list offers a nice variety of Italian selections.

ENGLISH SPOKEN Yes

FACILITIES AND SERVICES Air-conditioning, bar, direct-dial phones, hair dryers, TVs, office safe

NEAREST TOURIST ATTRACTIONS Accademia Gallery, Zattere, Gesuati Church, Guggenheim Collection

RATES
Single L165,000, double L255,000, triple L300,000; discount rates for stays over four nights; Continental breakfast included; half-pension, prix fixe meals (L50,000 for one meal, L80,000 for two meals a day, beverages extra)

(33) ALBERGO ANTICO CAPON ★
Campo Santa Margherita, 3004-B; first floor
7 rooms, all with shower and toilet

Everything—well, almost everything—you will need or want is right here on the Campo Santa Margherita: pizza places with large outside seating areas, one of the best ice cream makers in the city, a supermarket, a locksmith, a bookstore, bars, restaurants, and a laundry. Most mornings the *campo* has stalls selling fruit, vegetables, and fresh fish. The best time to catch the market flavor is early on a Saturday morning, when there are more stalls set up. In late afternoon, the area becomes a playground for the neighborhood children and a place for their mothers to catch up over a cappuccino. Later on in the evening, its pizzerias and bars are popular gathering places for the many students who attend the nearby university.

TELEPHONE AND FAX
041-528-5292

CREDIT CARDS
None, cash only

CLOSED
Never

RATES
Single L120,000, double L150,000, triple L180,000; lower off-season rates; breakfast (L8,000 extra per person)

All this brings me to the Antico Capon, a one-star walk-up above a pizza joint. It used to be the consummate Cheap Sleep, run by a little old *signora* who spoke no English and never invested in one upgrade all the years she ruled the roost. Now it has a new owner, Elias Manna, who is full of ideas and plans that he works on in his hallway office or sitting at one of the outdoor tables at the pizza place downstairs.

But the old saying "You can't make a silk purse out of a sow's ear" rings true here. Unless the building is razed and something totally new is put up in its place, the Albergo Antico Capon is and always will be a one-star with few apologies. To his credit, Elias wants to expand to eleven rooms, enlarge the bathrooms, and redo the sagging stairs. It's only a question of money. He even went so far as to suggest that the owner of the building along the back replant his window boxes so guests at the Albergo would have a prettier view. That is a question of someone else's money! At present, the rooms are surprising: large and freshly painted, with decent furniture and acceptable bed coverings. Things generally match. Three rooms overlook the *campo* and all the action, which can be loud and lengthy on weekends. Four face the back, and hopefully those replanted flower boxes. But if you can live with thin towels and metal phone-booth-style showers squeezed into the corners of the rooms, this is still the consummate Cheap Sleep.

ENGLISH SPOKEN No

FACILITIES AND SERVICES Office safe

NEAREST TOURIST ATTRACTIONS Campo Santa Margherita, Accademia Gallery; close to two *vaporétto* stops

(35) HOTEL AMERICAN ★★★ ($)
San Vio, 628
29 rooms, all with shower or bath and toilet

TELEPHONE
041-520-4733
FAX
041-520-4048
E-MAIL
hotameri@tin.it
CREDIT CARDS
AE, DC, MC, V
CLOSED
Never

An old-world Venetian formality reigns at the completely restored Hotel American on the San Vio Canal, away from the hustle and bustle, yet close enough for easy exploration of art galleries, shops, and good restaurants (see *Cheap Eats in Italy*). A large, inviting lobby furnished with period pieces, Oriental rugs, and the ever-popular Murano glassware sets the tone for the rest of the hotel. A first-floor, vine-covered terrace is a delightful place for summer breakfasts. In winter, you will eat in a gold-colored dining room on red-velvet chairs at linen-covered tables.

Be sure to request one of the nine rooms that face the canal, or any one with a terrace. Two top-floor rooms require some extra stair climbing, but occupants will be rewarded with views of the canal and of gondolas drifting by. I also like No. 23, with three canal-view windows. Green wallcoverings are complemented by the green paisley-print bedspread and the hand-painted furniture. Plans are to redo all the bathrooms to the standard found in room No. 11, which means you will have a well-lighted bath with a marble sink, extra shelves, a tub and a shower, and heated towel racks. The hotel is owned and managed by Salvatore Sutera, who also owns the very nice Hotel Falier (see page 277).

ENGLISH SPOKEN Yes

FACILITIES AND SERVICES Air-conditioning, bar, direct-dial phones, elevator to three floors, hair dryers, minibars, satellite TVs, in-room safes

NEAREST TOURIST ATTRACTIONS Accademia Gallery, Guggenheim Collection

(see page 277)

RATES
Single L225,000, double L340,000–360,000; extra bed L80,000; lower off-season rates; buffet breakfast included

(36) HOTEL GALLERIA ★
Rio Terrà Antonio Foscarini, 878-A
9 rooms, 7 with shower or bath and toilet

The Galleria face-lift is amazing, especially for a one-star. Years ago, this seventeenth-century *palazzo* at the foot of Accademia Bridge was cut and pasted into a hotel. The furniture you sold at your last garage sale, along with those rolls of red flocked wallpaper, were alive and well in the rooms, creating a potpourri of colors, patterns, and styles blended into a faded Venetian charm that appealed to many.

But new owners can mean many things in the hotel business, not always positive. Not so with Stefano, the debonair new owner of the Galleria. His stiff broom swept the place clean of dusty clutter, replacing it with better furniture and some antiques. He polished the floors and accented them with Oriental rugs, added Art Deco stylized lights to the inventory of chandeliers, put in a new hall bathroom, plus five others in the rooms, and made sure the flowers in the window boxes were in full bloom from May to October. At least six of the rooms have commanding views of the bridge and/or the Grand Canal. Everyone's favorite is No. 8, with a raised platform and two bamboo chairs in which you can sit and almost reach out and touch the canal below. Another top choice is No. 3, with views of both the bridge and

TELEPHONE
041-523-2489

FAX
041-520-4172

E-MAIL
galleria@tin.it

CREDIT CARDS
AE, MC, V

CLOSED
Never

RATES
Single L95,000 (no bath), double L125,000–200,000; extra bed 30 percent of room rate; Continental breakfast included

the canal. The hotel is small and there is no dining room, so breakfast will be served to you in your room.

ENGLISH SPOKEN Yes

FACILITIES AND SERVICES Direct-dial phones

NEAREST TOURIST ATTRACTIONS Accademia Gallery, Guggenheim Collection

(37) HOTEL MESSNER ★★
Fondamenta de Ca' Bala, 216/217
35 rooms in hotel and annex, all in hotel with shower and toilet, 19 in annex with shower and toilet

TELEPHONE
041-522-7443

FAX
041-522-7266

E-MAIL
messner@doge.it

CREDIT CARDS
AE, DC, MC, V

CLOSED
Never

RATES
Hotel: single L150,000, double L230,000, triple L285,000, quad L320,000; buffet breakfast included. Annex: single L135,000, double L185,000, triple L245,000, quad L265,000; buffet breakfast included. Both hotel and annex: lunch or dinner if a group is having it (L30,000 per person, beverages extra)

Let the groups stay in the annex, you want to sleep in the hotel itself. Not that there is anything radically wrong with the annex, but I have noticed several student groups booked here and I don't think many Cheap Sleepers want the noise that enthusiastic travelers with youth and great amounts of energy on their side can cause. Also, in the main part of the hotel, your very neat and tidy room will come with satellite TV and air-conditioning. The rooms are basically all the same, with green carpeting, beige furniture, a bathroom with a stall shower and lighted mirror, and a closet/storage unit built around the bed. Best bets overlook one of the nicest gardens in Venice, where in warm weather you will be seated in comfortably padded chairs surrounded by vine-covered walls and listening to a bubbling fountain. A breakfast buffet is included in the price, and if there is a group dining here either for lunch or dinner, individual guests are invited to join them for a set-price lunch or dinner (L30,000 per person, beverages extra).

On foot it is a walk and a half to St. Mark's Square, but by *vaporetto,* a matter of minutes. The area is non-touristy, yet very close to Madonna della Salute, one of the most beautiful, and certainly one of the most photographed, churches in Venice. In addition, it's not far from the Peggy Guggenheim collection and the Accademia.

ENGLISH SPOKEN Yes

FACILITIES AND SERVICES Hotel: air-conditioning, direct-dial phones, hair dryers, satellite TVs, in-room safes. Annex: direct-dial phones, hair dryers, in-room safes.

NEAREST TOURIST ATTRACTIONS Madonna della Salute Church, Accademia Gallery, Guggenheim Collection

(38) HOTEL TIVOLI ★★
Cá Larga Foscari, 3838
22 rooms, 18 with shower or bath and toilet

If you are in Venice between Christmas and New Year's, you will not be able to stay at the Hotel Tivoli because it will be closed. During the rest of the year, this smart two-star plays to a full house of contented regulars and visitors who have found it through word of mouth. The hotel, which is now ably run by Andrea Bottacin, offers exceptionally good value and comfort along with friendly service in one of the most interesting sections of Venice.

If you are traveling with a family, ask for No. 34, a sunny triple with a sloped ceiling and a private terrace. Seven of the rooms look onto the garden, where breakfast is served on warm mornings. Two of these garden rooms are No. 7, with a hardwood floor and white-tiled bathroom, and No. 30, with dark wood furniture, quilted bedspreads, and two windows. If there are two of you, No. 24, one of the best in the hotel, has high ceilings, reproduction furniture, and a large bathroom with a window and an enclosed shower. In most of the other rooms, the furnishings are of the hose-down type and the spreads bright chenille, but they are all clean and well maintained.

The beamed garden-side breakfast room, done in a Country Italian theme, is one of the prettiest in Venice, with its collection of pitchers, masks, and wrought iron. Its well-spaced tables are set with blue-and-white china.

ENGLISH SPOKEN Yes

FACILITIES AND SERVICES Bar, direct-dial phones, hair dryers, satellite TVs, office safe

NEAREST TOURIST ATTRACTIONS Campo Santa Margherita, Accademia Gallery

TELEPHONE
041-524-2460

FAX
041-522-2656

CREDIT CARDS
None, cash only

CLOSED
Dec 25–Jan 1

RATES
Single L100,000–135,000, double L220,000, triple 265,000, quad L300,000; lower off-season rates; Continental breakfast included

(39) LOCANDA CA' FOSCARI ★
Calle della Frescade, 2887-B
11 rooms, 5 with shower or bath and toilet

Valter and Giuliana Scarpa's hotel has always been good . . . and they are constantly making improvements. It is located between Campos Santa Tomà and Santa Barnaba, an upper-middle-class area filled with locals going about their daily lives. You will find many small shops, bakeries, bars, *caffès,* and restaurants (see *Cheap Eats in Italy*), but few are geared specifically to the tourist trade.

TELEPHONE
041-710-401

FAX
041-210-817

CREDIT CARDS
None, cash only

CLOSED
Nov 15–Feb 1

Locanda Ca' Foscari is a family run place, where the rooms are well cared for and maintained regularly. The walls are covered half with fabric and half with white paint. Each room is different, but they are coordinated and do not have sleazy chenille bedspreads or hodgepodge junk furniture. The top floors are filled with morning sunshine, and the beds are good, even though they look like army issue. Room 5 is viewless, but the heated towel racks and stall shower *with* a door might be trade-offs for some. Number 6 has a long bathroom and two windows on a private garden, which has a lovely green tree and exquisite lavender wisteria vines in springtime. Room 9 has corner window light and a green and rose pink floral quilt bed covering. The hall facilities are excellent, so if you are trying to sleep really cheap, a bathless room here is the ticket. If there are twelve or more in your party, Valter will cook dinner for you . . . but you must discuss this when you book your room.

ENGLISH SPOKEN Yes, also French and Spanish

FACILITIES AND SERVICES Office safe

NEAREST TOURIST ATTRACTIONS Campo Santa Tomà, Campo Santa Barnaba

(40) LOCANDA MONTIN ★
Fondamenta delle Eremite, 1147
8 rooms, 3 with shower only

Exacting guests will probably want to look elsewhere, but those who thrive on nostalgia, funky charm, and character will adore the Locanda Montin for its refreshing change from antiseptic anonymity. The hotel, which is off Calle Lunga Santa Barnaba and Calle d. Spezier, bears a faded look from years of attracting artists, writers, and musicians on prolonged visits to Venice. Up the stairs and along the corridors is the hotel's collection of original art from the fifties and sixties done by artists who were regulars at Antica Locanda Montin, the popular restaurant below the hotel (see *Cheap Eats in Italy*). Now it is somewhat of a cult hotel, appealing to would-be bohemians who do not mind hall plumbing and thin walls.

Despite its quirky quarters, it is becoming increasingly difficult to get a reservation. If you do succeed, you will be staying in a room that is filled to the brim with an assorted array of furnishings, and, in one case, history. Number 12, a double with a canal view, was occupied from 1915 to 1918 by war hero Gabriele d'Annunzio and actress Eleanora Duse. The same bed and armoire they used are there today. Another good choice is No. 5, also on the canal, with a balcony and a shower and sink. The hotel is situated just off Campo Santa Barnaba. It is not the easiest address to find, but once you reach the Fondamenta di Borgo, which runs off Calle Lunga Santa Barnaba, look for the black carriage lamp hanging over the front door with the name Locanda Montin marked on it.

ENGLISH SPOKEN Yes

FACILITIES AND SERVICES Office safe, 1 A.M. curfew

NEAREST TOURIST ATTRACTIONS Campo Santa Barnaba, Campo Santa Margherita, Accademia Gallery

(41) PENSIONE ACCADEMIA (VILLA MARAVEGE)
★★★ ($)
Fondamenta Bollani, 1058
27 rooms, 24 with shower or bath and toilet

The Pensione Accademia, occupying one of the most romantic settings in Venice just off the Grand Canal, offers charm and serene beauty at prices many can afford. It began as a villa in the seventeenth century, was occupied as a private mansion until early 1900s, and was then used as the Russian consulate before World War II. It was also the fictional residence of Katharine Hepburn in *Summertime*. The stately villa is surrounded by lush gardens that give you the pleasant feeling of being a million miles away, while actually only being minutes away from central Venice. On one side of the villa a graceful patio faces the canal, with tables and chairs placed among flowering plants. Along the other side is a garden with wisteria vines, fruit trees, and blooming roses.

The inside of the Accademia is just as appealing, with classic Murano chandeliers, Victorian and Venetian furnishings, and polished wooden floors. There is a cozy upstairs tearoom and a formally set breakfast room overlooking the rose garden. The adjoining bar has an ornamental fireplace. The reception area and main lobby open onto the large back garden. The rooms all vary and have either canal or garden views. Number 44, done in blue and yellow, can be pressed into service for three, but it is much better used as a double. It has an inlaid wooden floor, three windows on the canal, a large bath with a tub, and a small entry framed with mirrors.

TELEPHONE
041-521-0578, 523-7846

FAX
041-523-9152

CREDIT CARDS
AE, DC, MC, V

CLOSED
Never

RATES
Single L175,000, double L300,000, suite or garden cottage "Thelma" L350,000; lower off-season rates; Continental breakfast included

Single travelers are not reduced to closet-size accommodations. Room 27 on the top floor is an exceptionally nice choice for solo travelers. I like the beamed ceiling, wooden floor, pretty Art Deco lamp, and the view over the front garden and the canal. The shower not only has doors but a small seat. The first floor of the hotel has been completely renovated, so the rooms here now have air-conditioning, TVs, and private safes. While every room in the hotel has virtues to recommend it, my absolute favorite Accademia accommodation is "Thelma," the private garden cottage named in memory of a guest from Brighton who died in an automobile accident. She came often to the hotel and especially loved the garden, so when the hotel built the cottage, they dedicated it to her. Isn't that a lovely thing to do? The beamed cottage has a spacious sitting room with Oriental rugs on the stone floor, and comfortable sofa and chairs for pleasant lounging. The superior-class bedroom and bathroom have all the extras to make you want to check in forever. Outside, there is an inviting terrace set with a table and chairs, the perfect place to remember Thelma and admire the lovely gardens she so loved.

As you can imagine, reservations are essential, and in some cases a year in advance. The fiercely loyal clientele often reserve their favorite room or suite for the next year during this year's stay.

NOTE: Also under the same ownership are the Hotel Ala (see page 260) and the Hotel Do Pozzi (see page 262). Guests from the Pensione Accademia are given discounts at the Ristorante da' Raffaele (see Hotel Ala).

ENGLISH SPOKEN Yes

FACILITIES AND SERVICES Some air-conditioners, bar, direct-dial phones, hair dryers, satellite TVs, video in the bar, office safe and some in-room safes, parking (discounts arranged)

NEAREST TOURIST ATTRACTIONS Accademia Gallery, Guggenheim Collection

(42) PENSIONE LA CALCINA ★★★
Fondamenta Zattere al Gesuiti, 780
29 rooms, 26 with private shower or bath and toilet

TELEPHONE
041-520-6466
FAX
041-522-7045
CREDIT CARDS
AE, DC, MC, V
CLOSED
Never

Beloved by British and American guests, La Calcina is the same pensione where the writer John Ruskin lived during his 1876 stay in Venice. It has mellowed well with age and today stands out as a delightful respite from modernity, and an excellent Cheap Sleep value. Beautifully positioned on the Giudecca Canal, it provides guests with modern comforts while maintaining its old-world charm. On the ground floor is a small bar and formal breakfast room that faces the lagoon. When the weather is warm, breakfast is served on a wide terrace built over the water. Guests are encouraged to enjoy this picture-perfect spot during the day, as well as the panoramic roof terrace with a million-dollar view of Venice. This terrace is so small it can accommodate only two people at a time, therefore, guests are requested to reserve their time here.

The twenty-nine rooms are individual in decor, but uniform in amenities, including individually controlled air-conditioning and heating in each room. All have been recently redone with parquet floors and original furnishings. Rooms 37, 38, and 39 have terrace views and are especially appealing, but so is No. 2, with a three-window view of Giudecca, the lagoon, a small side canal, and the bridge over it.

ENGLISH SPOKEN Yes

FACILITIES AND SERVICES Air-conditioning (individually controlled), bar, direct-dial phones, hair dryers, in-room safes

NEAREST TOURIST ATTRACTIONS Accademia Gallery, Guggenheim Collection

RATES
Single L120,000–160,000, double L220,000–290,000; buffet breakfast included

(43) PENSIONE SEGUSO ★★
Zattere al Gesuiti, 779
40 rooms, 20 with shower or bath and toilet

The old-fashioned, elegantly upper-crust Seguso exudes an air of European tranquillity that is rarely found today. The pensione serves breakfast, lunch, and dinner (and will even make picnics) to its devoted guests, who enjoy gracious surroundings filled with antiques and family mementos—all for the price that a room alone costs in many Venetian hotels. While not for the traveler who likes marble, wall-to-wall carpeting, uniformed porters, and fax/computer modems, the Seguso is the ideal answer for hopeless romantics who yearn for and appreciate the leisurely lifestyle and value of a bygone era.

In front of the pensione is a large terrace with tables set under colorful umbrellas. Guests can sit here and look out across the Giudecca Canal, which separates the main part of Venice from Giudecca Island. Meals are served in a formal dining room set with fresh flowers,

TELEPHONE
041-522-2340, 528-6858

FAX
041-522-2340

CREDIT CARDS
AE, MC, V

CLOSED
Dec–Mar

RATES
Single L200,000–230,000, double L310,000–330,000, triple L450,000–480,000; half-board (lunch or dinner) is required in high season and reflected in these rates; low season rates on request; Continental breakfast included

linens, and lovely silver serving pieces. The homey bedrooms are decorated with tasteful simplicity. Some have
ornate ceilings; others brass beds. Several overlook the
terrace, and the prime ones on the corner have canal
views but are bathless. One of my favorites is No. 41,
which has wraparound windows on two sides offering
sensational canal views. I like the painted furniture, the
comfortable armchairs, and the settee, as well as the
private shower and toilet. Another good choice is No.
23, done with antiques, a comfortable leather armchair,
and a dressing table in addition to a massive armoire and
a marble-top chest of drawers. Doors open onto a small
balcony that has a view of the S. Vio Canal on one side
and the Giudecca Canal in front. This room has a sink in
it and a private toilet and shower in the bathroom. If you
want either of these rooms, get your request in as soon as
possible.

The pensione has been in the Seguso family for more
than a hundred years, and most of the staff have been
with them for all of their working lives. Everyone is
treated like family, and you will be, too, making you
feel, as most of the returning guests do, that this is a
wonderful home away from home in Venice.

ENGLISH SPOKEN Yes

FACILITIES AND SERVICES Bar, elevator, office safe, restaurant

NEAREST TOURIST ATTRACTIONS Accademia Gallery,
Guggenheim Collection

San Marco

This district has always been the heart and soul of
Venice. It was on the area we now know as Piazza San
Marco that the early rulers built the Palazzo Ducale, and
established their most important church, Basilica di San
Marco. The Basilica became one of the richest churches
in Christendom and the Palazzo Ducale the seat of a
government that lasted longer than any other Republi-
can regime in Europe. The public space of San Marco is
so revered that it is the only one in Venice granted the
name *piazza*. All the other Venetian squares are either
campos or *campiellos*.

Piazza San Marco is important for another reason:
almost every visitor to Venice passes through here and
spends some money. Even if they just sit at one of the
caffès and listen to the music while sipping an espresso,

they will spend a lot of money. Away from the piazza, along the Merceria and Calle de Fabbri, are some of the city's most expensive boutiques and shopping opportunities. In addition, San Marco is dense with hotels and restaurants of all categories and price ranges.

(45) ALBERGO AL GAMBERO ★★
Calle dei Fabbri, 4687
28 rooms, 16 with shower or bath and toilet

There are two sides to the Al Gambero: a plus side and a negative side. First, the good news. More than half the rooms are new and have private bathrooms, satellite TVs, room safes, and hair dryers. The old rooms are clean, the location is good, and the hall bathrooms do not need extra dousings with Lysol. The bad news? The noise, especially on the weekends. But wait a minute, you're not in Kansas anymore—this is the center of magnificent Venice, and noise has been reverberating off these ancient buildings for centuries. It is just part of the price one pays for being here.

Some room suggestions to follow when reserving in the newer section: No. 404 has a beautiful bathroom with heated towel racks and a bedroom with gold damask wall coverings and hand-painted lamp shades. Number 401 is small, but it's the only room with a terrace, and if you want to hear the gondoliers serenading their passengers as they float by on the canal, reserve No. 203. You will save money sleeping in one of the older rooms, and not be unhappy about that Cheap Sleep if you book No. 43, an aging room with a canal view and a bathroom.

ENGLISH SPOKEN Yes

FACILITIES AND SERVICES All rooms: direct-dial phones, office safe. New rooms: air-conditioning, hair dryers, satellite TVs, in-room safes.

NEAREST TOURIST ATTRACTIONS St. Mark's Square, Rialto Bridge, shopping

TELEPHONE
041-522-4384, 520-1420

FAX
041-520-0431

E-MAIL
gambero@tin.it

CREDIT CARDS
MC, V

CLOSED
Never

RATES
Single L95,000–170,000, double L155,000–240,000, triple L200,000–310,000; buffet breakfast included (deduct L5,000 if not taken); discount to *Cheap Sleeps* readers

(46) ALBERGO SAN SAMUELE ★
Salizzada San Samuele, 3358
10 rooms, two with shower and toilet

My notes read: Be sure to recheck for the 1999 edition to see if it has either been sold or redone; otherwise, forget it.

My notes continue: Great! New owners! Have imagination and lots of plans! Keep it!

TELEPHONE AND FAX
041-522-8045

CREDIT CARDS
None, cash only

CLOSED
Dec or Jan

What can you expect? First, I must caution Cheap Sleepers about the approach through a dank courtyard. Let's just say the curb-appeal factor is missing. Once you get beyond this and upstairs, the lobby is much better than you would expect, and so are the revised, cleaned-up, livable rooms. Starting with No. 1, you will be occupying a big room with a sunny view of the street. The original tile floor has been revealed, the pedestal sink saved, and a wardrobe and modern desk added. Number 6, the prettiest, is a smaller corner room with a view of the archway and street beyond. Nice curtains hang in the wood-frame windows. Number 3 is for four Cheap Sleepers, with plenty of flat surface space for luggage. The hall facilities are fine; in fact, I recommend saving a few lire and opting for a bathless room, even though there is an extra L2,000 charge for a towel. Let's hope that charge will be dropped as soon as possible. The two rooms with bathrooms, on the first floor, have ghastly views—but the towels are free. Breakfast is extra. Save this hotel expense, be Venetian, and go out to a *caffè,* stand at the bar, and get a jump start on your day with a strong espresso or frothy cappuccino.

ENGLISH SPOKEN Yes

FACILITIES AND SERVICES Office safe

NEAREST TOURIST ATTRACTIONS Accademia Gallery, St. Mark's Square

(47) ALBERGO SAN ZULIAN ★★★
Calle San Zulian, 534
19 rooms, all with shower and toilet; plus 4
apartments near Campo St. Antonin

From a Cheap Sleeper's viewpoint, the Albergo San Zulian offers sound comfort and a host of impressive amenities for rates that will not deplete most budgets. Good management skills from a devoted owner have added a star and moved it to a top slot in the ranks of the better three-star hotels near St. Mark's Square. A nice balance has been struck between new and old, harmonized by fabrics and furnishings that recall Italy's artistic heritage and at the same time offer a splash of contemporary sophistication.

The rooms are all good—not a poor choice in the bunch. They are intelligently outfitted with muted wall coverings, carpeted floors, ample closet space, luggage racks, and hand-painted furniture. Honeymooners will want to request No. 304, which has a beautiful wooden ceiling and a private terrace. Another special room is No. 203, which is done in shades of red with a carved settee, swag headboard, white watermarked wallpaper, gold-framed mirror, and a built-in closet. Room 104 is a large double with Oriental throw rugs, a sofa, two chairs, and a bathroom with a stall shower. The hotel is an ideal command post for walking to the Rialto Bridge area or to St. Mark's Square. There is also a choice of good restaurants within a short stroll (see *Cheap Eats in Italy*).

New! Four wonderful apartments, all in the same building near Campo St. Antonin, a pleasant stroll about ten minutes from St. Mark's Square. Named after famous Venetian painters, the attractive units vary in size from a large studio to two bedrooms. I like them because of their quality and the ease of livability evidenced in the nice furnishings, sunny views of neighboring rooftops and canals, maid service, air-conditioning, private safes, and equipped kitchens with refrigerators stocked for your first breakfast (you will only need to buy the bread). Everything is included in the price except telephone calls. Airport and train pickups can be arranged with advance notice (there will be a cost for this convenient service). Guests are requested to reserve a three-night-minimum stay.

ENGLISH SPOKEN Yes

FACILITIES AND SERVICES Air-conditioning, direct-dial phones, hair dryers, minibars, TVs, in-room safes

NEAREST TOURIST ATTRACTIONS Rialto Bridge, St. Mark's Square

(49) HOTEL AI DO MORI ★
Calle Larga San Marco, 658
11 rooms, 5 with shower or bath and toilet

Not long ago Antonella Bernardi's Hotel ai do Mori could charitably be described as a dump. Not anymore, thanks to her hard work and dedication to making her dream of owning a hotel come true. Recent improvements include new hall carpeting, new mattresses, two new bathrooms, and a coat of paint. Plans are to install bathrooms in all the rooms by the end of 1999.

Prices, unfortunately, have hit the tip-top of the one-star scale, but if you are talking location, this one ranks high—a minute from St. Mark's Square and the Grand Canal and close to the Rialto Bridge and more shopping and Cheap Eats (see *Cheap Eats in Italy*) than you will have time to try in ten visits to Venice.

TELEPHONE
041-520-4817, 528-9293

FAX
041-520-5328

CREDIT CARDS
MC, V

CLOSED
Jan, dates vary

RATES
One or two persons L130,000–160,000, triple L160,000–210,000, quad L200,000–280,000, suite for five L320,000, lower off-season rates; no breakfast served

The hotel has eleven rooms on three floors, most with reach-out-and-touch views of San Marco and the Basilica. Please remember, this *is* still a one-star, so there will be stairs to climb, and very small rooms when you get to them, no breakfast served, some noise, and probably not much closet space to accommodate steamer trunks full of clothing. Room 4/5 is a suite for five with a new bathroom that has a tub, but you will have to forego the view. In No. 6, four voyagers can look out the two windows at St. Marks and the Clock Tower, and go down the hall to share a bathroom with only one other room. For romantics willing to have a real workout climbing to the top floor, Room 11, called the Painter's Room, pays off its winded guests with an absolutely unbeatable view to the Basilica, San Marco bell tower, and more, not only from the room but from the bathroom and the private terrace. To get this panorama you must sacrifice space inside, and plan to do your living on the terrace. On rainy days or in winter, cabin fever could set in if you try to spend time in a room that is furnished basically with a bed and a closet.

ENGLISH SPOKEN Yes

FACILITIES AND SERVICES Air-conditioning, direct-dial phones, hair dryers, satellite TVs, office safe

NEAREST TOURIST ATTRACTIONS St. Mark's Square, Grand Canal, shopping, Rialto Bridge

(50) HOTEL ALA ★★★ ($)
Campo Santa Maria dei Giglio, 2494
87 rooms, all with shower or bath and toilet

TELEPHONE
041-520-8333
FAX
041-520-6390
E-MAIL
alahtlve@gpnet.it
INTERNET
www.hotelala.it
CREDIT CARDS
AE, DC, MC, V
CLOSED
Never
RATES
Single L210,000, double L300,000–340,000, triple L390,000; lower off-season rates; buffet breakfast included

For those wanting to be in the historic center of Venice, only minutes by foot from St. Mark's Square, the Hotel Ala is one answer. It is a neighbor of the famous Gritti Palace Hotel, where rooms start at around $500 per night, so you know you are in an exclusive area. If romance is on your agenda, plan to arrive at the hotel's private dock via gondola or water taxi.

While the hotel cannot be termed glamorous, it does have a pleasing air that has been discovered by loads of *Cheap Sleeps in Italy* readers. The large lounge and the breakfast room are hung with local artwork. These rooms also display Murano glass chandeliers, a mixture of old and new furniture, and an interesting collection of firearms. Most of the rooms are inviting for long stays because they have enough room for you and your belongings. Many display original beams and frescoed ceilings. Four have balconies, three have terraces, half look onto the canal, ten are specifically nonsmoking, and one is nonallergic.

Everyone has a favorite they ask for when reserving, with the possible exception of No. 101, a nice but dark room that faces a cement wall. Also viewless is No. 139. Many Cheap Sleepers like Nos. 240 and 241, which can be combined to form a large suite. The rooms are attractively outfitted with light furniture highlighted with floral accents and the balcony view is onto a canal. Number 108, also on a canal, is a standard double with wood beams, luggage space, and a nice bathroom with a tub, heated towel racks, and monogrammed towels. Room 460, on the top floor, has blue graphic wallpaper and a balcony view of the leaning tower at San Stefano. The ceiling alone could sell No. 243, a twin in blue and light gold with a tapestry in back of the bed.

For special occasions, my unequivocal favorite is the Antonia Suite, with sweeping views all the way to Lido. Trust me, once you check in you will start thinking about becoming a permanent resident . . . just as Antonia was. Antonia was an old lady who lived in this part of the hotel for more than twenty years. When she finally died late in her nineties, the hotel redid her quarters and named them after her. I like the living room with its big desk and large-screen television, the bedroom with a reproduction Guardi painting over the bed, the bathroom with an automatic skylight, and, of course, that million-dollar view.

The hotel operates the Ristorante da' Raffaele and offers discounts to guests who eat there. The setting alongside a canal is picture-perfect and the food equal to the setting.

NOTE: Also under the same ownership are the Pensione Accademia (see page 253) and the Hotel Do Pozzi (see page 262).

ENGLISH SPOKEN Yes

FACILITIES AND SERVICES Air-conditioning, bar, direct-dial phones, hair dryers, minibars, satellite TVs, elevator in part of the hotel, office safe and some in-room safes, restaurant

NEAREST TOURIST ATTRACTIONS St. Mark's Square, shopping

(51) HOTEL DIANA ★★
Calle d. Specchieri, 449
27 rooms, all with shower or bath and toilet

TELEPHONE
041-520-6911, 522-1561
FAX
041-523-8763
CREDIT CARDS
AE, MC, V
CLOSED
Dec and Jan
RATES
Single L180,000, double
L230,000, triple L300,000;
lower off-season rates;
Continental breakfast included

Calle Specchieri does not suffer from a shortage of hotel rooms, and the competition to attract guests is intense. The best two-star value by far along the stretch is the Hotel Diana. The rooms are uniform and do not subscribe to any particular style other than "international hotel." This means there will be no surprises—only a clean, reliable room with all the whistles and bells that make it a good deal. For many Cheap Sleepers, the elevator alone is reason enough to reserve here.

While some rooms are on the small side from an American's perspective, they are not cramped, thanks to built-ins and mirrored closets that give the illusion of more space. Gray carpets, white walls, maroon laminated headboards, a desk, a luggage rack, and the best two-star marble baths in San Marco are yours at the Diana. The top-rated bathrooms have ample sink space and tub-and-shower combinations with water shields. Air-conditioning, double-glazed windows, and insulated doors keep noise to an absolute minimum. The only rooms I found lacking were No. 401, which required extra steps to reach and was too tiny for much comfort; No. 101, with a bad view; and No. 204 because of the dim light in the bathroom. From this address, you are in walking distance to almost everything, from St. Mark's Square to dozens of good restaurants and tempting shops dotting the maze of twisting, narrow streets to the Grand Canal and Rialto Bridge.

ENGLISH SPOKEN Yes

FACILITIES AND SERVICES Air-conditioning, direct-dial phones, hair dryers, minibars, satellite TVs, individual guest safes in the office, elevator

NEAREST TOURIST ATTRACTIONS St. Mark's Square, shopping, Rialto Bridge

(52) HOTEL DO POZZI ★★★
Via XXII Marzo, 2373
35 rooms, all with shower or bath and toilet

TELEPHONE
041-520-7855
FAX
041-522-9413
CREDIT CARDS
AE, DC, MC, V
CLOSED
Sometimes in Jan

Of the three hotels in this Venetian group (see Pensione Accademia, page 253, and Hotel Ala, page 262), the Do Pozzi is the least flamboyant. The location, off Corte due Pozzi, is quiet yet central to the best shopping and most tourist must-dos in the city. Hanging throughout the hotel are paintings from the owner's private collection. Downstairs near the reception desk is a small glass case displaying old Japanese *katanda* (individually designed sword shields). The coordinated modern-style bedrooms are not blessed with decoration overkill, but they are fully equipped with all the extras and have compact bathrooms. The best rooms are definitely the dozen that overlook the garden. Families should consider No. 47, a two-room suite with twin beds in a small room off the hall and a double bed in the main room. The view is onto the Turkish and Moroccan tourist office.

Guests are given a discount at the Ristorante da' Raffaele, a canal-side restaurant that puts the *R* back into romance. At night, if you sit outside on the terrace with someone you love and watch the serenading gondoliers float by in the moonlight, you will know what I am talking about.

ENGLISH SPOKEN Yes

FACILITIES AND SERVICES Air-conditioning, direct-dial phones, some hair dryers, minibars, TVs, elevator, office safe

NEAREST TOURIST ATTRACTIONS Shopping, St. Mark's Square

RATES
Single L190,000, double L270,000; extra person L80,000; lower off-season rates; Continental breakfast included; set lunch or menu at da' Raffaele (L50,000, or 10 percent discount for à la carte)

(53) HOTEL FIRENZE ★★★ ($)
Salizzada San Moisé, 1490
26 rooms, all with shower or bath and toilet

If a San Marco location is a priority and your pocketbook is flexible, the Hotel Firenze sits on a prime parcel of real estate only thirty meters from St. Mark's Square. The building was rebuilt at the end of the nineteenth century and has an Art Nouveau facade of marble and iron. The exceptional pink-and-white breakfast room (no smoking, please) shows off leaded stained-glass windows and has comfortable banquette and settee seating.

A solid room choice is No. 301, a large double (or triple if you must) with soothing seafoam-green painted furniture trimmed in gold, blue, and pink, colors that are carried out in the Murano chandelier. The bathroom has all the perks, including a telephone and ample light. Number 302 is another good room, with a streetside view, built-ins, and a luggage rack. The rooftop terrace has breathtaking views of Giudecca, the bell tower and dome of St. Mark's Basilica, the reconstruction of La Fenice Theater, and beyond.

ENGLISH SPOKEN Yes

TELEPHONE
041-522-2858

FAX
041-520-2668

CREDIT CARDS
AE, DC, MC, V

CLOSED
Never

RATES
Single L260,000, double L360,000, triple L565,000; much lower off-season rates; Continental breakfast included

FACILITIES AND SERVICES Air-conditioning, bar, direct-dial phones in rooms and most bathrooms, elevator, minibars, radios, satellite TVs, in-room safes
NEAREST TOURIST ATTRACTIONS St. Mark's Square

(54) HOTEL LA FENICE ET DES ARTISTES ★★★ ($)
Campiello de la Fenice, 1936
75 rooms, 73 with shower or bath and toilet; 2 apartments

TELEPHONE
041-523-2333
FAX
041-520-3721
CREDIT CARDS
AE, DC, MC, V
CLOSED
Never
RATES
Single L200,000, double L350,000, triple L430,000, suite L400,000–500,000; lower off-season rates; Continental breakfast in room or buffet breakfast in dining room included

The Hotel La Fenice et des Artistes is a venerable Venice institution as famous for housing artists in varying stages of their careers as the Algonquin was in its New York heyday. Passing through the entry and the series of sitting rooms, some of which look onto sunny gardens, is like strolling through a bygone era, when hotels catered to guests who arrived with mounds of luggage and stayed for "the season." The hotel takes its name from the Teatro La Fenice, the opera house that was next door, but so tragically burned a few years ago. A rebuilding project has run into financial and political hassles, so it is anyone's guess when it will be reopened, but I can assure you that Venetians love their opera house and they will not let it remain closed forever.

The hotel is divided into old and "new" (built thirty years ago) sections. The old portion has no lift, plenty of steps, and many single rooms. The rooms in both parts vary widely, tending to be rather run over at the heels and mired in the past, with very few of the modern appointments found in most other hotels in this category. However, the ambience and prospect of staying here, soaking up its past history, and *maybe* running into someone who is famous, even mildly so, make up for this faded feeling for most of the dedicated guests.

Room 304, a suite in pink and blue, is better than No. 204, which has the same general layout overlooking the courtyard but needs redoing (starting with the thin upholstery). One of the best singles is No. 351, which is light, on the canal, and has a television. The drawback is the hall toilet, but it is private, for this room only. The room itself has a shower, sink, and bidet. Room 356 has three windows from which you can see the rebuilding of the opera house, La Fenice, and the courtyard around it. The bath here is good, with an enclosed shower, wide sink space, and a lighted mirror. Guests definitely want to avoid No. 251, a dizzy mix of orange and red with a glow-in-the-dark bedspread and an old bathroom. Room

405, another single with high windows and more space, has a big bathroom with a regulation-size tub. The flip side, No. 404, has its own terrace and lots of sunshine, but the marred wallpaper, wrinkled carpeting, and cramped bathroom put it on the "out" list. When reserving, be sure to ask if the bathtubs are full- or half-size— some of the half-size numbers remind me of nothing more than a laundry sink. As you can now see, this hotel is a mixed bag . . . but it still has great appeal.

NOTE: The hotel also has two large two-bedroom apartments (one with a terrace) in another building that are in demand year-round. The advantages here include space, decent bathrooms, a fitted kitchen, and all charges except the telephone are included. There is also weekly maid and linen service. As in the hotel, the decor gets mixed reviews. In one of the apartments some lovely antiques are interspersed with garish yellow plastic barstools and a stretch slipcover pulled over the sofa. They cost L1,900,000 per week, and stays of three weeks or more receive a 10 to 15 percent discount. Hotel La Fenice also owns the Hotel Piccola Fenice (see page 270).

ENGLISH SPOKEN Yes

FACILITIES AND SERVICES Most have air-conditioners, bar, direct-dial phones, elevator to some rooms, minibars in suites, satellite TVs, most have in-room safes

NEAREST TOURIST ATTRACTIONS St. Mark's Square, shopping

(55) HOTEL FLORA ★★★ ($)
Calle Larga XXII Marzo, 2283-A
44 rooms, all with shower or bath and toilet

There is absolutely no question about it, the Flora is one of the best three-star hotels in Venice. Its old-fashioned warmth and hospitality are in evidence from the minute you arrive until you reluctantly leave. For many of its devotees, it is the perfect example of a romantic hotel, to which many others are compared but never quite measure up.

This small hotel is owned and operated by Alex Romanelli and his son, Ruggero, who are carrying on the family tradition of hoteliers. Quality and impeccable taste show throughout. The entry is off Calle Larga XXII Marzo and down a narrow lane from which you can see the garden through the glass doors as you arrive. This garden oasis in the middle of Venice is dominated by an old well and several pieces of statuary. It is all bordered

TELEPHONE
041-520-5844

FAX
041-522-8217

E-MAIL
htlflora@doge.it

CREDIT CARDS
AE, DC, MC, V

CLOSED
Never

RATES
Single L250,000, double L340,000; extra bed L80,000; lower off-season rates; large Continental breakfast included

by twisting vines and beds of hydrangeas, pansies, and camellia bushes. Breakfast and afternoon drinks are served here in warm weather, and several of the rooms open onto it. During the cooler months, breakfast is served in the wood-paneled dining room, where pink-covered tables are laid with English floral-print china and pieces of family silver.

A beautiful hand-painted stairway leads to the bedrooms, all individually decorated with respect to the atmosphere of the hotel. Number 47 is among the most popular, thanks to its enviable antiques and its postcard view of the Salute Church. Number 34 is another well-loved choice, with two windows overlooking the garden, an ornate, velvet-covered headboard, and a matching armoire and side tables. Soft beige walls, Murano lights, a detailed ceiling, and a small green-and-white-tiled bath round it out. Number 36, for two to four guests, overlooks the Palazzo Contarini, the historical palace of Desdemona and Othello. Besides comfortable chairs and enough space to live in, the bathroom is new. Even the smallest rooms are very well done, especially No. 38, a ground-floor selection with two windows opening onto the garden. When reserving, please state your size requirements and remember that all the rooms are nice, but the *very* best overlook the gardens.

When you arrive, you will be warmly welcomed, and throughout your stay, well cared for. "The most important thing we have to offer our guests is our service and our best hospitality," Ruggero Romanelli told me. You will find these important ingredients, and many more, during your stay at the Hotel Flora, which is high for a Cheap Sleep but wonderful for a Big Splurge.

ENGLISH SPOKEN Yes

FACILITIES AND SERVICES Air-conditioning, bar, direct-dial phones, elevator, hair dryers, satellite TVs, in-room safes, room service for light snacks, screens on some of the windows, two rooms for the handicapped, Internet and cellular telephones available

NEAREST TOURIST ATTRACTIONS Premier shopping, St. Mark's Square

(56) HOTEL GALLINI ★★
Calle della Verona, 3673
50 rooms, 43 with shower or bath and toilet

TELEPHONE
041-520-4515
FAX
041-520-9103

The Hotel Gallini offers Cheap Sleepers not only value for their money but a discount if they mention the book when reserving and show a copy when they arrive. Adriano Ceciliati and his brother have owned and personally managed the Gallini since 1953 and are both at the hotel every day to provide not only five-star service, but five-star-plus friendliness. Adriano's charming wife comes early every morning to oversee the breakfast service and makes sure that everyone leaves satisfied. This committed, hospitable approach to the business has earned the family and their hotel an impressive roster of repeat international visitors, many of whom have been coming here since they opened.

The platinum location puts guests within easy walking distance of St. Mark's Square, La Fenice (the opera house), marvelous shopping, and the Rialto Bridge. The closest *vaporetto* stop is just a few minutes away on the Grand Canal, and guests are able to come directly to the hotel by gondola or water taxi. The building was once the site of the brothers' family home. When they converted the original seven-room flat into a hotel, they named it after their mother. The two personally rebuilt the hotel, putting it together piece by piece, even laying the intricate flooring. Every year the hotel is closed from November through February, which is when they paint and do repairs and remodeling projects.

The basic rooms do not sizzle with personality, nor do they sport fine antiques or expensive fabrics. They are well-coordinated, however, and large enough to be comfortable. They are also the cleanest in Venice, thanks to Piera and Bruna, two sisters who have worked here as the cleaning staff for thirty years. The pride they take in their job is certainly evident, and it also says a great deal about the Ceciliatis and how they treat their employees. All of the rooms are good, but I would have to give the edge to those on the third floor. Number 300 is a sunny, light, two-room suite; No. 308 is a double with three windows; Adriano was born in No. 352; and No. 354 was the original kitchen, where the boys played when they were growing up. Views from many of these rooms are directly on the Verona Canal, and from them you can almost hang out and touch the hats of the gondoliers who ply by throughout the day, serenading their passengers, and you as well. One never tires of this wonderful scene, not even Adriano and his brother. I know because I was lucky enough to stay in the hotel during a portion of my last trip to Venice. During the day when I would hear the gondoliers singing, I would rush to the

CREDIT CARDS
AE, MC, V

CLOSED
Nov 1–Mar 1

RATES
Single L180,000, double L230,000, suite L290,000; discounts given to *Cheap Sleeps* readers; Continental breakfast included

window. Many times, standing on the bridge over the canal, were the two brothers, listening to the music along with the rest of us. It was a very tender picture.

A final note: When you stay here, please be sure to say hello to the *real* manager and boss of this very special hotel, the handsome Mr. Pallino, a black cat who had the good sense to adopt the hotel, move in, and now takes his job of surveying the daily scene and generally keeping tabs on everyone very seriously. During the day you will find him stretched out along his sunny front window perch. After his breakfast and morning walk, you will find him purring on the back of a chair, or, more likely, in someone's lap.

ENGLISH SPOKEN Yes, and it is excellent

FACILITIES AND SERVICES Air-conditioners in most rooms, direct-dial phones, hair dryer available, minibars and TVs in suites, office safe

NEAREST TOURIST ATTRACTIONS St. Mark's Square, excellent shopping, La Fenice, Rialto Bridge

(57) HOTEL LISBONA ★★★ ($)
Off Campo San Moisè, 2153; along Via XXII Marzo
15 rooms, all with shower and toilet

TELEPHONE
041-528-6774

FAX
041-520-7061

CREDIT CARDS
AE, DC, MC, V

CLOSED
Never

RATES
Single L240,000, double L340,000; Continental breakfast included

The Hotel Lisbona was the hotel I stayed in many years ago on my first visit to Venice. I was traveling with a school friend and we requested a "room for two with a bath." What we wanted was a room for two with twin beds and a private bath. What we got was a room slightly bigger than a walk-in closet with one bed and a bathroom so tiny you could literally touch both sides of the walls at the same time. It was the middle of the summer and we were stuck . . . there was nothing better here, and everything else was fully booked. Despite the miniature quarters, we loved the location of this hotel and when I started writing *Cheap Sleeps in Italy,* I wanted to include it, but nothing had changed. The rooms were still really drab and rundown, not to mention so small you almost had to go outside to change your mind. But I never gave up, always going back, hoping it had changed. On my last visit . . . *bingo!* The hotel has been improved 100 percent, the rooms slightly enlarged, and a new owner is at the helm. All is finally well at the Lisbona and I am glad I can finally recommend it to you.

Talk about a photo op! If this one doesn't inspire you to load up the camera, nothing else in Venice will. Some of your neighbors will be the high rollers staying at the

Bauer-Gruenwald across the little canal and paying five or six times your room rate. These people you probably won't get to know. You *will* get to know the cluster of handsome gondoliers who park their colorful vessels alongside the Lisbona, and use the walkway under the arch leading to the hotel as their gathering place for playing cards, kibitzing, and flirting between gondola rides.

I must admit, the rooms are still small, but they are now livable enough that you don't have to go outside to turn around, or to change your mind. They have been completely redecorated with coral damask wallcoverings, new carpeting, better furniture, and improved baths. You definitely want one of the twelve that have canal views. Number 11 is a bigger perch for two, with double windows and a little balcony where you will use up plenty of film shooting the gondola activity below. I would avoid Nos. 14, 21, and 31. They are really too small unless you are a single with one very little piece of luggage, although they do have canal views and a tiny balcony. From the hotel door you are minutes from St. Mark's Square, the best shopping in Venice, good restaurants (see *Cheap Eats in Italy*), and *vaporetto* stops to take you any place you want to go.

ENGLISH SPOKEN Yes

FACILITIES AND SERVICES Air-conditioning, bar, direct-dial phones, hair dryers, minibars, satellite TVs, in-room safes

NEAREST TOURIST ATTRACTIONS St. Mark's Square, the gondoliers around the hotel

(58) HOTEL LOCANDA FIORITA ★
Campiello Nuovo, 3457
10 rooms, 8 with shower or bath and toilet

Cheap Sleepers will want to share this great find: an affordable hotel that is smart, clean, and exceptionally nice. The ten-room establishment is off Campo San Stefano on Campiello Nuovo, an inconspicuous square in the premier San Marco district between the Accademia Gallery and the Palazzo Grassi. The entrance is upstairs, through a contemporary reception area with a beamed ceiling, a collection of Venetian Carnivale masks hung on gray walls, and a display of Murano glass. Breakfast is served here around four tables with cane-seated bentwood chairs. In summer you can have your coffee and rolls served on the terrace below.

TELEPHONE
041-523-4754

FAX
041-522-8043

E-MAIL
locafior@tin.it

CREDIT CARDS
AE, MC, V

CLOSED
Never

RATES
Single L75,000–110,000, double L120,000–150,000; extra person L35,000; sometimes lower rates; Continental breakfast included

The thoughtfully planned rooms and baths are really amazing for a one-star, for many two-stars for that matter. The rooms are carpeted or tiled and have some exposed beams, a framed black-and-white print of Venice, a small desk, and an adequate-size wardrobe. The bathrooms have stall showers and lighted mirrors over the sinks, so you can see what you are doing while dressing for the day. The towels are Italian cotton. Two of my favorite rooms are still No. 1, a large double that opens onto a courtyard, and No. 9, fit for four, with two view windows onto the street. It is not surprising to know that this hotel books up fast, so get your reservations in just as soon as you know your arrival date in Venice.

ENGLISH SPOKEN Yes

FACILITIES AND SERVICES Direct-dial phones, hair dryer available, office safe

NEAREST TOURIST ATTRACTIONS St. Mark's Square, Campo San Stefano

(59) HOTEL PICCOLA FENICE ★★★ ($)
Calle della Madonna, 3614
7 suites, all with shower or bath and toilet

TELEPHONE
041-520-4909

FAX
041-520-4949

CREDIT CARDS
AE, DC, MC, V

CLOSED
Never

RATES
Suites from L350,000–450,000 for up to four persons; extra person L50,000; discounts for long stays; breakfast (L15,000 extra)

The moment the Hotel Piccola Fenice opened its doors it was a hit. Owned by Hotel La Fenice et des Artistes (see page 264), it consists of two-room luxury suites suitable for up to six persons who want more space and amenities than usually associated with a hotel room.

The deluxe suites are all fashionably chic, with the latest in colors, styles, and accoutrements. Number 1 features a sitting room with a sofa bed. The faux-finished furniture fits in nicely with the beamed ceiling, dark hardwood floors, and Murano light fixtures. The bedroom's armoire affords plenty of storage space and has four mirrors across the front. Other benefits include a quiet view and a blue-and-white-tiled bathroom. The other six suites are similar in taste and feel. Number 6 has a tiny balcony, a fine bathroom with a shower and sink space, and a walk-in closet. Number 7 is on the top floor and requires additional steps once you are in the flat. The best feature about this choice, aside from its size, is the terrace off the sitting room where you have a bird's-eye view of St. Marks and the reconstruction of La Fenice Theater. Number 3, the smallest, has only one large room and no cooking facilities at all. The "kitchens"—which are not intended for any serious cooking—

in the rest of the units are limited to a coffeepot, a toaster, and the few dishes you will need to lay out and serve breakfast.

The office hours of the hotel for booking are Monday to Saturday 9 A.M. to 7 P.M., and Sunday 9 A.M. to noon. If you belong to the time-share RCI, the Fenice is affiliated, so you are eligible to trade your time-share for one of these in Venice for a week.

ENGLISH SPOKEN Yes

FACILITIES AND SERVICES Air-conditioning, direct-dial phones, elevator to first floor, hair dryers, minibars, TVs, VCRs, in-room safes, limited kitchens, maid services daily

NEAREST TOURIST ATTRACTIONS La Fenice, St. Mark's Square, shopping

(60) HOTEL SAN STEFANO ★★★ ($)
Campo San Stefano, 2957
11 rooms, all with showers and toilets

TELEPHONE
041-520-0166

FAX
041-522-4460

CREDIT CARDS
AE, MC, V

CLOSED
Never

RATES
Single L265,000, double L340,000, triple L445,000; lower off-season rates; Continental breakfast included

The Hotel San Stefano is located right on the colorful Campo San Stefano, which boasts a pretty church, several outdoor cafes, and interesting local activity. The hotel is intimately charming, with views onto the *campo* from many of the rooms. A tiny garden patio along the front provides a place for warm-weather breakfasts or a calm oasis for postcard writing. Not too long ago, the hotel was sold to Roberto Quatrini (who also owns the Hotel Celio in Rome, see page 141). He spent three months and mega-lire upgrading the corridors with marble floors, resparked the breakfast room and lobby area by adding painted beam ceilings, installing special armchairs, and putting in a new bar.

The compact rooms are thoughtfully done and attractively decorated with typical Venetian hand-painted furniture, subdued fabrics, including watered silk, and crystal lights. My favorite room is No. 11, the only one on the top floor; it has a view of the square and the San Maurizio Tower, and is large enough to fit in a sofa with two chairs and a pretty Venetian-style painted wardrobe with two drawers. If you are a light sleeper, ask for a room away from the square, as it can get noisy at night, especially in summer. During the off-season, good discounts are offered.

ENGLISH SPOKEN Yes

FACILITIES AND SERVICES Air-conditioning (L10,000 extra per person, per day), direct-dial phones, elevator, hair dyers, minibars, satellite TVs, office safe, laundry service, nonsmoking rooms

NEAREST TOURIST ATTRACTIONS St. Mark's Square, Grand Canal

(61) HOTEL SERENISSIMA ★★
Calle Goldoni, 4486
36 rooms, all with shower or bath and toilet

TELEPHONE
041-520-0011
FAX
041-522-3292
CREDIT CARDS
AE, MC, V
CLOSED
Nov 15–Mar 1; reopens for Carnivale
RATES
Single L100,000–165,000, double L150,000–240,000; lower off-season rates; Continental breakfast included

No groups are accepted at the Serenissima, a distinct difference, and advantage, over the tour bus dinosaur hotel across the street, which grinds them in and grinds them out with as little as possible offered along the way. The theme here is cordial service and rooms that are dusted, polished, and maintained. The furniture in the white rooms is postmodern and the colors are coordinated. The bathroom showers have doors, along with a shelf for your toiletries. An added note is the owner's interesting modern art collection, which is hung in the hotel. A sketched portrait of her as a young girl marks the top of the second-floor landing. Prices in the off-season should appeal to most Cheap Sleepers looking for a real deal.

ENGLISH SPOKEN Yes

FACILITIES AND SERVICES Air-conditioning, bar, direct-dial phones, hair dryers, TVs, office safe

NEAREST TOURIST ATTRACTIONS St. Mark's Square, Rialto Bridge

(62) LOCANDA CASA PETRARCA ★
Calle degli Schiavine, 4386
7 rooms, 3 with shower or bath and toilet

TELEPHONE
041-520-0430
CREDIT CARDS
None, cash only
CLOSED
Never
RATES
Single L90,000, double L125,000–150,000; extra person 35 percent of room rate; discounts for long stays; Continental breakfast (L8,000 extra)

You probably would never find the Locanda Casa Petrarca if someone did not tip you off to it. When you book your room, Nellie, the hospitable English-speaking owner, will give you specific directions on how to get to her seven-room hideaway tucked at the end of Calle degli Schiavine. As you approach it, look for the flower boxes in the archway windows by the main entrance.

The rooms redefine *tiny,* but they are clean and cheerful, with tiled floors, bedside rugs, and the type of furniture you would put in a child's room. They are often filled with guests on long stays and the hotel can easily adopt a boardinghouse atmosphere. Three of the rooms look onto a canal, and one of them, No. 1, is a new double with a bathroom. The small reception area is done in wicker, and a bookcase provides guests with all sorts of good reads for borrowing. If you decide to eat breakfast here, Nellie will serve it in your room, which could add the perfect touch to your stay, depending on your roommate.

ENGLISH SPOKEN Yes
FACILITIES AND SERVICES Office safe
NEAREST TOURIST ATTRACTIONS St. Mark's Square, shopping, Rialto Bridge

San Polo

The smallest *sestiere*, San Polo, has one of the most important destinations for visitors and locals alike: Rialto Market. For hundreds of years the Rialto Market was the center in Venice for buying and selling everything from the finest gold and laces to the humble potato. The area developed into a rabbit warren of shops, taverns, offices, and street stalls. Not much has changed today. The Rialto Bridge is lined with one stall after another and at the foot, along the canal, are the famous fruit, vegetable, meat, and fish markets. For visitors, this is a must-see part of a trip to Venice.

(64) LOCANDA STURION ★★★ ($)
Calle del Sturion, 679 (sometimes spelled Storione)
11 rooms, all with shower or bath and toilet

If you dream of a room on the Grand Canal but have nightmares about the astronomical prices most hotels charge, fret no more and reserve a room at the Locanda Sturion, a hotel with a long history dating back to the thirteenth century, when it housed merchants bringing their wares to the Rialto Market.

The best rooms are the two large ones that overlook the Grand Canal. Because these are the *only* two with canal views, they are extremely popular, so get your request for one of them in early. The walls in the rooms are covered in red or pink brocade that matches the bedspreads. Tea and coffeemakers with a packet of cookies are welcoming touches. In the tiled bathrooms you will find lighted mirrors over the sinks bordered with artistic tile frames, a supply of toiletries, and heated towel racks. There are two rooms, Nos. 9 and 10 on the top floor, that guests either love or hate. Getting to them requires more stair climbing (see note below) for a romantic room—one has a pitched dormer roof and a

TELEPHONE
041-523-6243
FAX
041-522-8378
E-MAIL
sturion@tin.it
CREDIT CARDS
AE, DC, MC, V
CLOSED
Never
RATES
Single L220,000, double L315,000, triple L400,000; extra person L50,000; lower off-season rates; buffet breakfast included

bird's-eye view; the other is a quiet two-room suite that works well for a family. Breakfast is served in a dining room with a canal view. You will no doubt want to linger here over a second cup of coffee while scribbling a few cards to friends back home, suggesting you may never return from Venice.

NOTE: *Warning!* For most, the four flights of stairs (sixty-nine steps straight up) to the reception area and hotel proper will be a piece of cake. For some, however, they might pose a problem. Once you get to the reception, you could have more of a hike, depending on the room location.

ENGLISH SPOKEN Yes

FACILITIES AND SERVICES Air-conditioning, bar, direct-dial phones, hair dryers, minibars, parking (special rates at Tronchetto Park), satellite TVs, special Venetian travel videos and children's Disney (Italian) cartoon videos in the lounge, in-room safes, tea and coffeemakers in the room, discount at their restaurant, Bistro de Venise (see *Cheap Eats in Italy*)

NEAREST TOURIST ATTRACTIONS Rialto Bridge

Santa Croce

Named after the fourteenth-century Benedictine monastery of Santa Croce, this *sestiere* was located along the Grand Canal where the Fascist regime created the Piazzale Roma, the monstrous car park at the end of the bridge leading to Venice from Mestre.

(65) ALBERGO AL GALLO ★
Calle Amai, Corte dei Amai, 1976
7 rooms, 5 with shower and toilet

TELEPHONE
041-523-6761

FAX
041-522-8188

CREDIT CARDS
None, cash only

CLOSED
Jan 6–Carnivale

RATES
Single L65,000–95,000, double L115,000–145,000, triple L175,000, quad L195,000; Continental breakfast served in rooms (L10,000 extra per person)

The Albergo al Gallo is an all-purpose Cheap Sleep pleaser that houses guests in simple, clean rooms that do not subscribe to the garage-sale-gothic school of interior decorating. To keep ahead of deferred maintenance, the owner, Alex Basile, repaints yearly. To stay two steps ahead of the competition, he keeps his rates low and makes breakfast an extra. Good idea. Number 2 is a double with space enough to add bunk beds for children. The hall facility situation isn't bad when you consider that only two rooms use them and there is a toilet on each floor. The hotel is not far from the railway station and Piazzale Roma, the big car park.

ENGLISH SPOKEN Yes

FACILITIES AND SERVICES Fans available, office safe

NEAREST TOURIST ATTRACTIONS Near train station, across the Grand Canal from St. Mark's Square

(66) ALBERGO CASA PERON ★
Calle Vinanti, Salizzada S. Pantalon, 84
11 rooms, 7 with shower or toilet

This heaven-sent retreat for Cheap Sleepers is in a calm, attractive neighborhood midway between Piazzale Roma and the Grand Canal. Gianrico Scarpa and his wife, Luana, put a great deal of effort into keeping their hotel in tip-top shape. This shows from the minute you step into the lobby and reach your tidy bedroom until you sit on the peaceful upstairs terrace filled with fragrant jasmine, roses, vines, flowering plants, and boasting a view of the nearby bell tower. The eleven nests are sunny, bright, and reasonably spacious, with simple furniture displaying not a nick or scratch. Seven have private bathrooms; the rest have only private showers. My top choice is No. 5, with a private shower and toilet and the bonus of a small terrace with white jasmine and red roses blooming on it.

The dining room is small, with only four tables and a poster of one of Gianrico's departed birds. Be sure to notice the wooden chest that Gianrico found in a trash heap and refinished himself. He is also an amateur painter and has hung his work in the dining area and in many of the bedrooms. The Scarpas live in the hotel and are dedicated to every detail of its operation. Offering colorful help is their beautiful parrot, Perino, who considers himself to be the "assistant manager" and often rides on Gianrico's shoulder.

ENGLISH SPOKEN Yes

FACILITIES AND SERVICES Office safe

NEAREST TOURIST ATTRACTIONS Interesting neighborhood; fifteen-minute walk to *vaporetto* stop on the Grand Canal; close to car parks at Piazzale Roma

TELEPHONE
041-710-021, 711-038

FAX
041-711-038

CREDIT CARDS
MC, V

CLOSED
Jan

RATES
Single L75,000–95,000, double L110,000–145,000, triple L150,000–190,000; Continental breakfast included

(67) HOTEL AI DUE FANALI ★★★ ($)
Campo San Simeone Profeta, 946
16 rooms, all with shower or bath and toilet; 5 apartments

Beautiful rooms await guests at the desirable ai due Fanali, a hotel created in what was the ancient school of the Church of San Simeon Grando—you can see a bas-relief of the saint inside the hotel portico. The location,

TELEPHONE
041-718-490

FAX
041-718-344

INTERNET
www.venicehotel.com/ai2fanali

CREDIT CARDS
AE, DC, MC, V

CLOSED
Never
RATES
Single L270,000, double
L350,000; lower off-season
rates; Continental breakfast
included; apartment rates on
request

across the Grand Canal from the train station and
Piazzale Roma, on a quiet square in Santa Croce, is
prime for many.

The handsome lobby has polished marble floors, intricate wood ceilings, and period furnishings. The
friendly staff keeps everything right on the mark, and
the rooms are well-conceived and done with impeccable
taste. The singles benefit from Grand Canal views, and
the best rooms in the house are on the top floors. Of
these, No. 301, a twin-bedded double, has the best view.
Not to be overlooked is No. 201, in soft blue and yellow,
which has the original wooden ceiling beams, a French
marble fireplace, and a view of the square in front of the
hotel. The soft yellow bedspreads complement the
painted headboard. The bathroom, like all the others, is
exceptional, with chrome and gold fittings and marble
fixtures, plus a water shield for the shower, ample shelf
space and light, and plenty of towels. In the morning, a
generous breakfast of juice, rolls, cereal, and yogurt is
served either on the top-floor terrace or in the third-floor
breakfast room.

NOTE: Now available near Piazza San Marco, at Calle
del Cagnoletto, 4084, are handsome apartment suites
with extraordinary views. From the windows facing the
Riva degli Schiavoni you can overlook the San Marco
basin and the island of San Giorgio Maggiore. (If you
want to have the best all-around view of Venice, take the
vaporetto from Riva degli Schiavoni across the lagoon to
San Giorgio and go to the top of the San Giorgio
Maggiore Church. The spectacular vista is better than
from the Basilica of San Marco.) The apartments are
decorated in the best of taste, employing just the right
balance of tradition with whimsy. They have all the
services offered at the hotel, but if you need anything
extra, there's a direct telephone line to the hotel.

ENGLISH SPOKEN Yes

FACILITIES AND SERVICES Hotel and apartment suites:
air-conditioning, bar, direct-dial phones, hair dryers,
minibars, TVs, in-room safes

NEAREST TOURIST ATTRACTIONS Hotel: across Ponte
degli Scalizi from the train station and Piazzale Roma.
Apartments: St. Mark's Square

(68) HOTEL FALIER ★★
Salizzada San Pantalon, 130
19 rooms, all with shower or bath and toilet

Completely restyled from top to bottom in 1992, the Hotel Falier remains an excellent two-star hotel. It is well located and close to Piazzale Roma (where you can park your car if you have one) and the train station. The area is not touristy, but it is lined with good neighborhood restaurants (see *Cheap Eats in Italy*) and shops that are fun to stroll by and browse in.

The stylish open lobby, complete with Doric columns, French furniture, and potted palms, faces a street and a canal. At the back of the lobby is a corner breakfast area with banquette seating where you can watch the equivalent of *Good Morning America* on the television with your strong coffee, rolls, and jam. Each room, though small, reflects excellent taste. I like their uniformity, lacy window curtains, flowered bedspreads, built-in furniture, luggage racks, and modern baths with good shelf space. Two little terraces for guests are brightened by potted flowers and rooftop views. One of the most requested rooms, No. 41, with a pitched roof, looks out onto one of these terraces. The room has a fan, but in the dog days of August, you might sizzle.

NOTE: The owner, Salvatore Sutera, also runs the three-star Hotel American (see page 248).

ENGLISH SPOKEN Yes

FACILITIES AND SERVICES Bar, direct-dial phones, fans in rooms, hair dryers, office safe

NEAREST TOURIST ATTRACTIONS Train station, Piazzale Roma, Campo S. Rocco, Frari Church

TELEPHONE
041-710-882, 711-005

FAX
041-520-6554

CREDIT CARDS
AE, MC, V

CLOSED
Never

RATES
Single L205,000, double L235,000; very good off-season rates; Continental breakfast included

(69) HOTEL MARIN ★
Calle del Traghetto di Santa Lucia, 670-B
18 rooms, 14 with shower or bath and toilet

I remain very impressed with the Hotel Marin . . . . This is one terrific Cheap Sleep value.

The hotel is in a quiet neighborhood only a few minutes walk from Piazzale Roma, where motorists leave their cars, and the train station. Though not on my original list of new Venice entries to check for the last edition of *Cheap Sleeps in Italy,* as I walked by, I couldn't help but notice the blooming cinerarias and camellia bushes framing the entrance and terrace in front of the hotel. It was late, I was tired, and I was in no mood to evaluate another one-star. I vowed to come back, but

TELEPHONE
041-718-022, 721-485

FAX
041-718-022

E-MAIL
htlmarin@gpnet.it

INTERNET
www.gpnet.it/hotels/DB/ HOTELS/Ve__marin.htm

CREDIT CARDS
AE, MC, V

CLOSED
Nov 15–Dec 26

RATES

Single or double with shower, no toilet L135,000, with toilet and shower L145,000, triple L185,000, quad L220,000, lower off-season rates; Continental breakfast included

didn't make it until the last afternoon of my last day in Venice, and the payoff was great. I liked it very much, considered it a real Cheap Sleep discovery, and was happy to include it. When I returned to reevaluate it for this edition, I found it to be even better, and can still tell you without hesitation that this is one terrific value.

When Bruno and Nadia Scotton took over this place, it was a run-down number no one would consider. Nadia, who never settles for second best, told me, "We don't have quantity, only quality. We are only a one-star, but it's a good star." And I will add that it is shining brightly. At Nadia's insistence, each room has two wood-framed windows to let in light and air. The furniture is standard and includes a one-piece bed and closet unit, a desk, one or two chairs, a full-length mirror, tile floors, a picture on the wall, and quilted spreads. You could eat off the floor . . . any floor. Fourteen of the rooms now have private toilets and showers, while the remainder all have a shower and share the hall toilets. Nadia's green thumb is evident in the sitting room, which is filled with blooming azaleas and cyclamens. More greenery warms the pretty dining room, which has a delicate hand-done ceiling.

ENGLISH SPOKEN Yes

FACILITIES AND SERVICES Direct-dial phones, hair dryers, TVs on request, office safe

NEAREST TOURIST ATTRACTIONS Piazzale Roma, train station

Giudecca Island

One of the big present claims to fame on Giudecca—an otherwise tourist-free zone—is the Hotel Cipriani, where rooms start around $650 per night and more than double to $1,400 for a suite—breakfast, taxes, and service included. If you'd rather spend slightly less, have a meal or a drink at Harry's Dolce, also on Giudecca, which is less pricey than Harry's Bar in San Marco. Otherwise, call the Cipriani at (800) 223-6800 for reservations. For lodgings, see Instituto Suore Canossiane and Ostello Venezia in "Student Accommodations," page 289.

Lido Island

Lido is known for its beaches, gambling casinos, and as the site of the Venice Film Festival. You can get to Lido from San Zaccaria in Venice in about ten or fifteen minutes by *vaporetto,* but you will be light years away from the true spirit and unique romantic charm of Venice. The best way to explore Lido is on a bicycle, which you can rent at several locations. Lido also has many old-fashioned-type hotels, where families have come for generations and stayed for "the season." The season now is probably a week or ten days, and some of these dowager hotels seem to be relics of a bygone era.

Tourists flock to Lido during the warm months, drawn by the casino, the memories of the society life during the heyday of the twenties and thirties, and the long stretch of beach. Unfortunately, hotels control the best sections of the beach, and unless you stay at a hotel that rents beach cabanas, you will be relegated to the public beaches at the northern and southern ends of the island, where the water is not always clean. Even if you do not go to lounge on the beach, Lido is great: you can still play tennis, golf, water-ski, windsurf, parasail, ride horses, bicycle, and walk.

(72) HOTEL ATLANTA AUGUSTUS ★★★ ($)
Via Lepanto, 15
31 rooms, all with shower or bath and toilet

The motto at the Hotel Atlanta Augustus is "Cleanliness, Professionality, and Comfort." This promise becomes a reality thanks to owner Ricardo Polacco, his able assistant Marco, the superb cleaning staff headed for twenty-two years by Adrian, and Leonardo the cat, who gives every guest a warm welcome. With this unbeatable combination, it is no wonder it has such a loyal clientele. All this is only part of the great package you will get at this comfortable hotel on a quiet street in one of the best sections of Lido. The Liberty-style villa has thirty-one modern bedrooms, six of which have balconies and two of which have small corner kitchens. Starting with the standard rooms, No. 10 on the back is a quiet, sunny double with a small balcony. For a canal view and a balcony, request No. 3. For larger quarters, ask for a two-room suite, either Nos. 502 or 503, with mezzanine bedrooms and a small kitchen downstairs. These are modern in tone, with bleached Swedish

TELEPHONE
041-526-1205

FAX
041-526-5604

E-MAIL
atlanta@venicehotel.com

INTERNET
www.venicehotel.com/atlanta

CREDIT CARDS
AE, MC, V

CLOSED
Dec and Jan

RATES
Single L230,000, double L360,000, suite L490,000; lower off-season rates; buffet breakfast included

furniture accented by red, blue, and yellow sconces, three windows, and a double sink in the bathroom. Everything matches, even the coat hangers. Honeymooners will want a special room, and that is No. 501, with a canopy bed draped in white and blue. A large buffet breakfast served in the two-room dining area or in the garden provides enough energy for the day until you return to the American Bar, which features a nightly happy hour. During the day you can rent a bicycle from the hotel and pedal around the island, exploring all of its pretty neighborhoods, beaches, and parks.

ENGLISH SPOKEN Yes

FACILITIES AND SERVICES Air-conditioning in some rooms, fans in all, bar, direct-dial phones, hair dryers in some rooms (also available on request), elevator, free parking, TVs, some in-room safes, office safe, nonsmoking rooms, bicycle rentals

NEAREST TOURIST ATTRACTIONS Lido; thirty minutes to Venice proper, via foot and *vaporetto*

(73) HOTEL BELVEDERE ★★★ ($)
Piazza le Santa Maria Elisabetta, 4
30 rooms, all with shower or bath and toilet

TELEPHONE
041-526-0115

FAX
041-526-1486

CREDIT CARDS
AE, DC, MC, V

CLOSED
2 weeks in Nov, dates vary

RATES
Single L190,000–220,000, double L250,000–320,000; lower off-season rates, Continental breakfast included; pensione plan for set-priced meals (half-board L40,000 per person for either lunch or dinner; L60,000 per person for both)

The Belvedere, owned and managed by the same family since it was built in 1857, is one of the mainstays on Lido Island, overlooking the lagoon and across the street from the landing stages for the water taxis that take you to Venice proper. The dependably clean rooms have been modernized and are enhanced by dedicated upkeep and above-average bathrooms, all with showers. Fourteen of them have views and rent for the same price as the viewless chambers. The hotel is open fifty weeks of the year, rents beach cabanas, which they offer *free* to singles in summer, and has parking. The hotel also operates a good restaurant and snack bar, but this part of the hotel operation is closed on Mondays and from November until Carnivale (see *Cheap Eats in Italy*).

ENGLISH SPOKEN Yes

FACILITIES AND SERVICES Air-conditioning, bar, direct-dial phones, radios, TVs, office safe, elevator, free parking, free beach cabanas

NEAREST TOURIST ATTRACTIONS Lido Beach; ten minutes by boat to Venice

(74) HOTEL CRISTALLO ★★
Gran Viale Santa Maria Elisabetta, 51
24 rooms, all with shower or bath and toilet

It's improved!

Everyone likes manager Andrea Leone because he is helpful, considerate, friendly, funny, and treats guests like family. The hotel has a lot going for it as well, including air-conditioning, an elevator, free parking, and if you stay at least three nights, free beach cabanas on the posh Lido Beach. The Cristallo is in the center of the wide boulevard that runs through the small commercial section of Lido from the ocean to the lagoon.

All the bedchambers come with their own bathrooms and four have front-facing balconies. Everything on the third floor has been redone, including the white paint in the halls and blue carpeting. Number 32 is a corner site with two windows looking onto a garden and over rooftops. Just wait until you see the new gray marble sink and tub in the bathroom. Andrea said, "In room 22, we should rent the bathroom rather than the room." The room is fine, but he is right, the bathroom is really great. Number 34, one of the biggest and brightest, sleeps four and is on the street. The Hotel Pensione Wildner, page 242, is under the same ownership.

ENGLISH SPOKEN Yes

FACILITIES AND SERVICES Air-conditioning, bar, direct-dial phones, elevator, satellite TVs, office safe, free parking; free beach cabanas if your stay is three or more nights

NEAREST TOURIST ATTRACTIONS Lido Beach; ten-minute *vaporetto* ride to Venice

TELEPHONE
041-526-5293

FAX
041-526-5615

E-MAIL
wildnercolpowil@Tin.it

CREDIT CARDS
AE, MC, V

CLOSED
Nov 15–Mar 15 (reopens one week after Christmas and for Carnivale)

RATES
Single L160,000, double L220,000; extra person L50,000; lower off-season rates; Continental breakfast included

(75) HOTEL HELVETIA ★★★
Gran Viale Santa Maria Elisabetta, 4/6
56 rooms, all with shower or bath and toilet

On the main street, look for the red building on your right as you leave the boat that brought you from Venice. The Helvetia may be a three-star, but it can hardly be defined as an enclave of elegance. This is the Buster Brown–Oxfords type of sturdy hotel, meaning it has not changed in decades and has no plans to do so. Here you will find extended families who have been coming every year at the same time for generations. They come for the relaxation, sun, sand, and fun of being on Lido, and they do not need glittering surroundings to enjoy it. It is an easy place to stay in. They have a private beach and

TELEPHONE
041-526-0105, 526-8403

FAX
041-526-8903

CREDIT CARDS
MC, V

CLOSED
Nov–Easter

RATES
Single L140,000–275,000, double L190,000–335,000, triple L240,000–430,000; lower off-season rates; pensione plan (set meal L40,000 extra for lunch or dinner); Continental breakfast included

entrance is free, but the cabanas will set you back L50,000 to L100,000 per day. There is a pensione plan available for lunch and/or dinner, a large bar where guests catch up with friends made on past visits, and utilitarian rooms with private facilities that are ideal for families with children because nothing in them can be damaged. Fast-trackers will go crazy, but families in search of a beach vacation with as little hassle as possible will be thrilled.

ENGLISH SPOKEN Yes

FACILITIES AND SERVICES Bar, direct-dial phones, elevator, room fans, parking (L15,000 per day), office safe, beach cabanas (L50,000–100,000 per day)

NEAREST TOURIST ATTRACTIONS All of Lido; ten-minute *vaporetto* ride to Venice

Other Options

Apartment Rentals

Before reserving any apartment in Venice, please refer to "Tips on Renting an Italian Apartment," page 13. In addition to the establishments described here, Rental Directories International (see Rome, "Rental Agencies," page 188) can also set you up with an apartment rental in Venice, as can Rentals in Italy (and Elsewhere!) and Villas International (see Florence, "Rental Agencies," pages 115 and 116).

(44) STUDIO OPERAZIONI IMMOBILIARI
Calle Lunga Santa Barnaba, 2633 (Dorsoduro)
6 apartments

Dottore Cristiano Bacci, whose clients include members of the Cipriani and Gucci families, is in the business of selling apartments. Often the properties he sells are vacation homes that the owners are willing to rent when they are not in residence. Such is the case with the six apartments—probably more by now—he has available in Venice. What are they like? Ranging in size from a generous studio to a two-bedroom extravaganza, they are downright wonderful, with decorator-inspired furnishings, marble bathrooms, plenty of wardrobe space, and well-equipped kitchens with microwaves and real stoves, not just a hot plate. Dishwashers and washing machines come with the larger units, but as of press time, telephones were not available in any units. Hopefully that will change. For short stays, utilities are included, and for all the apartments, lower rates are possible for extended stays. All the standard reservation and cancellation policies apply.

ENGLISH SPOKEN Yes

FACILITIES AND SERVICES Dishwashers and washing machines in some; TVs, equipped kitchens with stove and microwave in all. No telephone, but that may change. Be sure to ask if the lack of one would be a problem during your stay. Maid service is extra.

NEAREST TOURIST ATTRACTIONS Several are in Dorsoduro, others are scattered

TELEPHONE AND FAX
041-528-5959

E-MAIL
Cribacci@tin.it

CREDIT CARDS
None, but hopes to have them, so ask

CLOSED
Aug and Christmas–Jan 7

RATES
From L2,400,000 per month for a studio to L1,000,000 per week for larger apartments

Hotels with Apartments or Kitchen Suites

(47) ALBERGO SAN ZULIAN ★★★
See "San Marco," page 258.

(67) HOTEL AI DUE FANALI ★★★ ($)
See "Santa Croce," page 275.

(18) HOTEL AL PIAVE ★★
See "Castello," page 236.

(72) HOTEL ATLANTA AUGUSTUS ★★★ ($)
See "Lido Island," page 279.

(59) HOTEL PICCOLA FENICE ★★★ ($)
See "San Marco," page 270.

(13) LOCANDA AI SANTI APOSTOLI ★★★ ($)
See "Cannaregio," page 232.

Camping

Forget white stretches of picturesque beaches where you can pitch a tent under the starry sky. That just is not happening in Venice. Most of the campsites are in dreary, drab Marghera or, worse, in Cavallino. The tourist office issues a long list, but don't expect too much beauty with your Bunsen burner. Another downer, there are no true Cheap Sleep campsites, only those that are slightly better than another. Here is a biased listing of the lesser of the evils.

CAMPING FUSINA
Via Moranzani (Fusina)
1,000 campsites

In summer, the *vaporetto* 16 connects Fusina to Venice. Otherwise, you have to take the bus to Mestre and get to Venice from there. This translates to twenty minutes by boat to Venice or 1½ hours by bus, foot, and boat. There is a store, restaurant, and bar, and the showers are free. You can buy a ferry pass when it runs: L15,000 round-trip, L30,000 three-day pass; children L8,000 round-trip, L21,000 three-day pass. They have caravan spaces, and, oddly enough, it is better to rent theirs than to come with your own.

ENGLISH SPOKEN Yes

FACILITIES AND SERVICES Bar; restaurant for breakfast, lunch, dinner, pizza; free showers, coin laundry, cyber access

TELEPHONE 041-547-0055

FAX 041-544-0050

CREDIT CARDS MC, V

CLOSED Never

RATES L20,000 a day plus L10,000 per day, per person, if you arrive in your own caravan; L22,000 per day if it is theirs, and you do not have to pay the additional L10,000 per person fee; sheets and blankets are included; L12,000 for a tent plus the per-person charge; children under five stay free, under twelve, L8,000 per day

CA' PASQUALL
Via Fausta, 33 (outside Venice)
2,000 campsites

The campground has a store, a restaurant, laundry facilities, and a swimming pool. You will need a car or bus to get to the boat, which takes an additional forty minutes to get to Venice. There is a seven-day minimum stay.

ENGLISH SPOKEN Yes

TELEPHONE 041-966-1100

FAX 041-530-0797

CREDIT CARDS AE

CLOSED Sept 18–May 9

RATES L11,000 per day for adults, L8,000 per children under six in tent or caravan; tents on the beach L30,000 per day, off the beach L25,000; caravans L60,000–100,000 per day; free showers; seven-day minimum stay

MARINA DE VENEZIA
Punta Sabbioni, Via Montello, 6 (outside Venice)
2,800 campsites

This mammoth campground has a better setting than the others included here, with two restaurants, thirteen bars—five on the beach!—a market, two swimming pools, tennis, mini-golf, laundry facilities, a barber shop, a jeweler, and a train to take you around. You can spend all day on the beach, but can't sleep there at night. There are no tent rentals, but you can bring your own. The access to Venice is terrible: it is a two-kilometer walk from the campground to the ferry, which takes forty minutes to get to Venice.

ENGLISH SPOKEN Yes
TELEPHONE 041-966-146
FAX 041-966-036
CREDIT CARDS None, cash only
CLOSED Oct–mid-April
RATES Camping in a tent or caravan L15,000 per person, children one to five L9,000 per day and L30,000 for your own tent or caravan; bungalows L140,000–210,000 per day for four to six people; lower off-season rates

Student Accommodations

In summer and during Christmas and other school vacation periods, accommodations to please most hard-core Cheap Sleeper budgets can be found in dormitories run by various schools and religious organizations. They are spartan at best. Some have strict rules and regulations, most have curfews and daytime lockouts, and only a few serve low-cost meals.

NOTE: Students interested in accommodation and other discounts in Venice should consider purchasing a Rolling Venice Card, see page 218 for details. All students and teachers should also purchase an ISIC card, which entitles them to significant savings almost across the board. For details about the ISIC card, please see page 16.

(34) DOMUS CAVANIS
Rio Terrà Antonio Foscarini, 896 (Dorsoduro)
59 rooms, 29 with shower or bath and toilet

This Catholic-run establishment has quarters for singles, families, and groups from June 15 to September 30. The prices aren't among the cheapest, but you will be in one of the most central locations in Venice. There is a midnight lockout.

ENGLISH SPOKEN Yes
FACILITIES AND SERVICES None
NEAREST TOURIST ATTRACTIONS Accademia Gallery, Guggenheim Collection
TELEPHONE AND FAX 041-528-7374
CREDIT CARDS None, cash only
CLOSED Oct–June 14

RATES Single L70,000, double L65,000 per person; discounts with a student card and for stays over two nights; Continental breakfast L8,000

(48) DOMUS CILIOTA
Calle delle Muneghe, 2976 (San Marco)

The Ciliota, near Campo San Stefano, is as friendly as you will get, and besides, they offer deals for Cheap Sleeping students. It accepts young ladies, families, and organized groups. Breakfast is included; lunch is extra. Curfew is at midnight, and it's open from June 15 to September 15.

ENGLISH SPOKEN Yes
FACILITIES AND SERVICES None
NEAREST TOURIST ATTRACTIONS San Marco
TELEPHONE 041-520-4888
FAX 041-521-2730
CREDIT CARDS None, cash only
CLOSED Mid-Sept–mid-June
RATES Single L65,000–85,000, double L105,000–125,000; set lunch (L23,000, beverages extra); Continental breakfast included

(63) DOMUS CIVICA
Calle d. Campazzo, 3082 (San Polo)

Domus Civica is near the train station and open daily to all Cheap Sleepers from June 15 to October 15. Most rooms are doubles with cold running water; showers, sheets and towels are free; and breakfast is served only to groups. There is a 20 percent discount with an ISIC card or a Rolling Venice Card (see pages 16 and 218 for descriptions of these two excellent discount programs). The reception desk is open from 7:30 A.M. to 11:30 P.M. Curfew is at 11:30 P.M.

ENGLISH SPOKEN Yes
FACILITIES AND SERVICES Elevator
NEAREST TOURIST ATTRACTIONS Train station
TELEPHONE 041-721-103, 524-0416
FAX 041-522-7139
CREDIT CARDS None, cash only
CLOSED Oct 15–June 15
RATES Singles L45,000 per person, doubles L35,000 per person in double room; breakfast served to groups only

(17) FORESTERIA VALDESE
Calle Lunga Santa Maria Formosa, 5170 (Castello)
**50 beds, no rooms with private shower or toilet;
2 apartments have private shower and toilet**

Housed in the crumbling Palazzo Caragnis at the end of Calle Lunga Santa Maria Formosa, the building dates back to the Doges and is now a national monument. In 1868, the Waldesian Protestant Church purchased the *palazzo*. The primary focus was to help needy children. In 1908, the grand hall was turned into a church for the Waldesian evangelical services. In 1925, the villa was opened to boarding guests, and today it operates as a hostel welcoming groups, families, and singles. The dorm rooms are basic, and so are the two flats with kitchens, which are good deals if there are several Cheap Sleepers in your group and you plan to only sleep and change clothes in your room. No towels are provided for the dormitory rooms. Several rooms have balconies, the location is nice, and the rules are: no smoking in the rooms, no booze, clear the table after breakfast, be out of your room from 10 A.M. to 1 P.M. (but there is no maid service, so I wonder why), and, for obvious reasons, you must keep your bed in order. It is part of the same religious group that runs Istituto Gould in Florence (see page 71) and Casa Valdese in Rome (see page 173).

The reception desk is open Monday to Saturday from 9 A.M. to 1 P.M. and 6 to 8 P.M., and on Sunday from 9 A.M. to 1 P.M. Reservations are accepted by phone or fax only.

ENGLISH SPOKEN Yes, but it can be limited

FACILITIES AND SERVICES None

NEAREST TOURIST ATTRACTIONS St. Mark's Square, Rialto Bridge

TELEPHONE AND FAX 041-528-6797

E-MAIL valdesi@doge.it

INTERNET www.doge.it/valdesi/01.htm

CREDIT CARDS None, cash only

CLOSED 3 weeks in Nov, dates vary

RATES Dorm: L30,000 first night, L1,000 less for successive nights, double L90,000–130,000, triple L120,000, quad L170,000; Continental breakfast included. Apartment: L180,000–190,000 per day; no breakfast

(27) ISTITUTO S. GIUSEPPI
Calle Cassellaria, 5420 (Castello)
240 beds, no rooms with private shower or toilet

Accommodations in dorm-style rooms are available all year except during Christmas and Easter. The central location has a garden. Families are preferred. Reservations should be made one month in advance and secured with a deposit.

ENGLISH SPOKEN Yes

FACILITIES AND SERVICES None

NEAREST TOURIST ATTRACTIONS St. Mark's Square, Rialto Bridge

TELEPHONE 041-522-5352

FAX 041-522-4891

CREDIT CARDS None, cash only

CLOSED Christmas and Easter

RATES L45,000 per person

(70) ISTITUTO SUORE CANOSSIANE
Fondamenta del Ponte Piccolo, 428 (Giudecca Island)
35 beds, no private facilities

Stern nuns with more rules than many care to read, let alone adhere to, signify this "ladies only" spot on Giudecca Island across from Venice. It operates as a school during the day. Guests must be out of the building from 9 A.M. to 4 P.M., and in bed by 10 P.M. in winter and by 10:30 P.M. in summer. Registration is from 9 A.M. to noon and from 3 to 6 P.M. No smoking, no drinking, no men, and probably not much fun allowed.

ENGLISH SPOKEN Very limited

FACILITIES AND SERVICES None

NEAREST TOURIST ATTRACTIONS Fifteen-minute boat ride from Venice

TELEPHONE 041-522-2157

CREDIT CARDS None, cash only

CLOSED Never

RATES L22,000 per person; no breakfast; showers free

(71) OSTELLO VENEZIA
Fondamenta di Zitelle, 87 (Giudecca Island)

This hostel requires guests to have a valid International Youth Hostel card and to submit reservations by April if they plan to stay here in the busy months of July and August. Rules, rules, and more rules, including lights *out* (at the master switch) by 10:30 P.M., even though curfew is not until 11:30 P.M. The price of the room includes sheets and breakfast; dinner is available for L17,000. Guests cannot leave before 7 A.M., must be out of their rooms from 9:30 A.M. to 1:30 P.M., and can only check in from 1:30 to 10:30 P.M. The office is open from 7 to 9:30 A.M. and 1 to 11:30 P.M. Got that?

ENGLISH SPOKEN Yes

FACILITIES AND SERVICES None

NEAREST TOURIST ATTRACTIONS Across lagoon from Venice; fifteen minutes by boat to St. Mark's Square

TELEPHONE 041-523-8211

FAX 041-523-5689

CREDIT CARDS MC, V

CLOSED Never

RATES L29,000 per person; Continental breakfast included; dinner available for L17,000; guests must have an IYH card (costs L30,000 if purchased here)

SHOPPING: CHEAP CHIC

Throughout history, Italians have known and appreciated good taste and fine quality. The "made in Italy" label is recognized as the best available the world over. The high quality of Italian life is evident everywhere you look, from gourmet food and fine wines to designer clothing, imaginative furniture, and unique handcrafts. In these days of standardization and mass production, Italian artisans are still creating original and beautiful objects. Italian ceramics, embroidery and lace, gold and silver jewelry, glassware, and paper and leather goods have established the country as a leader in the world market. Many believe that the Italians are some of the best-dressed people in Europe, if not the world. They dress with style, and they look with disdain at foreigners who wear shorts and T-shirts and the latest in athletic shoes, all in the name of "I am on vacation and *will* be comfortable at all costs."

Born shoppers simply cannot spend all of their vacation time taking in the sights, eating wonderful meals, and staying in quaint, charming hotels. To maintain their sanity, they have to go shopping. The good news is that the possibilities are endless. The bad news is that nothing comes cheaply. It is sad but true that the days of finding one bargain after another in Italy are over. The dollar now buys about 30 to 40 percent less than it did just ten years ago. That, along with soaring inflation, has made shopping here almost prohibitive for most of us, unless, that is, you know where to go, when to shop, and what to buy. This section devoted to Cheap Chic shopping will help you do just that, and in the bargain, you will certainly find keepsakes to bring home that you will enjoy for a lifetime.

Discounts are not easy to find. The government red tape has gone so far as to mandate the time and duration of major sales and the amount a store can discount its prices at these sale times. This is unbelievable to most Americans, but it is a fact of life for the Italians. There are two government-sanctioned sale periods each year: from mid-January until the end of February, and all of July. Prices tend to drop as the sales wear on. This is the time to buy, as prices are cut by as much as 50 percent on top-name and quality goods—not cheap items brought in especially for the sale. During nonsale times, look for shops with signs saying *sconti* (discounts) or *vendita promozionale* (promotional sale). These are not government-sanctioned sales, and the discounts will be minimal, but it is *something.*

The following shops in Florence, Rome, and Venice are by no means an exhaustive list, nor do they always represent the cheapest prices. They represent an eclectic choice of shops that represent good quality and value and are included to encourage you along your way to great shopping adventures of your own. Good luck and happy shopping!

Cheap Chic in Italy Shopping Tips

1. When you see it, like it, want it, and can afford it . . . buy it. Do not plan to think it over too long because you probably will not have time to get back, and even if you do, the item may be gone. Worse yet is leaving the store and never being able to locate it again.

2. Pack an empty soft folding suitcase in your luggage so you can bring your purchases home with you—avoiding the expense and hassle of mailing and insuring. Even if the airline charges you an excess-baggage fee (usually around $100), it will be cheaper and much easier than mailing several separate packages.

3. Do some preliminary shopping research before you leave home. Make a list of sizes, and check prices in your local stores. That way you will be able to spot a bargain, and have a focus to your shopping excursions. However, do not get caught up in sticking to an exact list. Be flexible.

4. At flea markets and outdoor markets, despite the competition, you can expect only a 10 to 15 percent discount as a result of hard bargaining. You will always get the best price if you pay cash.

5. *Never* change money in a store. Go to a bank, an American Express office, or an ATM for the best rate.

6. Bring a pocket calculator to avoid asking, "How much is that in dollars?"

7. Nothing is returnable. Buy with care.

8. Sales are held from mid-January through February, and again in July. The price reduction can be as much as 50 percent—and this includes all the big-name designers.

9. Keep a list of your purchases along with the receipts to show when you return to the United States. It will make it much easier to fill out the forms for the Italian tax rebate (see "*Detasse*," below).

10. Every person returning to the United States receives a $400 duty-free allowance, even a week-old baby gets one. This applies *only* to purchases you carry with you. If you are over your limit, apply your extra to any of your companions who are under the limit.

Detasse (Export Tax Rebate)

Americans left behind an estimated $50 billion in Value Added Taxes in Europe last year. Maybe shoppers did not spend enough to qualify for a refund, or maybe they just didn't know they were eligible for a refund. The amount you get back varies from country to country. In Italy it is 20 percent, the highest in Europe.

Most Italian shopkeepers are not eager to promote this, but you should take advantage of the savings *detasse* offers. It's very simple: you are entitled to a tax refund if you spend L300,000 or more at any one store. You can have multiple purchases at that store, but you cannot tally up purchases made at two or three branch locations, such as a sweater at a Benetton shop in Rome, three blouses at two of their Florence stores, and a coat from their store in Venice. When you are paying for your purchase, show your passport and ask for a formal receipt and refund form from the seller. Fill out the refund-form paperwork and keep all receipts. When you leave Italy, stop at customs, show them what you bought (not always required, but be ready), and get the refund forms stamped. Mail the stamped refund forms to the merchants. The merchant will mail you your refund, although maybe not right away (it sometimes takes up to three months). Most stores are reliable and will give you your rebate. It is easier for both the store and you if you use a credit card for your purchases, and then the rebate can be credited back, thus avoiding changing an Italian lire check into dollars at your bank (if they can even do such a thing). Final word: Some stores will offer you a big discount to forget all about the *detasse*. Best advice: take the *sconto* (discount) and run!

Size Conversion Chart

Women's Dresses, Coats, and Skirts

American	6	8	10	12	14	16	18
Continental	36	38^1/$_2$	40	42	44	46	48

Women's Blouses and Sweaters

American	6	8	10	12	14	16	18
Continental	34	36	38	40	42	44	46

Women's Hosiery

American	8	8^1/$_2$	9	9^1/$_2$	10	10^1/$_2$
Continental	1	2	3	4	5	6

Women's Shoes

American	5	6	7	8	9	10
Continental	36	37	38	39	40	41

Children's Clothing

American	3	4	6	8	10	12
Continental	98	125	145	150	155	160

Men's Suits

American	34	36	38	40	42	44	46	48
Continental	44	46	48	50	52	54	56	58

Men's Shirts

American	14^1/$_2$	15	15^1/$_2$	16	16^1/$_2$	17	17^1/$_2$	18
Continental	37	38	39	41	42	43	44	45

Men's Shoes

American	7	8	9	10	11	12
Continental	41	42	43	44	46	47

NOTE: Sizing is *not* standardized in Italy as it is in the United States. Often you will find widely different fits in the same size. If you have the measurements of the absentee person you are shopping for, making a decision will be much easier, and certainly more of a sure thing.

Shopping in Florence

Florence has long been renowned for its wonderful shopping. First-time Cheap Chic shoppers may find the number of shops overwhelming, but have heart . . . the city's small size puts almost everything within walking distance. Florentine artists today maintain the same high level of originality and attention to detail that they did centuries ago. The specialties of Florence are hand-embroidered linens, gold, ceramics, leather, handmade paper goods, and bookbinding. Many families have worked in the same shops for generations and take enormous pride in the workmanship that bears their name and upholds their reputation for quality. This means that often the prices are as high as the quality. So where does this leave the Cheap Chic shopper? First of all, remember you are getting top quality for your money, so be prepared to spend a little more and forget all about finding "a steal." For trinkets, not treasures, shop in the outdoor market stalls at the San Lorenzo Central Market and at the Straw Market, where you will find many imaginative items to accommodate even the slimmest budget. The competition is stiff in these two markets, but prices do not vary much from one stall to another. Sometimes you can bargain a few lire, but nothing significant. It all comes down to buying from the seller you like the best.

Shopping Hours
WINTER: Mon afternoon and Tues–Sat 9 A.M.–1 P.M., 3:30–7:30 P.M.; closed Mon morning and Sun
SUMMER: Afternoon hours 4–8 P.M.; closed Sat afternoon and all or part of Aug
FOOD SHOPS: Closed Wed afternoon
NOTE: Some shops in the center of town stay open from 9:30 or 10 A.M. to 7:30 or 8 P.M. Monday to Friday.

Important Shopping Note
Watch carefully! In 1999, new laws will go into affect enabling shops in Florence to be open nonstop during the day, on Monday mornings, and, if you can believe it, fifteen Sundays a year. This law doesn't say they *must* be open, it just gives them the right to be if they so choose. At press time, things were still in such a state of flux that it was decided to stay with the old system of hours because it is a sure thing. If you are going to a specific shop during one of the proposed new opening times, I suggest you call ahead to see if the shop is going with the new system or adhering to the old.

The letter in parentheses before each shop corresponds to a letter that marks the shop's location on the Florence map on pages 38–41.

Bookstores

(A) AFTER DARK BOOKSTORE
Via de Ginori, 478r (San Lorenzo Central Market)

An excellent selection of English-language books and popular American magazines, such as *People* and the *New Yorker*. Also, cards, gift wrap, postcards, and good used books. Owner Norman Grant will let you trade in your guidebooks for other used ones in stock. You can also bring in your other used books and receive a credit toward anything in the store. He also has a notice board—take a look, there might be something of interest.

TELEPHONE AND FAX 055-294-203
CREDIT CARDS AE, DC, MC, V
HOURS Mon–Sat 10 A.M.–2 P.M., 3:30–6:30 P.M.
ENGLISH Yes

(B) BM BOOKSHOP
Via Borgo Ognissanti, 4r (Piazza Goldoni)

American Libbie and her Italian husband, Francesco, opened the first English-language bookshop in Florence in 1963, featuring an excellent selection of books dealing with art, travel, fiction, cooking, design, and fashion. They also do mail order. They will ship your excess books back home for you, thus saving you the red-tape nightmare of trying to figure out the post office's bureaucratic rules for this simple task. In addition to a great shop, Libbie, Francesco, and their staff are friendly and very welcoming.

TELEPHONE AND FAX 055-294-575
CREDIT CARDS AE, MC, V
E-MAIL bmbookshop@dada.it
HOURS Mon–Sat 9:30 A.M.–1 P.M., 3:30–7:30 P.M. Closed 2 weeks in mid-Aug.
ENGLISH Yes

(C) ENGLISH BOOKSTORE AND PAPERBACK EXCHANGE
Via Fiesolana, 3r (Piazza Salvemini)

This is the unofficial community center for English-speaking visitors and residents in Florence. They will trade their secondhand books for yours, or give you a store credit. In addition to being one of the major university textbook suppliers, they specialize in new and used books on art history, humanities, Italian studies, political science, travel, and popular fiction. The store is owned by American Emily Rosner and her husband, and they are plugged into everything going on in Florence.

TELEPHONE 055-247-8154
FAX 055-247-8856
E-MAIL papex@dada.it
INTERNET www.dada.it/paperback

CREDIT CARDS AE, DC, MC, V
HOURS Mon–Fri 9 A.M.– 7:30 P.M.; Sat 9 A.M.–1 P.M., 3:30–7:30 P.M.
ENGLISH Yes

(D) LIBRERIA IL VIAGGIO
Borgo degli Albizi, 41r (Il Duomo)

If it's a travel book, information about trekking, or a map you are looking for, you will probably find it at Libreria il Viaggio. On my last visit, the *Cheap Eats* series was on display. Who couldn't love such a travel-book store?

TELEPHONE AND FAX 055-240-489
CREDIT CARDS MC, V
HOURS Winter: Mon 3:30–7:30 P.M., Tues–Sat 9:30 A.M.–1 P.M., 3:30–7:30 P.M., Summer (end of June–end of Sept): Mon–Fri 9:30 A.M.–2 P.M., 3–8 P.M., Sat 9:30 A.M.–2 P.M.
ENGLISH Limited

China and Ceramics

(E) CERAMICHE ARTE CRETA
Via del Proconsolo, 63r (Il Duomo)

Elisabetta di Costanzo has been creating handmade ceramics here for ten years, and has built a steady clientele for her whimsically imaginative pieces. She designs and makes everything in her shop, which is a great place to pick up gifts for lucky people back home. Very good quality and service. Packing and shipping service.

TELEPHONE 055-284-341
CREDIT CARDS AE, MC, V
HOURS Mon–Sat 9 A.M.–7 P.M.
ENGLISH Yes

(F) DINO BARTOLINI
Via dei Servi, 30r (Il Duomo)

A big store filled with every kitchen gadget imaginable; along with a spectacular selection of china, pottery, crystal, and silver. They have good sales at the end of January and February.

TELEPHONE 055-211-895
FAX 055-264-281
CREDIT CARDS AE, MC, V
HOURS Tues–Sat 9 A.M.–12:30 P.M., 3:30–7 P.M. Closed in Aug.
ENGLISH Yes

(G) LA MAIOLICA
Via Guelfa, 31r (San Lorenzo Central Market)

One of the friendliest ceramic shops (and certainly the most interesting) in Florence is La Maiolica. You can watch the artist/designer Salvatore

Rabbene create his wares in the tiny shop window, where you can also see his kiln and displays of his work. Salvatore speaks English and is used to dealing with Americans because he exports his work to several West Coast shops (at triple the prices you will pay in his shop). He will make things to order, personalize any of his designs, and have your purchases insured and shipped to your home. The quality is excellent and so is his service. All pieces are dishwasher-safe and lead-free.

TELEPHONE 055-280-029
FAX 055-437-8677
CREDIT CARDS AE, DC, MC, V
HOURS Winter: Mon 3:30–7:30 P.M., Tues–Sat 9 A.M.–1 P.M., 3:30–7:30 P.M.; summer: Mon–Fri 9 A.M.–1 P.M., 3:30–7:30 P.M., Sat 9 A.M.–1 P.M.
ENGLISH Yes

Clothing

(H) ALFREDA E MANUELA EVANGELISTI
Borgo dei Greci, 33r (Piazza Santa Croce)

Ties, scarves, and shawls are sold all over Florence and the quality ranges from flea-market polyester to beautiful Gucci silks. For a happy medium, yet still very high quality, let the mother-daughter duo of Alfreda and Manuela help you select a silk tie or scarf or a dramatic shawl. The prices are very good, and there is a discount if you pay in cash.

TELEPHONE Not available
CREDIT CARDS MC, V
HOURS Winter: Tues–Sat 9:30 A.M.–6:30 P.M.; summer: daily 9:30 A.M.–6:30 P.M.
ENGLISH Yes

(I) BALLOON
Via del Pronconsolo, 69r (Il Duomo)

Balloon has shops in most Italian cities (see "Shopping in Rome," page 311). They specialize in a selection of traditional clothing for thirtysomethings. Many of the items are made in China, so check the quality carefully.

TELEPHONE 055-212-460
CREDIT CARDS AE, MC, V
HOURS Mon 3:30–7:30 P.M., Tues–Sat 9:30 A.M.–1 P.M., 3:30–7:30 P.M.
ENGLISH Yes

Cosmetics and Perfumes

(J) FARMACIA MUNSTERMANN
Piazza Goldoni, 2r

Clarissa Petruzzi is carrying on the tradition established by her parents in running this wonderful pharmacy and cosmetics shop. Here you can buy her handmade natural and homeopathic cosmetics, which have been carefully prepared and packaged in the old-fashioned manner. There is a fine stock of products for body and skin care, sun lotions, hair preparations, fragrances for men and women, plus facial cosmetics. There is a catalog available in English, but you must place a minimum L100,000 order. Clarissa and her shop have my highest recommendation, not only for the products but for the care and consideration Clarissa extends to every customer, whether a first-time visitor or a sweet neighborhood couple who have been shopping here for decades.

TELEPHONE 055-210-660

CREDIT CARDS DC, MC, V

HOURS Mon–Fri 9 A.M.–1 P.M., 4–8 P.M. Closed two weeks after Christmas and two weeks in Aug.

ENGLISH Yes

(K) OFFICINA PROFUMO FARMACEUTICA DI SANTA MARIA NOVELLA
Via della Scala, 16r (Piazza Santa Maria Novella)

This is *not* a pharmacy but an *erboristeria,* a shop selling natural herbal-based cosmetics, remedies, and a new baby line in what was once the chapel of a Renaissance monastery. It is worth a visit if only to view the spectacular frescoed vaulted ceilings in the only thirteenth-century monastery pharmacy in Florence that still has its unaltered, preserved, original appearance. The Dominican monks who once ran the pharmacy have gone, but you can still purchase their medicinal liqueurs or Catherine Deneuve's favorite face cream. They are also famous for their pomegranate soap. They will ship.

TELEPHONE 055-216-276, 230-2437

FAX 055-288-658

CREDIT CARDS AE, MC, V

HOURS Mon 3:30-7:30 P.M., Tues–Sat 9:30 A.M.–7:30 P.M.

ENGLISH Yes

Department Stores

(L) COIN DEPARTMENT STORE
Via del Parione, 10r (Piazza Goldoni)

This is Italy's answer to Target, Mervyn's, and J.C. Penney's. It has a good housewares section in the basement.

TELEPHONE 055-215-684

CREDIT CARDS AE, DC, MC, V·

HOURS Winter: Mon 3:30–7:30 P.M., Tues–Sat 9:30 A.M.–1 P.M., 3:30–7:30 P.M.; summer: Mon–Sat 9:30 A.M.–1 P.M., 3:30–7:30 P.M.

ENGLISH Very little, depends on clerk

(M) LA RINASCENTE
Via degi Speziali, 17–21r (Piazza della Repubblica)

The Rome-based department store is now in Florence. The quality is good, but most of the merchandise you can find at home, and for less money.

TELEPHONE Not available
CREDIT CARDS AE, DC, MC, V
HOURS Mon 3:30–7:30 P.M., Tues–Sat 9:30 A.M.–1 P.M., 3:30–7:30 P.M.
ENGLISH Yes

(N) STANDA
Via dei Panzani, 31r (Piazza Santa Maria Novella)

Standa sells budget housewares, clothing, and cosmetics. Some locations also sell food, but the quality of the fresh produce is below par. There are other locations at Via dei Mille, 140r, and Via Pietraplana, 42r.

TELEPHONE 055-283-071
CREDIT CARDS MC, V
HOURS Mon 2–7:30 P.M., Tues–Sat 9 A.M.–7:30 P.M.
ENGLISH Depends on clerk

Fabrics and Trimmings

(O) PASSAMANERIA TOSCANA
Piazza San Lorenzo, 12r (San Lorenzo Central Market)

This store has the most beautiful selection of fabrics, tassels, braids, tapestries, exclusive handmade cushions, curtain holders, fringes, borders, laces—even mosquito netting—under one roof. Worth a visit even if you just buy some decorative braid.

TELEPHONE 055-214-670
FAX 055-239-6389
CREDIT CARDS MC, V
HOURS Mon–Sat 9 A.M.–7:30 P.M., Sun 10:30 A.M.– 7:30 P.M.
ENGLISH Yes

(P) PASSAMANERIA VALMAR
Via Porta Rossa, 53r (Piazza della Repubblica)

For a very Florentine gift that is easy to tuck into even the smallest piece of luggage, don't miss this colorful shop on the street leading from the Ponte Vecchio toward Il Duomo. It offers one of the most complete assortments of *passementerie,* which are: tassels for keys and tieback curtains, drawer sachets, hand-embroidered cushions, plus a dizzying collection of cords, ribbons, and fringes.

TELEPHONE 055-284-493
FAX 055-218-957
CREDIT CARDS MC, V
HOURS Mon and Sat 9 A.M.–1 P.M., Tues–Fri 9 A.M.–7:30 P.M.

Gifts and Handicrafts

(Q) CARTOLERIA ECOLOGICAL LA TARTARUGA
Borgo Albizi, 60r (Il Duomo)

This happy place sells an unusual selection of paper goods and hand-painted wooden toys to delight the child in all of us. Everything is made from natural ingredients, and all the paint is antitoxic. Prices are within every budget, even a child's.

TELEPHONE 055-234-0845
CREDIT CARDS MC, V
HOURS Mon 1:30–7:30 P.M., Tues–Sat 9 A.M.–7:30 P.M.
ENGLISH Yes

(R) CERTINI
Via di San Niccolò, 2r (San Niccolò)

Walter Certini's name is already known to shoppers in the United States from Gump's in San Francisco and through the Horchow, Smithsonian, Bergdorf Goodman, and Neiman-Marcus catalogs. These references alone should tell you that this is very good merchandise. What is it? Beautifully crafted pieces made from painted wrought iron and metal. Walter is a master, and he has created everything from massive chandeliers to pieces of furniture, picture and mirror frames, light fixtures, wine carafes, candleholders, and much, much more. You will just have to go to his studio/shop/workplace and see for yourself. He will ship, and his English is excellent.

TELEPHONE AND FAX 055-234-2694
CREDIT CARDS MC, V
HOURS Mon–Fri 8 A.M.–noon, 3–6 P.M.; closed Sat, Sun, Aug.
ENGLISH Yes

Herbal Products

(S) AUX HERBES SAUVAGES
Via dei Cimatori, 2r (Piazza della Repubblica)

Rita Redi has been selling herbs and aromatherapy products from her corner shop not far from the American Express office for almost twenty-five years, and I can attest to the fact that she knows her herbs and aromatherapy backward and forward. I had very severe eye allergies, and no one but Rita correctly diagnosed the problem and then found an herbal product to take care of the debilitating situation. Besides being knowledgeable, Rita is delightful, and her English is excellent.

TELEPHONE 055-217-570
CREDIT CARDS MC, V
HOURS Tues–Sat 9:30 A.M.–1 P.M., 5–7 P.M.
ENGLISH Yes

Internet Providers

(T) CIMA LIBRERIA
Borgo degli Albizi, 37r (Il Duomo)

This bookstore/café attracts a young, intellectual audience, and is a good place to hang out and while away a few hours at one of the Internet stations browsing the net or e-mailing your friends back home. The bookstore has a limited selection of English-language books, but if you read Italian, there are bargains to be had. The café opens at noon and serves hot lunches until 2:30 P.M. After that, you can have a sandwich, savory tart, salad, or pastry. Internet usage is based on an hourly rate of L11,000, or if you are going to be in Florence for any amount of time, they have six-month and yearly contracts available.

TELEPHONE 055-247-7245
CREDIT CARDS MC, V
HOURS Daily 10:30 A.M.–7:30 P.M.; Tues, Thurs, and Sat also opened from 9:30 P.M.–1 A.M.; and the last Sun of the month, open 10:30 A.M.–7:30 P.M.
ENGLISH Yes

(U) NETGATE
Via Sant' Egidio, 10r (Il Duomo)

Netgate has more than fifteen workstations with access to the Internet, and the rate is around L12,000 for thirty minutes. The staff is young and smart, and can also troubleshoot questions if you are having problems with your own computer you brought on the trip.

TELEPHONE 055-234-7967
FAX 055-263-8527
INTERNET www.netgate.aspide.it
HOURS Daily 10:30 A.M.–8 P.M.

Jewelry

(V) ANGELA CAPUTI
Borgo Sant' Jacopo, 82r (Ponte Vecchio)

The striking jewelry is all designed by Angela Caputi and sold exclusively in her shop in Florence by her sister Paola. Whenever I wear one of her designs, I am always asked, "Where did you find that wonderful necklace, marvelous pin, or those beautiful earrings?" The prices are reasonable when you consider you are getting one-of-a-kind pieces that you will wear for years.

TELEPHONE 055-212-972
CREDIT CARDS AE, DC, MC, V
HOURS Mon 3:30–7:30 P.M., Tues–Sat 10 A.M.–1 P.M., 3:30–7:30 P.M.
ENGLISH Yes

(W) THE GOLD CORNER
Piazza Santa Croce, 15r

The gold here is sold by weight, which makes it work out to be *slightly* less expensive. The selection is huge, and you are certain to find something in your price range. The prices are discounted 15 to 20 percent if you pay cash. There is an additional 14 percent discount for every purchase over L300,000 (see *"Detasse,"* page 292). Ask for the owner, Rosy Miranda Bordo, who speaks English well. She also carries Raymond Weil and Fendi watches and cameos.

TELEPHONE 055-241-971
FAX 055-247-8437
CREDIT CARDS AE, DC, MC, V
HOURS Winter: Tues–Sat 9:30 A.M.–7:30 P.M.; summer: daily 9 A.M.–7:30 P.M.
ENGLISH Yes

(X) SEZIONE AUREA
Via dei Servi, 46r (Ponte Vecchio)

This shop and its sister store offer a beautiful selection of handmade, Florentine Renaissance–inspired acrylic jewelry at affordable prices. These are one-of-a-kind pieces you will not see elsewhere.

The second shop is just before the Ponte Vecchio at Lungarno Acciaioli, 3r (tel: 210-233). It is open Mon–Sat 10:30 A.M.–1 P.M., 3–7 P.M., Sun 2–7 P.M.

TELEPHONE 055-239-6143
CREDIT CARDS AE, DC, MC, V
HOURS Mon–Sat 10 A.M.–1 P.M., 3:30–7 P.M.
ENGLISH Depends on sales personnel

Leather

(Y) THE LEATHER SCHOOL
Piazza Santa Croce, 16r

Bags, belts, boxes, briefcases, frames, loads of little gifty items, handbags, suitcases, and more are sold at this commercially run leather store in the old dormitory of the Franciscans, next to the sacristy of Santa Croce Church. You can also enter through the garden behind the church, at Via Giuseppe, 5. The Leather School was founded by the friars at the end of World War II to renew the tradition of leather tooling and gilding, which had been done centuries earlier at the monastery. Everything is still made on the premises and can be customized or personalized. The first American shopper was General Dwight D. Eisenhower, who ordered things from here. Since then, they have designed a bag for Diana, Princess of Wales, and the Emperor of Japan. Some of the smaller merchandise can be shopworn, so look over several pieces of the same item before you buy it. They also have a catalogue and can ship worldwide. Staff attitude and attention to customer service has improved.

TELEPHONE 055-244-533, 244-534

FAX 055-248-0337

E-MAIL leatherschool@leatherschool.it

INTERNET www.leatherschool.it

CREDIT CARDS AE, DC, MC, V

HOURS Winter: Tues–Sat 9 A.M.–12:30 P.M., 3–6 P.M.; summer: Mon–Sat 9 A.M.–6:30 P.M., Sun 10 A.M.–12:30 P.M., 3–6 P.M.

ENGLISH Yes

(Z) MADOVA GLOVES
Via Guicciardini, 1r (Pitti Palace)

This shop, in business since 1919, sells only leather gloves made in its own factory. The quality is unsurpassed. They can make a pair of gloves from the tracing of a hand, or for hands that are difficult to fit. The gloves come in every type of leather and color and are lined in cashmere, silk, sheepskin, or wool. The prices in the catalog include shipping.

TELEPHONE 055-239-6526

FAX 055-210-204

INTERNET www.web.tin.it/Madova

CREDIT CARDS AE

HOURS winter: Tues–Sat 9:30 A.M.–7:30 P.M.; summer: daily 9:30 A.M.–7:30 P.M.

ENGLISH Yes

Linens

(AA) TAF
Via Por Santa Maria, 17r (Ponte Vecchio)

Table linens, towels, and sheets are in one store, and then there is more of the same across the street—household linens, children's clothing, women's blouses, christening gowns made for angels. Many handmade items. Not cheap, but the quality is lovely.

TELEPHONE 055-239-6037

CREDIT CARDS AE, DC, MC, V

HOURS Mon 3:30–7:30 P.M., Tues–Sat 9:30 A.M.–1 P.M., 3:30–7:30 P.M. These seem to be the basic hours, which can vary with the month, day of the week, or whim of the boss.

ENGLISH Yes

Paper Products

(BB) FANTASIE FLORENTINE
Borgo Sant' Jacopo, 50r (Ponte Vecchio)

All of the gift items here are covered in marbleized paper by a sweet lady and her sister, who have been doing this for more than thirty years, fifteen in this location. The prices are low and the selection limited, but it is a great source for gifts that are light and easy to carry.

TELEPHONE 055-210-436
CREDIT CARDS None
HOURS Mon–Sat 10 A.M.–1 P.M., 3–7 P.M.. Closed last half of Aug.
ENGLISH Yes

(CC) IL TORCHIO
Via dei Bardi, 17r (San Niccolò)

Anna Anichini is a true Florentine craftswoman and artist who works with marbleized paper, one of Florence's specialties. All of her pieces are designed and made here in her workshop, which doubles as a showroom. Because everything is made here, she is able to offer some of the best prices and a wonderful selection. She does everything from photo frames to wedding and photo albums, diaries, address books, jewelry boxes, and papered pencils to match a covered scratch-paper holder. If you do not see what you want, she can make up sets to order. She is very friendly, easy to work with, and offers fast service.

TELEPHONE 055-234-2862
CREDIT CARDS AE, MC, V
HOURS Mon–Fri 9 A.M.–7:30 P.M., Sat 9 A.M.–1 P.M. Closed two weeks in mid-Aug.
ENGLISH Yes

Shoes

(DD) MANNINA
Via Guicciardini, 16r (Pitti Palace)

For beautiful shoes, many handmade and all with the perfect fit, I shop at Mannina every time I am in Florence. These are shoes you will wear and enjoy for a long time. The winter line debuts in August, and the summer around the end of February. If you time your visit during the winter or summer sales, the prices are reduced sometimes by 50 percent. The sale dates, which can vary slightly, are: winter from January 10 to March 10; summer from July 7 to September 1. There is another location at Via de' Barbadori, 23/24r; tel: 055-211-060.

TELEPHONE AND FAX 055-282-895
CREDIT CARDS AE, DC, MC, V

HOURS Summer: daily 9:30 A.M.–7:30 P.M.; winter: Tues–Sat 9:30 A.M.–7:30 P.M., second and fourth Sun of every month 10 A.M.–6 P.M.
ENGLISH Yes

Markets

(EE) MERCATO NUOVO (STRAW MARKET)
Loggia del Mercato Nuovo, Via Por Santa Maria (Piazza della Repubblica)

When I first went to Florence years ago, this was a bargain paradise. Not so anymore. Although you can find some straw products (chiefly hats), most stalls sell the same things you can find at the San Lorenzo Central Market (see below) and for about the same price. They do have fake designer bags, jewelry, linens, and tourist kitsch. The stall owners speak English and are not about to reduce their prices, but it is still worth a look.

TELEPHONE None
CREDIT CARDS Depends on the stall
HOURS Daily 9 A.M.–5 P.M., sometimes later in summer
ENGLISH Depends on seller, but most of them do

(FF) MERCATO DI SAN LORENZO (SAN LORENZO CENTRAL MARKET)
Piazza del Mercato Centrale

A visit to this colorful indoor market is a required experience, even if you aren't a foodie. Two floors display every type of edible you can imagine. On the ground floor are stands selling meat and fish, cheese, bakeries, household items, and groceries. There are places to grab a cappuccino and a pastry with the sellers if you arrive early, or eat a sandwich washed down with a beer or a glass of sturdy red wine. Upstairs you will find stand after stand of fruits and vegetables. Around the outside, hundreds of vendors hawk leather, Florentine paper goods, scarves, umbrellas, bags, T-shirts, you name it. The prices outside are sometimes negotiable. Always watch for quality and hope the seller is honest. Stand No. 4 has fake Gucci scarves. This entire shopping experience is part of a trip to Florence. Plan to come for the morning and have lunch at the sandwich stall in the market or at one of the nearby trattorias (see *Cheap Eats in Italy* for suggestions).

TELEPHONE None
CREDIT CARDS None at the food market, but at the stalls around the outside, some do take plastic
HOURS Indoor food market: Mon–Sat 7 A.M.–1 P.M. Outside stalls: daily 9 A.M.–8 P.M. in summer, Tues–Sat 10 A.M.–6 P.M. in winter
ENGLISH Depends on the seller

(GG) MERCATO DI SANTO SPIRITO
Piazza Santo Spirito

On the second Sunday of the month, it's a combination hippie flea market, flower market, organic food market, and general junk. On the third Sunday, it is a biological market, worth your time if you are a swap-meet fan, or if you want a change of pace. Plan on lunch at one of the restaurants around the piazza (see *Cheap Eats in Italy*). There is also a small produce and flower market on the piazza Monday through Saturday from 8 to 11 A.M.

TELEPHONE None

CREDIT CARDS Depends on stall

HOURS Tues–Sat 8–11 A.M., a few produce stalls; large flea market on the second Sun each month 10 A.M.–7 P.M.; third Sun 9 A.M.–4 P.M., biological market; no Sun markets in August

ENGLISH Depends on seller

Shopping Streets

Almost every street in Florence has interesting shops of some sort. This very short list is only meant to get you started. I encourage you to wander about and discover your own special Florentine shopping finds.

BORGO DEI GRECI (PIAZZA SANTA CROCE)

This street is loaded with one leather shop after another, selling everything from tiny boxes to handbags, shoes, and coats. There is lots of junk along with competition, so be sure to look at several stores before you decide what to buy.

LUNGARNO ACCIAIOLI (PONTE VECCHIO)

One shop after another lines this street, which runs along the Arno River from Piazza Goldoni to the Ponte Vecchio. All are lovely and most are expensive, as are the jewelry shops that border the Ponte Vecchio. In fact, one wonders just *who* can afford such dazzling finery.

VIA GUICCIARDINI AND BORGO SANT' JACOPO (PITTI PALACE)

Via Guicciardini continues after the Ponte Vecchio and leads to the Pitti Palace. Naturally almost every tourist hits this section of Florentine pavement and encounters the interesting shops along it. Just after crossing the bridge, parallel to the river, is Borgo Sant' Jacopo, another prime shopping territory.

VIA TORNABUONI (IL DUOMO)

The premier shopping street in Florence, with all the big-name designers. Side streets worth seeing are Via della Vigna Nuova, Via delle Spade, and Via delle Sole.

Shipping—How to Get It All Home

(HH) FRACASSI INTERNATIONAL FORWARDERS
Via Santo Spirito, 11r (Piazza Santo Spirito)

You can't always take everything with you. If this is the case, get rid of those bulky purchases and let Fracassi take care of them, by packing, insuring, and shipping them worldwide. I have used their services and they are reliable, plus everything arrived in perfect order. They accept cash only.

TELEPHONE 055-283-597
CREDIT CARDS None, cash only
HOURS Mon–Fri 9 A.M.–noon, 3–6 P.M.
ENGLISH Yes

Shopping in Rome

Rome is not the shopper's paradise that Milan, Florence, and Venice are. And nothing is cheap. There are many beautiful shops, but the prices are very high unless you are lucky enough to be in Rome during the twice-yearly sales that take place from around mid-January to the end of February and again in July. For the best buys, look for leather, knits, jewelry, and shoes. If you want religious items, blessed by the pope, head for Via Conciliazone, which leads to St. Peter's Square. Leather goods used to be available for next-to-nothing at street markets. Today, cheap leather is just that: cheap. Be sure that any leather you buy is stamped *vero cuoio,* a sign that means the leather is real, not imitation.

An occasional visitor to Rome never makes it to the Vatican at all, but no one misses the Piazza di Spagna (Spanish Steps). This is the heart of the best shopping in Rome, where deluxe boutiques of the big-name designers beckon crowds of shoppers who admire and buy, especially during the sales, when they snap up $150 silk scarves as if they were napkins. Just two blocks from these shops is Via Frattina, where you will find the same high-quality merchandise, but designer names that are not as famous and prices that are *slightly* less. Cheap Chic shoppers will love the neighborhoods around Campo de' Fiori and the winding, narrow streets of Trastevere. Less expensive shops are across the Tiber on Via Cola di Rienzo and Via Ottaiano, but you will get what you pay for here and the quality is not always tops. Dedicated bargain hunters will want to check out the Sunday morning flea market at Trastevere, but don't expect to find any hidden bargains . . . go for the fun of it, and if you find something you like and want, all the better. It is beyond the scope of *Cheap Sleeps in Italy* to detail all the shopping possibilities in Rome. Listed below, however, are a few to get you started. After an hour or so on the job, you will be off on your own, discovering all sorts of wonderful places.

Shopping Hours

WINTER (OCT–JUNE): Mon 3:30–7:30 P.M., Tues–Sat 9 A.M.–1 P.M., 3:30–7:30 P.M.

SUMMER (JUNE–SEPT): Mon–Fri 9 A.M.–1 P.M., 4–8 P.M., Sat 9 A.M.–1 P.M.

FOOD SHOPS: Mon–Wed, Fri–Sat 8:30 A.M.–1 P.M. and 5–7:30 P.M., Thurs 8:30 A.M.–1 P.M. These hours are observed year-round.

HOLIDAYS: If a holiday falls during the week, shops stay open on Mon and close on the holiday, but this does not apply to food shops.

NOTE: Shopping times are hardly set in stone, and are subject to change according to the whims of small-shop owners.

The letter in parentheses before each shop corresponds to a letter that marks the shop's location on the Rome map on pages 124–29.

Bookstores

(A) AMERICAN BOOK SHOP
Via della Vite, 27 & 57 (Spanish Steps)

A tiny English-language bookshop loaded with guidebooks, art history titles, architecture books, and paperback fiction. The prices are high, but the selection is good.

TELEPHONE 06-679-5222
FAX 06-678-3890
CREDIT CARDS AE, DC, MC, V
HOURS Winter: Mon 3:30–7:30 P.M., Tues–Sat 9 A.M.–1 P.M., 3:30–7:30 P.M.

Summer (July–Sept): Mon 3:30–7:30 P.M., Tues–Sat 9 A.M.–1 P.M., 4–8 P.M. Closed mid-Aug for one week.

ENGLISH Yes

(B) ANCORA BOOK SHOP
Via della Conciliazione, 63 (Vatican)

A Catholic bookshop. Look upstairs for the English-language titles.

TELEPHONE 06-656-8820
CREDIT CARDS AE, DC, MC, V
HOURS Mon–Fri 9 A.M.–1 P.M., 3:30–7:15 P.M., Sat 9 A.M.–12:45 P.M.
ENGLISH Generally

(C) THE CORNER BOOKSHOP
Via del Moro, 48 (Trastevere)

Owner Claire Hammond and her crowded corner bookshop are well-known fixtures in Trastevere. If she does not have the English-language title you are looking for, she can order it for you.

TELEPHONE AND FAX 06-583-6942
CREDIT CARDS AE, MC, V
HOURS Mon 3:30–8 P.M., Tues–Sat 10 A.M.–1:30 P.M., 3:30–8 P.M., Sun 11 A.M.–1:30 P.M., 3:30–8 P.M. Closed Sun in Aug.
ENGLISH Yes

(D) ECONOMY BOOK CENTER
Via Torino, 136 (Train Station)

The Goldfield family runs a great bookshop. Bring in your used English-language books, and you will receive store credit toward your purchases. There is a wide selection of cards, children's books, videotapes, books on tape, and travel books. Very accommodating.

TELEPHONE 06-474-6877
CREDIT CARDS AE, DC, MC, V
HOURS Winter: Mon 3–8 P.M., Tues–Sat 9 A.M.–8 P.M.; summer: Mon–Fri 9 A.M.–8 P.M., Sat 9 A.M.–2 P.M.
ENGLISH Yes

Clothing

(E) BALLOON
Piazza di Spagna, 35 (Spanish Steps)

A clothing store with many outlets in Italy, including several in Rome, Balloon has good prices on tailored clothes for men and women, most of which is designed in Italy and made in China. This means you must look carefully for poor workmanship and flimsy silks, but they are still worth a look, especially for the traditionalist. Racks hold one piece in every size, and then you choose the color you want from a bin or wall display. I have two words to say about them: they wrinkle. To keep the stock looking its best in this store, two full-time ironing ladies are employed.

To find it, look for the green doors at the rear courtyard on the left side of the American Express office. There are benches in the courtyard for your nonshopping pals, or they can look for step space and join the crowds people-watching on the Spanish Steps.

TELEPHONE 06-678-0110
CREDIT CARDS AE, DC, MC, V
HOURS Mon 3:30–7:30 P.M., Tues–Sun 10 A.M.–7:30 P.M.
ENGLISH Yes

(F) MARISA PIGNATARO
Via S. Maria dell'Anima, 42 (Piazza Navona)

Marisa Pignataro designs wearable clothes that never go out of style, yet appeal to creative women who do not allow themselves to become fashion victims. Her prices are not low, but her quality is high. These comfortable, packable, easy-care garments travel beautifully. Mixing and matching her skirts, tops and pants, and pulling them together with colorful fabric belts makes a dynamic fashion statement.

TELEPHONE 06-689-6476
CREDIT CARDS MC, V
HOURS Mon noon–8 P.M., Tues, Thurs–Sat 4–9:30 P.M., Wed 11 A.M.– 6 P.M.
ENGLISH Yes

Department Stores

(G) LA RINASCENTE
Via del Corso, 189 (Trevi Fountain)

By American standards, this is a very small department store, but they do offer daily one-stop shopping if you are desperate. Ask for the Hostess Tourist Service, which will help you locate what you want to buy. Don't forget to get the *detasse* (export tax refund) if you spend L300,000 or more here. Piazza Colonna is just off Via del Corso.

TELEPHONE 06-679-7691

CREDIT CARDS AE, DC, MC, V

HOURS Mon 2–9 P.M., Tues–Sat 9:30–9 P.M., Sun 11 A.M.–8 P.M.

(H) STANDA
Viale di Trastevere, 62–64 (Trastevere)

Standa is a far cry from fashionable, but it is fun to look at what most Italians can afford. Every once in a while you will find something great . . . especially in the underwear department. Other branches are located at Via Cola di Rienzo, 173, and Viale Regina Margherita, 117.

TELEPHONE 06-589-5342

CREDIT CARDS MC, V

HOURS Mon 3:30 P.M.–7:30 P.M., Tues–Sat 9 A.M.–8 P.M.

(I) UPIM
Via del Tritone, 172 (Trevi Fountain)

Utilitarian goods, some with a hint of style. The prices are reasonable for Rome. Good place to pick up the cosmetic-of-the-moment. Another branch is at Via Nazionale, 222.

TELEPHONE 06-678-3336

CREDIT CARDS AE, DC, MC, V

HOURS Winter: Mon noon–8 P.M., Tues–Fri 9 A.M.–8 P.M., Sat 10:30 A.M.–8 P.M.; summer: Mon–Fri 9 A.M.–8 P.M., Sat 10:30 A.M.–8 P.M.

Discount Shopping

(J) BABIES DRESS AGENCY
Via Angelo Brunetti, 31 (Piazza del Popolo)

Italians adore their children and obviously are willing to spend lavishly to clothe them. It is nothing to see price tags on infant and toddler clothing reach the triple digits. For those of us suffering from permanent sticker shock at prices that are higher than we would pay at home for ourselves, let alone children, there is now help in Rome. The Babies Dress Agency is an elegant resale shop where Italian mothers can buy very gently worn children's clothes for at least half the original price. The quality is excellent. Recognizing the need for this type of shop, the savvy owner has opened one for the moms. Dress Agency is right around the corner from this store, making it easy to outfit nearly everyone in the family for much less.

TELEPHONE 06-322-0431

CREDIT CARDS AE, DC, V

HOURS Mon 3–7:30 P.M., Tues–Sat 10 A.M.–7:30 P.M.; closed all of August

ENGLISH Yes

(K) DISCOUNT SYSTEM
Via Viminale, 35 (Train Station)

Located at Via Viminale and the corner of Via Napoli, the biggest discount clothing game in town for both men and women has 50 percent off made-in-Italy designer clothes, luggage, belts, bags, and umbrellas. It doesn't mean everything is cheap, but you will get your Armani for less.

TELEPHONE 06-482-3917

CREDIT CARDS None

HOURS Mon 3:30–7:30 P.M., Tues–Sat 9 A.M.–1 P.M., 3:30–7:30 P.M.

ENGLISH Usually

(L) DRESS AGENCY
Via del Vantaggio, 1-B (Piazza del Popolo)

The shop attracts women who want to dress well and spend less for designer clothes that are barely worn. This is the grown-ups version of Babies Dress Agency, see page 312. The clothes are current, in good condition, and fairly priced. They also carry shoes and bags.

TELEPHONE Not available

CREDIT CARDS DC, MC, V

HOURS Mon 3–7:30 P.M., Tues–Sat 10 A.M.–1 P.M., 3–7 P.M.

ENGLISH Yes

(M) IL DISCOUNT DELL'ALTA MODE
Via Gesù e Maria, 16-A (Piazza del Popolo)

This must be the last-chance spot to buy dated, shopworn overstocks of designer labels such as Giorgio Armani, Jean-Paul Gaultier, and Claude Montana at about 40 to 50 percent off. The selection and quality varies. If you are in the neighborhood, give it five minutes. Who knows? You may hit pay dirt.

TELEPHONE 06-361-3796

CREDIT CARDS None, cash only

HOURS Mon 3:30–7:30 P.M., Tues–Sat 9:30 A.M.–1 P.M., 3:30–7:30 P.M.

ENGLISH Some

(N) LEONE CIMENTARI
Via d. Portico di Ottavia, 47 (Jewish Quarter)

A huge discounted china store selling almost every pattern known at discounts ranging from a few cents to big bucks. This is not for the delicate shopper clad in pastels. This is a big, dirty, dusty barn, and you must do a lot of the searching and digging on your own. Bring gloves and a rag to wipe the dust off the plates to see if there are any defects. If you are trying to match a specific pattern, bring a small item of it. They will ship. In addition to china, look for crystal, silver, pots, pans, and kitchenware. Plan on one hour just to case the place, then go back and make your selection. It is a good place to fill in your own china pattern, but don't forget to calculate in shipping charges if you do not carry your purchases yourself. It is worth the trip and the long waits, especially on Saturday when it is filled with prospective brides and grooms, and women who have finally convinced their husbands that they *do* need new china. When ready to buy, ask for an English-speaking clerk.

TELEPHONE 06-654-689
CREDIT CARDS AE, DC, MC, V
HOURS Mon 4–7 P.M., Tues–Sat 9:30 A.M.–1 P.M., 4–7 P.M.
ENGLISH Yes

(O) MAS
Piazza Vittorio Emanuele (Santa Maria Maggiore)

If you love Pic-n-Save, Tati in Paris, or Filene's bargain basement, and *never* pay retail, you are a candidate for Mas. There are bins and bins of clothes, shoes, suitcases, sundries, umbrellas, hats, scarves, sweaters (even cashmere if you look hard enough!), fur coats, bedding (Bassetti, sometimes), zippers, and more at prices you won't believe. If you approach on Via Carlo Libero, you will pass one fake jewelry and hair ornament shop after another. This shopping excursion takes time and is recommended *only* for the hard-core Cheap Chic shopper. Your husband/boyfriend will go absolutely crazy here. There are dressing rooms and clerks. Fashions run the gamut from toddler to senior citizen . . . but again, it is all the luck of the draw. The first time I was here, it was a gold mine. The last time I struck out. In between it has been worth the safari.

In the square across the street is a huge outdoor market. The clothing here is awful, but the food is interesting (see Piazza Vittorio Emanuele, page 316). However, *please* watch out for the gypsies who swarm in around 12:30 P.M. as it is about to close. They are fast and clever and can (and will if you are not careful) take your purse and wallet in a heartbeat.

TELEPHONE 06-486-8078
CREDIT CARDS AE, MC, V
HOURS Mon 3:30–7:30 P.M., Tues–Sat 9 A.M.–1 P.M., 4–8 P.M.
ENGLISH Don't plan on it

Gifts

(P) AI MONASTERI
Piazza della Cinque Lune, 76 (Piazza Navona)

Ai Monasteri sells products made in Italian monasteries, plus beer from their Belgian and German brothers. They sell a variety of natural cosmetics, wines, grappas, and natural elixirs, jams, honey, oil, vinegars, chocolates, essential oils, soaps, and more. The prices are reasonable, but the display could use improvement.

TELEPHONE 06-688-02783
CREDIT CARDS None, cash only
HOURS Winter: Mon–Wed, Fri–Sat 9 A.M.–1 P.M., 4:30–7:30 P.M.,

Thurs 9 A.M.–1 P.M.; summer: Mon–Fri 9 A.M.–1 P.M., 5–8 P.M., Sat
9 A.M.–1 P.M.
ENGLISH Yes

Markets

(Q) CAMPO DE' FIORI
Campo de' Fiori

This is the most photographed outdoor market in the heart of Rome.
The market begins around 7 A.M., except Sunday, and closes between 1
and 2 P.M., when everyone escapes to nearby restaurants for lunch. Life on
the *campo* picks up in the early evening, and by midnight it is filled with
people spilling out of the cafes around it.

TELEPHONE None

CREDIT CARDS None

HOURS Mon–Sat 7 A.M.–1 P.M. (or thereabouts)

ENGLISH Not much

MERCATO DEI FIORI
Via Trionfale, 47–49 (Edges of Rome)

This indoor wholesale flower market is open to the public on Tuesday
morning only. Bargain prices. Take the metro Ottaviano or the bus to
Piazzale Clodio.

TELEPHONE None

CREDIT CARDS None

HOURS Tues 10:30 A.M.–1 P.M.

ENGLISH Not much

(R) MERCATO DI PORTA PORTESE-TRASTEVERE
**Between the Tiber and Viale di Trastevere, from Ponte Sublicio to
Ponte Testaccio (Trastevere)**

All roads on Sunday lead to this huge open-air flea market. Over a
thousand sellers offer everything you can imagine, and some things you
cannot: some fakes, some hot, some not. Watch out for pickpockets and
try to bargain down (about 10 to 20 percent). To get there, take bus
number 75 to Porta di Portese, or take Via Ippoliot Nievo off Via di
Trastevere.

TELEPHONE None

CREDIT CARDS None

HOURS Sun 7 A.M.–2 P.M., sometimes earlier

ENGLISH Not much

(S) PIAZZA FONTANELLA BORGHESE
Piazza Fontanella Borghese (Spanish Steps)

The stalls at this small market at the end of the Borghese Square
sell prints, stamps, old postcards, books, some jewelry, and assorted

knickknacks. The prices are not cheap, but there may be an old print that will catch your eye. You can bargain from 10 to 15 percent off, and cash helps.

TELEPHONE None
CREDIT CARDS Depends on stall
HOURS Mon–Sat 9 A.M.–6 P.M.
ENGLISH Some

(T) PIAZZA VITTORIO EMANUELE
Piazza Vittorio Emanuele (Santa Maria Maggiore)

A covered outdoor market with stalls jammed with every edible product from the animal, vegetable, and fruit worlds . . . as well as some things that do not *look* edible. This is in an area where there are many immigrants, so you can expect to see stores selling Arab, Chinese, Korean food. Some vendors hawk cheap clothing. Watch out for pickpockets, especially when the stalls are beginning to close down and the gypsies swoop in for their handouts. Be careful: These people and their children are pros, and you won't know what hit you!

TELEPHONE None
CREDIT CARDS None
HOURS Mon–Sat 7 A.M.–1 P.M.
ENGLISH Not much

(U) VIA DELL' ARANCIO
Via dell' Arancio, at end of Via di Ripetta (Spanish Steps)

This small fruit and vegetable market in a high-end Roman neighborhood makes up for in quality what it lacks in size. If you keep going back to the same stall, after four or five visits you will be treated like a regular.

Shopping Streets

The following streets are lined with beautiful shops and are well worth a stroll. You will not be alone in your *passeggiata* (strolling), especially late in the afternoon or on Sunday, when it seems as though all of Rome is out browsing and window-shopping. Most of these stores are expensive, but now and then you will find something you can afford, especially during the January and July sales.

VIA BORGOGNONA (SPANISH STEPS)

Chic and expensive shops with lovely displays.

VIA COLA DI RIENZO (VATICAN)

Be sure to stop in Castinori, a huge gourmet grocery store, at No. 99. This street has some of Rome's more modestly priced shops, including Standa, the lowest-price supermarket in Rome.

VIA CONDOTTI (SPANISH STEPS)

Probably the most famous shopping street in Rome.

VIA DEI GAMBERO (SPANSH STEPS)

Boutiques.

VIA DEL CORSO (PIAZZA VENEZIA)

Midpriced shops with blaring music and clothing aimed at youthful shoppers with bodies to match.

VIA DEL BABUINO (SPANISH STEPS)

Designers.

VIA DEL GOVERNO VECCHIO (PIAZZA NAVONA)

Secondhand clothing with style and attitude.

VIA DELLA CROCE (SPANISH STEPS)

Luscious food shops.

VIA FRATTINA (SPANISH STEPS)

More famous and near-famous designers.

VIA MARGUTTA (SPANISH STEPS)

Art galleries and antiques.

VIA SISTINA (SPANISH STEPS)

From the top of the Spanish Steps to Piazza Barberini. Small shops, high prices, excellent quality.

VIA VITTORIO VENETO (VIA VENETO)

La dolce vita is still here—just look at all those double-parked Mercedes, their owners wearing sunglasses at all hours while talking on their cell phones. Shops tend to veer toward the gaudy . . . think gold lamé.

Shopping in Venice

Beginning with Marco Polo, the Venetians controlled trade with the East, bringing silks and spices to the European continent. The trading spirit continues to this day, as millions of visitors flock to the city not only to enjoy its unique beauty and art but to purchase handmade lace, beautiful glassware, art prints, and papier-mâché Carnivale masks. Most shopkeepers speak English and are used to tourists and anxious for their business.

The maze of winding streets crisscrossed by canals and bridges will prove frustrating for the shopper with limited time and patience. It is easy to get turned around in Venice, but this is not the same as being lost. Please do not worry about getting a little mixed up; everyone does, even the natives, and it is part of the charm and adventure of Venice. Besides, who knows? You may discover some sumptious restaurant, the perfect hotel, or a hidden shop you otherwise would have missed.

Venice is divided by the Grand Canal, which winds like an S through the most famous parts of the city. Every *sestiere* (district) has its main shopping street, with little alleyways wandering off of it, so you are almost guaranteed to find wonderful treasures no matter where you look. The Grand Canal, the Piazza San Marco (St. Mark's Square), and Rialto Bridge are the best-known landmarks, and shopping is concentrated in these areas: The Mercerie, a succession of streets winding from Piazza San Marco to the Rialto Bridge; the Frezzeria, a prime shopping street that starts at the far end of Piazza San Marco from the Basilica; and Salizzada San Lio, leading away from Rialto through Castello.

Shopping Hours
WINTER: Mon 3:30–7:30 P.M., Tues–Sat 9 A.M.–1 P.M., 3:30–7:30 P.M.

SUMMER: Mon–Sat 9 A.M.–1 P.M., 4–7:30 P.M., some open Sun afternoon and during lunch

FOOD SHOPS: Mon–Tues, Thurs–Sat 9 A.M.–1 P.M., 5–7 P.M., Wed 9 A.M.–1 P.M.

The letter in parentheses before each shop corresponds to a letter that marks the shop's location on the Venice map on pages 208–15.

Antiques

(A) ANTICHITÀ BROCANTE
Via L. Mocenigo, 5-A (Lido Island)
Catherine Alary has successfully transformed her hobby of collecting furniture, lace, and small objects d'art from the 1800s to the 1900s into a business on Lido. Her charming shop is just far enough from the tourist

trail to keep it authentic. In other words, she depends on locals as customers, not on the tourist trade Lido experiences about six months of the year. Of course, you probably won't buy one of her armoires, but she has plenty of other collectibles that fit easily into a suitcase. For instance, she has a large collection of vintage cigarette cases that would make perfect business-card holders, and some great old compacts.

TELEPHONE 041-526-5189
CREDIT CARDS None, cash only
HOURS Mon–Sat 10:30 A.M.–1 P.M., 4–7 P.M.; open Sun from May–Oct
ENGLISH Yes, and French

Art

(B) MAZZUCCHI ART GALLERY
Frezzeria, 1771 (San Marco)

Franco Mazzucchi sells his own watercolors of Venice at very fair prices. He also handles other artists. You can buy a print and some originals in a nice frame for $10 to $500, which when you consider the cost of framing alone in many places, is a fair price.

TELEPHONE 041-520-7045
CREDIT CARDS AE, DC, MC, V
HOURS Daily 10:30 A.M.–7:30 P.M.
ENGLISH Yes

Book Binding

(C) GIANNI L. PITACCO
Ruga Giuffa, 4758 (Castello)

Gianni Pitacco is a book-binding craftsman who can bind your books in leather or paper, do special orders, or create and customize just about anything you can think of that can form the pages of a book. Think about him for photo albums for new parents, the bride and groom, or yourself as a lasting memento of your stay in Venice.

TELEPHONE 041-520-8687
CREDIT CARDS None, cash only
HOURS Mon–Sat 9 A.M.–1 P.M., 3–8 P.M. Closed Aug 1–15.
ENGLISH Yes

Ceramics and Porcelain

(D) GIULIANA ROLLI
Salizzada S. Pantalon, 39 (Santa Croce)

Giuliana Rolli is the only artist in Venice who does hand-painted porcelain. She has been selling her beautiful and delicate work commercially since 1990, encouraged by friends and her husband, who is a violinist. When I first found her, she was working out of a space not much bigger than a closet in San Polo. Success brought her to this new, larger location in Santa Croce near Piazzale Roma and the train station. Here she has space to paint and fire her work, and then to display it after it is completed.

All the work you see in the shop is hers, and there is bound to be some special piece you will find to give as a gift, or to take home as a keepsake of your trip. She has adorable doll dish sets, a great series based on the artist Kandinsky's work, ornaments, cups, saucers, teapots, and painted eggs. All are dishwasher safe. She also can personalize any item. Her English is excellent, and she is a delight. Be sure to tell her hello from me.

TELEPHONE 041-524-0789

CREDIT CARDS AE, MC, V

HOURS Mon 11 A.M.–12:30 P.M., Tues–Sat 10 A.M.–1 P.M., 4–8 P.M., open on festival Sundays, and after 8 P.M. in summer. Closed end of Dec–mid-Jan and last week of July until Aug 2.

ENGLISH Yes

Department Stores

(E) COIN DEPARTMENT STORE
Salizzada San Giovanni Grisostomo, 5787 (Cannaregio)

This nationwide department store chain was founded in Venice after the end of the Second World War. It sells middle-of-the-road goods, a step or two above Standa and Upim. This is one of their best stores, with four floors of clothing for the whole family. There is also a small housewares section and, across the street, a complete cosmetics and perfume department.

TELEPHONE 041-522-7192

CREDIT CARDS MC, V

HOURS Mon–Sat 9:30 A.M.–1 P.M., 3:30–7:30 P.M.

ENGLISH Yes

(F) STANDA
Strada Nova, 3660, Campo San Felice (Cannaregio)

The Standa chain was started during the height of Fascism. Today it is the K-Mart of Italy, stocking inexpensive (for Italy) cosmetics, clothing, housewares, and some toys. There is a supermarket in the Cannaregio and Lido stores and they are both above average for their type. There are other locations at Calle del Magazen, 4540 (San Marco) and Via Corfu, 1 (Lido Island).

TELEPHONE 041-522-2543

CREDIT CARDS MC, V

HOURS Daily 9 A.M.–7 P.M.

ENGLISH Limited

Dolls

(G) TRILLY
Fondamenta dell' Osmarin, 4974 (Castello)

Next to glass and masks, the most popular items in Venice seem to be dolls and puppets. As with the masks, many are mass produced, the quality varies widely, and the unknowing consumer inevitably has a hard time sifting through all the choices to find the true handcrafted item.

Trilly offers an exclusive collection of one-of-a-kind porcelain dolls and puppets handmade by the artist from the best materials and fabrics. She sews all the costumes and hand-paints the sweet faces. The hair on the smaller doll heads is fiber, but on the larger dolls, it is real hair. When you arrive at her shop, do not be put off by the tacky assortment of glass dust collectors . . . zero in on her specialty, beautiful dolls and puppets.

TELEPHONE AND FAX 041-521-2579
CREDIT CARDS MC, V
HOURS Daily 11 A.M.–7:30 P.M.
ENGLISH Yes

Glass

For more on Venetian glass, see "Murano," page 327.

(H) AL CAMPANIL
Calle Lunga Santa Maria Formosa, 5184 (Castello)

Sabrina, recognized by many as one of the top glass designers in Venice, specializes in museum copies and hand-painted glass. She also has a limited selection of very nice Venetian-inspired jewelry.

TELEPHONE 041-523-5734
CREDIT CARDS AE
HOURS Mon–Sat 9:30 A.M.–12:30 P.M., 3:30–7 P.M.
ENGLISH Yes

(I) FRATELLI TOSO
Fondamenta A. Colleoni, 7 (Murano)

If you love glass, do not miss Fratelli Toso.

The Toso brothers are carrying on their family tradition, begun in 1854, of creating exquisite glass. Theirs is not only one of the most recognized factories, but the oldest on Murano. The dusty, rather cluttered shop is obviously not there to attract the casual glass buyer of beads or glass objects—in fact, they don't do beads at all. If you go upstairs to their museum, you will see wonderful examples of their work, starting from the early days and continuing to the present, and quickly realize that everything they do is a handcrafted work of art, aimed toward serious buyers. Ask to see their collector's line called Maestro Glasses, and you won't leave without at least two for yourself. They also design beautiful lights, can make anything to order, and ship worldwide.

TELEPHONE 041-739-060, 739-089
FAX 041-739-688
CREDIT CARDS AE, MC, V
HOURS Mon–Fri 7 A.M.–noon, 2–5 P.M., Sat 9 A.M.–1 P.M.
ENGLISH Yes

Glass Beads and Jewelry

(J) ANTICLEA ANTIQUARIATO
San Provolo, 4719-A (Castello)

Rita and her daughters are carrying on a family business started more than twenty years ago by Rita's parents. Their specialty is antique jewelry and beads, beaded bags, and beaded flowers. They sell their pieces in a tiny shop along a canal filled with all sorts of interesting treasures besides the beads and beaded objects, including old postcards, prints, and a few antiques. It takes a while to absorb it all, so plan time to just look at what she has before you decide.

TELEPHONE 041-528-6946
CREDIT CARDS AE, MC, V
HOURS Daily 10 A.M.–1 P.M., 3:30–8 P.M.
ENGLISH Yes

(K) DONÀ MARIA LUISA
Calle dei Saoneri, 2738 (San Polo)

Good quality glass bead necklaces and glass objects at reasonable prices.

TELEPHONE 041-522-2884
CREDIT CARDS AE, DC, MC, V
HOURS Daily 10 A.M.–7:30 P.M.
ENGLISH Yes

(L) GALLERIA BUBACCO
Ruga Vecchia S. Giovanni, 1077-A (San Polo)

Leslie Genninger, a designer from Cincinnati, Ohio, has demonstrated what imagination, American drive, and hard work can do to make a dream come true. Leslie left a career as an investment banker and came to Venice in 1988, where she fell in love with Murano glass, and at the same time was sad to realize that few new designs were being made. So she started her own design studio, the Murano Class Act, and now her exclusive, custom-made jewelry designs are selling as fast as she can produce them. She uses some old beads as well as her own creations to make the most wearable necklaces, bracelets, earrings, cufflinks, pins, buttons, and stickpins I've seen in Venice. Also on display are works of art by other noted Venetian glass designers. Her other locations are Calle del Frutariol, 1845 (San Marco), tel: 041-523-9494; and Fondamenta de Ca'Rezzonico, 2793-A (Dorsoduro), tel: 041-522-5565

TELEPHONE 041-522-5981
FAX 041-522-5565
VOICE MAIL USA: 513-784-7989
CREDIT CARDS AE, DC, MC, V
HOURS Winter: Mon 2:30–7:30 P.M., Tues–Sat 10 A.M.–1 P.M., 2:30–7:30 P.M.; summer: daily 10 A.M.–1 P.M., 2:30–7:30 P.M.
ENGLISH Yes

(M) NINFEA
Calle Lunga Santa Maria Formosa, 5228 (Castello)

For many years, Francesca has been acquiring "Venetian Pearls" dating from the end of the last century to 1940. Her collection of originally designed necklaces, bracelets, and accessories made with these antique beads are unique. She also has a good selection of yesterday's things—Bakelite, paperweights, little antique items . . . all interesting.

TELEPHONE AND FAX 041-522-2381
CREDIT CARDS AE, MC, V
HOURS Tues–Sat 10:30 A.M.–12:30 P.M., 4:30–7:30 P.M.; closed Mon, Aug 1–20
ENGLISH Yes

(N) RIALTO 79
Ruga degli Orefici, 79 (San Polo)

Venetian glass jewelry is a dime-a-dozen bauble. Everywhere you look you will see strand after strand of cheap necklaces and gaudy earrings. Nowhere is the selection any tackier than along and around the Rialto Bridge, with, that is, the exception of this shop. Armando and his wife, Luisa, stock an excellent selection of handmade glass beads, many of which are designed by Luisa. I especially like her silver and gold necklaces strung so they appear to be floating around your neck. There is something for every budget, and there are no hard-sell tactics. Look for their shop on the right side as you cross away from the Rialto Bridge.

TELEPHONE 041-522-0647
CREDIT CARDS AE, DC, MC, V
HOURS Daily 9 A.M.–7 P.M., closed Dec 20–Feb 1
ENGLISH Yes

Lace and Vintage Clothing

For more on lacemaking, see "Burano," page 327.

(O) ANNELIE PIZZI E RICAMI
Calle Lunga S. Barnaba, 2748 (Dorsoduro)

A wonderful selection of antique and new linens and laces, old dresses, blouses, curtains, baby clothes, and table coverings. The sachets made from old scraps of lace are charming gifts that take up no space in your suitcase. Monogramming is available and the prices are very good.

TELEPHONE 041-520-3277
CREDIT CARDS AE, MC, V
HOURS Mon–Fri 9:30 A.M.–12:45 P.M., 4–7:30 P.M., Sat 9:30 A.M.–12:30 P.M.
ENGLISH Yes, and German

(P) CAPRICCI E VANITÀ
San Pantalon, 3744 (Dorsoduro)

The ironing board in front serves as a reminder of the care required for these lovely laces and vintage clothing. This charming one-of-a-kind shop specializes in Italian and imported laces, old folk costumes, and clothing from the forties, fifties, and sixties.

TELEPHONE 041-523-1504
CREDIT CARDS AE, MC, V
HOURS Mon 4–7 P.M., Tues–Fri 10 A.M.–1 P.M., 4–7:30 P.M., Sat 10 A.M.–1 P.M.; closed Aug
ENGLISH Yes

Markets

The most famous markets in Venice are the *pescheria* and the *erberia,* which run alongside the Rialto Bridge. The Ruga degli Orefici, the street leading off the bridge to the markets, is lined with one touristy stall after another. You will probably get your Venetian T-shirts here, but, with few exceptions, don't count on it as a quality stretch of merchandise. Traditional outdoor fairs are held during the major Venetian festivals. A week before Easter, the whole length of Strada Nuova, Campo Santa Bartolomio, and Campo San Luca are filled with market stalls selling clothes, leather, sweets, and some craft items. Just before Christmas and Easter there is an antiques market in Campo San Maurizio. There is also an outdoor market at Campo Santa Margherita (Dorsoduro), a block of stalls along Strada Nova (Cannaregio), and along Rio Giuseppe Garibaldi (San Marco).

(Q) RIALTO BRIDGE
(San Polo)

Rialto is *the* market in Venice, and has been for hundreds of years. The *erberia* (fruit and vegetable stalls) sells everything the *pescheria* (fish market) does not. This is definitely worth a trip, and don't forget your camera.

Lining the Rialto Bridge and beyond are scores of cheesy tourist traps selling plastic gondolas, plates with pictures of the Doge's Palace, T-shirts, imitation gondolier hats, and more. However, there is the occasional item of quality, and if you are shopping for T-shirts, here's the place. Bargains are rare.

TELEPHONE None

CREDIT CARDS None

HOURS Fish market: Tues–Sat 8 A.M.–1 P.M.; fruit and vegetable market: Mon–Sat 8 A.M.–1 P.M.; other stalls: Mon–Sat 10 A.M.–7 P.M. in winter, daily in summer

ENGLISH Sometimes

Masks

(R) LA VENEXIANA
Frezzeria, 1135 (San Marco)

The streets of Venice are lined with one mask and costume store after another, very few of them selling the real thing . . . handmade, hand-painted masks and hand-detailed costumes. Every piece you see at La Venexiana is handmade exclusively for their stores. At their two shops you will find papier-mâché masks from famous opera characters to Mickey Mouse, and fabulous costumes to wear at Carnivale, to your next masked ball, or to wow your friends at Halloween. Second location: Ponte Canonica, 4322 (Castello), tel and fax 041-523-3558.

TELEPHONE 041-528-6888

CREDIT CARDS AE, DC, MC, V

HOURS Daily 9:30 A.M.–7:30 P.M.

ENGLISH Yes

(S) VENANZIO TEMPORIN-BOTTEGA D'ARTE ARTIGIANALE
Barbaria delle Tole, 6360-A (Castello)

At this tiny, jumbled mask shop, the artist and his dog, Lio, sit out front to greet customers. There are loads of mask shops throughout Venice, and you may find your own favorite, but this one has a personal feel to it. Don't be put off by the garish ceramic figures . . . look at the masks, and remember that the artist can customize one for you. Everything is original and made here. The prices are very good, even better if you pay cash. Babaria delle Tole is off Campo San Giovanni e Paolo.

TELEPHONE 041-528-6818, 520-8367

CREDIT CARDS DC, MC, V

HOURS Mon, Wed–Sun 11 A.M.–7:30 P.M.; closed Tues

ENGLISH Limited, but he does speak French

Photography

(T) ARICI GIANLUIGI
Calle d. Miracoli, 5401-C (Cannaregio)

Finding a place to have your photos developed or to buy a roll of film or a postcard doesn't take much in Venice. However, finding the *best* place isn't always so easy. This photo shop, owned by Gianluigi and his wife, Norma, is a well-loved neighborhood institution. I know because during my last research trip to Venice, I passed it several times a day on my way to and from my flat. I was first attracted by his line of quality postcards, later on when he graciously helped me with a camera problem, and finally when my friend left a package containing several leather card holders in his shop and he faithfully kept them for her until he saw me again and told me he had her package. So, if you need film or film developing, a nice postcard, or help with your camera, stop in and be sure to tell Gianluigi hello from me . . . and my grateful friend.

TELEPHONE 041-523-6030

CREDIT CARDS None, cash only

HOURS Mon–Sat 9:30 A.M.–1 P.M., 3:30–7:30 P.M.

ENGLISH Yes (his son is studying to be a doctor in the United States)

Silk

(U) DIMODÍ
Campo S. Filippo e Giacomo, 4523 (Castello)

There is no shortage of tie and silk scarf shops in Venice, but this one has a wide selection and favorable prices, especially if you can find something on the end-of-season discount rack. They also have a good selection of umbrellas and men's sweaters. They subscribe to the tax-free plan if you spend more than L300,000 (see *"Detasse,"* page 292).

TELEPHONE AND FAX 041-523-5187

CREDIT CARDS AE, DC, MC, V

HOURS Winter: Mon 3–7:30 P.M., Tues–Sat 9:30 A.M.–1 P.M., 3–7:30 P.M.; summer: daily 9:30 A.M.–10 P.M.

ENGLISH Yes

Stationery

(V) GIANNI BASSO
Fondamenta Nuove, Calle del Fumo, 5306 (Cannaregio)

Anyone who appreciates the fine art of hand printing should consider a visit to Gianni Basso a required stop on a trip to Venice. Gianni Basso is a master craftsman who designs and prints every piece he turns out the old-fashioned way, by hand. He is well-known and loved not only in Venice, but by clients who come to him from around the world. His business cards are nothing short of fabulous, as is all of his printed stationery. He also does a limited edition of Pinocchio cards and scenes of Venice. He works in his shop every day but Sunday, occasionally assisted by his wife and their vagabond dog, Lilly.

TELEPHONE 041-523-4681

CREDIT CARDS None, cash only

HOURS Mon–Fri 8:30 A.M.–1 P.M., 2–7 P.M., Sat 8:30 A.M.–1 P.M.; closed 10 days in mid-Aug, Dec 23–Jan 6
ENGLISH Yes

Shopping Destinations

BURANO

The island of Burano is as charming and homespun as Murano is touristy and hard-sell. You can do both islands in a day, and that is what I recommend. Burano is known for two things: fishing and lace. Artisans still make the lace by hand, and the prices are astoundingly high. However, you should be able to find beautiful hand-done hankies, sachets, and other little gifts at affordable prices. The lace-making school began in 1872 and is open to the public, selling goods from their stunning modern and traditional collection of table and bed linens. There is also a museum that displays magnificent pieces of old lace. I recommend going there first, before shopping, so you will be able to recognize the hand-sewn from the machine-made when you hit the shops. When you start your shopping, browse first, then go back and buy, all the time trying not to be too confused by the endless selection. Burano is also known for its rich, eggy cookies and its gaily painted houses. Bring your camera and allow time to wander . . . this is a photo opportunity for sure.

How to get to Burano: If you are already on Murano, get the number 12 to Burano. If you are leaving from Venice, you can get the number 12 from the Fondamente Nuove (in Cannaregio).

MURANO

Though Venice's major glass makers have shops around San Marco, it is much more interesting to see them all together on Murano. The prices are somewhat competitive. You may be able to negotiate on large purchases but not on the little souvenirs. Do not fall for the many hawkers touting "a free trip to Murano." These con artists prowl the wharf along the Grand Canal and the streets leading to it with offers of free boat trips to the island. Once you are on one of these boats, you are steered to the shops these guys represent, and they get a kickback on whatever you buy. Be assured that buy you will with these high-pressure salesmen, who make the worst used-car salesman at home look like a cupcake. You can go by yourself from stop number 5 along the Grand Canal at San Zaccaria in front of the Danieli Hotel, or at number 12 from Fondamente Nuove in Castello. You will need to allow at least three hours; you can combine this with a trip to the island of Burano to see the handmade lace there, and that is what I recommend.

Glossary

Although the staff of most hotels speak English, many owners of smaller pensiones have a limited command. Thus it is important to try to master a few words to get by in a pinch. Your efforts will be rewarded by smiles and appreciation that you are at least trying to communicate.

Basics

Good morning	*Buon giorno*
Good afternoon/evening	*Buona sera*
Good night	*Buona notte*
Hello/goodbye (informal)	*Ciao*
Goodbye	*Arrivederci*
Yes	*Si*
No	*No*
Please	*Per favore*
Thank you	*Grazie*
You are welcome	*Prego*
All right/okay	*Va bene*
How are you?	*Come sta?*
I am fine, thank you	*Bene, grazie*
And you?	*E lei?*
Do you speak English?	*Parla inglese?*
I do not speak Italian	*Non parlo italiano*
I do not understand	*Non capisco*
I do not know	*No lo so*
Can you please repeat slowly?	*Può ripetere lentamente?*
Excuse me	*Mi scusi/Prego*
Excuse me (in a crowd)	*Permesso*
I am sorry	*Mi dispiace*
Today	*Oggi*
Tomorrow	*Domani*
Day after tomorrow	*Dopodomani*
Yesterday	*Ieri*
In the morning	*Di mattina*
In the afternoon	*Nel pomeriggio*
In the evening	*Di sera*
Here/There	*Qui/La*
Good/Bad	*Buono/Cattivo*
Big/Small	*Grande/Píccolo*
Cheap/Expensive	*Económico/Caro*
Hot/Cold	*Caldo/Freddo*
Vacant/Occupied	*Líbero/Occupato*
Help!	*Aiuto!*

Stop!	*Alt!*
Look out!	*Attenzione!*

Questions and Directions

How?	*Comè?*
Where is ——— ? (a hotel, the station)	*Dov'è ——— ? (un albergo, la stazione)*
When?	*Quando?*
What, what is it?	*Cosa?, Cos'è?*
Why?	*Perché?*
What time is it?	*Che ora sono?*
Which	*Quale*
Left/Right	*Sinistra/Destra*
Straight ahead	*Sempre diritto*
Where are the restrooms?	*Dov'è il bagno?*

Numbers

1	*uno*
2	*due*
3	*tre*
4	*quattro*
5	*cinque*
6	*sei*
7	*sette*
8	*otto*
9	*nove*
10	*dieci*
11	*undici*
12	*dodici*
13	*tredici*
14	*quattrodici*
15	*quindici*
16	*sedici*
17	*diciassette*
18	*diciotto*
19	*diciannove*
20	*venti*
21	*ventuno*
30	*trenta*
40	*quaranta*
50	*cinquanta*
60	*sessanta*
70	*settanta*
80	*ottanta*
90	*novanta*
100	*cento*

101	*centuno*
110	*centodieci*
200	*duecento*
500	*cinquecento*
1,000	*mille*
10,000	*diecimila*
50,000	*cinquantamila*

Days of the Week

Monday	*lunedì*
Tuesday	*martedì*
Wednesday	*mercoledì*
Thursday	*giovedì*
Friday	*venerdì*
Saturday	*sabato*
Sunday	*domenica*

Months

January	*gennaio*
February	*febbraio*
March	*marzo*
April	*aprile*
May	*maggio*
June	*giugno*
July	*luglio*
August	*agosto*
September	*settembre*
October	*occobre*
November	*novembre*
December	*dicembre*

At the Hotel

Hotel	*Hotel/albergo*
Do you have a room?/I would like a room.	*Ha una cámera?/Vorrei una cámera.*
For one/two/three people	*Per una/due/tre person (a/e)*
For one/two/three nights	*Per una/due/tre nott (e/i)*
For one/two weeks	*Per una/due settiman (a/e)*
With a double bed	*Con un letto matrimoniale*
With two beds	*Con due letti*
With a private shower/bath	*Con una doccia/un bagno privato*
With a balcony	*Con una terrazza*
How much is it?	*Quanto costa?*
It is expensive	*È caro*
Is breakfast included?	*È compresa la prima colazione?*
Do you have anything cheaper?	*Ha niente che costa di meno?*

Full-board/Half-board	*Pensione completa/mezza pensione*
Can I see the room?	*Posso vedere la càmera?*
I will take it	*La prendo*
I would like to reserve a room	*Vorrei prenotare una càmera*
I have a reservation	*Ho una prenotazione*
A key	*Un chiave*

Changing Money

Is there a bank near here?	*C'è una banca qui vicino?*
Is there an exchange bureau?	*C'è una cassa di cambio?*
Can I use my credit card?	*Posso usare la carta di credita?*

Signs

Entrance/Exit	*Entrata/Uscita*
Free entrance	*Ingresso líbero*
Gentlemen/Ladies	*Signori/Signore*
WC	*Gabinetto*
Open/Closed	*Aperto/chiuso*
Closed for holidays	*Chiuso per ferie*
Closed for restoration	*Chiuso per restauro*
Pull/Push	*Tirare/Springere*
Out of order	*Guasto*
Do not touch	*Non toccare*
Danger	*Perícolo*
Ring the bell	*Suonare il campanello*
No smoking	*Vietato fumare*

Index by City

Alphabetical Listing of Accommodations in Venice

($) Indicates a Big Splurge

Big Splurges in Venice

Other Options in Venice

Readers' Comments

Every effort has been made to provide accurate information in this guide. The publisher and author, however, cannot be held responsible for changes in any of the listings due to rate increases, inflation, dollar fluctuation, political upheavals, the passage of time, or changes in management.

Cheap Sleeps in Italy is updated and revised on a regular basis. If you find a change before I do, or make an important discovery you want to pass along to me, please send me a note stating the name and address of the hotel or shop, the date of your visit, and a description of your findings. Your comments are very important. I investigate every complaint, hand out every compliment you send me about a hotel or shop, and personally answer every letter I receive. Thank you very much for taking the time to write.

Please send your comments to: Sandra A. Gustafson, Cheap Sleeps in Italy, c/o Chronicle Books, 85 Second Street, Sixth Floor, San Francisco, CA 94105.